THE WORLD IS CHRIST'S
A CRITIQUE OF TWO KINGDOMS THEOLOGY

THE WORLD IS CHRIST'S
A CRITIQUE OF TWO KINGDOMS THEOLOGY

WILLEM J. OUWENEEL

ezra press.

www.EzraInstitute.ca

Published by Ezra Press
Ezra Institute for Contemporary Christianity
9 Hewitt Avenue, Toronto, Ontario, Canada M6R 1Y4

Book design by Janice Van Eck

ISBN 978-0-9947279-6-1

CONTENTS

PART I: THINGS TO BE SAID FIRST

PART II: THEOLOGICAL TOPICS

PART III: PHILOSOPHICAL TOPICS

APPENDICES

FOREWORD

The unstinting author of this substantial work, Willem Ouweneel, is surely right when he says, "Apart from the Bible's teaching about the divine persons of the blessed Trinity, I would say that the Kingdom of God is arguably the most universal and concise summary of the contents of Scripture." As such, there is perhaps no subject more important for Christians to understand today than the meaning and implications of the kingdom of God under the Lordship of Jesus Christ. And yet, few seem to have grappled with this theme as they should or rightly handled the Word of truth with respect to it.

There is so much error and bewilderment in the contemporary church regarding the origin, nature, scope and power of *God's kingdom* that it is hard to see what could be more necessary in this regard than the publication of a thorough, clear and consistent scriptural statement expounding this profound reality. Given the centrality and importance of this hermeneutical key to the Bible, the book you hold in your hand stands tall, not only as an orthodox and faithful account of the kingdom from a man committed to the full inspiration and authority of the Scriptures, but as a mineral-rich mountain to be mined for the treasures hidden within. It is, therefore, a genuine joy and privilege for me to be able to write the foreword to this outstanding book from the pen of an extraordinary man who happens to be my friend.

I first met the author several years ago in the Toronto area whilst he was visiting Canada from his native Netherlands on a speaking tour, and I soon after began reading his keen published works, deriving much pleasure from them. This enjoyment was not simply because I have a love of reading theological and philosophical books. It is true that the writer of Ecclesiastes poignantly reminds us of a wearisome reality—of the making, and indeed, study, of many books, there is no end—but every now and then one comes across a person who has written something so timely, coherent and penetrating, even prophetic, it makes one very glad of books and a little sad when one in fact reaches the end.

Willem Ouweneel's book, *The World is Christ's*, is such a work because it emanates from the mind of not just a brilliant scholar with three doctoral degrees in diverse fields, but a cultural prophet with fire in his bones—a wise man who both understands the times in which we live, and yet lives to serve the Lord of all times with wisdom and understanding. Consequently, before Willem is a polemicist he is an accomplished and diligent scholar; before he is a scholar, he is a preacher of the Word of God; and before he is a preacher of the Word, he is a warm-hearted man of faith in the Lord Jesus. It is for this reason that one can read this extensive polemical and prophetic work and find that its goal is neither sectarian nor self-serving, but aims only at the edification and blessing of God's people. The reader will discover that though the book contains a sustained critique of faulty understandings of the kingdom of God, the entire work is permeated by an atmosphere of humility, ecumenical generosity, good humour and a deep love for Christ and his eternal purposes.

To illustrate the self-effacing good-humour the author possesses, I can relate that over lunch one day at a symposium I had invited Willem to speak at in Ontario, he asked me in his Dutch accent if I had heard the story about the Dutchman who had been stranded alone for years on a desert island. Learning that I had not heard the story (despite my own Dutch roots!), he proceeded to tell me with a grin on his face that when they found the poor marooned man, they noticed he had erected three distinct structures on the island. When asked what they were the Dutchman explained that one was his home, the second was his church and the third was the church he *used* to go to! I soon learned that unnecessary divisions and separations in the church were something that truly grieved Willem Ouweneel. Despite the polemical title, the heart behind this book is one that strives for unity in the body of Christ, for the kingdom of God.

I am conscious in writing these opening words for such a critical book that, though well-known in his own country, the name Willem Ouweneel will be unknown to most English-speaking readers; Willem is a Dutchman who has spent most of his professional life in Europe and his works have only recently begun to appear in English in North America. But the obscurity of the name should not mislead anyone regarding the originality and eminence of the author. Indeed, this book breaks new ground insofar as, to the best of my knowledge, it is the first coherent book-length critique by a single author of an increasingly ubiquitous 'Two Kingdoms Theology,' from the pen of a man inimitably qualified to engage the subject.

Moreover, *The World is Christ's* is more than a narrow critique. It is a sweeping volume on Christian worldview that effectively expounds the gospel's relationship with culture in the context of the kingdom of Christ. In the process, the damaging myth of neutrality in human thought is decisively destroyed; false dualisms in Christian teaching inherited from Greek philosophy are perceptively exposed; the science of theology is helpfully de-privileged as the sole discipline able or qualified to speak "Christianly" and scripturally about the world, life and culture; and the foundations of a biblical philosophy for social order are instructively laid. In short, although I cannot follow Willem at every single point, anyone wanting to understand the profound importance of the kingdom of Christ for all human life and thought will not fail to be challenged, enriched and enlightened by reading this wonderful book.

Crucially, this work is not merely theoretical, it is immensely practical and filled with promise as it directs us to the transforming reality of the work of the Holy Spirit in the cosmos and specifically in our lives. In Willem's own words, pregnant with hope:

Already now, the kingdom of God is a spiritual reality in this world because Christ is on the throne. The kingdom is manifested wherever the Holy Spirit is working, and wherever we find people who—though in weakness—submit their lives and their societal institutions to the authority of the king in the power of the Holy Spirit.

Thank God the world is indeed Christ's—a world he is reconciling to himself—Ouweneel helps us to see both how and why! Thank you, Willem.

Rev. Dr. Joseph Boot
July 2017

PREFACE

Some Christians seem to be under the impression that theology is a hobby-horse of theologians. What average churchgoers really care about theonomy or reconstructionism, transformationalism (Kuyperian or not), and scholasticism? Do subjects like "cultural mandate," "common grace," "natural law," and "one kingdom" or "two kingdoms," really make the average Christian tick? To some extent such questions are understandable. Some theological discussions are very theoretical; they are only the gourmet's cup of tea. However, in other cases, it turns out that behind the scholarly terms very practical, everyday problems are concealed. Suddenly, the theoretical terms come to life; they land on your doorstep!

It is like this with the problems that I am going to discuss in the present book. Behind them, there are questions hidden such as: Must I, as a Christian, send my child to a Christian school, or is that not necessary, or is it even undesirable? I am a Christian *and* a politician; should my Christian convictions direct how I vote on bills, and should I even *publicly explain* my Christian convictions, or is that in fact basically wrong? Can I, as a Christian, shop at stores that support anti-biblical actions? Should Christians work for a more Christian character of society, or would that be a basic error? Are there Christian ways of doing science, the arts, psychology, economics, or politics? Or is that just as silly as asking whether there is such a thing as Christian plumbing? By the way, does my church have any say in issues like these? Formally or morally?

Not so long ago, for many Christians the answers to these questions were relatively easy and self-evident. They firmly believed that Jesus was Lord over all of their lives, and that everything in life was "religious," that is, involved their relationship with God. Therefore, they believed in the necessity and legitimacy not only of Christian churches, but also of Christian marriages, Christian families, Christian schools, Christian associations, and they extended their commitment to imagining what a Christian company or a Christian political party might look like. It was self-evident to them that, when they prayed "Thy kingdom come," they were not thinking only of Christ's second coming, but also of the way this kingdom was to be realized in this world, here and now. They understood that, if you prayed such a petition, it returned like a boomerang: it is through us that God wants to realize his kingdom, every day a bit further, in every domain of life in which we are active.

Today, this picture has changed drastically. The revision began with Presbyterian theologian Meredith Kline, and other Presbyterian theologians at Westminster Seminary California (Escondido, CA) followed in his wake, such as Michael Horton, Darryl Hart, and David VanDrunen. An entire generation of theology students have been trained in a totally new way of thinking, and they are preaching this new view nowadays from the pulpits. I say "totally new," but one of the interesting things is that the Escondido theologians want to make us believe that *their* view is nothing but the continuation of the thought of Augustine, Luther, Calvin, and their followers! Not so long ago some thought they were very Reformed if they believed in the Three Forms of Unity, and in line with them, in what I call a one-kingdom theology: the one kingdom of God. Now, suddenly, the tables are turned: you are allegedly truly Reformed only if you believe their new doctrine, which looks like an ellipse with two focal points: natural law and the two-kingdoms model (the theory of the sacred and the secular kingdoms). Even if the new doctrine is at odds with the Forms of Unity and with the Westminster Standards, they insist that no one is truly Reformed who does not adopt this new trend.

What does the new trend entail practically for you? The Triune God providentially rules the entire world, but the glorified Man Jesus Christ is *not* King of the entire world, but only of a limited part of it: the church. So you have a Christological problem here. Apart from going to church and your private prayers, your life is lived out largely in a secular sphere, called the "common kingdom." So you have an ecclesiological as well as a philosophical problem: your Christian worldview is at stake. You may tell people that you are a Christian, but in no way should your Christian convictions ever interfere with anything that goes on in this "common (secular, actually neutral) realm." So you also have a psychological problem: in the public arena you keep your mouth shut about what is the most precious thing in your life. At best you can appeal to "natural law" (whatever that may be), but you may never appeal overtly to your Christian beliefs.

Formerly, some might have thought that secularization was a very regrettable thing—but now they are told that the secular domain has been instituted by God himself, already as part of the Noahic covenant! God does not even *want* you to make your Christian convictions explicit in the public domain; you would trespass his rules for the "common kingdom." Formerly, secularization was bad—now it turns out not only to be the view of Luther and Calvin, but even *God's own* will that there is this secular domain. We always thought that secularization was the work of atheists and agnostics within our Western society—now it turns out that they unconsciously understood God's ideas about society better than traditional Protestants did!

You see what this entails? In fact, we cannot legitimately speak of *Christian* marriages, *Christian* families, and *Christian* schools (at best we can speak of the marriages, families, and schools of Christians) because marriages, families, and schools belong to the "common realm." They are *not* aspects of the kingdom of God, as many of us had always thought. Why did we and our spiritual forebears always think so? The answer some give is that this was "a Dutch thing" (Abraham Kuyper, Herman Bavinck, Herman Dooyeweerd), and partly a "Dutch-American thing" (Geerhardus Vos, Cornelius Van Til). Well, here I am, another Dutchman, supported by a Dutch-American editor (Nelson Kloosterman), and a Dutch-Canadian publisher (John Hultink). (Interestingly, one of our greatest opponents, David VanDrunen, is another Dutch American! I don't know whether he has ever been in the Dutch town of Drunen—I have. The Drunen dunes are lovely.)

Let me warn the reader that this debate is very nebulous. Apparently, some two-kingdoms books are quickly becoming outdated because the authors of those books are constantly softening their position in lectures, at conferences, and in magazine articles (not necessarily in their courses at Westminster Seminary California!). One sensitive point is this: one particular two-kingdoms theologian asserts that the *Man* Christ Jesus is not ruler of the common kingdom, but when attacked he, or another, will state that of course Christ is ruler of the common kingdom, but without accepting the obvious consequences of this view. One particular two-kingdoms theologian will claim that the Bible has no decisive authority in the public square, but when attacked he, or another, will admit that, of course, Christians should be good witnesses to the truth in all spheres. One particular two-kingdoms theologian will maintain that what Christians do within the common realm has no eternal significance, but when attacked he, or another, will state that, of course, all good things we do have lasting value. So how can you have a meaningful discussion with such opponents? My answer is: I will stick to what they have *written* in *books*, and pay no attention to all kinds of backtracking movements apart from their books.

In the present book, I am not trying to come up with the one and only true interpretation of Luther and Calvin on these matters. I do not defend the Dutchmen and Dutch-Americans mentioned above. I do not defend Kuyperianism or neo-Calvinism as such. I wish only to present a *biblical* model of Christians living under the kingship of Christ in every domain of life, in continual interaction with all the relevant authors that I came across, whether opponents or congenial thinkers. I presume that my opponents will shout: "Biblicism!" Don't worry; I will deal with all these aspects in the present book.

Bible quotations in this book are usually from the English Standard Version. I thank Dr. Nelson D. Kloosterman again very warmly for his expert editorial work on the manuscript of this book. And I am again deeply thankful to my publisher, John Hultink, for his constant encouragement in this entire project. Both have also contributed considerably to the contents of this book, and I am much indebted to them. The final result is entirely my own responsibility.

Willem J. Ouweneel
October 2016

ABBREVIATIONS

EBC   Gaebelein, F. E., ed. *The Expositor's Bible Commentary*. 12 vols. Grand Rapids, MI: Zondervan.

EDR   Ouweneel, W. J. *Evangelische Dogmatische Reeks*. 12 vols. Heerenveen: Medema.

NICNT   *New International Commentary on the New Testament*. Grand Rapids, MI: Eerdmans.

RD   Bavinck, H. 2002–2008. *Reformed Dogmatics*. Edited by John Bolt. Translated by John Vriend. 4 vols. Grand Rapids, MI: Baker Academic.

WA   *Luthers Werke* (Weimarer Ausgabe). Wimar: Böhlau Verlag, 1883–2009.

PART I
THINGS TO BE SAID FIRST

1

A REFORMED DEBATE

PREPARATORY PONDERINGS

1. Before you read any further, what is more plausible: that the glorified Man Jesus Christ is King over all the world, *or* only over a limited part of the present world?
2. How can we (insofar as we are familiar with these problems) find a *biblical* road in the midst of all the controversies between Kuyperians and Klineans, between Old Princeton and New Westminster, between Reformed and Presbyterians?
3. Do the controversies about who is most genuinely Reformed appeal to you? What purpose might they serve? What injury might they do?
4. Do you think that a European theologian might throw any light on these matters? Or are these things that North Americans themselves must solve?

1.1   ONE OR TWO KINGDOMS?

1.1.1   A Neo-Scholastic Model

In this book, one of the main things I am doing is trying to refute the two-kingdoms model as conceived and articulated by David VanDrunen and some congenial thinkers.[1] VanDrunen has described this view as follows: "God rules the church (the spiritual kingdom) as redeemer in Jesus Christ and rules the state and all other social institutions (the civil kingdom) as creator and sustainer, and thus these two kingdoms have significantly different ends, functions, and modes of operation."[2]

John Frame called the two-kingdoms (hereafter: 2K) theory the Escondido theology because several of its proponents have worked, or work, at Westminster Seminary California (WSC).[3] As the quote above indicates, adherents of this 2K model believe that Christians live in two kingdoms: a sacred realm and a secular realm. The former is what the Bible calls the "kingdom of God;" in the present age, it is supposed to coincide more or less with the visible church.[4] This is the redemptive, supernatural kingdom. The other kingdom is the realm of our common duties and vocations, which are neither holy nor unholy. The former kingdom stands under the kingship of the glorified Christ, the latter stands under the general providence of the (Triune) God ("secular" supposedly does not mean godless).

In contrast with this, I present a "one kingdom" view: the *entire* world stands under the kingship of the glorified Man at God's right hand, including the work of the Christian plumber, and in a certain sense, *even including the work of the non-Christian plumber*. I believe that this is the implicit testimony of Scripture (Matt. 28:18; Eph. 1:20–23; Col. 1:15–18; 1 Pet. 3:21–22; these passages will be investigated later in this book).

The opponents of 2K theologians are first and foremost the (transformationalist) neo-Calvinists, and after them also theonomic theologians (or reconstructionists, or dominion theologians), and (free church) evangelicals.[5] The first group allegedly makes the mistake of believing that the entire

---

[1] VanDrunen (especially 2006; 2009; 2010a; 2010b; 2014); also see Horton (1995/2002a; 2006), Hart (2006), Clark (2008), and Stellman (2009, xiv, xix, xxvii, 22, 32, 53).

[2] VanDrunen (2010b, 1).

[3] Frame (2011).

[4] Cf. VanDrunen (2010a, 30, 101, 106, 123, 133–34).

[5] See extensively, Littlejohn (2012a).

society is under the kingship of Christ, or has to be actively brought under it ("transformation"). The second group allegedly errs because they believe in, and long for, a worldwide Christian society brought under the Mosaic Law. And the third group is alleged to be wrong because of its supposed biblicism and its devaluating the institutional church (as the term "free church" already indicates). We see that we are dealing with at least four views here, which mutually exclude each other. Is one of them right, or should we look for a fifth view?

1.1.2   Two Comments

Let me immediately make two comments here. I have enjoyed reading especially David VanDrunen's book *Living in God's Two Kingdoms*. It is expertly written, it presents the two-kingdoms case very well, and it contains a lot of practical Christian wisdom. The same is true for Jason Stellman's *Dual Citizens*. It is just a pity that, in my opinion, the core thesis of these books is entirely mistaken. It is not heresy (it falls within the lines of the Nicene Creed)—yet it is mistaken, and even misleading. Scripture does not teach two kingdoms (except in the very different sense of Matt. 12:25–28, the "kingdom of Satan" and the "kingdom of God"), neither explicitly nor implicitly. The present book tries to explain what is wrong with the 2K model, how such a model could possibly arise, and what damaging effects it has.

Second, I am not a reconstructionist nor, I hope, a biblicist (cf. §2.4). I am a transformationalist in the sense that God by his Spirit transforms the hearts of people (Rom. 12:2; 2 Cor. 3:18), and from there changes their lives, including their functioning within their various societal relationships, and from there even influences culture as a whole. But I am not necessarily a transformationalist (or neo-Calvinist) in the sense that I would believe in a Christian-cultural task that aims at transforming the entire world into the kingdom of God, or into the new heaven and the new earth.[6] Moreover, I do not like the triumphalism and cultural optimism that has often characterized this approach, apart from the eschatological problems connected with it (see especially chapter 9).

In the North American Reformed and Presbyterian scene, it may sometimes look as if one has to choose between these two approaches, neo-Calvinism and 2K theology (reconstructionism being in retreat). Some

---

[6] See, e.g., Plantinga (2002); Wolters (2005); Goheen and Bartholomew (2008); cf. also Seerveld (2014a; 2014b); all these have been strongly influenced by Dooyeweerd (see, e.g., 1960; 1979; 1984).

have presented a Third Way, which tries to avoid the problems of both the 2K approach and transformationalism.[7] Perhaps my approach could also be called a kind of Third or Fourth Way.

Nelson Kloosterman spoke of "A Third Way" as well.[8] In his counting, theonomy/reconstructionism is the "first way," and "religious secularism" (read: 2K theology) is the "second way." Both ways are extensively reviewed, although his discussion of the "second way" is now a little outdated because of newer publications.[9] Kloosterman called his "Third Way" "Worldview Christianity." I feel very much at home here, especially because he wrote: "In our generation, the Lord seems to be surprising and humbling Calvinists with the reality that worldview Christianity is being championed by non-Calvinists around the world. These are Christians who are coming to see that the Christian faith provides an integrative-comprehensive understanding for all of living in the world." I am thankful to belong to this group.

1.1.3   Scholasticism and Reformation

I intend to show in the present book that 2K theology is a kind of neo-scholasticism—and this in an age in which Reformed thinking was finally liberating itself from its ties with scholasticism. In their essences, Reformational thinking and scholasticism do not fit together. Luther and Calvin brought Christian life back to the Word of God, although scholastic elements remained in their own thinking. No wonder—it is extremely difficult to get rid of this bug, certainly at such an early stage of renewal (early sixteenth century). Therefore, after these two Reformers, scholasticism was soon reintroduced into the German-speaking world by Luther's successor, Philip Melanchthon, and into the French-speaking world by Calvin's successor, Theodore Beza, as we will see. It is hard to blame them: there was little else at hand. One of the things Luther and Calvin failed to do was to develop a Christian philosophy, that is, a Christian-philosophical basis for our thinking about nature and culture, state and society, justice and economy, etc.

Of course, someone like VanDrunen is aware of the accusation of scholasticism.[10] His response to this is quite remarkable: there is no actual response. This is an interesting tactic: he does not hesitate to quote extensively the

---

[7] See, e.g., Aniol (2013).

[8] Kloosterman (2008).

[9] E.g., VanDrunen (2009; 2010a; 2010b; 2014); Stellman (2009); see on VanDrunen (2010b): Kloosterman (2012a).

[10] Boot (2016) has wondered whether VanDrunen imbibed scholasticism at Loyola University, a private Roman Catholic university in Chicago.

objections that his critics level against 2K theology[11]—and subsequently does not explicitly answer any of these objections. Presumably, his critics are invited to follow his arguments, and then conclude for themselves that they are wrong. Similarly, VanDrunen extensively quotes the accusation that his approach is nothing but the ancient scholastic nature-grace dualism[12] but, although he enters into certain detailed questions (e.g., does grace perfect nature?), he hardly enters into the factual question: Is 2K nothing but a variety of this nature-grace dualism, and might this be a problem?

The basic difference between Reformational thinking and scholasticism was and is this: the great power of the Reformation was to place again the entire world, and people's entire lives, under the authority of Scripture and under the kingship of Christ. Scholasticism, however, placed only the spiritual (sacred) domain under the authority of Scripture and under the kingship of Christ, whereas the natural (secular) domain was placed under the authority of pagan thinking, especially Aristotle (d. 322 BC). This is the well-known nature-grace dualism of scholasticism. In the course of the sixteenth century, the Lutheran and Calvinist universities were gradually placed entirely under the sway of scholasticism, though this time it was covered with a Reformational frosting. The nature-grace dualism of scholasticism led to the idea of a Christian theology versus a supposedly "neutral" (read: Aristotelian; today: humanist) philosophy.

Even today, many Christian theologians have great difficulty with the idea of a Christian philosophy, or they astonishingly claim that Christian theology as such constitutes this Christian philosophy. For instance, during a lecture at the Free University in Amsterdam (1970), the great German dogmatician Wolfhart Pannenberg claimed that theology is the true philosophy.[13] He certainly was in line with Augustine (d. 430) here—but that does not make it correct. Whatever one can say of Thomas Aquinas, the premier practitioner of scholastic thinking, he at least knew how to distinguish between theology and philosophy.

In his battle with French modernist philosopher René Descartes (d. 1650), who lived for a while in the Netherlands, the greatest Dutch Reformed theologian of the seventeenth century, Gisbert Voetius (d. 1676), called Aristotle "our philosopher."[14] No wonder: Voetius was the premier exponent of *Reformed* scholastic thinking in the Netherlands. Please note:

---

[11] E.g., VanDrunen (2010a, 18–19).
[12] VanDrunen (2010b, 27–36, 526–27).
[13] Quoted by Strauss (1971, 64).
[14] Ouwendorp (2012, 149).

against Descartes, he placed not a Christian philosophy (he probably was not even able to imagine what such a thing might involve), but a pagan philosophy. I don't know how the ghost of scholasticism within Reformed thinking could have been exposed in a more painful way.

1.2 UNDERLYING PROBLEMS

1.2.1 Theology versus Philosophy

A great number of the issues brought up by VanDrunen are, strictly speaking, not theological problems at all, such as "natural law," the "cultural mandate," the meaning of "religion," the relationship between theology and the sciences, or the arts, or politics, etc.; a Christian view of culture, a Christian view of the state, the separation of church and state, the relationships between the church, the state, and other societal relationships, and so on. It is typically scholastic to either declare all these topics to be "theological," or to declare them to be philosophical, and thus present us with "neutral" (secular, common, non-Christian, sometimes outright apostate-Christian) solutions for these problems.[15]

The *former* idea ("all is theology") is objectionable because Scripture does not contain a view of science, of art, of culture, or even of theology for that matter—so theologians cannot derive such ideas from it. Theology (at least the core of theology: exegetics and dogmatics) must expound Scripture, and nothing else.

The *latter* idea ("neutral philosophy") is objectionable because it denies the universal authority of Scripture and the universal kingship of Christ. There *is* no neutral domain within cosmic reality, as we will see. It does not help if one objects to the term "neutral" by emphasizing God's universal providence ("God is always 'involved' in some way or another").[16] I call a domain "neutral" or "secular" if it is thought to be *not* under the universal kingship of the glorified Man Christ Jesus, and *not* under the universal authority of Scripture. These two things mean the following:

(a) As to the former point, I do not just speak of the kingship of "Christ"

---

[15] Advocates of 2K do not like the term "neutral" (see, e.g., VanDrunen 2010a, 179); I will nevertheless use the term at all places where the "common kingdom" is viewed as religiously neutral.

[16] VanDrunen (2010a) prefers the term "common(ality)," but I find this insufficiently specific. By "neutral" I do not mean "apart from God," for this is not what VanDrunen intends, but "apart from the explicit guidelines of God's Word and the kingship of the glorified Man Christ Jesus."

because of the bizarre doctrine that the sacred domain is under the *Logos sarkos* ("incarnate Word," read: the glorified Christ), and the secular domain under the *Logos asarkos* ("non-incarnate Word," read: the Second Person in the Godhead).[17] This doctrine is bizarre because there is no *Logos asarkos* at present, and there will never again be any such person. The Son is both God and Man, but we can no longer speak of his deity apart from his humanity (see §8.5.2).

(b) As to the universal authority of Scripture, of course, 2K theology does not deny that the Christian as an individual, living and functioning as a member of a state, a family, a working environment, etc., is under the authority of Scripture. But it does deny that states, families, schools, and companies *as such* are under the authority of Scripture; that is, it denies that Scripture as such supplies us with a Christian worldview that helps us to develop a Christian view of marriage, of the family, the school, the company, the association, and even the state.

In contrast with all these views, which I consider to be erroneous, I wish to present what I believe to be a truly Reformational picture, one in which the entire world is viewed as being under the authority of Scripture and under the kingship of Christ. For me and many others, this implies that there is, or must be, a Christian(-philosophical) view of religion, a Christian(-philosophical) view of culture, a Christian(-philosophical) view of the state, of science, of the arts, and even a Christian(-philosophical) view of theology. Where this is denied, we again encounter scholastic dualism, no matter what new garment it may be wearing.

In its simplest form, scholasticism is always this: there is a spiritual (sacred, Christ-ruled) domain and a natural (secular, common, neutral) domain, which have to be carefully kept apart. There is a domain under the authority of God's Word and a domain that is supposedly governed by the God-given "natural law" but, as we will see, actually by pagan (or apostate-Christian) principles. There is a domain under the kingship of Christ and a "neutral" domain (which is at best a domain that falls under God's general providence). Such a dualism is a fundamental attack on the spirit of the Reformation: God's Word has its sway over all of reality; for instance, a notion such as that of "natural law" *has no meaning apart from God's Word*, which provides its underpinning, its nature, and its meaning (see chapter 4).

---

[17] Bolt (1983, 30); cf. VanDrunen (2010b, 75–76, 426–27).

1.2.2   A Historical Snare

I realize that I may be accused here of falling into the snare into which, in my view, 2K theologians have fallen. They claim: 2K theology is the original (Lutheran and) Reformed view, whereas the so-called "neo-Calvinism" of Abraham Kuyper and Herman Dooyeweerd is supposed to constitute a deviation. So if you want to be a good Reformed Christian, you ought to follow the 2K line, not the Kuyper–Dooyeweerd line. That is, you must follow the straight line, not the deviation. This is what Christian sects do, too (which does not mean that I am calling 2K theologians sectarians!): our group represents the oldest form of Christianity (or Reformational Christianity), and all others are deviations.

I presume that each of the almost seventy (!) Reformed or Presbyterian denominations in North America considers itself to be *the* most faithful representative of good old Reformed/Presbyterian persuasion—what else would be their *raison d'être*? So the others are a bit less faithful—if otherwise, why not unite with them? I find this one of the most pathetic aspects of the 2K discussion: let the real Reformed version please stand up! As if in the light of eternity, anyone will still care about the most "authentic" brand of Reformed/Presbyterian persuasion.

To narrow it down a bit, for years now there has been a fierce debate in North America on who represents the truly Reformed tradition: is it the neo-Calvinist (Kuyper-Van Tilian) line, as it had been for such a long time at Westminster Theological Seminary (WTS) in Philadelphia? Or is it the 2K line as it has now been developed at WSC?[18] Who is the true representative of Luther and Calvin, and of the Reformed and Presbyterian confessions? I ask again this revolutionary and "biblicistic" question: For whom are these questions actually relevant? Who cares? Should not only one question prevail in the end: What is the most *biblical* (or if you like, theologically purest) approach?

Now I myself do not want to fall into a similar historical-theological snare. That is, I am not going to attempt to show that the Kuyper-Dooyeweerd line, or the Kuyper-Van Til line, is the most faithfully Reformed because it supposedly corresponds with the earliest Lutheran and Calvinist views. On the contrary, I would rather defend the position that there was still too

---

[18] An interesting exception at WSC seems or seemed to be its president, W. Robert Godfrey, who wrote (2009): "The implication of the universal kingdom of Jesus is that there is no neutral realm in this world. All are either honoring him or rebelling against him. Clearly all Christians must seek to think and live as Christians in all that they do. In everything, we acknowledge Jesus as king." These are great words at a school where, nowadays, the kingship of the glorified Man Jesus is limited to the domain of the church.

much scholasticism in those older views, and that Kuyper and especially Dooyeweerd pointed to a way of breaking out of these scholastic bonds (see chapter 2). This is why I will hardly enter into the views of Luther and Calvin, and other early Reformational thinkers.[19] I would rather focus on the question what is the purest biblical-theological position in line with the most basic of all Reformational insights: *sola Scriptura*, that is, the recognition of the universal authority of God's Word in all domains of life and society. As John Frame said courageously regarding the accusation of biblicism: "My own critique of the Escondido Theology is based on Scripture, not on the history of Reformed thought."[20] This is my desire as well.

Moreover, I maintain the Reformation's *solus Christus*, the universal mediatorship and kingship of Christ (cf. §7.5): "For there is one God, and there is one mediator between God and men, the man Christ Jesus" (1 Tim. 2:5). There are not *two* mediators: the Man Christ Jesus (for the sacred realm), and the *Logos asarkos* (for the secular realm). As I said, since the Incarnation there *is* no longer a *Logos asarkos*: "The Word became flesh" (John 1:14); not part of the Word became flesh, and another part remained *asarkos*. Of course, we must clearly distinguish between the divine and the human natures of Christ,[21] but we may not separate them. The whole idea of a *present* non-incarnate (part of the) *Logos* is a grave Christological error.

1.2.3 A Positive Approach

Refuting a certain theory, such as the 2K model (hereafter: NL2K[22]), is a negative (antithetical) enterprise. My main goal is rather a positive (thetical) one, namely, to explain and underpin the one kingdom model: the glorified Man at God's right hand is King over the entire universe (Matt. 28:18), no domains excepted. Moreover, I wish to do so, not from a historical-theological angle but from a biblical-theological one. So far, a large part of the discussion surrounding NL2K has been a historical analysis. What did NL2K say Augustine said, and was this correct? What did NL2K say Martin Luther said, and was this a balanced presentation? And what about Calvin, or the early Reformed theologians? Or how did NL2K deal

---

[19] For Calvin, I refer, e.g., to Wedgeworth (2010), C. Venema, and G. Haas in McIlhenny (2012, 3–63), and Tuininga (2016); for Luther and Calvin, see Kloosterman (2012a) and Littlejohn (2012b; see on their successors: 2012c–e). For Kuyper and Bavinck, respectively, see Kloosterman (2012a) and N. D. Kloosterman in McIlhenny (2012b, 65–81).

[20] Cf. Frame (2011, 20 note 12).

[21] See extensively, Ouweneel (2007b).

[22] "The doctrine of Natural Law and Two Kingdoms." I suppose this abbreviation was first used by Kloosterman (2012a).

with Abraham Kuyper and Herman Dooyeweerd? Did NL2K quote Luther, Kuyper, Bavinck, etc., in a selective way to support their own theory, or did they properly represent them?

This is not my approach; it is a blind alley. First, what is the profit gained by it? We can go on for decades arguing what Luther, Calvin, or Kuyper said, or did not say, or intended to say. Perhaps in the end we will come to an agreement (although I doubt it). This will be highly interesting for some historical theologians, but hardly for dogmaticians, and certainly not for the public at large. After all, Luther, or Calvin, or Kuyper may have been wrong—or even *all three* may at certain points have been mistaken. As good Protestants, we want to know in the end: *what is written?* Back to the Word!

This is why I follow a biblical-theological approach, that is, what does the Bible say about our subject—one or two kingdoms—and not primarily what did Augustine, Luther, or Calvin say about it. I can guess what the response will be from the VanDrunen camp: biblicism! I realize the danger of my approach. We stand on the shoulders of our predecessors, and should never assume that we could reinvent the theological wheel anew. The "Spirit of truth" will "guide" us "into all the truth" (John 16:13), but he does this primarily collectively, not so much individually. That is, it is God's normal order to teach his children through the "teachers" of the church (Eph. 4:11–14).

However, I also see the opposite danger. We blame Roman Catholic theologians for accepting, in addition to the Bible, (ecclesiastical) tradition as an authoritative source of knowledge. We ourselves must beware of turning the Reformers into a kind of unassailable tradition, especially when such a tradition has been solidified in confessional documents, either the Three Forms of Unity (the Heidelberg Catechism, the Belgic Confession, and the Canons of Dort) or the Westminster Standards (the Westminster Confession of Faith, and the Westminster Shorter and Larger Catechisms). Such confessional documents are binding for church members as such, but they can never be so for academic theologians (see §§10.4.2 and 10.5). Don't confuse the church and the academy![23] I fear the danger of biblicism (see §2.4)—but I dread the danger of confessionalism as well (see §2.5).

The path of truth is a narrow path between these two "-isms." Yet, I insist that I am not primarily interested in a Lutheran or a Reformed model, but in a model that I, as an orthodox Protestant, can defend biblical-theologically with a good conscience. During his defense at the Diet of Worms (1522), Luther said that he would believe neither the pope, nor the councils, since they had often erred, and often contradicted each other. He said he only

---

[23] See extensively, Ouweneel (2013, chapter 10; 2014c, chapter 5).

believed the biblical passages that he had quoted, and his conscience was bound by the Word of God (see at the end of the next chapter). Let me, very immodestly, say the same—just as I think *every* Protestant thinker should say: I do not believe Luther, Melanchthon, Calvin, or Beza, since they have often erred, and often contradicted each other. I do not even wish to choose between Kuyper and Kline, or between Van Til and VanDrunen. As a good Protestant, I maintain *sola Scriptura*; my conscience is bound by this alone. I am convinced that only in this way can I be (at least as far as this point is concerned) a genuine Lutheran!

N. T. Wright reportedly said that one third of his books were false—he simply did not know *which* third. This is probably true for all of us. The popes and councils were wrong on certain points, Luther and Calvin were too, Kuyper and Kline were, and we are as well. This is not relativism—just modesty. The only thing we can do is not hide behind the backs of past giants, but study Scripture as thoroughly as possible and remain faithful to our consciences. It is a great thing if we can truly say: "I am speaking the truth in Christ—I am not lying; my conscience bears me witness in the Holy Spirit" (Rom. 9:1). *If* we err on certain points, then at least let us do it with a good conscience.

1.3   HOW REFORMED IS THE DEBATE?

1.3.1   What Is Reformed?

These few paragraphs have already yielded a number of problems that have to be dealt with in the rest of this book: What exactly does the 2K doctrine entail, and what does the one-kingdom doctrine entail? What is scholasticism, and is it acceptable or objectionable? To what extent has early Protestantism been infected with scholasticism? Is there room for such a thing as Christian philosophy, and what does it entail? What is the proper relationship between (Christian) theology and (Christian) philosophy? If a Christian view of science, or culture, or the state, or "natural law" cannot be derived from the Bible, how do we arrive at such views? What is the role of Christian philosophy in this? What exactly is biblicism? What is confessionalism? What is the relationship between the two? What are the dangers in them?

There is another question to be raised here. The entire debate surrounding NL2K has been a Reformed one;[24] apparently it is hardly a subject for

---

[24] I am ignoring here the fine theological distinctions between "Reformed" and "Presbyterian" theology. They both claim to be Calvinistic, but their historical development has been

outsiders.[25] One must be Reformed to truly savor it. Why is this so? Why is
NL2K a Reformed issue at all? Can a person reject this theology, and still be
Reformed? Apparently this is possible, for there are many Reformed theologians who thoroughly disagree with NL2K (although I realize that both
parties quickly accuse the other party of "not being genuinely Reformed"[26]).
Or, we might ask the reverse: Can a person accept this theology without
being Reformed? I would say, Why not? In other words, why was this such
a Reformed discussion in the first place? Is there any room at all for a not-
so-Reformed theologian mingling himself into this discussion?

At the same time, the question may be raised as to what the term
"Reformed" actually means. As I said, I count almost seventy different
denominations in North America that call themselves Reformed or
Presbyterian (as is well known, the Reformed in the narrower sense are
usually Calvinists of Dutch (sometimes German) descent, and Presbyterians
are usually Calvinists of Scottish and English descent). Almost seventy
Calvinistic denominations! Catholics, Lutherans, and Anglicans will not
envy such a painful dissension. Who is in a position to define what is
Reformed? And if we do not think in terms of denominations but of parties,
who would dare say that, for instance, non-Klineans (who, as far as I can
see, form the great majority of the Reformed world) are not Reformed?[27]

To make it simple, let us assume that a person is Reformed if he fully and
wholeheartedly subscribes to the Three Forms of Unity. But is it that simple? What about the Reformed Baptists (a group that included such godly
men as John Bunyan [d. 1688], Joseph C. Philpot [d. 1869], and Charles H.
Spurgeon [d. 1892])? What about the present-day Reformed who reject the
idea of an eternal decree of reprobation? Or are these people simply not
Reformed? But also: in what sense do the Three Forms of Unity cast light
on the one- or two-kingdoms debate? If the Forms are decisive about what
is the truly Reformed approach, then NL2K is obviously the loser.[28]

---

quite different. Moreover, there are (not unimportant) theological differences between the
much earlier Forms of Unity and the much later Westminster Standards. The gourmets of
Calvinist theology sometimes smell right away whether some treatise has a Presbyterian or a
Reformed flavor. In the present book, I use "Reformed" in the wider sense of "Calvinistic."

[25] As excellent exceptions, I mention the Anglican Craig Bartholomew (2017); Bartholomew
and Goheen (2013); Goheen and Bartholomew (2008); the Southern Baptist Russell D. Moore
(see, e.g., 2004; 2015), and the Evangelical Gideon Strauss—all of whom obviously sympathize
with Reformed thought.

[26] E.g., Clark (2008, 3–4); VanDrunen (2010b, 348–50); Frame (2011, xxxix).

[27] Cf. Frame (2011, 193–94 note 4, 249, 305).

[28] See Kloosterman (2012a, 33–34).

1.3.2   The Heidelberg Catechism

First, let us listen to the Heidelberg Catechism (Q/A 50; also cf. Q/A 31):[29] "Q. Why is it added: 'And sitteth at the right hand of God'? A. Because Christ ascended into heaven for this end, that He might there appear as the Head of His Church (Eph. 1:20–23; Col. 1:18), by whom the Father governs all things (John 5:22)."[30] These words implicitly deny that Christ, the *Logos Sarkos* (the "Word incarnate"), is King only over a spiritual realm, the church; he is the One "by whom the Father governs *all things.*"

The Catechism refers here to Matthew 28:18 (where Jesus, as the risen *Man*, says, "All authority in heaven and on earth has been given to me"), Ephesians 1:20–23 (where it is said of the risen *Man*, God "put *all things* under his feet"), and Colossians 1:18 ("He is the beginning, the firstborn from the dead, that *in everything* he might be preeminent"). It is the same One who made purification for sins who now exercises supreme authority at God's right hand (Heb. 1:3–4). It is the risen Man Jesus Christ "who has gone into heaven and is at the right hand of God, with angels, authorities, and powers having been subjected to him" (1 Pet. 3:21–22).

It is simply false to assert that the glorified Man Jesus is King over some "kingdom of God" in the limited sense of the (visible) church, but not over some secular realm. Ephesians 1 makes the falsity of this distinction very clear: God "put all things under his [i.e., Christ's] feet and gave him as head over all things to the church, which is his body, the fullness of him who fills all in all." He who is the head of the body (the church) is the same person who, at the same time, is head over "all things." Either the body and these "all things" are here two different matters, or "all things" includes the church but is a much wider concept. If Christ is King over the kingdom of God, this kingdom contains not only the church, but, in Jesus' own words, it contains the entire world (cf. Matt. 13:38, the "field" is "the world"). Also the earthly "rulers and authorities" (Titus 3:1) stand under Christ's kingship (Eph. 1:20–21; Col. 1:15–18; 1 Pet. 3:21–22).

Please note that, in the passages quoted, it is not the Second Person of the Godhead—in this quality—who rules over all things. From the beginning of creation, the Triune God has ruled over the world, and this included, and includes, God the Son. However, the quoted passages indicate that a new situation has emerged: it is the Man who went through death and resurrection, and is now gloriously seated at God's right hand, who is the King of the world. He is still God the Son, the Second Person of the Godhead—but it

---

[29] Ouweneel (2016d, 155–58; cf. 93–97).
[30] Dennison (2008, 4:780).

is as the risen and glorified *Man* that he is now King, not just of the church but of *all things*. This is a key point for the remainder of this book: the Man Christ rules over all the domains of this world.

1.3.3   The Belgic Confession

Second, the original version of the Belgic Confession (Art. 36) says, God

> has invested the magistracy with "the sword for the punishment of evil-doers and for the protection of them that do well." Their office is not only to have regard unto and watch for the welfare of the civil state, but also that they protect the sacred ministry, and thus may remove and prevent all idolatry and false worship, that the kingdom of antichrist may be thus destroyed and the kingdom of Christ promoted. They must, therefore, countenance the preaching of the Word of the gospel everywhere, that God may be honored and worshipped by every one, as He commands in His Word.[31]

The text unequivocally says that it belongs to the God-given task of the government *to promote "the kingdom of Christ,"* and to further "the preaching of the Word of the gospel everywhere," so that God may be honoured by *everyone*. Also the modified version drafted by the Synod of the Christian Reformed Churches (1958) still says that the civil rulers carry out their task "in order that the Word of God may have free course; *the kingdom of Jesus Christ may make progress*; and every anti-Christian power may be resisted" (italics added). This includes the anti-Christian powers that dominate most nation states in the world. The Belgic Confession knows of no neutral realm in this regard.

Compare this with the Westminster Confession of Faith (23.3): The civil magistrate (!)

> hath authority, and it is his duty, to take order that unity and peace be preserved in the Church, that the truth of God be kept pure and entire, that all blasphemies and heresies be suppressed, all corruptions and abuses in worship and discipline prevented or reformed, and all the ordinances of God duly settled, administered, and observed (Isa. 49:23; Ps. 122:9; Ezra 7:23, 25–28; Lev. 24:16; Deut. 13:5–6, 12; 2 Kings 18:4; 1 Chron. 13:1–9; 2 Kings 24:1–20; 2 Chron. 34:33; 15:12–13). For the better effecting whereof, he hath power to call synods, to be

---

[31] Ibid., 4:447.

present at them, and to provide that whatsoever is transacted in them be according to the mind of God (2 Chron. 19:8–11; 2 Chron. 29–30; Matt. 2:4–5).[32]

Of course, there has been much debate surrounding these confessional statements. Is it true that the civil authorities have the right to interfere with church matters, and even have the power to "call synods"? Today, few Reformed thinkers would agree with this (the relevant paragraphs were even revised at the foundation of the Presbyterian Church in the United States in 1788). We believe in the "separation of church and state" (although this expression is often misunderstood; see §5.5). But the point at stake here is that apparently it would have been unthinkable for the divines who wrote the Belgic Confession (Guido de Brès, d. 1567) and the Westminster Confession to accept the idea that the "secular" state falls outside the kingdom of God. How can this be reconciled with the idea of two kingdoms, one of which is the secular state that is *not at all* called to promote God's kingdom, and does not even belong to this kingdom?

For me it is not decisive what the Belgic Confession and the Westminster Confession say on this matter. However, for those who quibble about who the "real Reformed" are, it should be very illuminating that the Reformed/Presbyterian confessions speak in a way very different from NL2K.

1.3.4 The Canons of Dort

Third, the Canons of Dort (3/4.4) say,

There remain, however, in man since the fall, the glimmerings of natural light, whereby he retains some knowledge of God, of natural things, and of the difference between good and evil, and shows some regard for virtue and for good outward behavior. But so far is this light of nature from being sufficient to bring him to a saving knowledge of God and to true conversion that *he is incapable of using it aright even in things natural and civil.* Nay further, *this light, such as it is, man in various ways renders wholly polluted, and hinders in unrighteousness,* by doing which he becomes inexcusable before God.[33]

This view conflicts radically with Horton's and VanDrunen's idea of the natural law ruling the secular kingdom without any need of the light of God's

---

[32] Ibid., 4:262.
[33] Dennison (2008, 4:135); italics added.

Word-revelation being cast upon that natural law. NL2K's idea of natural law is an excellent example of a theological theory that has a kernel of truth (see chapter 4), but began to lead a life of its own, and in the end was inflated so strongly that its adherents began to "read" it everywhere into the Bible and into (Reformed) literature. In my view, Horton and VanDrunen[34] are clear examples of this. In opposition to them, Joseph Boot describes natural law as "an originally Stoic concept filled with difficulties, the *actual content* of which nobody seems to know with any clarity."[35]

Notice the Canons' reference to Romans 1:18, "For the wrath of God is revealed from heaven against all ungodliness and unrighteousness of men, who *by their unrighteousness suppress the truth*." To be sure, there is some knowledge of God and his law within natural persons: "They show that the work of the law is written on their hearts" (2:15)—but in combination with 1:18 this shows that such knowledge is totally corrupted by sin (see extensively §4.1). Whatever awareness of divine things they may have is suppressed by their unrighteousness. It is impossible to found a state or a society upon natural law alone in such a way that such a state or society could be pleasing and honouring to God (see the Belgic Confession again).

Reviewing the testimony of the Three Forms of Unity, plus that from the Westminster Confession of Faith, I do not see how Horton, VanDrunen, and their fellow thinkers (Clark, Hart, Stellman) can be viewed as truly standing in the Reformed tradition. They may be called orthodox Christians, for they subscribe to the Apostolic and the Nicene Confessions. But if they claim for themselves that *they* stand in the true Reformed tradition, they are mistaken—at least if the Forms of Unity are viewed as faithful representations of this Reformed tradition.

1.4   DO I QUALIFY?

1.4.1   Am I Reformed Enough?

I wonder whether I myself qualify for participating in the NL2K debate. If one must definitely belong to the Reformed camp—in whichever of its nearly seventy varieties—then I may be disqualified. Although I have about fifteen thousand Dutch Reformed (*Nederduits Gereformeerde*, since 1816 *Nederlands Hervormde*) ancestors, I have never been a member of one of the more than twenty (!) Reformed denominations that, since my birth,

---

[34] Horton (1995, 196–98); VanDrunen (2006; 2010a; 2010b; 2014).
[35] Boot (2016).

have existed in the Netherlands. I have been raised among the (Plymouth) Brethren,[36] but today I prefer to call myself an orthodox-evangelical Protestant. I do subscribe to the Five Points of Calvinism, though with a few nuances.[37] I recognize the importance of the notion of the covenant,[38] although I do not see how one could call *all* relationships between God and humans "covenantal" (such as, for instance, the Father–children relationship).

As far as my education is concerned, I went to a Christian primary school where the teachers were Reformed. I went to a Christian secondary school where at least the teachers of religion were Reformed. I received my first doctorate, in the natural sciences (1970), at a University—that of Utrecht— whose founders were Reformed; its motto is still *Sol Iustitiae, Illustra Nos* ("Sun of righteousness, illuminate us;" cf. Mal. 4:2). I earned my second doctorate, in philosophy (1986), at the Free University of Amsterdam, whose founders were Reformed, and whose philosophical department was still largely Reformed. The subject of my dissertation was the philosophical anthropology of Reformed philosopher Herman Dooyeweerd (d. 1977). The two promoters, Andree Troost (d. 2008) and Evert H. van Olst (d. 2012), were Reformed. I obtained my third doctorate, in theology (1993), at the University of the Orange Free State in Bloemfontein (South Africa), where the theological department was Reformed. All the members of the theological examining committee were Reformed professors: my promoter Sybrand A. Strauss, and the examiners Andree Troost (d. 2008), Danie F. M. Strauss, and Ludie F. Schulze.

As to my academic posts, in 1977 I was one of the four founders of the Evangelical College (Evangelische Hogeschool) at Amersfoort (the Netherlands); the other three were Reformed. I have taught at this College until my retirement in 2009. From 1990 till 1997, I was a professor in the philosophy of the natural sciences at the Potchefstroom University for Christian Higher Education (South Africa), where the term "Christian" was practically synonymous with "Reformed." From 1995 until my retirement in 2014, I was a professor on the Evangelical Theological Faculty in Leuven (Belgium), an international theological school with an international academic staff; the majority of the Dutch and the South African professors were Reformed. From 1996 until 2001, I was a professor in philosophy, theology, and psychology at the State-Independent Theological Seminary

---

[36] So, too, were twentieth-century Bible scholars, such as the Scotsman Dr. Frederick B. Bruce (d. 1990), the Irish Dr. David W. Gooding (b. 1925), and Dr. John Lennox (b. 1943).

[37] See Ouweneel (2016i, §12.3).

[38] See Ouweneel (2016g).

in Basel (Switzerland), whose rector, Samuel R. Külling (d. 2003), as well as part of the academic staff, were Reformed.

As to my preaching, I move as easily within the Dutch Reformed Church (since 2004, after merging with the Dutch Lutherans and the Kuyperian *gereformeerden*, called the Protestant Church in the Netherlands)—where I have preached dozens of times—as within the Evangelical free churches, from Baptist to charismatic. I have preached in Reformed churches both in the Netherlands and in South Africa. I wrote a book of daily devotionals on the Heidelberg Catechism,[39] and five dogmatic volumes in which I evaluated, in a sympathetic-critical way, the most important areas of Reformed theology.[40]

What does this mean? First, according to the Three Forms of Unity, Michael Horton, David VanDrunen, and their friends in several important respects cannot be called Reformed. Second, in several important respects, I do qualify as a philosopher and theologian strongly shaped by the Reformed tradition. And third, what does it all matter? Do Reformed theologians have a monopoly on the issue about whether there is one kingdom of God in this world, or two kingdoms of God? Of course not. Therefore, let me break open this discussion by interjecting my not-so-Reformed, or not-entirely-Reformed contribution.

1.4.2   I Am Dutch!

There is a second "problem:" I am not American or Canadian (or Australian or British), but Dutch. I have visited about fifty different countries, I have preached or lectured in about thirty countries, and I have been affiliated with academic institutions in four countries (Belgium, the Netherlands, South Africa, Switzerland). Yet, I have never spent more than twelve weeks in a row in any other country than the Netherlands. I have visited the United States and Canada almost twenty times, and I have visited about half of all the American states. I think I know a little about that part of the world, as well as its mentality. Yet, I am still Dutch.

Funny enough, my main opponents as well as my main fellow thinkers all have Dutch surnames (a little alphabetical selection: Berkhof, Dooyeweerd, Haas, Kloosterman, Kuyper, Plantinga, Stob, Tuininga, Vander Goot, VanDrunen, Van der Waal, Venema, Vos, Wolters, Zylstra, etc.), so the debate almost seems to be a Dutch one anyway—without disregarding Meredith Kline, Darryl Hart, Michael Horton, and Jason Stellman, of

---

[39] Ouweneel (2016d).
[40] Ouweneel (2016e–i).

course. Or is the "Dutch" VanDrunen the great exception here? Is this in fact a battle between the Reformed of Dutch descent and the Presbyterians of British descent? I find this question highly interesting—not because of the Dutch-British contrast, of course, but the Reformed-Presbyterian contrast. Some other theologian might try to figure this out. In any case, I am on the "Dutch" side.

The question is quite important from a linguistic point of view. Some NL2K theologians who oppose Kuyper and Dooyeweerd are not even able to read these opponents, and so many of their fellow thinkers, in Dutch. They are dependent on English translations, which cover only a limited part of the work of so many relevant Dutch theologians. For instance, how many Presbyterians are able to read the almost 1,750 (!) pages of Kuyper's majestic *Pro Rege, of het koningschap van Christus* ("Pro Rege, or the Kingship of Christ"),[41] which is only now for the first time being published in English translation? I have had these three volumes on my shelves for decades, and I cannot imagine how a person like VanDrunen could write a refutation of Kuyper's views on Christ's kingship without having read this monumental work. The very first lines explain the purpose of the entire work: "*Pro Rege* is being written with the aim of removing the separation between our life *inside* the church and our life *outside* the church …. "[42] Great! *This* is one of Kuyper's works that VanDrunen badly needs to read!

In orthodox-Reformed North America, being Dutch is hardly an advantage nowadays, especially if one has studied at the Free University, like me. To reassure my readers I may tell them that I believe in the full inspiration and divine authority of the Scriptures,[43] and that I am resolutely opposed to abortion and homosexual practice. I do not wish people to say, He is from the Netherlands, and he is an alumnus of the Free University, so he can't be any good. If I'm not "any good," that is not due to *these* reasons.

I apologize for talking in these two sections only about myself. But this seemed unavoidable. I would appreciate it if NL2K theologians were prepared to listen to a philosopher-theologian who is not only not-entirely-Reformed but also Dutch. Nelson Kloosterman already wrote of those who

---

[41] Kuyper (2016b); see for an English summary of his views Kuyper (2009); cf. Kloosterman (2012a, 45–47). This series is now appearing in English translation: *Pro Rege: Living Under Christ's Kingship*; vol. 1: *The Exalted Nature of Christ's Kingship*, edited by John Kok and Nelson D. Kloosterman, translated by Albert Gootjes; Abraham Kuyper, *Collected Works in Public Theology* (Acton Institute for the Study of Religion and Liberty / Lexham Press, 2016).

[42] Kuyper (2016b, xxxii).

[43] See, e.g., Ouweneel (2012b; 2016b).

discard the present debate as "just a Dutch thing."[44] One need think only of Abraham Kuyper, Herman Bavinck, Herman Dooyeweerd, a Dutch-American like Cornelius Van Til, and those other so-called neo-Calvinists (Geerhardus Vos, Bernard Zylstra, Al Wolters, all born in the Netherlands).

Incidentally, I see a tremendous advantage in being a European philosopher-theologian. I do not know personally anyone who teaches at WTS Philadelphia and WSC. I have neither studied, nor taught, nor lectured at these places. I have never been under the enormous impact of a genius like Meredith Kline (d. 2007); I have never been tempted to become a Klinean, nor to become one of his mortal enemies. I have never been a disciple of Norman Shepherd or John Murray; I have never felt the possible tensions between Reformed and Presbyterians, or between Princeton and Westminster, or between Kuyperians, Van Tilians, and their opponents. When reading John Frame's *The Escondido Theology*,[45] I often think: he *knows* all those people far too well. I do not. I do not know their formidable (or not so formidable) personalities, but I do know (some of) their writings. To be sure, neither have I personally known Kuyper, Bavinck, and Dooyeweerd.

Of course, I know very well why some authors are Klineans: they studied at WSC. But I do not hold that against them. I judge them by what they write. I do not care which of them are the "most Reformed," I care only about their orthodoxy. That is to say, are they in line with the Nicene-Constantinopolitan Creed, and with what I understand of the Bible, the divinely-inspired, infallible, and authoritative Word of God?

1.4.3   An American Problem

John Frame wrote,

> The two kingdoms view, as the Escondido theologians understand it, goes beyond Reformation theology in important ways. Indeed, except for the law/gospel dichotomy, its distinctive positions are American, not European. It was in America that the Westminster Confession was revised to eliminate the possibility of state control of the church. It was in America that Presbyterians developed the doctrine of the "spirituality of the church" that forbade the church to speak or act in matters secular.[46]

---

[44] Kloosterman (2012a, 56–58).

[45] Frame (2011).

[46] Frame (2011, 5; also see 19–20 notes 9 and 10).

Of course, as a thorough European I find this highly interesting. I think Frame is absolutely right. In the Netherlands, Reformed thinking has been strong from the sixteenth century to the present (though much less so since the middle of the twentieth century). It would be difficult to imagine the development of Reformed thinking in North America without the influence of the Dutch theologians, or the influence of theologians who were born in the Netherlands, spent their early youth there, and grew up in a Dutch-American family steeped in Reformed thinking. Yet, in no Dutch Reformed mind could the idea ever arise that "the church"—usually what is meant is: individual Christians—is/are not supposed to try to influence the state and society by means of explicit Christian values, norms, and ideas.

In the Netherlands, there have been Christian political parties since the beginning of parliamentary democracy (1848). They have all been thoroughly democratic; otherwise they could not have participated in the political process. Yet, they were not, and until today are not, ashamed to appeal to Christian norms and principles in Parliament. And where they participated in coalition governments—as they usually did—they sought to implement as much of their Christian ideas as they could, though always respecting the democratic process. It is interesting that NL2K really thinks that Christian politics is inconceivable and undesirable. I would recommend that they study the history of Christian politics in the Netherlands.[47]

Christian Democracy has flourished, or still flourishes, in Austria, Belgium, Finland, Germany, Hungary, Ireland, Italy, Luxembourg, Malta, Norway, Poland, Portugal, Romania, Spain, Sweden, Ukraine, and Serbia (alphabetical order) (although I must admit that I am not convinced in every case of the confessional depth of such a party). We cannot say that it did not work in the United States because unfortunately it simply has never been tried—and I cannot see that this was because Americans were wiser than Europeans. I fear it was more the influence of the Enlightenment on the Founding Fathers. I would recommend that advocates of NL2K should devote study to European Christian Democracy. It might help them overcome their bizarre and narrow-minded prejudices toward "Christian" politics. Historian Darryl Hart in particular might greatly profit from this.[48]

And how does NL2K relate to countries where Christians are persecuted? As Joseph Boot says, "Sociologically, this culturally retreatist *theology* [i.e., NL2K] is emanating from the comfortable academic halls of white,

---

[47] Some introductory reading: Bosmans (2004); Lucardie (2004); see further Galetto (1990); Kalyvas (1996); Kaiser (2007).

[48] See Hart (2006).

middle-class, *Christian* enclaves like Escondido and Grand Rapids—not the fires of persecution in the Syrian or Pakistani church. I do not believe it is viable to take 2K theologies seriously in most of the rest of world where Christians are suffering, sometimes terribly, in lands dominated by false religion. It is all too easy to speak of a 'common kingdom' governed by norms we can all agree on from the comfortable academic chairs of a culture deeply transformed by the gospel for centuries. What can really be said of the notion of a 'common kingdom' governed by 'natural law' that all essentially agree upon, in places where Christians are being beheaded and raped, or their children murdered in front of them?"[49]

A little later in his article, Boot writes:

> Perhaps VanDrunen's most bizarre conclusion comes when he argues that, *"The odds are good, in fact, that if you ask your unbelieving neighbor whether he believes in freedom, satisfaction of basic needs, ecological responsibility, fair trade and healthy local businesses, he will heartily agree."*[50] This statement makes it obvious to me at least that these scholars advocating 2K theology need to leave their sheltered academic cloister in Christianized leafy communities in Escondido and Grand Rapids and go and live in the Islamic world for twelve months before promoting their doctrine. And in fact there is little need to go to Pakistan to question this assumption. Come to West Toronto and you can't get agreement from your neighbor that there are two genders and that marriage is between a man and a woman! Ask my progressivist community about "freedom" in the sense of the Western political tradition and they believe it is obsolete in light of the need for a socially just society.

These points are well taken. NL2K may work only in a neat white American middle-class community *that has some centuries of Christian civilization behind it*. Chances are good that VanDrunen's "unbelieving neighbor" is an apostate Christian, or a (grand)child of apostate Christians, who—usually unconsciously—has retained a lot of Christian values. NL2K's "common kingdom" is a dream world. Come out of your comfortable chairs, American NL2K theologians, and begin to study, on the one hand, Christian-democratic parties in Europe and, on the other hand, how you would apply

---

[49] Boot (2016).

[50] VanDrunen (2010a, 194); cf. Mattson's (2011) comment: "No. Actually, outside of the Western world, the odds are not nearly so good."

NL2K in extreme Muslim countries, where the "common kingdom" is dominated by false religion—or even in the slums of your own large cities. Is this the trilemma: a neutral state, or a state of anarchy, or a state based on false religion? Is there not a fourth option: a state based on true religion, or at least a state with one or more strong Christian-democratic parties?

During 2016, the most powerful woman on earth was a pastor's daughter, Angela Merkel (b. 1954), the *Christian*-democratic Federal Chancellor (i.e., prime minister) of Germany, a lady who is not ashamed to witness about her faith. And Germany's president was Joachim Gauck (b. 1940), a Protestant pastor, and an anti-communist human rights activist during the time of the German Democratic Republic (communist East Germany).

1.5   WHAT THIS BOOK IS NOT ABOUT

I fully realize that, if we wish to do full justice to NL2K, we would have to view it within the framework of the entire "Escondido theology" (as John Frame has called it). And this theology ought to be considered within the framework of Presbyterian theology, possibly in relation to Reformed (Dutch-German Calvinist) theological traditions, and at any rate against the backdrop of the Westminster Standards.[51] It is impossible within the scope of the present book to deal with all this material. However, I am glad that I have dealt with a number of relevant issues in my "Eternal Series:"

(a) For the problems involving "law and gospel" I refer to my book on the Mosaic Law.[52]

(b) VanDrunen sees a direct relationship between NL2K and the "traditional" Reformed doctrine of justification.[53] For my views on this subject I refer to my work on justification.[54]

(c) Those who are familiar with the Escondido theology know about the profound conflict between Meredith Kline and Norman Shepherd concerning the covenant(s) (with issues such as the Mosaic covenant viewed as a "republication" of the covenant of works at Mount Sinai, etc.). For these issues, I refer to my book on the covenants.[55]

(d) As an introduction to the subject of one or two kingdoms, I suggest reading my book on the kingdom of God.[56]

---

[51] See Frame (2011, 1–21) for a historical overview.
[52] Ouweneel (2016f).
[53] VanDrunen (2010a, 21).
[54] Ouweneel (2016h).
[55] Ouweneel (2016g).
[56] Ouweneel (2016e).

(e) For the vigorous debate about "theonomy" (the view that the Mosaic civil laws apply to states today), see my books on eschatology and the Torah.[57]

(f) For those who feel that no Reformed/Presbyterian discussion can ever occur without mentioning matters like the counsel of God, predestination, election, and the like, I refer to my book on these matters.[58]

I humbly suggest that the present book should be considered against the backdrop of this entire "Eternal Series," in which I evaluate the most important Reformed/Presbyterian issues of the present time. In addition to this, for those who read Dutch, I may point to my twelve-volume Evangelical Dogmatic Series (Evangelisch Dogmatische Reeks).[59] For instance, for my extensive treatise on "natural revelation" (NL2K would say: "natural law," which basically amounts to the same[60]) I refer to this Series.[61]

WORKING IT OUT / **CHRISTIAN CULTURAL ACTIVITY**
Some people claim that the New Testament says little or nothing about Christian cultural activity. Is this claim correct?

Let us first establish what we wish to understand by cultural activity. The shortest definition of culture that I know is this: culture is developed nature. This development leads to agriculture and body culture, but also to (practical and theoretical) knowledge, art, beliefs, morals, a judicial order, an economic order, civilization, society. All people are engaged in certain forms of cultural activity: working the land, working their bodies, working their minds (schooling, self-study, science), being part of society as families, as members of churches, associations, political parties, as citizens (voters, taxpayers), as road users, as sellers and buyers, as writers and readers, as producers and consumers, as employers and employees, as painters and enjoyers of painting, as musicians and as enjoyers of music. All people have vocations,[62] including their jobs, from which other people are supposed to profit.

[57] Ouweneel (2012a; 2016f).
[58] Ouweneel (2016i).
[59] Ouweneel (2007a–2013).
[60] Cf. Frame (2011, 128, 148 note 3).
[61] Ouweneel (2012b, chapters 1–4).
[62] "Vocation" means literally "calling," which originally is God's calling. Luther linked *Beruf* ("profession") with *Berufung* ("calling") so that, in his view, the maid was as much "called" by God as the king or the pastor (see, e.g., WA 14.18b.11 etc.).

Now what is *Christian cultural activity*? This is an ambiguous phrase. Because we are Christians, in a sense all our cultural activity is Christian cultural activity: we are Christian citizens, road users, sellers, buyers, and so forth. In this sense, the New Testament naturally speaks about Christian cultural activity because it views the Christian in all his various cultural activities: Peter, John, and James were fishermen (John 21:2–3); Paul, Aquila, and Priscilla were tentmakers (Acts 18:3); other believers (-to-be) were shepherds, soldiers, tax collectors, tailors, treasurers, sellers of purple, household servants (Luke 2:8; 3:14; 7:8; 8:27; 19:2; Acts 9:39; 10:1; 16:14; 1 Pet. 2:18 [*oiketai*]), etc. The apostles were travellers (e.g., Acts 19:29); Christians are buyers at the meat market (1 Cor. 10:25); singers and musicians ("singing" in 1 Cor. 14:15 is literally "strumming" [a string instrument]; cf. the harp players in Rev. 5:8; 15:2), taxpayers (Rom. 13:6–7); etc. In all these cultural activities, Christians must be honest, fair, dedicated.

Of course, this is not the most interesting meaning of the phrase *Christian cultural activity*. What people would like to know is whether any cultural activity is *specifically* Christian in manner or method. Did Paul make tents differently after his conversion, and did Lydia sell purple differently after her conversion? Do plumbers plumb differently after they have become Christians? Later in this book, we will see that this absurd question is asked frequently, and that the negative answer is used as an argument that there cannot be such a thing as "Christian" culture (science, art, politics, etc.), just as there cannot be such a thing as "Christian plumbing" (§11.4.2). But this is not the point at all. Jesus did not primarily transform culture as such; he transformed *culturally active people*, and he did so knowing that one day these transformed people would begin asking questions about their cultural activities on the basis of their Christian beliefs. They would look for *thought frameworks* that enabled them to be culturally active Christians in a responsible way.

For instance, there is no Christian manner or method of tentmaking or plumbing. But sooner or later Christians began to ask fundamental questions about technical activities in general, and ultimately this led to an explicitly Christian view of technology.[63] There is no Christian manner or method of using a sword or a rifle. But sooner or later Christians began to ask fundamental questions about military activities in general, and ultimately this led to an explicitly Christian view of warfare.[64] There is no Christian manner or method of fishing. But sooner or later Christians

---

[63] See, e.g., Schuurman (1987; 2003); Schuurman et al. (1993).
[64] See, e.g., Clouse (1991).

began to ask fundamental questions about hunger in the world, and dealing with the environment, which led to an explicitly Christian view of creation care (e.g., pollution of the seas, depletion of species).[65]

There is no Christian manner or method of buying and selling. But sooner or later Christians began to ask fundamental questions about "the market" (the economic order) in general, and ultimately this led to an explicitly Christian view of economics.[66] Christian economists have outspoken ideas about the un-Christian character of both communism and (extreme) capitalism, and try to find their own, more biblically responsible way.

There is no Christian method of taxing or paying taxes. But sooner or later Christians began to ask fundamental questions about how far taxing can go, and for what purposes taxes may be used, and ultimately this (and many other similar questions) led to an explicitly Christian view of politics and of the state (see extensively chapter 12).

There is no Christian method of putting paint on cloth or wood. But sooner or later Christians began to ask fundamental questions about the visual arts in general, about the way art reflects our present society and civilization, and ultimately this led to an explicitly Christian view of art.[67]

Indeed, the New Testament says little or nothing about *specifically* Christian cultural activity; it simply was too early for that. However, it does give us the general guidelines for a Christian lifestyle, which sooner or later led to elaborated and explicated Christian views of reality. In my view, the only way to guarantee coherence in our Christian thinking is to do this within the framework of a universal Christian-philosophical cosmology and epistemology (see extensively chapter 11). Although the New Testament as such can in no way be called philosophical, it does contain the starting points for such a Christian-philosophical view of cosmic reality.

---

[65] Some recent works: Bouma-Prediger (2010); Toly and Block (2010); Liederbach and Bible (2012); Wirzba and Bahnsen (2012).

[66] See, e.g., Keizer (1986).

[67] See, e.g., Rookmaaker (1994); Seerveld (1995; 2000; 2005).

SCHOLASTIC THEOLOGY

PREPARATORY PONDERINGS

1. "Two-kingdoms theology is nothing but a variety of an age-old (medieval) dualism between the natural and the spiritual (in fact, between pagan and Christian thinking)." Do you think this claim is fair or exaggerated?

2. In your view, to what extent are Luther's and Calvin's works, as well as the early Protestant confessions, normative (formally, morally, or both) for present-day Protestants?

3. This also involves the question: How important is it, in your view, that present-day theologians figure out, as precisely as possible, exactly what Luther and Calvin, as well as later Protestant theologians, wrote and meant?

4. What is the greater danger to your own soul: biblicism or confessionalism? Can you explain? Or are you free of these dangers? Or do you not see them as dangerous at all?

2.1 THEOLOGY AND PHILOSOPHY

2.1.1   A Plan for This Book

One consequence of the approach that I outlined in the previous chapter is that I am less interested in exactly what Luther, Calvin, and early Reformed theologians taught. Others may quibble about that; I will not interfere. Instead, there are two main parts in this book.

(a) First, I will enter into the biblical-theological aspects of the matter (chapters 3–10). For some people, this seems almost superfluous. It is generally known that, at the early Lutheran universities in Germany, there were no such disciplines as Old and New Testament exegesis. The core of the theological faculty was dogmatics. Exegesis was hardly deemed necessary, because the meaning of the Bible text had been decided once and for all by the patristic and scholastic expositors, as well as by Luther and Calvin and their immediate successors. What was there to be added? It was only in the time of, and partly as a consequence of, the Enlightenment that theologians began to rethink this position. Exegesis came into vogue again, and today it sometimes seems as if some theologians would prefer to throw out dogmatics rather than exegesis.

Understandably so. Exegesis is, and must always remain, the alpha and the omega of all theology. We must look again at Genesis 1:28 because of the so-called "cultural mandate." Similarly we must look again at the Noahic and the Abrahamic covenants, and their supposed significance for Christians today. The same goes for the expressions "the age to come" and "the world to come." Ditto for Romans 2:15 because of the so-called "natural law." We must also look at the many texts in which the apostle Paul deals with the Mosaic Torah, seemingly in both a positive and a negative way. Very important is Colossians 1:15–18 because of the kingship of Christ, both cosmologically and soteriologically. And so on. I am afraid that David VanDrunen was so busy with the historical questions that he forgot to do this basic homework (with a few exceptions). One cannot adduce arguments for the NL2K model by referring to Augustine, Luther and Calvin, and their early successors. Good Protestants incessantly demand a thoroughly biblical-theological foundation.

(b) Second, I will enter into the philosophical aspects of this issue (chapters 11–12). This is another problem with scholastic theology, of which Horton and VanDrunen are representatives. It is the idea that anything that is spiritual, or biblical, or religious, belongs to the "upper storey" of grace (or supernature), and thus to the domain of theology. Today, Horton, VanDrunen, and sympathizers may use different terms—the secular and the sacred realms, Christ's kingdom and the common kingdom—but in essence they are talking about the same things. All the other topics, including philosophy, the sciences, and the humanities, belong to the "lower storey" of nature (the common realm). In this "storey," the Bible has hardly anything to say. In practice, this means that, in the Middle Ages, it was Aristotle who was authoritative in the natural realm, whereas today it is all kinds of humanist (neo-pagan or apostate-Christian) thinkers.

Elsewhere, I have tried to show the great error in this type of scholastic thinking.[1] Here are a few mistakes.

1. There *is* a thoroughly Christian philosophy, and, although little understood, it is much older than Kuyper and Dooyeweerd. We could think, for instance, of Bonaventure (d. 1274), who spoke of *lumen cognitionis sensitivae*, the "light of the empirically obtained knowledge," and *lumen cognitionis philosophiae*, the "light of philosophical knowledge," which form the transcendental conditions for the various sciences and humanities. Ultimately, he reduced these *lumina* to the one *lumen superius scripturae*, the "higher light of Scripture," and thus to the voice of Christ, the incarnate Word of God.[2] A Christian philosophy entails a Christian comprehensive view of the entire empirical cosmos, and as such it underlies the entire Christian scholarly enterprise.[3]

2. Christian epistemology (including Cornelius Van Til's presuppositionalism, see Appendix 1),[4] and the external prolegomena of theology, and more generally questions about paradigms and scientific theory building, including theological theory building, do not belong to theology at all. And the subjects just mentioned do not belong to some area of "natural law," either, that is, to a domain where the Word of God supposedly has nothing to say. No person in the world has any "philosophical premises" written on his heart!

3. Theologians *as such*, in this capacity, are unable to develop a Christian view of nature, or of culture, or of law, or of the state, or of the relationship between church and state, or of politics, or of art, or of science, etc. All these subjects belong to the domain of Christian philosophy, even though we readily admit that theology, as the interpreter of Scripture, may be helpful in developing the biblical starting points for a Christian worldview

---

[1]   Ouweneel (2012b, chapters 6–14; 2014a; 2014c).

[2]   Quaracci ed. 1883, quoted by Schlink (1983, 25–26).

[3]   Examples of how this may be worked out are found in my *Academic Series for Beginners*: Ouweneel (2014a; 2014b; 2014c; 2015; 2016a; 2016b).

[4]   See Ouweneel (2016b).

underlying such a philosophy. Nevertheless, a Christian philosophy is never derived from Scripture, and even less from theology. It is founded in a Christian worldview, which itself is inspired by what Herman Dooyeweerd has called the biblical *ground motive*, that is, a driving force, ultimately of a transcendent, existential nature, that drives the human heart.[5]

In these few words I have indicated the plan for part of what has to be further explained in the coming chapters of this book.

2.1.2 Scholasticism

Before we move on, there are a few essential terms that I would like to explain a little further. These are scholasticism, neo-Calvinism, biblicism, and confessionalism. Of course, I am not going to give an extensive treatise on each of these subjects. My only goal is to explain how these terms function in the argument of the present book.

Take, for instance, scholasticism. In the widest sense, this is a collective term for a variety of very different theological-philosophical schools within the Western world, roughly between the Carolingian Renaissance (c. 800) and the beginning of the Modern Age (c. 1500). Before this period, Patristic thought led the way in our Western world, and after about 1500, it was modern philosophy (today we would add: post-modern philosophy). The term "scholasticism" arose because this was taught and practiced at "schools" (Latin: *scholae*): first the cathedral schools, later, since c. 1100, at the brand new universities (Bologna, Paris, Oxford, etc.). Historians generally view it as ceasing in influence around 1500, with the rise of modern philosophy; but at the Protestant universities it continued to be influential until the time of the Enlightenment. Strictly speaking, scholasticism still leads the way at the traditional Roman Catholic theological faculties, because in 1879, Pope Leo XIII, in his encyclical *Aeterni Patris*, declared Thomism (the theology and philosophy of Thomas Aquinas, d. 1274), which constitutes the high point of scholasticism, to be the official philosophy of the Roman Catholic Church.

Scholasticism was first of all a method of learning. It developed a method of dialectical reasoning, whereby one theological truth was derived from another by building up logical inferences. We are reminded of this approach in the Westminster Confession of Faith (1.6): "The whole counsel of God concerning all things necessary for His own glory, man's salvation, faith and life, is either expressly set down in Scripture, or *by good and necessary*

---

5 See Ouweneel (2014a).

consequence may be deduced from Scripture."[6] Elsewhere I have tried to show that this principle is correct only if the biblical terms involved refer to concepts, which in theology is often not the case. All basic terms in theology refer to ideas, not concepts.[7] For instance, from the concept of a (human) father it follows "by good and necessary consequence" that this person must be of the male sex, and must have fathered one or more children through sexual intercourse with at least one woman. However, from the *idea* of God's Fatherhood, it does *not* follow that he is of the male sex and has had sexual intercourse with one or more women. We can predicate of God's Fatherhood only those things that Scripture itself predicates of it. Therefore, in its generality, the Westminster statement is wrong.

It was believed that, through the scholastic method, an enormous, magnificent building could be constructed out of Christian truths, truths that were all coherent and consistent, that is, without inner contradictions. The basic elements of this building were never empirical facts; rather, they were truths that had already been well established by the "authorities:" especially Augustine in the sacred realm, and Plato (d. 347 BC), later Aristotle (d. 322 BC), in the secular realm. From these elements, higher truths were inferred using the dialectical method. The result was often what we call "scholastic" in the pejorative sense: dull, pedantic. It was the heyday of Christian rationalism, which after 1500 was continued by the theological faculties of the new, Protestant universities. Its absolute apex was reached in the thirteenth century, in the thinking of Albert the Great (Albertus Magnus, d. 1280) and his brilliant pupil, Thomas Aquinas, who died before his master (d. 1274). As I said, his thought system is called Thomism.

Not everything in Thomism is objectionable, of course. The Reformers learned a lot from it, and so do we. Many elements are tremendously valuable.[8] In the present book, when I speak of scholasticism as underlying NL2K, I refer specifically to the nature-grace dualism, which I find disastrous. It is my conviction that the distinction between the "common kingdom" and the "redemptive kingdom" is nothing but a variety of this nature-grace dualism, which has plagued not only medieval scholasticism but also early Lutheran and Reformed thinking.

---

[6] Dennison (2008, 4:235); italics added.
[7] Ouweneel (e.g., 2014a; 2014c).
[8] Cf. Frame (2011, 205–207).

2.1.3   The Scholastic Ground Motive

The ground motive of Thomism is the *nature-grace dualism*.[9] Thomas followed Albert both in the latter's distinction between nature and grace,
and in the latter's attempt to keep the two together in a harmonic unity.
The lower realm of nature contains matters like philosophy, reason, the
body, the state, the earth, general revelation, natural law, and so forth. The
upper realm of grace contains theology, faith, the soul, the church, heaven,
special revelation, and so forth. Thomas did distinguish nature from grace,
yet he saw nature as *related* to grace. First, the "natural truths," investigated by reason, are also part of the divine revelation (cf. Rom. 1:19–20;
2:15). Second, nature is not separated from theology, for natural reason
investigates also that part of theology that is called "natural theology." This
is the knowledge about God that may be acquired apart from Scripture.
Third, natural reason "leads" to "grace:" natural theology belongs to the
praeambula fidei, "preambles of faith."

In the domain of nature (the secular realm), human reason possesses a
relative autonomy (so Thomas). At the Fall, humanity preserved its intellect
almost entirely, so that reason, by its own light, is still able to discover
natural truths. This is the task of philosophy (and today we would add, it
is also the task of the sciences and humanities that issued from it). Reason
is proper to believers and unbelievers, so that they can argue together, and
together are able to fathom the natural or secular sphere (i.e., NL2K's "common kingdom"). This includes the fact *that* there is a God. However, reason
cannot demonstrate supernatural truths, for instance, *what* or *who* God is,
and further truths such as the Trinity, the incarnation, the resurrection,
redemption, the last judgment. At best, reason can try to refute arguments
that are adduced against these truths.

In the supernatural (or sacred) domain of grace, reason is totally
dependent on the divine inscripturated revelation and faith. Thus, the
actual proofs for faith are not of a philosophical nature, but Thomas saw
them, for instance, in biblical miracles and fulfilled prophecies. Reason
and faith each know their own types of proofs. Thus, grace does not annul
nature, but it perfects it (*perficit naturam*). Although, because of the strict
separation of nature and grace, we do speak of a dualism, Thomas himself
still saw them as a harmonic unity.[10] It was only during late scholasticism,
especially with William of Ockham (d. 1347), that the two were separated,
and this has continued to this very day: religion and science (and society,

---

[9] See Ouweneel (2000, chapter 9).
[10] Ouweneel (2016c, §§6.4.3–6.4.4).

and politics, etc.) are matters that must not be mixed up. For the same reason, NL2K wishes to keep the sacred and the secular realms strictly apart. If NL2K claims to follow Luther in this regard, this claim is to a certain extent correct; Luther said of himself, *Ich bin von Occams Schule* ("I am of Ockham's school").[11]

In Thomism, philosophy is still entirely the handmaiden of theology (*ancilla theologiae*). This means that it serves only as an instrument for theological purposes. In this view, neutral philosophy is useful to lay the foundations, after which Christian faith can be introduced by virtue of the philosophical arguments. In reality, Thomist philosophy was not neutral at all; it was submitted to a dogmatically adapted (Christianized) Aristotle, with whom Thomas was very impressed. The central error here is the totally unbiblical separation between nature and grace, that is, between reason and faith, between philosophy (together with all the sciences and humanities that proceeded from it) and theology, between natural and ecclesiastical life, between natural law and the Mosaic Law, between state (or world, society) and church. After the Reformation, which was such a monumental return to Scripture, these errors were perpetrated in the newly arising Lutheran and Reformed scholasticism. *Here lies the origin of* NL2K, which is rooted in this Protestant scholasticism.

As an example I mention Francis Bacon, the English philosopher, statesman, and lawyer of clear Calvinist orientation, who developed a methodology for the natural sciences. His ideal has been described as follows:

> Nature and grace were two separate kingdoms or departments of the *potentia Dei ordinata* [i.e., God's ordering power]: the kingdom of nature was accessible through the arts and sciences based on human reason and observation; the kingdom of God was accessible through the forgiveness of sins based on the teachings of Scripture. Ultimately the two were united in God; one was based on his works, the other on his word.[12]

The former was based upon God's general revelation and common grace; the latter on God's special revelation and redemptive grace. If this is a correct rendering of Bacon's view, it is the medieval scholastic dualism revived, and one of the many precursors of NL2K.

---

[11] Cf. WA 6.195 and 600; WA 581, 5; WA Tr 2, 516. Scholars agree, however, that it is very difficult to assess the extent to which Ockham really influenced Luther's theology; see, e.g., Bosch (2000, 60).
[12] Kaiser (1991, 138).

2.2 THE REFORMATION

2.2.1 Introduction

Of course, we are making huge leaps through history here, moving from the thirteenth to the sixteenth century. But we need to be brief. The Reformation cannot be severed from the great movement of Renaissance and humanism, which had begun a little earlier. The Renaissance aimed at a revival of the thinking of antiquity, and the Reformation aimed at a revival of biblical Christianity.[13] At the same time, there were clear correspondences: like the Renaissance, the Reformation had a nationalistic trait, through which national churches arose in opposition to the catholic (universal, worldwide) church of Rome. Like the Renaissance, the Reformation was individualizing; it emphasized the priesthood of all believers, a personal relationship to God, and personal study of the Bible. The Reformation, too, aimed at a religious renaissance (regeneration) and a return to the ancient thinkers, in this case, the church fathers, especially Augustine.

However, in line with the Bible, the Reformers were especially concerned with a Scriptural rebirth and with personal salvation; with the *sola fide* ("by faith alone") and the *sola gratia* ("by grace alone"). Above all, the Reformation entailed the rediscovery of the *sola Scriptura*, "Scripture alone," *in all matters of Christian doctrine and Christian practice.* Protestants recognize many authorities above them—parents, elders, magistrates—but each of these authorities is seen as subordinate to the Scriptures. Indeed, the main discovery of the Reformation was the insight that Scripture has divine authority over the *entire* human life, *both individually and societally* —not only over the domain of grace (the sacred realm), but also over that of nature (the secular realm). Total natural depravity demands a total redemption of the person, and hence also a total reformation of human life and society under the guidance of God's Word and Spirit.

The natural awareness of God was no longer viewed as depending upon scholastic proofs of God but as a deep, inner consciousness (*sensus divinitatis*[14])—in the heart, not in the *ratio* (reason)—of God beyond us, although this consciousness was corrupted by sin. This implied a rejection of natural theology. In this way, the Reformation gave its own revolutionary answer to the medieval problem of authority in matters of faith. The

---

[13] Jaspers (2010, 66).
[14] The term comes from Calvin, *Institutes* 1.3.1.

answers are no longer viewed as depending on a more or less autonomous *ratio* (*contra* the earlier and later rationalists and humanists), nor on the authority of "the" church (contra Roman Catholics, including the Counter-Reformation), nor on the mystical experience of one's own soul (*contra* the medieval, but also the later Catholic as well as Protestant mystics), but only on Scripture. This was thought to be true not only for theological issues but for all matters of life and society. It was *this* Reformational view that had enormous consequences for the development of the sciences.[15]

2.2.2 Martin Luther

Just like Calvin later was, Martin Luther (1483–1546) was direct, biblical, and sharply opposed to the Thomistic synthesis of Patristic and Aristotelian teaching. Above all, as one whose thought lay beyond mysticism and rationalism, he was the preacher of the *Word* concerning human sin, the cross of Christ, and justification by faith alone. He fiercely opposed all philosophy that preached autonomous reason and human free will, and thus human self-justification. However, he did not totally reject the philosophical tradition, including Aristotle—although he also heavily criticized the latter—but left open the possibility of a Christian philosophy. All the more regrettable, then, that he and the other Reformers failed to develop a consistent Christian-philosophical view of cosmic reality. As a consequence, their impact upon the domains of science and scholarship remained limited. On the contrary, too much scholastic thinking remained in Luther's views.

The effects of this failure were rather drastic. Among their collaborators and successors we find the same division that was encountered already during high and late scholasticism: on the one hand, an irrationalistic mysticism,[16] and on the other hand, a rationalistic synthesis philosophy (like Thomism was). Today we find the former, for instance, in certain charismatic circles, but also in hyper-Calvinism (pietism, with its strong emphasis on pious sentiments); and we find the latter, for instance, in NL2K. This new synthesis entailed a rationalistic "scientification" (theologizing) of the biblical doctrines of the Reformation, and a reintroduction of pagan philosophy; this led to "Protestant scholasticism." There is nothing here to be lauded or to be pursued, as NL2K wants to delude us. What we should follow is the original pure and uncompromised Reformational return to God's Word and the recognition of Christ's kingship—*not Reformed scholasticism.*

---

[15] Ouweneel (2000, §10.3).
[16] Ouweneel (2000, §9.3.3).

In Lutheranism, this scholasticism was introduced by Philip Melanchthon (d. 1560), who has been called the father of Protestant scholasticism. He sought a harmony between reason and revelation, between humanism and Lutheranism. His great work, *Loci communes* (1521), relied on medieval scholasticism, and became the foundation for Lutheran scholasticism as we find it with later Lutheran theologians such as Martin Chemnitz (d. 1586), Johann Gerhard (d. 1637), and David Hollaz (d. 1713).

Melanchthon introduced a softened Aristotelianism at the Lutheran universities, complete with Cicero's doctrine of the "natural light of reason," as well as natural theology. His textbooks have governed German education for a long time. It is no wonder that, even in our time, the well-known Swiss Lutheran theologian Gerhard Ebeling (d. 2001) entirely accepted the (scholastic) "duality" in our culture, tried to live with it, and tried to argue from that starting point.[17] His thought was rooted in Luther's dualism between philosophy (*sapientia humana*, "human wisdom") and theology.[18] The NL2K theologians who can read German might be thrilled with him.

2.2.3 John Calvin

The other great Reformer and superior thinker was John Calvin (1509–1564). Shortly after his transition to the Reformation, he wrote the first, as yet brief version of his main work, the *Institutio religionis christianae* (*Institutes* [i.e., Teaching] *of the Christian Religion*; published 1536). In terms of dogmatics he was in fact a radical Lutheran, without any humanistic elements, unlike Melanchthon. Philosophically, Calvin was important because of his emphasis on the law and on ethics, which (*contra* Luther) in his case was oriented toward the world in political, economic, and social activity, as a path leading toward the full realization of the kingdom of God. The latter were not elements that emerged first with Abraham Kuyper, as NL2K wish to make us believe; they were simply *revived* by Kuyper (see §2.3.2).

Calvin placed heavy emphasis on the natural sphere, which in line with humanism was viewed as a "wonderful work of art," but in this very sense as creation of God. Moreover, Calvin acknowledged the total depravity of nature through sin, so that also the so-called light of (natural) reason is "blinder than moles."[19] Scripture is the "pair of spectacles" that blinded humans must put on in order to find again the road to the Creator in created nature: "Just as old or bleary-eyed men and those with weak vision..., with

---

[17] Ebeling et al. (1986, 6:754-82 and 6:782-830).

[18] Weber (1907; 1908); Althaus (1914; cf. 1952, 2); Hägglund (1955, 13).

[19] Calvin, *Institutes* 2.2.18.

the aid of spectacles will begin to read distinctly; so Scripture, gathering up the otherwise confused knowledge of God in our minds, having dispersed our dullness, clearly shows us the true God"[20]—namely, in the natural world. As Richard Lischer said, "Using his famous figure of the spectacles, [Calvin] portrays the revealed word as bringing the universal revelation of God into focus."[21]

Please note, this involves the essential thought that the secular realm—if one wishes to use this expression—can be properly viewed only through the spectacles of the written Word of God, not the spectacles of natural law, as NL2K would have it. Thus, the *entire* earthly life, including state, society, and science, can be actively restored to God.

In 1559, Calvin founded in Geneva a Reformational university, and arrived at the idea of a *philosophia christiana* ("Christian philosophy"). It is doubtful, however, what he meant by this. In his *Institutes* he rarely used the term *theologia*—on purpose, thought Abraham Kuyper[22]—but he did use the term *philosophia nostra* ("our philosophy") or *philosophia christiana* ("Christian philosophy"), apparently in the sense in which Augustine used the term *theologia*, that is, the Christian doctrine of faith.[23] By thus confusing theology and philosophy, Calvin failed to discern the possibility of a consistent Christian-philosophical view of cosmic reality, distinct from theology. As a consequence, Aristotelianism was afterwards introduced into Calvinism as well, this time by his co-worker and successor, Theodore Beza (d. 1605),[24] just as Melanchthon had done in Germany (see §11.1.2).

2.3 LATER CALVINISM

2.3.1 Gisbert Voetius

Similarly, in the Calvinistic Netherlands, Gisbert Voetius (d. 1676) proved himself, in his conflict with René Descartes, to be a true Aristotelian, though dressed, of course, in Reformed garb. Especially Reformed theologian Willem J. van Asselt (d. 2014) in the Netherlands referred to Voetius several times as "Voetius the Reformed scholastic," apparently with

---

[20] Ibid., 1.6.1.
[21] Lischer (2002, 362).
[22] Kuyper (2008, 238).
[23] Cf. Van der Walt (1974, 439–44).
[24] Kickel (1967); Van der Walt (1974, 543–44); Spykman (1992, 24–25, 66-68); on the problem of dualism and its meaning in our present-day, see culture Walsh and Middleton (1984, 93–116).

satisfaction.[25] Over against Descartes, Voetius has no other defense than his Reformed theology—as if a secularized *philosophy*, or any philosophy, can be combated with *theology*. No one, however, saw yet the possibility of a Christian *philosophy*. If there was to be philosophy, then let it be a Reformationally adapted Aristotelianism.[26]

In Voetius' work we find such an abundance of scholastic distinctions and concepts that even the French Reformed theologian Samuel Maresius (d. 1673) accused Voetius of leading "the Dead Sea of the scholastics to the bath water of Siloam."[27] For Voetius, the term *scholasticism* strictly speaking refers to a method; but his theology shows how much method and content can go hand in hand.[28]

Another Reformed example is the famous *Synopsis purioris theologiae* (1625),[29] which, in its "purest theology" (!), followed Aristotle in many respects.[30] Even Herman Bavinck wrote rather naïvely about the way theology had borrowed from pagan philosophy. He claimed that Christian theology preferred Platonism and Aristotelianism because these were the most suited for developing and defending the truth.[31] This is no surprise when one considers how much Bavinck himself was still caught in scholastic dualisms, no matter how Reformationally adapted.[32]

It is no surprise either that, to this very day, every attack upon Aristotelian notions within theology, such as the Greek dualistic view of soul/spirit and body,[33] or the "incommunicable attributes" of God,[34] or the notion of "natural theology,"[35] is considered an attack on Protestant theology, or even on Scripture itself. We find the same attitude with NL2K. This position views every attack on Reformed scholasticism as an attack on the Reformed tradition, and of course there is a kernel of truth in this! It leads to the sad conclusion that each form of Reformed thought that endeavours to free itself from scholastic bonds is considered to be a *deviation* from early Reformed thought, *and is for that reason alone to be rejected.*

---

[25] Van Asselt (2007).

[26] See extensively, Van Ruler (1995).

[27] Van Asselt et al. (1998, 127).

[28] Ouwendorp (2012, 149).

[29] Polyander et al. (1964–1966).

[30] Cf. Van der Walt (1974, 559–609).

[31] Bavinck (*RD* 1:608); Calvin praised Plato for viewing the soul as an immortal substance (*Institutes* 1.15.6).

[32] Cf. Veenhof (n.d.); Troost (2004, 58 incl. note 19).

[33] See extensively, Ouweneel (2008a, chapters 5–8).

[34] See extensively, Ouweneel (2013, chapter 4).

[35] See extensively, Ouweneel (2012b, chapter 2).

Ultimately the entire NL2K debate comes down to this: the participants are for or against scholastic theology; those who are for it are viewed as the truly Reformed. This is a very important thesis for the present book: in the entire debate, one is either for or against scholasticism. Every participant in the debate is entitled to proclaim which approach he or she considers to be "truly Reformed."

The very fact that scholastic theology tried, and tries, to defend Aristotelian-Thomistic views by means of Bible passages, shows how far it has departed from Scripture. One of the consequences of this Protestant scholasticism, already in the sixteenth and seventeenth centuries, was that, in the domain of the sciences and humanities, pagan thinking exerted far too great an impact. The effect of the Reformation on ecclesiastical and societal life was enormous, but unfortunately its effect on science and culture was much smaller. In turn, the Renaissance had, socially speaking, only little impact in the seventeenth century, but it did manage to penetrate the new philosophy and sciences. As a consequence, during the Enlightenment (eighteenth century) the new, secularized (humanistic, counter-Christian) philosophy took the lead throughout all of Western culture.[36]

2.3.2 Abraham Kuyper

The theological-philosophical movement that began in the Netherlands especially with Abraham Kuyper (d. 1920) and Herman Bavinck (d. 1921) is often called neo-Calvinism.[37] It must not be confused with the "New Calvinism" that is sometimes spoken of in certain North American (especially Southern Baptist) circles. When I refer to neo-Calvinism, I mean Kuyperian/Bavinckian neo-Calvinism. Actually, I do not like the term at all. It plays into the hands of NL2K, which may triumphantly exclaim: You see, this is something neo, "new," that was not there before. So this cannot be the representative of the original Calvinistic views. It is a deviation—what we want is a return to the original views, not something revolutionary, which conflicts with those original Reformed views.

This objection is not new; it was expressed already by Bernardus D. Eerdmans[38] and Cornelis B. Hylkema,[39] and later in several publications by Theodorus L. Haitjema and Arnold A. van Ruler. We should not forget

---

[36] Klapwijk (1995, 20–21).

[37] As far as can be determined, this term was first used in 1887 by the liberal theologian Johannes Reitsma (d. 1902). Kuyper's first fellow thinker who used the term (1896) was the Reformed pastor Willem H. Gispen, Sr. (d. 1909); see Harinck (2014, 21 note 43).

[38] Eerdmans (1909).

[39] Hylkema (1911).

here that the latter two were Dutch Reformed (Nederlands Hervormd), and that Kuyper & Co. belonged to the Gereformeerde Kerken in Nederland, founded by Kuyper himself. It is difficult to view this conflict apart from the ecclesiastical conflict. But aside from this, Haitjema and Van Ruler objected to neo-Calvinism mainly for two reasons: Kuyper's view of regeneration (which does not concern us here), and his view of common grace, the grace of God manifested in his general providence, in culture, in the sciences and the arts (see §4.4.1). Nowhere does this come to light more clearly than in what perhaps has become Kuyper's most famous line: "There is not a square inch in the whole domain of our human existence over which Christ, who is Sovereign over *all*, does not cry: 'Mine!'"[40] Thus, Kuyper confessed the kingship of Christ in all domains of society: church and state, marriage and family, organization and association, the legal order and the economic order, the arts, the sciences and humanities—in my view *entirely in line with Luther and Calvin.*[41]

It has often been objected that, in this respect, Kuyper has gone too far. There is a thin line between *wereldmijding* ("avoiding the world") and *wereldwijding* ("consecrating the world"), which corresponds with the antithesis between cultural pessimism and cultural optimism. Some have argued that Kuyper's view of common grace was sometimes emphasized at the expense of emphasizing special grace. This may be true; some of his own followers have leveled their criticisms in this respect. However, what interests me much more right now is the question whether, as NL2K has claimed, neo-Calvinism implies a deviation from, or even an abandoning of, the views of Calvin and early Calvinists. Reformed theologian Simon G. de Graaf has extensively shown that the seeds of Kuyper's idea of common grace can be found already in Calvin's work.[42] Herman Kuiper has shown the same,[43] although he might have gone too far in suggesting that Calvin was the *father* of the doctrine of common grace.

2.3.3 NL2K Scholasticism

To the extent that NL2K advocates wish to be loyal to early Reformed theology, they of course also applaud scholasticism. No wonder: early

---

[40] Kuyper (1880, 26); the original Dutch reads: "*Er is geen duimbreed op heel het erf van het menselijk leven, waarvan Christus niet zegt: 'Mijn!'*"; the most accurate English translation, cited above, appears in Henderson (2008, 12).

[41] The best English introduction to Kuyper's thought is still his American "Stone Lectures" (repr. 2009).

[42] De Graaf (1939); see also his two essays (2012, 85–124), translated and introduced by Nelson D. Kloosterman.

[43] Kuiper (1928).

Reformed theology *was* thoroughly scholastic. Scholasticism is a plague that is very hard to combat. It is amazing how much Voetius and so many other Reformed theologians were still impressed with Aristotle. No philosopher, Christian or not, can fail to admire Aristotle as one of the greatest thinkers of antiquity, and perhaps of all of Western thought. But for theology, Aristotle is thoroughly unhelpful. Bavinck referred to Aristotle several times, but with significant demurrals—though when Bavinck and Kuyper spoke of the union of body and soul, for instance, and of the immortality of the soul, echoes of Aristotle reverberated loudly. Indeed, even in Kuyper and Bavinck, who in some sense are NL2K's real targets, numerous remnants of scholasticism can be found. As far as Kuyper is concerned, this is seen most tragically in his systematic-theological lectures.[44] When it comes to scholasticism, Kuyper and NL2K advocates are more closely related than the latter may be aware!

In the view of NL2K advocates, any attack on scholasticism is an attack on early Reformed thinking—and in a certain sense this is perfectly correct. Early Reformed thinking *was* to a large extent scholastic. Modern theologians who reject scholasticism for being speculative and abstract receive this reply from Michael Horton: "I contend that conservative evangelical theologies represent 'turgid scholasticism' not when they rely on the Protestant scholastics, but precisely to the extent that they abandon or (as is more frequently the case) ignore them."[45]

Please notice what is going on here. Apparently being "scholastic" is not the problem—because, according to Horton, we *should* "rely on the Protestant scholastics" and not ignore them—but being "turgid" is the problem. Whatever Horton means precisely, it is clear that he implicitly recommends relying on Protestant scholasticism. Horton's claim is precisely what the present book is opposing: if you want to be genuinely Reformed you must be a scholastic! If that is true, I will never be Reformed, at least not Klinean-Reformed (and this is the only strand of Reformed thinking that Klineans acknowledge as truly Reformed). If, in this connection, I long for anything, I long for a Reformed theology freed from all scholastic bonds, ancient and modern. I remember what Reformed philosopher and theologian Andree Troost (d. 2008)—one of my most appreciated teachers—wrote in reply to Reformed theologian Jochem Douma, whom he accused of scholastic tendencies.[46] Troost wrote that he had been fighting

---

[44] Kuyper ([1911]).
[45] Horton (2002b, 2).
[46] Troost (1977).

against Reformed scholasticism all his life, and at that moment in his life—he was 61—he could only hope that *in principle* he had overcome this power in his own thinking. Troost has deeply imbued me with the same hope.

Today, Aristotle is no longer in vogue; one will hardly find references to him in NL2K literature. But we must remember how the nature-grace dualism originated: alongside the sacred realm, a secular realm had to be created where Aristotle could be hailed as authority, and even as a "precursor of Christ" *in naturalibus* ("in natural matters"), as John the Baptist had been *in spiritualibus* ("in spiritual matters").[47] I suppose none of the ancient scholastics would have thought of calling this natural realm "neutral." It never was; it was dominated by a forerunner of Christ! Today it is different. NL2K's "common kingdom" is the spiritual descendant of the natural realm that for such a long time was governed by Aristotle. Here, the great question arises: By whom is this "common kingdom" governed today? Where are the "neutral" philosophers and scientists of today? They are not pagans anymore; in the Western world they are largely apostate Jews and Christians, or children of apostate Jews and Christians. NL2K advocates hold out to us a "common realm" in which Christians are not allowed to speak up for their faith (close your mouths, any whose name is Frame, Wolters, Plantinga, or Wolterstorff!), a realm which at the same time is dominated by the Aristotles of today: no longer pagans, but apostate Jews and Christians. Is this what NL2K advocates had in mind? Or where are their "common" artists, philosophers, and scientists?

2.3.4   Michael Horton and NL2K

I will have a lot to say about VanDrunen's works, but having just mentioned Michael Horton, I wish to say a few words about his work as well. I think especially of his book *Where in the World Is the Church?*[48] I consulted the first edition of this work in order to search for early traces of modern NL2K. I must say that, in many respects, I like the book very much. It is helpful when it comes to exposing and avoiding pietism, on the one hand (I call the Reformed version of it hyper-Calvinism), and worldliness (in the sense of the apostles Paul and John), on the other hand.[49] It helpfully reminds us of the rightful place of Christian art.[50] It still refers to Abraham Kuyper in a positive, and not yet in a negative tone.[51] On the whole, I find it quite a useful book.

---

47 Knowles (1989, 229).
48 Horton (1995/2002a).
49 Ibid., 141–45, 175–76.
50 Ibid., chapters 4–5.
51 Ibid., especially chapter 2.

Nonetheless, unfortunately, the elements of NL2K are present already here. Not yet in an intrusive way, but the traces are unmistakable: the distinction between "secular" and "sacred," or "common" and "holy;" the church being "separated from the common, the world," art and religion having "an independent existence;" "cultural activity is not sacred;" and "the 'two-kingdoms' approach that had been so influential in the Reformation's view of church and state."[52] "One does not have to 'bless' work or secular institutions with the adjective 'Christian,' or 'redemptive,' or 'kingdom' for it to be honorable to God.... There is going to be a division between the kingdom of Christ and the kingdoms of this world until Christ's return."[53] The "Christian plumber" argument is already present (cf. §11.4.2), as well as the reference to natural law.[54] But all of this is present in a moderate, inconspicuous form. I could imagine giving this book to someone seeking to understand better, for instance, the attitude of Christians toward the arts, along with the advice: "Don't pay too much attention to what Horton says about the relationship between the sacred and the secular."

However, things are very different in Horton's article of nine years later, "How the Kingdom Comes,"[55] where we find NL2K in full bloom. I have not read most of what Horton has written between 1995 and 2006; but I find it interesting to see how little the theory seems to have been developed since 1995. Yet, even here, we find statements that I will have to discuss in the present book because I view them as mistaken and misleading.

2.4 BIBLICISM

2.4.1 "Biblical" Theology

Theologians who do not wish to keep the discussion within historical theology but move it into biblical theology—"back to the Scriptures"—are easily accused of biblicism, and understandably so. There are many meanings of the term "biblicism," for that matter.[56] The term has been related to the doctrine of mechanical inspiration of the Bible, to an overestimation of special revelation in contrast to general revelation (Scripture as the exclusive source of true knowledge), to an a-contextual, a-historical application of biblical moral principles, and so forth.

---

[52] Ibid., 85, 89, 93, 125.
[53] Ibid., 187; cf. 193.
[54] Ibid., 194, 196.
[55] Horton (2006).
[56] Ouweneel (2012b, §9.4).

For our purpose, the most important description of biblicism involves the attempt to arrive at a kind of "biblical" theology, which is based directly and immediately on Scripture, without a fundamental theoretical reflection upon the starting points, the methodology, and the nature of such an enterprise,[57] and without consulting any earlier theological works. Such an irrational "theology" is often presented as the result of a rejection of all current "corrupt" doctrines, and of a "simple return to Scripture," under the "direct guidance of the Holy Spirit," without any human intervention. Often its adherents prefer to call this approach no "theology" at all.[58]

This is an often well intended but dangerous road, because it looks biblical but never is. The reason is that a "theology" that does not reflect upon its presuppositions and starting points has no other option than to adopt, unthinkingly and inadvertently, presuppositions and starting points from earlier centuries, or such as are automatically given with our present-day culture, and which we all take in through the air we breathe, as it were. These are never purely Christian presuppositions and starting points. Just think of rationalism and positivism, or rather the irrationalism and post-modernism, that haunt our culture, and also influence Christians, usually unconsciously. This form of biblicism threatens every Evangelical, Lutheran, and Reformed theology that does not sufficiently account for its presuppositions, in particular its philosophical prolegomena.[59] Such forms of so-called "biblical" theology or of this "no-theology-but-the-Bible" attitude invariably fall into scholastic or humanistic hands, or in both at the same time.

Actually, it is the same with the "natural law" debate (see extensively chapter 4). There is some natural knowledge of God and his law within people: "They show that the work of the law is written on their hearts" (Rom. 2:15). However, if we compare this with Romans 1:18, we see that this knowledge is totally corrupted by sin; the truth is suppressed by the unrighteousness of the wicked. Building a society upon natural law, without the guidance of the written Word of God and the Holy Spirit, is naïve; it is a denial of the total depravity of unregenerate people (cf. the first of the Five Points of Calvinism).

Usually, such forms of biblicism are a-historical, or even anti-historical. It is the attempt to acquire entrance to Scripture in a self-chosen, headstrong way without paying attention to almost twenty centuries of

---

[57] Insofar as NL2K is unaware of its philosophical premises, and believes that theology is derived directly and immediately from the Bible, it is in fact just as biblicistic!

[58] Cf. Davis (1984a, 57–58).

[59] See extensively, Ouweneel (2013, chapters 6–14).

Christian Bible exegesis, and to the great teachers of the church, with the
exception of the few leaders of one's own denomination ("sectarianism").[60]
Reformed theologian Valentijn Hepp distinguished between: (a) a *serious*
form of biblicism, which rejects all church dogmas and confessions, as
well as all theological theory building, (b) a *lighter* form, which allows the
formulation of confessions but insists on the regular revision of the church
dogmas, and (c) the *lightest* form of biblicism, which leaves the confession
unaffected but does not bother about the significance of every phrase in the
confession.[61] Interestingly, biblicism is here measured according to one's
attitude toward the confession (cf. §2.5): the more confessionalist, the less
biblicist—and vice versa!

2.4.2   Biblicism or Natural Law?

NL2K advocates employ a very special use of the term "biblicism." According
to Kloosterman, NL2K logic with regard to Abraham Kuyper runs as follows:

> If you say, Dr. Kuyper, that human sin vitiates every effort to base pol-
> itical theory on the study of general revelation, then you, Dr. Kuyper,
> must be committed to finding the rules of civil government in the
> Bible alone. Either you ground public social and political ethics in
> natural law, or you derive them from Bible verses only. Does that
> choice sound familiar? Critics of NL2K, those of us who insist that sin
> vitiates the grounding of public social and political moral standards
> exclusively in natural law, are given only one other choice: we must
> therefore be biblicists who want to have a Bible verse for every polit-
> ical policy and social moral standard. With Kuyper, we would defend
> the use of Scripture for public social and political ethics that illumines
> and directs proper appeals to natural law. The choice is not either the
> Bible or natural law, but both the Bible and natural law—*and in that
> epistemological order!*[62]

This is an important point, which is also related to what VanDrunen wrote
elsewhere about the relationship between biblical data and natural law.[63]
The point is this: from where do we get divine guidelines for our behaviour
in our private lives and in the various societal relationships in which we
function? Is this the choice: either from natural law, supposedly written

---

[60] See Ouweneel (2010b, chapters 13–14).
[61] Hepp (1936).
[62] Kloosterman (2012a, 42).
[63] VanDrunen (2010a, 175–76).

on our hearts, or directly from the Bible? Biblicists are those who think they can get such divine guidelines directly from the Bible. NL2K advocates reject biblicism—so do I—and thus—though unwarranted—they see only one option left: natural law (whatever this may be, and no matter how people imagine that they can deduce certain rules from it)!

I clearly see a third option: *from a radical-Reformed perspective*, the rules for civil government are neither explicitly found in the Bible, nor in natural law, *but in a radical-Christian philosophy* (see chapter 11), in this case especially a Christian philosophy of the state (see chapter 12). Later in this book, we will see that such a philosophy, as a rational, theoretical enterprise, is necessarily founded in a rational, pre-theoretical *Christian worldview*, which itself is rooted in the suprarational, pre-theoretical human heart. I come back to these important matters in subsequent chapters, especially in the last ones.

2.5 CONFESSIONALISM

2.5.1 "The Old Is Better"

Of course, the question is whether Hepp's approach (see at the end of §2.4.1) found the proper middle road between biblicism and confessionalism. On the one hand, the dangers of biblicism are, among many other things, individualism and pride. In brief: it ignores the guidance of the Spirit throughout church history (John 16:13). On the other hand, there are also the dangers of confessionalism: rigid collectivism, imprisoning Scripture in one specific favourite tradition, and closing oneself off forever to newer insights into Scripture, especially if they come from other traditions. In brief: it ignores the guidance of the Spirit in the *present* church situation. The Spirit led the men who wrote the Three Forms of Unity and the Westminster Standards, and that's it. Who are we to know better than these men?

Or, to put it this way: biblicists are eagerly digging for new sources of water, ignoring the sources that have been dug up long before: "always learning and never able to arrive at a knowledge of the truth" (cf. 2 Tim. 3:7). Confessionalists, by contrast, have "hewed out cisterns for themselves, broken cisterns that can hold no water" (cf. Jer. 2:13). They stick to what is familiar and secure; considering the possibility that some confessional elements might not hold water (to preserve the metaphor) shakes them to the core.

I remember once buying at a market in a Dutch fishermen's town a Dutch translation of a book written by Puritan theologian John Owen (d. 1683), in which the publisher had printed as a motto: "No one after drinking old wine desires new, for he says, 'The old is better'" (Luke 5:39). Of course, the publisher wanted to recommend Owen as "good old wine," without understanding that, in Luke 5, Jesus meant it in a negative way: the spiritual leaders of Israel were not open to Jesus' message because they stubbornly stuck to their own traditions.

Being constantly open to fresh biblical insights is commendable, but biblicism is dead wrong. Respect for ancient and well-tested confessions is commendable, but confessionalism is dead wrong. Against this background the NL2K debate has been very off-putting when authors have argued vigorously about the true interpretation of Luther and Calvin, and other early Protestant writers. As if the most important question is whether author P or Q is "truly Reformed," or who is most faithful to the "Reformed tradition" (see the next section). The question becomes even more precarious when we consider two typical characteristics of the NL2K position, which we have considered before in this and the previous chapter:

(a) In the light of the Three Reformed Forms of Unity, the NL2K position fails immediately, as we have seen (§1.3). Does this mean it is not really Reformed, or not sufficiently Reformed? If NL2K theologians insist on their faithfulness to the Reformed tradition—and neo-Calvinism's lack of faithfulness—this should be a great concern to them.

(b) The "Reformed tradition" with which NL2K connects turns out to be nothing but Reformed scholasticism. If neo-Calvinism has any surpassing merit, it consists—so it seems to me—in trying to break free of this scholasticism (i.e., the remnants of a Greek and medieval past)—an endeavour in which, in my view, the post-Kuyper/Bavinck generation, including Sytse U. Zuidema (d. 1975), Herman Dooyeweerd (d. 1977), Dirk H. Th. Vollenhoven (d. 1978), Klaas J. Popma (d. 1986), Johan P. A. Mekkes (d. 1987), and Hendrik G. Stoker (d. 1993), succeeded better than their intellectual forbears. Personally, I would indeed rather connect with that form of the Reformed tradition in which this scholasticism has in principle been overcome. I say in principle, because we should not underestimate the tremendous power of scholasticism in Christian (both Catholic and Protestant) thinking. Who can truly say that he has thoroughly cleansed himself of it in every domain of his thinking?

2.5.2   NL2K and Confessionalism

John Frame calls R. Scott Clark,[64] who is a representative of NL2K, an excellent example of a confessionalist.[65] I fully agree, but I am afraid that Clark is not the only one. I know this is a sensitive matter, also for all *Reformed* thinkers who reject NL2K but who themselves are deeply attached to their Reformed tradition. I do not blame them; on the contrary, I have explained that I basically adhere to the Five Points of Calvinism, and I have written a book sympathetic to the Heidelberg Catechism.[66] Yet, it would be unthinkable for me, in order to underpin any theological standpoint, to use the Three Forms of Unity or the Westminster Standards as an objective criterion for the correctness of any view. We honour and respect such venerable documents, but they cannot be a standard of truth. As a good Protestant, I can accept Scripture alone as the standard of truth, even if I hear the word "biblicism!" reverberating all around me.

A striking example is David VanDrunen. In defending the concepts of "natural law" and the "two kingdoms," he devotes almost an entire book to the development of Reformed thinking on this matter.[67] This may be interesting to the historians of theology, but (a) many *Reformed* opponents of NL2K have given very different interpretations of the relevant statements by Augustine, Luther, Calvin, and many others;[68] (b) all these ancient authors do not prove NL2K to be right. Am I a biblicist if I reply that I am more interested in what *Scripture* says on the concepts of "natural law" and the "two kingdoms"? I will try to live with the accusation.

In the meantime, I cannot but establish the fact that even these *terms* ("natural law," "two kingdoms") do not occur in the Bible. Don't remind me of the fact that this also holds for the terms "Trinity" and "substitution." At least the contents of these terms are clearly there. However, as I try to show in this book, the *contents* of the terms "natural law" and "two kingdoms" are not in the Bible at all. Contrary to Karl Barth,[69] I do believe in the existence of natural revelation, but I also believe that it is impossible to work with the concept of a "natural law" apart from (a) the light that God's inscripturated revelation sheds on it, and (b) the work of the Holy Spirit in the souls of those pondering God's natural revelation (see chapter 4).

---

[64] Clark (2008).

[65] Frame (2011, 69–126, 152).

[66] Ouweneel (2016d).

[67] VanDrunen (2010b).

[68] See, e.g., chapter 1 note 19.

[69] See especially Brunner and Barth (1946); cf. Hauerwas (2002).

NL2K has inflated the subject "natural law and the two kingdoms" so much that it began reading it into every part of the Bible. This is a well-known phenomenon in theology,[70] if not in all scientific development. People discover a certain phenomenon, and they are so proud of their discovery that they begin to observe this phenomenon everywhere, and even feel tempted to base their entire discipline on it.

Let me give a clear example. VanDrunen defends the "active obedience of Christ" as a vital element in the Reformed doctrine of justification.[71] He reviews the Reformed literature on this point, even though he is strongly convinced even before the actual dogmatic argument begins. He repeats several arguments that were given by Luther, but never answers the one essential dogmatic question: What is the direct biblical evidence for the thesis that a person needs someone else vicariously fulfilling the law for him in order to be saved? We hear a lot of conclusions from conclusions—we call this "conclusivism"—but never any direct biblical evidence. Elsewhere I have argued that, in my view, the Bible speaks in a very different way.[72] But that is not the point that concerns me right now; it is the confessionalist background of the entire discussion: the argument is that it *must* be so, since our greatest men believed it.

This confessionalism reminds me very much of the Roman Catholic Church: *Roma locuta, causa finita* ("Rome has spoken, the matter is finished"). This time it is: *Reformatio locuta, causa finita* ("The Reformation [i.e., the Reformers] has/have spoken, the matter is finished"). Who are we to contradict the Reformers? There are three counter-questions to be asked: (a) What is the principal difference between Rome and the Reformation at such a point? (b) Why could there not be theologians today who, on certain points, see more clearly than the Reformers did (especially after five centuries of continued thinking)? (c) Why not pay attention to the Reformers' own attitude in matters like this? I refer again to the statement that Luther himself made at the Diet of Worms: "Unless I am convinced by Scripture and plain reason—I do not accept the authority of the popes and councils, for they have contradicted each other—my conscience is captive to the Word of God."[73] I think it would be wise and courageous if every Protestant theologian would make this statement his own, substituting "Reformers and early Reformed scholastics" for "popes and councils."

---

70 Cf. Ouweneel (2016g) on the covenant concept.
71 In Johnson and Waters (2006, 128–33).
72 See extensively, Ouweneel (2016h, chapter 4).
73 http://www.luther.de/en/worms.html.

WORKING IT OUT / **PUBLIC SCHOOLS**

Does the Bible allow me to send my children to state-governed public schools that actively teach values, ideas, and practices that are in direct conflict with the Bible?

How lovely it would be if the Bible gave us very clear-cut and specific answers to questions like this! But unfortunately, "state-governed public schools" are unknown in the Bible—and Christian schools, too, for that matter. It is difficult to find anything reminiscent of "schools" in the Bible.[74] The only reference that I can think of is rather vague: "Woe to you, scribes and Pharisees, hypocrites! For you travel across sea and land to make a single proselyte" (Matt. 23:15). The proselyte is a Gentile pupil, who is turned into a Jew. A beautiful Christian reference, though equally vague, is this one: "What you [i.e., Timothy] have heard from me in the presence of many witnesses entrust to faithful men who will be able to teach others also" (2 Tim. 2:2).

Where direct guidelines are lacking, we must look for indirect guidelines. One passage that comes to mind is this:

> I wrote to you in my letter not to associate with sexually immoral people—not at all meaning the sexually immoral of this world, or the greedy and swindlers, or idolaters, *since then you would need to go out of the world*. But now I am writing to you not to associate with anyone who bears the name of brother if he is guilty of sexual immorality or greed, or is an idolater, reviler, drunkard, or swindler—not even to eat with such a one (1 Cor. 5:9–11; italics added).

Note the phrase in italics. If we wish to avoid gross sins around us (including "values, ideas, and practices that are in direct conflict with the Bible"), we would have to go out of "the world," that is, withdraw to the desert or to an island. We protect our children as much as we can against such gross evil, but we cannot always avoid it. Children will encounter such sins on television, on the Internet, on the billboards along the streets, in the books they read. It is far better to try to *arm* them against evil than to try to keep them away from it, because we will not succeed in this.

---

[74] The "boy" in Judg. 8:14 (DRA, TLV), who apparently was able to write, may suggest a kind of school he had attended.

Of course, we realize that young children are far more sensitive than adults to bad influences. As they grow up, we try to arm them, but when they are very young, they first need to be protected. In that sense, a Christian school is usually a much better option than a state-governed public school. However, first, many parents simply cannot afford such private schools. Second, gross evil may occur at Christian schools as well; be aware of the fact that it is more difficult to protect your children against evil at a Christian school, because they take it for granted that things are okay at such a school. At a public school, you can warn your children beforehand.

In life we must often weigh pros and cons. Homeschooling might be an option, but it can have the enormous disadvantage that you may be robbing your children of important social contacts with peers, which are essential to healthy maturing. Christian schools might be an option but, as I said, they are often far too expensive for many parents, and it is more difficult to arm your children against things that go wrong at such schools. Please do realize that even at Christian schools you might not agree with everything that is taught there (except, perhaps, if it is a school of your own church denomination). Sometimes, a state-governed public school might not be the worst option, *if you invest time following what is taught and practiced at such a school.* Prepare your children for what they might expect at such a school. And help them, from your own Christian world and life view, to distinguish what is wrong at such a school, and arm them against it.

Let me add this remark on the term "education."[75] In English this covers two quite different things, which are distinguished in Dutch and German: *opvoeding/Erziehung* is the kind of education (raising, nurture, bringing up, training, instruction) that parents do at home, and *onderwijs/Unterricht* is the kind of education (giving lessons, teaching) that teachers do at school. To make it even more complicated: "Christian education" is what Christian parents do at home, what teachers do at Christian schools, but also what happens at many churches (Sunday school, Bible study). When some people hear about "Christian education," the latter form is presumably what will come up in their minds first. Of course, families, schools and churches all contribute to children's education (not to mention radio and TV, the Internet, the street, scouting, sports clubs, etc.).

Christian parents wish to give their children a Christian education that is as thorough as possible. Because the school in many ways is an extension of the family, many parents rightly prefer a Christian school. I have mentioned one important reason for this: the Christian atmosphere at such a school,

---

[75] See extensively, Kloosterman (2008) on "Christian education" in relation to NL2K.

where prayer and Bible reading are practiced just as diligently as they are at home. But this argument is more of a utilitarian kind. There is a second important reason, which is of a far more principal nature. Christian parents want their children to be taught the natural sciences, history, art, music, literature, economics, etcetera, from a *Christian* perspective. This is the very reason why many NL2K advocates object to Christian schools: they do not believe in the possibility of a Christian approach to all these disciplines. In their view, both the school and the disciplines taught there belong to the "common realm," which is neutral and secular. So why should we need Christian schools?

In the rest of this book I hope to show how mistaken this view is. But already at this point I ask: Can you imagine studying history from a "neutral" perspective? Dry data and dates, without any deeper ideological, and even religious connection? Studying world history in a way entirely separated from redemptive history?[76]

Or imagine teaching music without being able to point out in what sense Bach and Mendelssohn wrote Christian music—I am not talking only of the *words* they put in music!—and Karlheinz Stockhausen and John Cage wrote anti-Christian music. This becomes clear if you study the worldviews of these various composers.

Or imagine teaching the visual arts without being able to point out in what sense Rembrandt van Rijn made Christian paintings, and Pablo Picasso made anti-Christian paintings. They used similar paint and canvas, but they worked from very different worldviews, which led to very different types of painting.[77]

Or imagine teaching economics without being able to point out in what sense communism constitutes an anti-Christian economic system, and what, for a Christian, is the blessing but also the danger of capitalism (leading to increased wealth but often also to increased selfishness and greed). Are such economic systems "neutral"? You would love a Christian teacher explaining this to your kids!

Or imagine teaching biology without being able to point out the dangers of evolutionism. What Christians would like to send their children to schools like that, where Charles Darwin and Richard Dawkins determine what children must think about these things? I am not advocating biblicist fundamentalism—but I do advocate an approach in which the Christian

---

[76] See extensively, Ouweneel (2016a; 2016c).

[77] On this point, Horton (1995, chapters 4–5) has made a good contribution.

teacher can point out the various ideological backgrounds, especially when it comes to questions about "beginnings."

Or imagine what your children may hear at school about psychology and sociology without having at their disposal a thoroughly Christian (theological and philosophical) anthropology.[78] There is hardly any discipline in which worldviews and ideologies play a greater role. Imagine an atheist or an agnostic explaining this to your kids!

Or imagine the state-governed school where atheists and agnostics explain to your children what "religion" is, and how dangerous religion is ("you only have to look at extreme Islam"), or how old-fashioned religion is in the light of our (post)modern values, norms, and principles!

And finally, imagine how naïve NL2K is to believe in common (neutral, unbiased) lessons in science, history, art, and religion! It is the old error of positivism—old because hardly any present-day philosopher still believes in it. This is the naïve faith in the objective empirical "facts." The state-governed school is seen as the "neutral" school where they give your kids the "straight facts." (Some might even blame the Christian school for burdening the kids with not only "facts" but also "Christian prejudices.") Don't believe this nonsense. You can better listen to parents who sent their children to state-governed schools, *and who took pains to carefully check what their kids were learning there.* Of course, there are some very good teachers at state-governed schools (some of them are Christians). I am referring to the others, who imbue your kids not with "neutral facts" but with the ideologies of an evil world.

---

[78] See extensively, Ouweneel (2015).

PART II
THEOLOGICAL TOPICS

CREATION THEOLOGY[1]

PREPARATORY PONDERINGS

1. Have you ever thought about whether you have a cultural task? If so, what does this task involve? In other words, what is your vocation?
2. You may view this as a God-given vocation but is it also a *kingdom* vocation? That is, does your vocation come from the King? Is it intended to further his kingdom, or is it a "common (neutral, secular)" task? Why?
3. Do you think there is good and bad culture, and how could we distinguish between the two? According to what criteria? Must these be neutral or Christian criteria?
4. Do you believe that Christian believers and unbelievers in the same country can more or less have a common morality (ethics), which is not specifically Christian and is not explicitly based on the Bible? (Do not think of a Western country only but, for instance, also of a country like India or Indonesia.)

---

[1] This chapter is a translation and elaboration of parts of chapters 4 and 14 in Ouweneel (2008a).

3.1   THE CULTURAL MANDATE

3.1.1   The Ones Called and the Calling

No exposition of natural law can do without the wider framework of a proper *ktiseology*, that is, a theological doctrine of creation. Such a doctrine must devote attention also to the creation mandate (see this and §3.2) and to the creation ordinances (§3.3), to prevent viewing the creation merely as an event in the past. The creation order continues to function until the end of time. This creation order was not damaged by sin; what was injured was only the functioning of the creation, especially of humanity, *under* that creation order.[2] For that reason, a proper treatment of soteriology and eschatology in particular (see chapter 9) cannot avoid dealing with the creation order.[3] The new creation does not exist *in opposition to* the old creation, but implies the restoration and exaltation *of* the old creation. For that reason, the creation order continues to function in the new creation.

In Genesis 1:26, 28; 2:5, 15; 3:17–19, 23—that is, both before and after the Fall—humanity is given the mandate (command) to develop ("enculturate") the many rich potentialities that the Creator has embedded within the creation. The "Father is working until now" (John 5:17), but he also delegates work. He creates and maintains; but he assigns to humanity the task of transforming his creation into culture. This must occur in both our personal lives and our collective lives, that is, within the various societal relationships in which human beings have been placed. Moreover, since the Fall, this must occur in opposition to the power of sin, the kingdom of Satan (Matt. 12:25–26), which is the same as saying: under the kingship of Christ, and under the leading and in the power of the Holy Spirit. This so-called cultural mandate[4] is the biblical calling by which *each* individual human being and *each* societal association is called by God to a particular life task, whether or not people acknowledge this vocation as coming from God.[5] Each person was created to glorify God in a general sense; but each person is called to do so in a very unique way, in terms of the service that God has

---

[2]   See extensively, Ouweneel (2008a, chapter 12).

[3]   See extensively, Ouweneel (2009a; 2010a; 2012a).

[4]   The notion of the "cultural mandate" (Dutch: *cultuurmandaat*) goes back especially to Reformed theologian Klaas Schilder (2016), who built upon, but at the same time contrasted this idea, with that of "common grace" as we find this with Calvin (*Institutes* 2.2.12–19) and Kuyper (2016a) (see §4.4.1).

[5]   Cf. chapter 1 note 58.

entrusted to him or her. This service was granted or given (Latin: *datum*, "given"), and it is a mandate (*mandatum*, "commanded, command").[6] It is both a God-given privilege and a responsibility.

Culture is "elaborated" or "developed nature" in the broadest sense of the phrase, whether this refers to raising crops (agri*culture*, horti*culture*) and livestock, or physical and spiritual formation, nurture and education, science, art, religious life, business life, associations, politics, etc. As Gordon Spykman put it: "According to the divine plan, the Garden [i.e., Eden] was destined to become a City"[7]—not like the city of Enoch (Gen. 4:17) or the cities of Babel and Nineveh (Gen. 10:8–12), but a city for God (cf. the "city of God" in Ps. 46:4; 87:3; cf. 48:1, 8; 101:8; Isa. 60:14; Matt. 5:35), as this would achieve full realization in the New Jerusalem (Rev. 21:9–22:5). In the words of Cornelius Plantinga: "We may think of the holy city as the garden of Eden plus the fullness of the centuries."[8] We are reminded here of Isaiah 60:5, 14 ("the wealth of the nations shall come to you…; they shall call you the City of the LORD") and Revelation 21:26 ("They will bring into it [i.e., the city of God] the glory and the honor of the nations") (see more extensively §9.3).

God created each human being as a true *homo culturalis*, which is perhaps a better term than *homo sapiens*.[9] Humans are cultural beings, which is to say, people with the innate urge to shape nature, to take hold of nature, to control it, to elaborate it, to develop it, to exploit it, to design it. Even the most primitive peoples do this, not according to specific instincts—like spiders weave webs, termites build mounds, and beavers make dams—but according to their own free design. The cultural mandate is a *command*—inherent to human nature—one that is at the same time inconceivable apart from notions like *freedom* and *creativity*. Nature is developed according to humans' own free design.

3.1.2   The Creation Mandate

The notion of "cultural mandate" has at times been somewhat misunderstood. This occurred especially because the notion of "culture" was often used in a very optimistic sense, as if "the" culture as we know it would be something very positive. Often this was the complaint of Dutch conservative (hyper-)Calvinists toward those of a Kuyperian Reformed orientation.[10]

---

[6] Spykman (1992, 178).
[7] Spykman (1992, 256).
[8] Plantinga (2002, 33).
[9] Cf. Danesi and Perron (1999, ix).
[10] See, e.g., in the field of Christian politics: dnpp.eldoc.ub.rug.nl/FILES/root/jb-dnpp/jb93/hippe.pdf.

To some extent this was quite understandable, because much of what we call "culture" is so thoroughly permeated with sin that the notion itself has become quite encumbered. For that reason one had perhaps better avoid the phrase "cultural mandate;" after all, we have definitely not received a mandate to produce the kind of (sinful) "culture" so prevalent around us.

Some prefer to speak of a "creation mandate," and use that phrase to identify the divine mandate to develop the potentialities that lie embedded within the creation in honour of God and in service to humanity. In what follows, I will use this less-encumbered phrase. This mandate remained even after the Fall: Christians still participate in opening up creation culturally as God has intended.

Not only is the creation mandate itself a norm, but its fulfillment is normed in every respect as well, just like all things humans do. Therefore, the fulfillment of the creation mandate must occur with the acknowledgement of the sovereignty and commandments of God, as laid down in Scripture. This *principle* remains valid, even though there are many places on earth where God's commandments were and are, or have become, unknown. This normativity applied before, but also after, the Fall because the Fall did not limit or even annul the validity of God's norms. As a consequence of the Fall, humans may no longer be able to fulfill God's commandments in their own strength—this is why believers have received new life as well as the power of the Holy Spirit—but that does not change at all the *validity* of these commandments.

We see an illustration of this in agriculture. Humans "worked the ground" before the Fall (Gen. 2:5), but also after the Fall (3:23; 4:2, 12). God told fallen Adam: "Because you have listened to the voice of your wife and have eaten of the tree of which I commanded you, 'You shall not eat of it,' cursed is the ground because of you; in pain you shall eat of it all the days of your life; thorns and thistles it shall bring forth for you" (3:17–18), and he told Cain: "When you work the ground, it shall no longer yield to you its strength" (4:12).

Since the coming, suffering, death, resurrection, ascension, and subsequent glorification of Christ, God's commandments are obeyed in the recognition of the kingship of Christ (or disobeyed because this kingship is disowned) (see extensively chapters 5–7). Today the creation mandate cannot be disconnected from the kingdom of God; on the contrary, it presupposes that kingdom.[11] After the coming of Christ, the fulfillment

---

[11] See extensively, Ouweneel (2016e); cf. Plantinga (2002, 109–113), who emphasizes that all cultural work is kingdom work. This is not understood by Horton (2011, 712–15), who

of this mandate occurs within the context of his solemn declaration: "All authority in heaven and on earth has been given to me" (Matt. 28:18). This declaration touches the heart of the kingdom of God, for this kingdom entails that God, the King of kings and Lord of lords (1 Tim. 6:15), has appointed Christ (God the Son), as the Man exalted and glorified at his right hand, to be King of kings and Lord of lords (Ps. 2:6; Rev. 17:14; 19:16; cf. Eph. 5:5; Rev. 11:15).

Thus, every vocation of the believing person exists within this eschatological context of the kingdom of God. This is not what NL2K advocates believe but what I believe, as I will develop and defend extensively. Because God's commandments retain their validity also for unbelievers, the latter are called as well to learn to view their vocation within the framework of God's kingdom, through regeneration and faith, under the guidance of the Holy Spirit. Thus, the world does not consist of "two kingdoms," but of those who are subjects within the one kingdom and those who are not yet subjects of this one kingdom but are called to submit to it. Each unbelieving scientist, artist, politician, etc., does carry out his scientific, artistic or political task *under the kingship of Christ, which he however disowns*. He is called to become a believing scientist, artist, politician, etc., who carries out his scientific, artistic or political task *not only under, but also in the joyful recognition of, the kingship of Christ*.

Again, this is in stark contrast to the views of "natural law" and "two-kingdoms" theology (NL2K). In the rest of this as well as in the following chapters, I intend to make clear why I choose the course that I follow here as the only biblical one.

3.1.3   Creation and Predestination

The creation mandate is also important in connection with the doctrine of predestination.[12] Too often the impression is created that predestination is related exclusively to a person's eternal destiny, in connection with which the believer's earthly life is nothing but a kind of "waiting room" available to get ready for heaven. No, the one who is elect is called not only to an eternal abode in heaven, but also to a cultural task (or creational task) on this earth in the broadest sense of the phrase. Please note, *theologizing and preaching are also cultural tasks* because they satisfy our description of culture: deploying the potentialities that God has laid within his creation,

---

creates a gulf between the cultural mandate and the Great Commission, by linking the former with "common grace" and the "common realm," and the latter with "God's saving grace" and the kingdom of God.

[12] See extensively, Ouweneel (2008b; 2016i).

in this case within humanity—a deployment that is possible only through regeneration and the power and guidance of the Holy Spirit. Culture is the transformation of nature; spiritual growth is the transformation of a person into the image of God's Son (Rom. 8:29; 2 Cor. 3:18), transformation by the renewal of his mind (Rom. 12:2).

Jesus said to his followers, "You are the salt of the earth" and "the light of the world" (Matt. 5:13–14). And Paul said to one of his pupils, "Fulfill your ministry [*diakonia*]" (2 Tim. 4:5; cf. Col. 4:17). Even believing slaves have a cultural task, with which "in everything they may adorn the doctrine of God our Savior" (Titus 2:10).

To give one example in connection with predestination, it is interesting to notice how the first part of Paul's letter to the Ephesians is stamped with the believer's *heavenly* calling:

> Blessed be the God and Father of our Lord Jesus Christ, who has bless-
> ed us in Christ with every spiritual blessing in the heavenly places,
> even as he chose us in him before the foundation of the world, that
> we should be holy and blameless before him. In love he predestined
> us for adoption as sons through Jesus Christ, according to the purpose
> of his will (Eph. 1:3–5).

However, in the second half of the letter, this is worked out in a very practical, *earthly* way: within the circle of faith (4:1–5:21, practical church life), within the circle of marriage and the family (5:22–6:4), and within the circle of our daily labour (6:5–9). Within all these spheres, the believer lives under the authority of the *Lord* (4:1, 5, 17; 5:8, 10, 17, 19–20, 22; 6:1, 4, 7–8). This can mean only one thing: he lives in the sphere of the king-dom of Christ and God, who is our Lord and King (cf. 5:5, where believers are referred to as heirs in the "kingdom of Christ and God"). This is one argument against NL2K: marriage, family, and daily labour belong just as much to the realm of the kingdom of God as the church. We will return extensively to this very important point.

A cultural task, or creation task, is a *vocation*, which means basically the same as "calling;" to receive this task, one must indeed first be called in the sense of 1 Peter 2:9: God "called you out of darkness into his mar-velous light." That is to say, the creation mandate is a mandate that after the Fall effectively comes to the *believer*, to the person who participates in regeneration through the Holy Spirit and in salvation in Christ. The creation mandate must never be secularized, something that is the ultimate consequence of NL2K. Since the coming of Christ, there is no such thing as a cultural task for some generalized "humanity." Ever since the Fall, the creation mandate remains in force for every person as an immutable divine norm, but it can be performed according to God's intentions only by virtue of regeneration, under the guidance of the Holy Spirit, and in the light of God's commandments, that is, within the sphere of the kingdom of God.

Unbelievers also fulfill their cultural task; virtually no person on earth can escape doing so. In terms of the horizontal dimension (qua "structure"), unbelievers often do this better than many Christians: they may be better painters, scientists, or magistrates. But in terms of the vertical dimension (qua "direction"), the unbeliever fulfills his cultural task in apostasy from God and his commandments (see on these two axes, "structure" and "direction," §§3.2.2 and 4.5). There is no neutral realm: there is Godward culture and there is apostate culture (and unfortunately we often see a mixture of the two). Unbelievers fulfill their task in servitude to apostate spiritual forces (idols, idolatrous ideologies). Or they do so entirely apart from any *mandate*, but—as they fancy—out of their own free choice, out of their apostate notion of autonomy, the self-determination of the free individual. To be sure, the person possesses the creaturely freedom to obey or not to obey the mandate; but that such a person is formally under that *mandate* is wrongly denied.

3.2 GOOD AND BAD CULTURE

3.2.1 Culture under God's Norms
Under the influence of the aforementioned cultural optimism, people easily make the mental error of thinking that, not only does the creation mandate entail cultural development, but the reverse is also true: every form of cultural development automatically entails the fulfillment of the creation mandate. This is the error of NL2K: in the one (sacred) realm, Christ is King, in the other (secular, neutral, not sacred) realm we are dealing only with God's providence. Here, people supposedly carry out their cultural task in obedience to the natural law. This is a double mistake: first, Christ is King of the entire cosmos, not just of the church; second, any cultural task carried out apart from regeneration and the Holy Spirit cannot be anything else than apostate.

As mentioned above, cultural development is *normed*. On the one hand, there is good culture, brought to development in faithful agreement with God's norms and ordinances. In principle, this is done by believers guided by the Holy Spirit, but because of the intrusive character of God's law order, even unbelievers are able to contribute satisfactory cultural achievements.

Please note, this is not because of some natural law in their *hearts* (cf. §4.1), but because of the intrusive law order in the surrounding *cosmic reality* (see extensively §3.4.4). On the other hand, there is bad culture, brought to development by unbelievers, but also by believers who are led by their sinful flesh more than by God's Word and Spirit. "Good" and "bad" have to do here with the vertical direction of things, not with the creation structures (see the next section). That is, a person may be a fantastic artist or scientist from the viewpoint of the creation structures, and a very bad artist or scientist if he uses his art or science to oppose God.

It is significant that the very first cultural development mentioned in the Bible was this kind of bad culture. We learn of the development, especially among the descendants of Cain, of an economic order (Jabal), of art (Jubal), and of technology (Tubal-Cain) (Gen. 4:20–22).[13] We do not learn of such matters among the descendants of Seth. From this, people in Anabaptist and pietist circles have often concluded that cultural development as such would be a wrong thing.[14] That claim cannot be maintained, of course; for then they would have to be consistent and live like the most primitive peoples—and even they are familiar with a certain degree of culture. Even the Amish have their culture, although in its development it got stuck somewhere in the eighteenth century. However, they do not live in trees; they have houses and horse-drawn buggies. No one can do without some form of culture—and maintaining an eighteenth-century culture as such does not make anyone holier than living in a twenty-first-century culture.

We are dealing here with a serious confusion between (horizontal) *structure* and (vertical) *direction* (see next section and §4.5). That is to say, what is wrong is not culture itself, nor a particular domain within culture, nor the culture of a certain century or of a certain part of the world, but the sinful manner in which any culture is given its shape. Jabal's economics, Jubal's art, and Tubal-Cain's technology may have been superb (horizontal), but they were part of a culture hostile to God (vertical).

3.2.2 Structure and Direction

With regard to its *structure* (including God's structural laws), we are referring to culture that meets the norms of the various cultural aspects. With regard, for example, to the aesthetic aspect of culture, we think of the difference between genuine art and kitsch. With regard to the logical aspect, we think of the difference between what is academically respectable

---

[13] Cf. on this VanDrunen (2010a, 78).
[14] See the criticism by De Graaff (1969, 275–77).

and what is pseudo-science. Regarding the historical aspect, we think of the difference between the norm of historical continuity, on the one hand, and basically a-historical reactionism *or* revolutionism, on the other hand. Regarding the social aspect, we think of a social society versus an asocial society. The economic aspect involves a balanced economy versus a lack of income *or* excessive expenses. The ethical aspect involves a developed morality versus a primitive morality. And so forth.

With regard to culture's *direction*, we think of a dimension perpendicular to that of *structure*. That is, we are referring to the question whether a certain culture envisions the glory of God or the dishonour of God, the latter being evident in terms of whether it focuses on serving human beings or even Satan instead of God. There is nothing common here: there is Godward culture, and there is apostate culture.

A culture that is less developed in terms of its structure can nevertheless envision the glory of God as far as its direction is concerned, and a highly developed culture can be oriented to the dishonour of God as far as its direction is concerned. To state this with more nuance: in every highly developed culture, even that of God-haters, there is something that gives glory to God in that his exalted norms become visible in such a culture—even though such God-haters are not serving God but themselves, to say nothing of their serving Satan, and even though they show no interest whatsoever in God's norms. As a development of God's own creation, every culture appeals to—in some cases, lives parasitically from—God's norms, even where no understanding of, or interest in, God's creation ordinances exists. The beautiful painting and the brilliant scientific theory point indirectly to the aesthetic or the logical-analytic creation ordinances (see §3.3), no matter how godless the painter or the scientist may be.

The creation mandate, the command to develop the potentialities of the creation, does not entail "extracting from creation what it contains"—which is by definition apostate culture—but subjecting creation to norms like: What glorifies God, and not primarily the culture builder? What serves the well-being of the individual neighbour and the society as a whole, and not primarily one's own self-interest? The development of the creation must not be maximized, but optimized. This norm obtained all the more urgency when, from the time of the Fall, the creation mandate was to be realized in a sinful world by people who, whether regenerated or not, had a sinful nature. In such a situation, cultural development cannot for a moment be separated from the notions that I have discussed elsewhere, notions like pilgrimage (Heb. 11:13; 1 Pet. 1:1, 17; 2:11; see chapter 8), suffering for the sake of righteousness (1 Pet. 3:14), looking ahead "eagerly" (Rom. 8:19) to a world that surpasses the most beautiful cultural world on earth (Heb. 11:16; see chapter 9), bearing the reproach of Christ (v. 26), seeking the things that are above, not the things on earth (Col. 3:1–2), not laying up treasure on earth (Matt. 6:19–20), placing intimate concourse with the Lord (Ps. 25:14) above every cultural effort, and so on.

3.2.3 Horton's Confusion

Let me give here a striking example of the confusion of structure and direction present in the thought of one NL2K advocate. Michael Horton wrote: "There is going to be a division between the kingdom of Christ and the kingdoms of this world until Christ's return."[15] This is a false contrast; it sounds as if the former and the latter, in spite of the differences, are comparable items. The only point of comparison is that all these kingdoms have a king. For the rest, the differences are not gradual but essential. The "kingdoms of this world" have to do with "horizontal structure," whereas the kingdom of Christ has to do with "vertical direction:" it can manifest itself *within* all "kingdoms of this world." The kingdom of Christ did indeed clearly come to light in various German lands and European countries (Scotland, England, the Netherlands) in which Protestant convictions dominated public life (sixteenth and seventeenth centuries). And apart from this, already today, Christ is King of the entire world, including the states in which apostate convictions are dominant (states dominated by false religions, or by modern secularization). I will endeavour to extensively substantiate this view in subsequent chapters.

Another example of the same confusion with Horton is this:

> There is a tendency in many circles today to speak in the following terms: "All of life is sacred," "all activity is kingdom activity," and so forth. This was true in Eden and it was true in the Jewish theocracy, but *now*, Jesus said, "my kingdom is from another place. It is no longer of this world" [cf. John 18:36]."[16]

However, first, Jesus did *not* say "no longer," as if at some earlier time his kingdom *had* been "of this world" (e.g., in Eden, or in Davidic Israel). *There was no kingdom of Christ before he had been glorified at the right hand of God* (cf. Matt. 28:18; Eph. 1:20–23; 1 Pet. 3:21–22; see extensively chapters 5 and 6).

---

[15] Horton (1995, 187).
[16] Horton (1995, 193).

Second, if Horton means God's kingdom in the general, providential sense (which is a very different matter), even then Jesus' statement does not apply: whether God's universal rule was "of this world" never was a question. Notice how Jesus said to his opponents: "You are from below; I am from above. You are of this world; I am not of this world" (John 8:23). This applied to God's providential kingdom as well: it *concerned* this world, but it was never *of* this world.

Third, once again we encounter here a confusion of structure and direction. Jesus meant that his kingdom was of a different category than the empire that Pilate represented, not only in the sense of good and evil, but in the sense that I tried to explain: the Roman Empire was part of "horizontal structure," the kingdom of Christ has to do with "vertical direction." This means that a connection between the *horizontal* Roman Empire and the *vertical* kingdom of Christ was definitely possible: after three centuries *the latter did come to light within the Roman Empire*, because, from about AD 313, the Roman emperor wished to rule under the authority of Christ, no matter how weakly this was realized. As far as I know, apart from Julian the Apostate (361–363), the Roman Empire, both in the West and in the East, had Christian emperors until its fall (ignoring for now how deep their Christian beliefs were).

Jesus' kingdom is not "of the world (*kosmos*)" in the sense that it is not part of the cosmic structures that God has created. But it is fully "in the world" in the sense that it is realized within all these cosmic structures (see further in §6.3).

3.2.4 "Christianity and Culture"

A remarkable example of the confusion between structure and direction is the way David VanDrunen speaks of "Christianity and culture."[17] My point may be insignificant, or even pedantic. Yet, I hope it is clear. "Christianity" belongs to the vertical dimension of direction, while "culture" belongs to the horizontal dimension of structure. That is, the two cannot be properly compared in this way. Christianity can be compared with atheism, and culture can be compared with nature. But "Christianity and culture" is a confusing, if not simply an erroneously coordinated construction. Any culture is Christian or it is not.

The juxtaposition of the two is comparable to that of "church and world," which is very common, yet equally confusing. That is, it is again a confusion of structure versus direction: a church denomination or a local congregation

---

[17] This confusion is present even in the subtitle of VanDrunen (2010a).

is one of the many societal relationships (structure), in which either "the world" (viewed as the domain of sin and Satan; cf., e.g., 1 John 5:19) or the kingdom of God manifests itself (or a mixture of both) (direction). Even if "world" is taken in a more neutral sense, such as that of society, the juxtaposition is equally wrong, for a church denomination or a local congregation is part of society just like any other societal relationship.

Another confusing comparison is that between "theocracy and democracy," which is again a confusion of structure versus direction: the term "democracy" refers to a specific structure of the nation state, whereas the term "theocracy" refers to a Christian versus a non-Christian, or even apostate character of the state, as we will see (§5.1.3).

Such misleading juxtapositions are category confusions (if you like: comparing cheese and chalk, or confusing apples with oranges). VanDrunen's juxtaposition of "Christianity and culture" suggests that we can first look at Christianity and culture separately, and then decide whether there is any connection between the two, and if so, what this might be. This is a serious mistake. On the one hand, there can be no Christianity in this world without cultural work in some form attached to it. *Even forming church denominations and founding local congregations is cultural work in the widest sense of the term.* On the other hand, there is not the slightest form of neutral culture. We will extensively argue that culture, like anything in this world, is thoroughly religious, that it is either in obedience oriented toward God or in apostasy oriented away from him. It is not Christianity *and* culture—it is either *Christian* culture, or it is *apostate* culture (or a mixture of both). There is no room for neutrality here. This will be extensively argued in chapters 5 and 6, and it will constitute one of the main issues of the present book.

3.3 THE CREATION ORDER [18]

3.3.1 Creation Ordinances

There is no doubt that there is something that might be called "natural law," or broader, "natural laws," including laws for culture, society, the state, the judicial order, the economic order, etc. Elsewhere, I emphasized, as Protestant theology has always done, that we must distinguish the work

---

[18] See Ouweneel (2008a, chapter 4). I have gratefully made use of Rouvoet (1992), Schaeffer-de Wal (1993), Schuurman et al. (1993), Spykman (1992, 178–91), Strauss (1980; 1991; 2009), Troost (1969; 1976), Wolters (1992), and others.

of divine maintenance ("upholding," Heb. 1:3) in addition to the work of creation.[19] The laws of nature may never be understood in terms of the worldview of deism, as if they are laws that God established once, at the time of creation, which since then have functioned autonomously, independently of God. The creation is not a gigantic robot. All things are continually dependent on the preservation of the creation by God, so that everything that happens in reality and in history can be related to God's direct action (see extensively Job 38, Ps. 29, and especially 104; Col. 1:17; Heb. 1:1–3).

The creation ordinances provide reality with stability and reliability: "We can orient ourselves in [the created world], feel secure in it, and make plans for its and our future. Its habitability depends on its knowability, and this knowability is that of a universe *governed by law*."[20] In this connection, Scripture distinguishes between, on the one hand, God's word as creation ordinances *for* cosmic reality, and on the other hand, God's deeds *in* cosmic reality (including his involvement in cultural and historical development). The creation ordinances, which constitute the law order *for* cosmic reality, are parallel with God's activity *in* cosmic reality. The Spirit of God who in Genesis 1:2 hovered over the waters, and the voice of God that called things into existence, substantially coincide. To express it more accurately in Christian-philosophical vernacular, God's *Word* is found on the law side of (i.e., is normative for) cosmic reality, God's *Spirit* is on the subject- or factual side of reality.[21]

Scripture is filled with the idea that the order that exists for cosmic reality is a *creation order*, that is, an order grounded in the creational will and power of God. All things are grounded in God's sovereign creational will (Rev. 4:11). All creatures obey God's *word* (Ps. 119:89; 148:8). The heavenly bodies obey God's *ordinances, word, statutes, commandments* (Job 38:33; Ps. 119:91; 148:6; Isa. 45:12; Jer. 31:35; 33:25). Earthly nature also obeys his *voice*, his *commandments*, his *word* (Ps. 104:7–8; 147:15, 18). God has established a *covenant* with day and night, which is to say: on account of God's covenant faithfulness day and night follow a fixed rhythm (Jer. 33:20, 25).

Speaking scripturally about ordinances in which creational reality is grounded points to the fixed regularity that is proper to the cosmos. We are dealing here with God's *law*. This law is a far wider notion than the Law of Moses; it relates to the entire order that God has established for all his creatures. Heavenly bodies, things, plants, animals, and humans are subject

[19] Ouweneel (2007a, §5.1.2).
[20] Berkhof (1986, 162); italics added.
[21] For this terminology, see Ouweneel (1995, chapter 2; 2012b, chapters 1–4).

to a law in the widest sense of the word—natural law. When we speak of a *creation order*, we recognize this order as a *law order*, that is, from the outset God has subjected his creation to laws. Stated concretely, natural laws apply for the physical-biotic reality, psychic laws for the perceptive-sensitive reality, norms and principles for spiritive reality,[22] and structural laws for individual things (inanimate things, plants, animals, humans), events and states of affairs.

3.3.2 God's Law, God's Word

This law, as we mentioned, is God's *word*; for this reason, the Christian believes that in the cosmic law order we are dealing with *divine revelation*. In the law order or creation order, God reveals *himself*, or at least something of himself. And just as God's law is revelation, so too God's revelation is always law, always a revelation of God's will, whether this involves his will as Creator or his will as Redeemer. In Psalm 19 we find one single revelation of God: whether this involves the law order in the works of nature, or the positivized law for human living—the Mosaic Law—we are dealing with one divine law, which means: one divine revelation.[23]

This is very clear in Psalm 119, which is an acrostichon, in which verses 89–96 constitute the twelfth stanza, called *lamed* (i.e., each line in this stanza begins with the Hebrew letter *lamed*, the twelfth letter of the Hebrew alphabet). This stanza evidently begins with speaking of the cosmic law order (vv. 89–91), but in the same breath it continues to speak of the normative Law of Sinai, especially the Ten Commandments. The cosmic law and the Sinaitic Law constitute a single law, a single revelation of God. We see this in Jeremiah 33:20, 25 (NIV) as well, where God's "covenant with day and night" and his "fixed laws of heaven and earth" are mentioned in direct parallel with his covenantal faithfulness toward the house of David. We find the same in Psalm 89:2–3, where God's (covenantal) faithfulness with respect to the heavens (i.e., the heavenly bodies) is paralleled with his covenantal faithfulness with respect to David (cf. vv. 5, 8, 28–29, 36–37).

If only on account of this intimate relationship between God's word or law or covenant in nature, and God's word or law or covenant in his relationships with people, we must be careful about making too sharp a distinction, let alone a separation, between (a) natural laws, on the one hand, and human norms (including the structural laws of society), on the

---

[22] For this terminology, see Ouweneel (2015).

[23] "Law" and "revelation" are close; see how Isa. 2:3 ("out of Zion shall go the *Torah* [law, teaching]") is rendered in *The Message*: "Zion's the source of the revelation."

other hand, and (b) a natural (general or creational) revelation, on the one hand, and a supernatural (special) revelation, on the other hand, that is: between a law order for nature and society, on the one hand, and an oral or written law of God for faith life, on the other hand. This view is totally opposed to the NL2K position, which does make such a separation between God's laws for the sacred realm and the natural law for the secular realm.

3.3.3 Natural and Special Revelation

In the Reformed tradition, we are used to the distinction between "general (or natural) revelation" and "special revelation." In the words of the Belgic Confession (Art. 2):

> We know [God] by two means: First, by the creation, preservation, and government of the universe; which is before our eyes as a most elegant book, wherein all creatures, great and small, are as so many characters leading us to "see clearly the invisible things of God, even his everlasting power and divinity," as the apostle Paul says (Rom. 1:20). All which things are sufficient to convince men and leave them without excuse. Second, He makes Himself more clearly and fully known to us by His holy and divine Word, that is to say, as far as is necessary for us to know in this life, to His glory and our salvation.[24]

In the next chapter, I will discuss this matter of the two revelations more extensively, but at this point I wish to make a few introductory remarks. The distinction between God's revelation in "the creation, preservation, and government of the universe" and God's revelation ("more clearly") in "his holy and divine Word," is not necessarily problematic in itself, as long as they are kept together. This is what we just found in Psalm 19 and 119. The distinction *becomes* problematic as soon as it is turned into a genuine *dualism*, corresponding to the scholastic nature-grace dualism. General revelation is then thought to belong to the "lower storey" of nature (the "common kingdom"), whereas special revelation is viewed as belonging to the "higher storey" of grace (the "kingdom of God"). In this way, special revelation is placed dualistically in opposition to the general (natural) revelation. Moreover, the "common realm" is thought to be *independent* of the "sacred realm," as if people who do not know—and often even do not *wish* to know—God's special revelation could nevertheless be guided by God's natural revelation (natural law, as NL2K would say).

---

[24] Dennison (2004, 4:425).

The Confession refers to Romans 1:20, God's "invisible attributes, namely, his eternal power and divine nature, have been clearly perceived, ever since the creation of the world, in the things that have been made." This verse, taken by itself, seems to point to a natural revelation that can be received independent of God's Word-revelation. However, the text continues: "So they are without excuse." This refers back to verses 18–19: "The wrath of God is revealed from heaven against all ungodliness and unrighteousness of men, who by their unrighteousness suppress the truth. For what can be known about God is plain to them, because God has shown it to them," and continues in verses 21–22, "For although they knew God, they did not honor him as God or give thanks to him, but they became futile in their thinking, and their foolish hearts were darkened. Claiming to be wise, they became fools."

Note Paul's argument carefully. *In principle*, God's power and divine nature can be recognized in his creation, but *in practice* people do not recognize it because of their wickedness. Or *if* they recognize it, they suppress this truth, and do not honour or thank the God who has thus revealed himself. On the contrary, they have turned to idolatry (v. 23). There is not the slightest basis in Romans 1 (nor in Rom. 2, as we will see; §4.1) to believe in some "natural law" that is known and acknowledged by all people, and that may govern some "common realm." In chapter 4, I will go into this matter more deeply.

3.4   NATURAL LAW AND SCHOLARSHIP

3.4.1   "Theological Ethics"

To the extent that Christian thinking today has any room left for talking about creation ordinances, these are often handled in a biblicistic manner. That means that they are deduced from the Bible in some "theological" ethics, rather than being developed and positivized in all the various scientific disciplines on the basis of a strictly Christian-philosophical paradigm: the norms for societal relationships in a Christian sociology (if you will: a Christian social philosophy); economic norms in a Christian science of economics (or a Christian economic philosophy); juridical norms in a Christian jurisprudence (or a Christian judicial philosophy); moral norms in a Christian (not a "theological"!) ethics (or a Christian ethical philosophy).

Ethics is an independent special science, which can be practiced in both a Christian and a non-Christian way (like *every* special science for that matter, including theology). Strictly speaking, it cannot be a part of theology, unless one, in a "scientistic"[25] way, equates "theological" with "Christian" or "biblical." A theological ethics is just as erroneous as a theological chemistry. The phrase "theological ethics" is a remnant of scholastic thinking, whereby everything that involves the sacred, faith, norms, morality, etc., belongs to the "upper" realm of "grace," and is studied by means of "sacred" theology, whereas the remaining ("profane," "secular"!) scientific disciplines plus philosophy belong to the "lower" realm known as "nature."[26] It is the kind of speaking that we, today, encounter with NL2K as well.

As long as we remain in this scholastic atmosphere, either there is no room at all for creation ordinances, or these are limited in a biblicistic manner to some "theological ethics," which is usually unable to deduce any more creational structures from the Bible than four or five: marriage and family; labour; the composite of people, state, and government; the church; and occasionally the "cultural mandate." This impoverished *under-estimation* of the creation ordinances is a result of the traditional scholastic *overestimation* of theology ("theologism;" see §§9.4.2, 10.4, and 11.3.2).[27] In reality, this discipline has the task of investigating the *nature* of the numerous creation ordinances, that is, of illuminating how they are the revelation of the multiplicity and richness of God's creational will. But it is the various scientific disciplines that must *elaborate* these various creation ordinances *from a Christian-philosophical viewpoint*. In fact, this is exactly the whole task of the special sciences: all the natural laws that the natural sciences discover, and all the cultural and societal laws that the humanities discover, are nothing but facets of God's creational will for nature, culture, and society, respectively.

In modern theology, the concept of creation ordinances is often rejected out of a (understandable) fear of all metaphysics. This concept, however, would degenerate into a purely metaphysical notion only if the creation order were separated from the great love commandment: "Love God above all, and your neighbor as yourself" (e.g., Luke 10:27). In this central religious commandment, the immense diversity of our daily life finds its unity and concentration. This means that our entire life is directed to Spirit-inspired love toward God and neighbour (cf. Rom. 5:5). Separated from this service of the human heart toward God, there is indeed no room for a

---

[25] "Scientism" is the absolutization of scientific thinking and speaking in contrast to every-day thinking and speaking.

[26] On this matter extensively, see Troost (2004, 388–94).

[27] See extensively, Troost (1977; 2004).

genuinely biblical notion of creation order. *There is no neutral ground here,* no "common kingdom," no secular realm.

Metaphysics involves the theory of "being-in-itself," of "objective facts," separated from their divine Origin and supporting Ground. This metaphysics, in whatever form, is the foundation for every so-called "neutral" science, every so-called "neutral" politics, every so-called "unprejudiced biblical exegesis," every "social gospel," every "Christian humanism," every notion such as the "solidarity" of the church and the world, and other horizontalistic approaches. In reality, the slogan, for example, of a so-called "neutral" state is necessarily permeated by a particular *faith commitment,* just as is every other view of the state[28] (see especially chapter 12).

3.4.2   The Positivizing of Laws

The response to both the traditional-scholastic and the modern-humanistic approaches—or the combination of the two in, for instance, NL2K—is, in my view, the return to a truly biblical vision of the creation order as the starting point for a Christian view of society. In the creation order, God reveals his will as a normative *principle.* This will is the *beginning* (the Latin word *principium* means both "beginning" and "principle"), the creative starting point, the religious plumb line that makes human life possible, provides such life with content, and directs that life in kingdom service toward Christ, the glorified Man at God's right hand, Lord and King of the entire cosmic reality. Because this involves a "principle," God allows all kinds of room for the human elaboration of, and giving shape to, God's creation word and redemption word.

The various scientific disciplines have a special task in this activity. They have the divine calling—even if scientists are usually not aware of this—to *positivize* the various creation ordinances that belong to the creation order. This means that they must deduce, elaborate, and formulate them. Naturally this will remain the flawed work of human beings. We must always distinguish sharply between the laws and norms that God has anchored in the creation order, and the concrete hypotheses, theories, "(natural) laws," norms, and societal structures as those are elaborated in and by means of scientific work. But this does not mean that there is no connection at all between them. On the contrary, this work of positivizing is precisely an essential component of the creation mandate given to humanity (see §3.1).

Through and since the Fall, this positivizing work has become even more burdensome. First, subjectively, because the sinful nature within us resists

---

[28] See extensively, Troost (1976).

the structural principles that God has put within the creation order. We ought not to trust, in any way, the mere elaboration of the "natural law," supposedly written in the hearts of all people (see §4.1),[29] without the light of God's Word and Spirit. Sinful people would prefer, for example, to invent their own form of marriage or of the state, rather than acknowledge the pre-established, normative structure of marriage or the state as that is fixed within the creation order. Please note that people can never entirely escape that divine structural law. This means that, when marriage is a real marriage, and the state is a real state, that normative structural law is always visible to a certain extent, even in the most corrupt marriage and the most deteriorated state.

However, autonomous people do not acknowledge this pre-established creation order, and in their positivizing of this structural law, they will incorporate various anti-normative elements. With respect to marriage, think of the parasitic phenomena of cohabitation or of homosexual partnerships, and with respect to the state, think of dictatorship, "popular sovereignty," the separation of religion and society, etc. No supposed "natural law" has *in itself* the capacity of discerning between such normative and anti-normative (apostate) elements; here, the light of God's Word-revelation is needed.

Second, objectively, sin affects the factual knowability of the creation order as well (that is, forget about the "natural law" in your heart; it does not help you a bit). This means that we cannot know the *creation order* (the laws) directly (except in those very few instances where it is [or they are] explicated in Scripture). What we *can* know directly is only the *ordered creation* (the "facts").[30] Creational principles function and come to light in the concrete empirical realities in which they are realized and embodied. However, since the Fall, these experienced facts are always connected to sin (anti-normativity). Not the creation order itself or its objective knowability as such has been affected by sin—God's revelation continues to be loud and clear, and free of sin—but our knowledge and our subjective capacities for knowing have been fundamentally corrupted. Stated concretely: only from the many sin-affected marriage and civic-state relationships that we know from the past and from the present, we must try to penetrate to the original creation *principles* of marriage and of the state. Had we known absolutely no marriages or states, we could not have the faintest idea of the normative structures for marriage and the state (no matter how much "natural law"

---

[29] I realize that VanDrunen (2010b, 1) limits the "natural law" to the *moral* law, but I do not understand why; if the natural law corresponds with God's natural revelation, this covers *all* God's creation ordinances.

[30] Hendrik Hart (1984) has beautifully compared this *world order* and this *ordered world*.

may supposedly be written on our hearts); but the marriages and the states that we *do* know are nonetheless all corrupted by sin.[31]

3.4.3 *Principium* and Elaboration

There are at least two wrong ways of detecting a certain creation principle. The one is the illusion of the "natural law," suggesting that we can find this principle written on our hearts (cf. §4.1). In our quest for the creational *principium* of marriage or state, we supposedly need only look within ourselves to find an innate awareness of what a marriage or a state ought to look like. Forget it. What we will find there is indeed an inner awareness, an intuition, a vague picture, but *one that is not innate at all* but only an impression formed by the culture in which we live and whose principles and ideas we have imbibed. This culture may be Christian, and is often not very Christian at all. We have fooled ourselves: we thought we had followed some "natural law," but what we in fact followed was the cultural patterns in which we had been socialized.

The second wrong way is to try to detect the creational principle by imitating biblical examples; in our quest for the creational *principium* of marriage or state, every form of biblicism must be avoided. Otherwise we will proceed to elevate *biblical historical* marriages like those of the patriarchs or Israel's kings to *normative* marriages, or elevate *biblical historical* civic-state arrangements like that of ancient Israel or of the biblical world empires (from Babylon to Rome) to *normative* civic-state arrangements, as though we could simply adopt and copy these historical examples. People are then forgetting that in those few cases where a direct appeal to Scripture passages is indeed possible, such an appeal is often misleading because such Bible texts do not at all provide us with a specific creational *principle*, but with a concrete (normative *or* anti-normative) *positivizing* of a creational principle in a particular historical context.

Both the civic-state arrangement of ancient Israel and that of Nebuchadnezzar were not examples of a principle, but of concrete positivizings *of* a principle; no normative structure for a state can be deduced from such examples. This normative structure must be detected and discovered *in reality itself*, and done so by studying *many* forms of civic arrangements, which must be observed and analyzed with careful thought before we may arrive at generalizations. Scripture itself points us in this direction, namely, in Isaiah 28:24–28: "When a farmer plows for planting, does he plow

---

[31] See extensively, Troost (2005, especially chapter 12); cf. also Strauss (1979; 1980; 1991; 2009).

continually? Does he keep on breaking up and harrowing the soil? When he has leveled the surface, does he not sow caraway and scatter cummin? Does he not plant wheat in its place, barley in its plot, and spelt in its field? *His God instructs him and teaches him the right way.* Caraway is not threshed with a sledge," etc.

Note what is italicized here: God teaches the farmer how he must perform his farming. How does God do that? He does *not* do this by some alleged "natural law" written in the farmer's heart, so that the farmer intuitively knows what to do. *Nor* does God teach him in a biblicistic way, that is, by means of isolated Bible verses that should guide him. The farmer does not look within himself to read what is written on his heart in order to find the rules for his work, nor does he look in his Bible. (It is good when farmers read the Bible, but not to discover the techniques of effective farming.) There is a *third direction*, and *this* is where the farmer has to look. God gives the farmer wisdom to investigate *nature*, to discern in nature itself the unique *creational features* of each crop, and to act according to these features. By way of the *ordered regularity* (i.e., complying with the standard of the divine law) of the creation, the farmer can identify God's *law* for the creation.

What is valid for the farmer is valid for a Christian cosmology (a philosophical view of cosmic reality). Exactly as in the case of the farmer, such a philosophy is not rooted in some "natural law," nor is it based upon isolated Bible passages. *It is rooted in cosmic reality itself.* By observing and analyzing this reality—a rational-empirical job—Christian cosmologists may hope to form an idea of the creational patterns needed for each discipline. Philosophy attempts to present the comprehensive view of total reality, and the special sciences develop partial views for their respective fields of investigation.

God does nothing but maintain in his covenant faithfulness his *law* for the creation, and people detect and discover this law by way of the *lawful regularity* of the creation. For that purpose a person must *believe a priori* in this law order. The supposed "natural law" written on his heart—if such a thing exists at all (§4.1)—is in no way sufficient. The humanist who does not believe in a pre-established, normative structure for marriage or the state will never "see" this. He may still believe in *natural* laws—the ordered regularity of nature is too striking not to—but he will not believe in the law structures of societal relationships. In fact, how many Christians even have difficulty with this? They accept with no problem the existence of natural laws, which are deduced not from Bible verses but from empirical reality. Why then do they not just as easily accept the law structure of societal relationships that are not deduced from Bible verses, but from empirical reality?

Again, I see only three options, and two of them are wrong:

(a) This law structure is not written on the hearts of people (only NL2K could believe that it is).

(b) This law structure is not written in the Bible, either (only biblicists could believe that it is).

(c) *This law structure is written in reality itself.* And it can be properly "read" from reality only in the light of a radical-Christian worldview, by the power of the Holy Spirit. Any other reading is by definition apostate reading. Again, there is no neutrality here. Those who believe there is, will repeatedly end up either in some scholastic approach (as does NL2K), or in some humanistic approach (as is so common in our secularized Western world), or in some biblicistic approach (as in the case of naïve fundamentalists).

WORKING IT OUT: **SHOPPING AT THE WRONG STORES**
Does the Bible give any direction for whether I shop at stores/businesses that support anti-biblical actions?

Let me repeat here what I wrote in the previous chapter: how lovely would it be if the Bible gave us very clear-cut and specific answers to questions like this! In many such cases, the best we can do is to look for very general, indirect guidelines. Also remember the statement by Paul that I quoted in the previous chapter, in which he says that, if you want to avoid all evil, you must go out of the world. I have places where I buy my clothes, other places where I buy my groceries. To tell you the truth, I have never thoroughly investigated what the stores and businesses involved stand for, what actions they support, what they do with their profits, and so on. First, it is often quite difficult to get reliable information on these questions (don't trust rumours told by others, even on the Internet!). Second, it may cost you a lot of time to make such investigations. Third, in the end you might discover that, actually, there is hardly any store left where you can buy with a good conscience.

I remember how, years ago, people began spreading the rumour that the logo of the American company Procter & Gamble was occultic. They saw all kinds of devilish pictures in it. Thousands of people were alarmed, and refused to buy products from this firm. Afterward, it turned out that all the interpretations of the logo were completely inaccurate. Sensationalists had alarmed people for nothing. Let this teach us the lesson that we should be very reluctant to believe bad rumours that are spread about stores and businesses. This is not to deny, of course, that certain companies are indeed worth avoiding.

Let me give you two Bible references here that might be appropriate. The first one is this: "Be not overly righteous, and do not make yourself too wise. Why should you destroy yourself?" (Eccl. 7:16). This is *not* recommending loose, indifferent behaviour. Rather, the Preacher recommends that you do not "destroy" yourself by imposing on yourself too harsh and severe regulations that make it impossible to function normally.

The other reference is this: "Eat whatever is sold in the meat market without raising any question on the ground of conscience. For 'the earth is the Lord's, and the fullness thereof.' If one of the unbelievers invites you to dinner and you are disposed to go, eat whatever is set before you without raising any question on the ground of conscience. But if someone says to you, 'This has been offered in sacrifice,' then do not eat it, for the sake of the one who informed you, and for the sake of conscience—I do not mean your conscience, but his. For why should my liberty be determined by someone else's conscience? If I partake with thankfulness, why am I denounced because of that for which I give thanks?" (1 Cor. 10:25–30).

What do we learn here? First, some of the meat in the meat market, or perhaps all the meat, may come from idolatrous ceremonies. Don't worry too much about that. Such meat will not hurt you, because *you* are not an idolater, and you did not take part in those ceremonies (cf. vv. 14–22). Second, if an unbeliever sets meat before you, you may have suspicions about the meat's origin, but again, don't worry. Third, if the unbeliever tells you that it is idolatrous meat, you refuse to eat, *not* because of *your own* conscience but because of his. Use the opportunity to explain to him why you do not want to have anything to do with idolatry. But personally you would be perfectly free to eat the meat. It will not affect you because you are not responsible for where the meat comes from.

If you do not feel free to shop at stores or businesses that support anti-biblical actions, *then don't do it.* "Whoever has doubts is condemned if he eats, because the eating is not from faith. For whatever does not proceed from faith is sin" (Rom. 14:23). Never go against your conscience (Acts 24:16; Rom. 13:5; 1 Tim. 1:5, 19; 3:9), even though you realize that your conscience may have been poorly trained (1 Cor. 8:7, 10, 12).

However, remember two things. First, you will not sin if you do shop at such stores because you are not responsible for their actions (but I can very well imagine that you do not wish to indirectly support such actions). Second, do not condemn other Christians who do shop at such stores. This is the whole subject of Romans 14: some Christians believe they are not allowed to do certain things, and condemn other Christians who do them. Conversely, some Christians believe they have the liberty to do certain things, and look down upon other Christians who refuse to do them. Both attitudes are wrong, as Paul explains:

> One person believes he may eat anything [in our case: can buy at any shop], while the weak person eats only vegetables. Let not the one who eats despise the one who abstains, and let not the one who abstains pass judgment on the one who eats, for God has welcomed him.... Why do you [i.e., those who do not eat (or do not buy at certain shops)] pass judgment on your brother? Or you [i.e., those who do eat (or do buy at certain shops)], why do you despise your brother? For we will all stand before the judgment seat of God.... Therefore let us not pass judgment on one another any longer, but rather decide never to put a stumbling block or hindrance in the way of a brother.... For the kingdom of God is not a matter of eating and drinking but of righteousness and peace and joy in the Holy Spirit. Whoever thus serves Christ is acceptable to God and approved by men. So then let us pursue what makes for peace and for mutual upbuilding.... Blessed is the one who has no reason to pass judgment on himself for what he approves. But whoever has doubts is condemned if he eats, because the eating is not from faith. For whatever does not proceed from faith is sin (vv. 2–3, 10, 13, 17–19, 22b–23).

NATURAL LAW THEOLOGY[1]

PREPARATORY PONDERINGS

1. Do you believe there is such a thing as a "natural law," laid down in creation as well as written on the hearts of people (believers and unbelievers)? Try to substantiate your answer.
2. Do you believe that, if they were just fair and honest enough, people could come up with common moral principles (e.g., about abortion, homosexuality, euthanasia, etc.), which are purely based on their intuition and about which a great majority of the people could agree?
3. In your view, can people live by the "natural law" in a neutral, secular way, that is, without the light of God's biblical revelation being shed on it? Explain your answer.
4. Do you believe that there is both a sacred realm and a profane realm, and that our lives are divided across these two realms, or do you believe that *all* our lives are "sacred" to God? If so, what exactly would this involve, do you think?

---

[1] This chapter is a translation and elaboration of parts of chapters 4 and 14 in Ouweneel (2008a).

4.1 ROMANS 2:12–16

4.1.1 Without or under the Torah

Michael Horton described the idea of natural law as follows: "There is a sufficient basis for 'natural law'—a discussion of right and wrong, truth and error, justice and corruption, beauty and horror, crime and punishment—even with nothing more than the human conscience."[2] A discussion of *truth* and *error* purely on the basis of the conscience? A discussion of *beauty* and *horror* purely on the basis of the conscience? Since when does my conscience tell me whether something is true or false, or is beautiful or ugly? A little later Horton wrote: "The nations have God's law written in their conscience, but the people of God have God's law written in Scripture.... If the Law of God is written on the conscience of the pagan who has never been acquainted with the Scriptures, then unbelievers can establish just societies."[3] To me this seems to be the denial of the first of the Five Points of Calvinism: the total depravity of humanity.

David VanDrunen has described natural law as follows:

> In affirming natural law, they [i.e., Reformed thinkers] professed belief that God had inscribed his moral law on the heart of every person, such that through the testimony of conscience all human beings have knowledge of their basic moral obligations and, in particular, have a universally accessible standard for the development of civil law.[4]

In the world of NL2K, this idea is of crucial importance. Yet, we do not find such a thing anywhere in the Bible. Of course, the verse that NL2K does refer to is Romans 2:15. The entire passage is as follows:

> For all who have sinned without the law will also perish without the law, and all who have sinned under the law will be judged by the law. For it is not the hearers of the law who are righteous before God, but the doers of the law who will be justified. For when Gentiles, who do not have the law, by nature do what the law requires, they

---

[2] Horton (1995, 196–97).

[3] Horton (1995, 197–98; cf. 2011, 140: "Everyone is aware of God's existence, even of his moral will (Ro 2:14–15). Neither Jews, who have the written law, nor Gentiles, who have the law written on their conscience, can plead ignorance."

[4] VanDrunen (2010b, 1).

NATURAL LAW THEOLOGY   85

are a law to themselves, even though they do not have the law. They show that the work of the law is written on their hearts, while their conscience also bears witness, and their conflicting thoughts accuse or even excuse them on that day when, according to my gospel, God judges the secrets of men by Christ Jesus (vv. 12–16).

In the first place, we must carefully observe the context.[5] In the first chapters of the letter to the Romans, the apostle Paul wishes to show that the whole world, both Gentiles and Jews, both "good" people and "bad" people, must be "held accountable to God…for all have sinned and fall short of the glory of God" (3:19–21). In Romans 2, Paul investigates the question whether being under the Mosaic Torah makes any difference as to one's position before God. Those who "have sinned without the law" (v. 12) are the sinning Gentiles, who have never formally been under the Mosaic Torah, even if its moral power ought to be valid for all humanity. Those who "have sinned under the law" (v. 12) are the sinning Jews, who since the Torah-giving at Mount Sinai stand formally and practically under the Mosaic Torah, and have trespassed it many times.

For one's outward position in this world it does make a lot of difference whether one belongs to the chosen nation that is under the Mosaic Torah, or whether one belongs to any of the other nations. But when it comes to the issue of one's sinful condition, there is *no* difference. Whether a person has sinned in the sense of formally trespassing the Torah, or sinned otherwise (because one cannot trespass a law under which one does not formally stand), makes no difference: he is a sinner. The former will be judged according to the Mosaic Torah, the latter will not. But they are sinners all the same because they do not meet the standards of God's own righteousness and holiness, which, by the way, are morally expressed in the Mosaic Torah. A person is not declared righteous simply because he stands under the Torah (v. 13) but because he lives according to the Torah in spirit and deed. But where this is so, Gentiles, who were never formally under the Torah but—unknowingly—live according to the spirit of the Torah (assuming that such people do exist), are declared righteous by God (vv. 14–15).

4.1.2 What Was Written?

Here follows the verse that is central to our discussion at this moment: "They show that the work of the law is written on their hearts" (v. 15).

---

5 See especially Murray (1968); Moo (1996); Shulam (1998); Wright (2002); also see T. R. Scheuers in McIlhenny (2012, 133–40).

Please note, first, that the verse does *not* say that some "law" is written on the hearts, but only "the work of the law." Second, in the entire context there is no mention at all of some "natural law" that encompasses all of human individual and societal life. The text speaks only of the Mosaic Torah, and this only in a moral-religious sense. There is no mention, here or elsewhere in Scripture, that all God's creation ordinances were written on the hearts of all people. We saw (§4.1.1) that VanDrunen limits the "natural law" to some *moral* law, possibly because of the way he interprets Romans 2:15. However, if the natural law corresponds with God's natural revelation, this would include *all* God's creation ordinances.[6]

What the verse does say is this: Gentiles who act in the spirit of the Mosaic Torah show in this way, *not* that the Mosaic Torah as such, or its core, the Ten Commandments, is written on their hearts, but that what God demands of them is written there. They are spiritually aware of what the holy and righteous God expects of them, without knowing the explicit formulation of what God expects as given in the Ten Commandments. "By nature" (spontaneously, naturally) they do what the Torah expects of people without knowing the Torah, and thus they show that their hearts are in the right place. At Mount Sinai, the Israelites said to Moses, "All that the LORD has spoken we will do" (Exod. 19:8; cf. 24:3, 7). Now the point is that the Lord has *not* spoken to the Gentiles, and yet, some of them do what the Lord expects of people who wish to serve and obey him.

As far as I can see, NL2K theologians make four mistakes with regard to Romans 2:15.

(a) They read far too much into the verse. The text speaks only of the Mosaic Torah, not of some general "natural law" that would contain *all* principles and norms of God with respect to societal, cultural, and moral life. Moreover, the text does not say that these principles and norms have been written on the hearts of all Gentiles, but only seems to suggest that some Gentiles may act according to what they understand of the moral demands of the holy and righteous God—and if they do, they are rewarded for it. Already Calvin made this mistake: "That inward law, which we have...described as written, even engraved, upon the hearts of all."[7]

(b) In addition, we should note that Paul places a theoretical case before us: how many Gentiles, in practice, have "done what the law requires" (v. 14), have sought "by patience in well-doing for glory and honor and immortality"

---

[6] See chapter 3 note 23, as well as the entire argument of chapter 3.

[7] Calvin, *Institutes* 2.8.1.

(v. 7), or simply have "done good" (v. 10), and, as "doers of the law," have as such been justified (v. 13)? In principle, doers of the law are declared righteous by God. But how many such people indeed exist? Is Paul's point not rather that "all have sinned and fall short of the glory of God" (3:23)? In other words, what use is it to speak of people who have some "natural law written on their hearts" if *in practice* no natural person would ever be able to *live* according to this supposed law?

(c) The next point ties in with this. It is impossible and irresponsible to separate Romans 2:15 from 1:18–21:

> The wrath of God is revealed from heaven against all ungodliness and unrighteousness of men, who by their unrighteousness suppress the truth. For what can be known about God is plain to them, because God has shown it to them. For his invisible attributes, namely, his eternal power and divine nature, have been clearly perceived, ever since the creation of the world, in the things that have been made. So they are without excuse. For although they knew God, they did not honor him as God or give thanks to him, but they became futile in their thinking, and their foolish hearts were darkened.

That is, people may have some awareness of God, or at least of "his eternal power and divine nature," but they are not able to live by it. Any awareness of the truth they may have is "suppressed by their unrighteousness." Where this is the case, how could some "common," secular realm, even under the providence of God, ever succeed, other than by the preserving grace of God? Much criticism has been leveled against Kuyper's view of common grace (see §4.4.1); but anything he said about it seems preferable to the idea of NL2K that a "natural law" written on people's hearts will suffice to maintain the secular realm.

John Frame rightly said, "I think it remarkable that VanDrunen says nothing more in his book[8] about the unbeliever's suppression of the truth. Certainly that complicates the role of natural law in providing moral knowledge to human beings. If there is a natural law, but man completely suppresses it, then it does not serve as a guide at all."[9] (By the way, as Frame continues, he tends to weaken the force of the word "completely.")

---

[8] VanDrunen (2006).

[9] Frame (2011, 131; cf. 147).

4.1.3   The Empirical Approach

The fourth mistake deserves a section of its own.

(d) If we understand by "natural law" what I have described above as the law order, or the creation order, the totality of creation ordinances, we must understand that this is nowhere described as written on the hearts of the believers. The fact that we have some idea of how to run society, politics, science, the arts, or whatever, is *not* because we have some basic awareness of such things written by the Creator on our hearts, but *by investigating reality* (cf. §3.4.3). It is the very difference between the medieval idealists and the later nominalists together with later empiricists. The idealists, in the wake of Plato, believed that we can work out how cosmic reality really is (natural laws), or ought to be (norms), because we have some inner awareness of these things, which stems from our dwelling in the "world of ideas" before we were born.

Even Aristotle, who in some sense may be called the father of nominalism, if not of empiricism, trusted more in what reason knew *a priori* to be right than in empirical observation. For instance, he believed it *reasonable* that heavier things fall faster than lighter things, until Galileo proved the *empirical fact* that all things fall at the same rate of speed by dropping two balls from the tower of Pisa (1589). By the way, the latter may have been a legend; at any rate, the experiment had already been carried out in 1586 in Amsterdam by Simon Stevin and Jan Cornets de Groot (father of Hugo Grotius [or de Groot]), who dropped two balls from the tower of the Nieuwe Kerk ("New Church").

Indeed, in the sixteenth century the tables were definitively turned, and empiricism replaced idealism. As a consequence, the natural sciences could make the tremendous progress that we have observed in the last four centuries. The idea of an innate "natural law" belongs in fact to the Platonic-scholastic past. Elaboration of creation ordinances in the various sciences and humanities, *by the light of a Christian worldview*, belongs to the present. It is no good claiming here that the former view is more in line with the Reformed tradition. This may very well be the case, but it is not relevant. The views of early Reformational thinkers regarding natural reality and the natural sciences were, on the whole, far more stamped by medieval ideas than by those of the pioneers of the natural sciences. We need only recall how early Protestant thinkers responded to Copernicus and Galileo.

One example: this is what Luther said about Copernicus in his *Table Talk*:

There is talk of a new astrologer who wants to prove that the earth moves and goes around instead of the sky, the sun, the moon, just as if somebody were moving in a carriage or ship might hold that he was sitting still and at rest while the earth and the trees walked and moved. But that is how things are nowadays: when a man wishes to be clever he must needs invent something special, and the way he does it must needs be the best! The fool wants to turn the whole art of astronomy upside-down. However, as Holy Scripture tells us, so did Joshua bid the sun to stand still and not the earth.[10]

It is thoroughly naïve to expect that people—believers and unbelievers— purely by means of their supposed "natural" awareness of principles and norms, can construct a properly working nation state, society, judicial order, or economic order. This "nature" is totally corrupt. In states, it has led to an intractable conservatism, or the reverse, to an all-destructive revolution- ism; to a repressive capitalism, or to an equally repressive communism; to rationalistic modernism, or to an equally destructive post-modernism; to a dangerous cultural optimism, or to an equally dangerous cultural pessimism. Perhaps the most constructive contribution of the Christian West has been democracy (unless this too was a product of the Enlightenment), which offers us a striking illustration of the corruption of "nature:" democracy is the least bad political system because it keeps all the evil powers within our society more or less in balance.[11]

In conclusion I must say that a common realm, separated from the kingdom of God, *not* standing under the direct authority of God's Word or under Christ's Lordship, but maintaining itself by a "natural law written on the hearts," is a farce, a fiction, an illusion. This may become clearer in the next sections.[12]

4.2   NATURAL REVELATION[13]

4.2.1   Two Revelations?

If natural law is connected to God's natural revelation, let us consider this revelation a little more closely. By faith we know and confess that God has

[10] Richard Pogge, "A brief note on religious objections to Copernicus," Ohio State University, last modified January 2, 2005, http://www.astronomy.ohio-state.edu/~pogge/Ast161/Unit3/response.html.

[11] Churchill (2008, 574) stated: "It has been said that democracy is the worst form of government, except for all those other forms that have been tried from time to time."

[12] See extensively, Frame (2011, chapter 11: "Is Natural Revelation Sufficient to Govern Culture?" He rightly answers the question with No).

[13] §4.2 consists of excerpts from Ouweneel (2012b, chapters 3–4).

created the world, and that this Creator God reveals himself to humanity in his created works (cf. Ps. 19:1–2; 29:3; Acts 14:17; Rom. 1:20). These passages implicitly indicate a very important point, totally overlooked by NL2K, namely, that we know of this self-revelation of God *in his works* only through his self-revelation *in Scripture*. It is only through God's *word* (or *Scriptural*) *revelation* that we recognize in the cosmos God's *work* (or *creational*) *revelation*. It is absolutely false to suggest, as NL2K does, that God's work-revelation can speak for itself; in reality we recognize it in its character of divine *revelation* in the light of God's *word-revelation* only.

Even the division (going back to the scholastic nature-grace dualism) into two types of revelation is not without danger.[14] Reformed dogmatician Johan Heyns summed up: (a) The all-sufficient and unique redemptive revelation in Jesus Christ is affected by the idea of natural revelation functioning apart from Christ. (b) If the aim of all revelation is to create an encounter between God and humans, this cannot occur purely by natural revelation; so *is* it actually a form of *revelation*? (c) The distinction between a natural and a biblical revelation can easily lead to a division, which would threaten the unity of God's revelation.[15]

It has been claimed that traces of natural revelation are found in all religions, but this is debatable.[16] The religions of the natural person are a product as much of the divine primordial revelation as they are a product of human sin.[17] That is, what little remnants the apostate religions may contain of God's original revelation have been heavily corrupted by sin and demonic blinding (cf. 2 Cor. 4:4). The light came into the world, and gave light to *each* person in the world, but the world has not "known" (recognized, acknowledged) him (John 1:9–10). The darkness "comprehended" it not (v. 5 KJV, etc.; others: "did not overcome it").[18]

Here we have to notice how VanDrunen views the matter. He *blames* Abraham Kuyper for his idea that "natural knowledge becomes of service only with the help of special revelation."[19] But there is nothing to blame here; it is exactly the view that I am seeking to defend, as well as the view of so many Protestant theologians. It is not original with Kuyper; it goes back to Calvin's idea of the "spectacles of Scripture" describing the necessity of

---

[14] Cf. Bavinck (*RD* 1, chapters 10–13); Berkouwer (1955); Vander Stelt (1978).

[15] Heyns (1988, 7).

[16] Cf. Buri (1956, 229–31, 234–37, 242–45, 249–54).

[17] Cf. Brunner (1946, 233–34; also see Wentsel (1982, 53–58, 87–90).

[18] Cf. Calvin, *Institutes* 1.3 and 1.6.

[19] VanDrunen (2010b, 280).

Scripture for properly apprehending natural revelation[20] (see §2.2.3)—not to mention that it goes back to Scripture itself. Would VanDrunen blame Calvin here just as severely as he has blamed Kuyper?

In view of the way NL2K has separated God's work-revelation and God's word-revelation we must now seek deeper insight into their precise relationship. If this relationship is viewed from a scholastic standpoint, as NL2K does, we are lost before we begin.[21] In the scholastic nature-grace dualism, general revelation belongs to the lower realm of nature (characterized by natural law), the domain of God's mediated acting, whereas special revelation belongs to the upper realm of grace (characterized by Scripture), the domain of God's immediate acting.

4.2.2 God's Work Is Word

Theologians have often been aware of the dualism just mentioned, and have tried to eliminate it. They did so, either by eschatologically enclosing nature within grace (Karl Barth),[22] or, conversely, by enclosing grace in nature by discarding the special revelation as a form of suprarationalism and metaphysics (liberal theology). Interestingly, such (fruitless) attempts usually keep presupposing the nature-grace dualism as such. The scholars involved cannot let go of it, cannot surpass it, because they have never learned about a decent alternative. To a large extent, the history of theology since the Middle Ages has been the story of a continual shifting between the poles of nature and grace, often frenetically kept together in a dialectical synthesis. At times it is the pole of the natural, at other times the pole of the supernatural, which is emphasized, and the reactions that are inevitably evoked are dismissed as "one-sided."

A more balanced view, more in the spirit of Scripture, involves much more than some vague talk about the "harmony" between nature and grace, including the supposed "harmony" between God's natural revelation and God's biblical revelation, as, for instance, Gerrit Berkouwer did.[23] As such, it is correct that Berkouwer points out that we should not pursue a theological quest for a cheap rational unity in God's revelational acting.[24] However, this does not mean that no synthesis concerning God's revelation would be possible, as long as one does not pursue this synthesis on the rational level.

---

[20] Calvin, *Institutes* 1.6.1. Kloosterman (2012a, 39–49) has pointed out how Kuyper himself referred to this idea of Calvin's.

[21] Cf. Troost (1978); Ouweneel (2008a, 128–31).

[22] Barth (1961, 49–50) and many other places; also see Brunner and Barth (1946).

[23] Berkouwer (1955, 316); cf. the comments of Troost (1978, 107, 121).

[24] Berkouwer (1955, 308).

What is theologically distinguished as word- and work-revelation does not find its unity somewhere "beyond faith," as Berkouwer says, but in faith, but then faith viewed in the ultimate, existential, religious meaning of the term. This is what the ancient theologians called the *fides qua*, a faith explicitly viewed as transcendent, not irrational but suprarational.

Here again, NL2K has fallen into the ancient scholastic snare because there is no "natural law" that could be considered apart from God's word-revelation. In fact, the work-revelation and word-revelation are one revelation because all creation, which is God's *work*, is nothing but the embodiment or manifestation of God's *Word*.[25] That is to say, God creates through his word (cf. ten times in Gen. 1, "And God said;" Ps. 33:6, 9; John 1:1–3; Rom. 4:17b). This is the same as saying that God's eternal Word receives a form within time in God's creation in Christ, who in his person is the Word of God. As such, Christ is also the Root of creation: all things have been created in/through/for him (cf. Col. 1:15–17; Heb. 1:1–3). In this connection, Reformed theologian-philosopher Andree Troost has written important things about the conspicuous *absence* of the expression "in Christ" in Article 2 of the Belgic Confession.[26]

Ultimately, work-revelation is itself *word-revelation*, namely, in the form of God's creational word in Christ. He speaks, and the world comes to exist (Ps. 33:6, 9), and through this world God is still speaking (19:2); in creation, we hear the "wordless" Word of God (vv. 4–5). God the Son upholds this world by the continual *word* of his power (Heb. 1:3). In this sense, God's Word is always *actual* (Latin: *actus*, act, action), that is, God's (creational and providential) *words* and his (creational and providential) *works* coincide here. God's word is deed, and his deed is word. This corresponds with the Hebrew *dabar*, which means both "word" and "thing, matter," sometimes with the meaning of "deed, action."[27] Also the Greek *logos*, "word," can mean "thing, matter" in the sense of "deed" (e.g., Acts 8:21; 15:6). The distinction between word-revelation and work-revelation fails because the sharp distinction between God's word and God's work cannot be biblically maintained.

---

[25] Cf. Troost (1978, 122–26; 2004, 272–73, 325–26).

[26] Troost (2004, 225–26, 272–73, 325–26, 330–34; cf. 437–39).

[27] See, e.g., DOTT 1:912–15.

4.3 VARIETIES OF NATURAL LAW

4.3.1   1 Corinthians 11:14

An interesting alternative to Romans 2:15 might seem to be this Pauline word: "Does not nature itself teach you that if a man wears long hair it is a disgrace for him, but if a woman has long hair, it is her glory?" (1 Cor. 11:14–15). However, first, there is no question here of any "natural law written on the hearts." The point is rather that we can apparently learn something from nature, not by our intuition (why would long hair be a disgrace for men?), or by some innate awareness, but by observation of the natural order of things.

This does not help us, though, to understand immediately what Paul is referring to in this passage. In what civilization did people ever learn from nature "that if a man wears long hair it is a disgrace for him, but if a woman has long hair, it is her glory?" I am not aware of any. I do know Christians who are very keen on hair length—short hair for men, long hair for women—but apparently they have never watched the portraits of great Reformed theologians in the seventeenth and eighteenth centuries, who had either long hair or long-haired wigs.

Our verse might very well be an example in which the word "nature" in fact means something like "custom" or "culture."[28] This is a good lesson for us. Too many people who have appealed to some "creation order," or to some "natural law," did not realize that, in fact, they were appealing to the specific customs of their ecclesiastical and societal traditions. This is one more reason why we should mistrust appeals to some "natural law written on the hearts."

For instance, a Christian view of the state cannot be derived simply from our intuition or some inner awareness. What we know, or think we know, about civic states is determined more by the Western culture and customs in which we have been raised. Nor can a Christian view of the state be derived from a select number of Bible verses. That would be biblicism, which often also entails forcing the verses quoted into some pre-conceived ideas about what the state is to be.

No, if we want to understand what the state is, or marriage, or proper male and female behaviour, we must *learn this from the very nature of the state, or marriage, or human behaviour, itself.* That is, analyze the phenomenon of

---

[28] Cf. Fee (1987, 526–27).

the state, or marriage, or human behaviour, as well as the many forms that states and marriages have had throughout history, and do this in the light of a coherent Christian-philosophical view of cosmic reality. Only in this way can you acquire some idea of the divine creational ordinance concerning the state.

4.3.2   "Sound Popular Sentiment"

What I am now going to say is not at all intended to be offensive. In no way do I wish to associate NL2K with Nazis. Yet we can learn something from the Nazi period that should be a warning to all of us. It is the use that the Nazis made of the term *gesundes Volksempfinden*, which means something like "sound popular sentiment." The idea was that the common people in Germany instinctively knew deep in their hearts what was best, especially in political and judicial affairs. It reminds me very strongly of the idea of "natural law" allegedly written on the heart. People supposedly have an inner awareness about how things should be, or should be done. Thus, the "common people" were assumed to be able to distinguish between genuine (i.e. Nazi-friendly) art and *entartete Kunst* ("degenerated art"), which was considered to be *volksfremd* ("foreign to the people"). From 1935 on, Nazi laws stipulated that those deeds had to be punished by the judicial system that deserved punishment according to "sound popular sentiment." Of course, it was the Nazi regime that determined what this "sound popular sentiment" was supposed to involve.

However, does "sound popular sentiment" know what is the best political system, or the best form of nation state? Or the best judicial system? Or the best economic order? Or the best types of visual arts, literature, or music? Or the best approach to the natural sciences? Or the best approach to education? Replace the term "sound popular sentiment" here with the term "natural law," and the questions remain precisely the same. My claim, stated here and repeated elsewhere throughout this book, is simply this: *in practice, "sound popular sentiment" or "natural law" is nothing but what we carry with us from tradition, either a scholastic, or a humanistic, or a biblicistic tradition, or a mixture of (some of) these three.* This "awareness" of things is not at all written on our hearts, but arises from our various cultural traditions.

If a person is a radical Christian, let him look for an equally radical Muslim or Hindu, and try to find out how much "natural law" the two have in common! Let him ask the Muslim in Saudi-Arabia, or the Hindu in India, how "sound popular sentiment" works in *their* countries. The majority of people in those countries know perfectly well how politics should be done, how the judicial system should function, what is genuine art or literature or music, and what not. If the investigator is an adherent of the "natural law" idea, his findings in such countries will not likely make him very happy. No wonder; the idea is false, at least in its NL2K form.

In addition to this, let me make a more effective suggestion: let the person do his homework, that is, develop a *radical*-Christian view of reality, or even better, a *radical* Christian-philosophical cosmology and epistemology, which can work like a sieve to sift his thoughts and eliminate all scholastic, humanistic and biblicistic elements. If he refuses to do so, he will invariably turn out to be a (cryptic) scholastic traditionalist, or a (cryptic) humanist, or a (cryptic) biblicist.

4.3.3 Examples

The next examples are mine. If "sound popular sentiment"—others would say, "natural law"—feels that abortion is murder, it should be forbidden. But if it feels that, because of the highly exalted ideal of individual freedom of choice, abortion is the responsibility of pregnant mothers only, it should be allowed. As John Frame put it:

> When people argue from natural law that abortion is wrong, they are essentially pitting their intuitions against the intuitions of others (intuitions which, when true, are often suppressed). Often such arguments are naturalistic fallacies, arguments from 'is' to 'ought:' e.g., unborn children are genetically unique organisms, therefore we ought not to kill them. Arguments from Scripture are not problematic in this way.[29]

Besides, who are we, especially in the "neutral" realm, to tell other people what they should or should not do, as long as we are no threat to the other (except to the unborn baby, of course)?

Second example: if "sound popular sentiment" feels that homosexual marriages are unnatural, they should be forbidden. But if "sound popular sentiment" argues that homosexuality occurs in the animal world as well, or that people themselves must decide whom they want to marry, again because of the ideal of individual freedom of choice, such marriages should be allowed. They are no threat to anybody else, so why not allow them? What is more decisive: *your* idea of what a marriage is, or the freedom of others? Imagine a situation in which "natural law" (whatever that may be) has to decide!

---

[29] Frame (2011, 147).

Please note that in the common realm it cannot be Scripture or arguments from Scripture that prevail. Scripture is valid only for the other realm, the kingdom of God. People believe in the separation of church and state—is this belief also a product of the "sound popular sentiment" or of "natural law"?—so religious arguments cannot be adduced in the common realm. Only "sound popular sentiment," or "natural law" if you like, may be allowed to decide.

But *whose* natural law? We need only wait for the (Reformed) theological leaders, at respected Reformed colleges and universities to *dictate* to us what this "sound popular sentiment" or this "natural law" entails. And I predict that what they propose will be either scholastic, or humanistic, or biblicistic; I can think of scarcely any other alternative. It is easy enough to dismiss the Kuyper-Dooyeweerd line, or any other radical-Christian-philosophical line. But try to imagine the alternatives. I definitely would not like to live in a society where the "natural law" of the people in power is going to decide in cases like abortion or so-called homosexual marriages.

The "struggle for life" and "the survival of the fittest"[30]—are these also aspects of "natural law"? Why? Or why not? Who decides that? According to what criteria? I am afraid that in this battle about what "natural law" entails, only the "fittest" (the most persuasive debaters) will survive. Again it will be the strong who will decide which "natural law" we must follow. Why not simply give up this foolish idea, and simply return to "it is written"? This is what Jesus said three times to the devil (Luke 4:4, 8, 10). It happened in the desert, and not for a second did Jesus wonder whether he was in the sacred realm or in the secular realm. Not for a second did he wonder: Can I appeal to Scripture here, or only to natural law? I would recommend that my readers do the same. Wherever you are, don't be afraid to appeal to the Bible! "In your hearts honor Christ the Lord as holy, *always being prepared* to make a defense to anyone who asks you for a reason for the hope that is in you" (1 Pet. 3:15).

4.4   THE FALL AND THE CREATIONAL STRUCTURES[31]

4.4.1   Common Grace

I repeat: the supposed "natural law" is written on people's hearts, but the creational ordinances are written on cosmic reality as such, so to speak,

---

[30] The latter term was coined by British philosopher Herbert Spencer (1864, 444).
[31] See Ouweneel (2014b).

and they must be read by careful investigators, within the framework of a Christian-philosophical view of this cosmic reality and these creational ordinances. If we choose otherwise, we will invariably land in scholasticism, humanism, or biblicism. Elements of all three are present in NL2K.

Let us look again at the creation structures, that is, the structural laws that the Creator has laid down in cosmic reality. Even after the Fall, the laws to which reality remains subject may be called *creation* ordinances. These are the laws God had originally instituted at the time of creation. In the way in which God has maintained the cosmic law order, even after the Fall, his grace toward fallen humanity comes to light. Especially since Abraham Kuyper, theologians sometimes speak here of *general grace*, or *common grace*; perhaps it would be clearer to speak of God's *providential* or *preserving* or *restraining grace*. It must be distinguished from "special grace," which comes to light in the gospel; perhaps it is better to call the latter saving or redeeming (or redemptive) grace.

Such a distinction is not without problems. Not only NL2K theologians suffer from the aftermath of scholasticism! The same scholastic nature-grace dualism that we have discussed above may also plague any distinction between a general and a special revelation, or a general and a special grace. The former may easily be placed in opposition to special grace, especially if the former is *not* viewed as a result of Christ's work on the cross, as is done, for instance, by Reformed hyper-Calvinist Henry Kersten[32] (see more extensively in §7.5.1). Yet, it cannot be denied that there is a divine grace by which God makes his sun rise on the evil and on the good (Matt. 5:45). Paul told certain Gentiles that God "did good by giving you rains from heaven and fruitful seasons, satisfying your hearts with food and gladness" (Acts 14:17). God's "invisible attributes, namely, his eternal power and divine nature, have been clearly perceived, ever since the creation of the world, in the things that have been made. So they [i.e., the Gentiles] are without excuse" (Rom. 1:20).

This matter of God's general or common grace had been discussed by John Calvin,[33] and was elaborated by Herman Bavinck, Abraham Kuyper, Simon Ridderbos, and others.[34] It was discussed and partly criticized by Klaas Schilder, Gerrit Berkouwer, Jochem Douma, Anthony Hoekema, Bruce Demarest, and others.[35] Doubtful elements in this doctrine include

---

[32] Kersten (1980, 1:76–77).

[33] Calvin, *Institutes* 2.2.12–19.

[34] Kuyper (2016a); Bavinck (1989); cf. *RD* 3:218–19; 4:38–40); Ridderbos (1949).

[35] Schilder (1939, 109–120); Berkouwer (1962, 148–62); Dooyeweerd (1963, 36–38); Douma (1966); Hoekema (1986, chapter 10); Demarest (1997, 76–83, 92–96).

the dangers of scholastic dualism, or cultural optimism, or both. In spite of these dangers, the doctrine is obviously important because it helps us understand how, on the one hand, the Fall was radical, and led to the total depravity of humanity, and how, on the other hand, a measure of "humanness" and altruism has remained.[36] However, the "good" works resulting from it, which have some usefulness and healthy effect with respect to temporal existence, have no value before God in the light of eternity.[37] At best they are "dead works" (Heb. 6:1; 9:14). This kind of works, no matter how benevolent, does not at all diminish the radical character of the Fall.

Due to the general (providential, preserving, restraining) grace of God, since the Fall the creation and human society have not been delivered up to the powers of evil. They have not totally fallen apart or disintegrated, but are preserved and maintained. In the succinct language of John Frame: "'Common grace' in the Reformed theological tradition is the blessings of God given to the reprobate.... Common grace is the limitation of the common curse."[38] I take this to mean that the reprobate receive *nothing* else than this type of grace; for it cannot be denied that the elect also profit from the rising sun and the fertile rains.

Michael Horton put it in even stronger terms:

As God gave wisdom to Daniel to understand secular literature and philosophy, so He graciously gives His common grace to all men and women bearing His image. It is not saving knowledge or saving wisdom, but it is a gift of the Holy Spirit nonetheless. Apart from this work of the Spirit in creation and providence, the world would be ugly, tyrannical, unjust, and unhappy—with absolutely no insight, education, laughter, pleasure, delight, or singing.[39]

I can go along with this, although I find it confusing to speak here of a "gift of the Holy Spirit." In Scripture, this refers to gifts to *believers* (Luke 11:13; Acts 2:38; 10:45; 1 Cor. 12:4; Heb. 2:4).

4.4.2   What Did the Fall Effectuate?

The Fall did not affect the law order as such, but the direction of the human heart was affected in that the heart turned away from God and his

---

[36] See extensively, Berkouwer (1962, chapter 5).
[37] Cf. Calvin, *Institutes* 2.3.4; 3.14.1–3.
[38] Frame (2011, 169).
[39] Horton (1995, 199).

commandments.[40] The Fall did not affect the *structures* or structural laws, but did affect the *direction* of the creation (see §4.5).[41] In other words, not the *essence* of a certain societal structure, for instance, the state, was affected (i.e., according to its law side), but its *historical* sense (according to its subject side). In the former sense, the state is still "normal," for its law structure has remained unchanged. In the latter sense, the state is "abnormal," for it is pervaded with sin.[42]

In other words, the radical antithesis between good and evil lies not on the law side but on the subject side of reality. In contrast with the *God-oriented* direction, which involves the reverent, obedient orientation toward God and his Word, we find the *apostate* direction, by which, on the subject side, apostate thoughts, statements, deeds, and also apostate marriages, families, churches, states, etc., arise. God-oriented and idol-oriented structures stand under the same divine law order, but they function with different (Godward or apostate) directions. Both in God-oriented and in apostate states, the normative structure of the nation state remains presupposed, otherwise states could not even be identified as states anymore. But the apostate states live parasitically on God's law in disobedience.

It is a sad mistake to suppose that, outside the kingdom of God, there can be such things as common states, common families, common marriages, common associations, common political parties, etc.—at least common in the sense of not standing directly under the authority of God's Word and under the kingship of the glorified Man Christ Jesus. The basic orientation of such societal relationships is *always* either Godward or apostate (often, of course, a mixture of both because of the sinful nature also in believers). The law structure of the state, as established by the Creator, always maintains its appeal to all citizens, both believers and unbelievers.

Incidentally, the idea that the existence of the state necessarily presupposes the Fall is at variance with the fact that, already before the Fall, humanity received the task of subduing the earth and having dominion over all that dwells upon it (Gen. 1:28). Human rule in principle presupposes the state. This mistaken idea ("the state is a consequence of the Fall") conflicts especially with the doctrine of the kingdom of God. God ruled over all things at all times, also before the Fall. And the ultimate fulfillment of the kingdom of God involves his royal dominion over all things, also when sin will have been removed from the cosmos (cf. John 1:29; 1 Cor.

---

[40] This is often not clearly distinguished; see, e.g., Noordegraaf (1990, 85, etc.).
[41] It is therefore inaccurate for König (2006, 403) to speak of "sinful structures."
[42] Heyns (1988, 183).

15:28; Rev. 22:5). The idea of rule, dominion, kingship, does not necessarily presuppose the presence of sin, and of sinful people who must be kept under control.

4.4.3 Normative Structures

Even when we are confronted with apostate families, churches, or states, we can still learn from them something about God's creation ordinance for the family, the church, or the state. Not because of some natural law "written on our hearts," as if by nature we have some awareness of what a family, a church, or a state is or ought to be. Rather, we *empirically* learn to recognize at least *something* of the normative structure of family, church, or state in even the most apostate families, churches, or states. Even sin always presupposes God's commandments because disobedience refers to norms that are not being obeyed. Even in norm-disobedient people and societal structures, the validity of the norms remains recognizable.

It is not true, as has sometimes been asserted, that speaking of creation ordinances, also within our present, sin-corrupted reality, would leave the Fall out of consideration—and thus also the re-creation, redemption, renewal, and consummation in Christ. It is not the doctrine of the creation ordinances as such that threatens to separate the creation from the Fall and the re-creation. On the contrary, it is scholastic theology and scholastic social philosophy—including NL2K—that do this. Here, creation, Fall, and redemption/consummation are separated in such a way that each of these motifs is turned into a starting point for one's idea of the state. Let me give an example of each erroneous approach.

(a) The Roman Catholic doctrine of the state bases its idea of the state on the motif of *redemption*. The redeeming grace of God in Christ is seen to be embodied in the church, which is seen as the dominating societal entity. From the upper storey of grace, to which the church belongs, the light of grace shines to the lower storey of nature, to which the state belongs. The separated motifs of creation and re-creation now become motifs that stand in a dialectical interaction within world history. In such a view, it is self-evident that the church rules over the state, as was the case during long periods of Western medieval history.

Incidentally, the reverse error is the state dominating the church. Thus, the British head of state is also head of the Anglican Church (although this is just a nominal function). In the seventeenth century, it was the States-General of the Netherlands who gave the order to hold the Synod of Dort (1618–1619), and to produce a new Dutch Bible translation: the States

Translation (Statenvertaling, 1637; cf. the King James Version in England, 1611). This is an age-old battle: which has the priority, the Christian state or the Christian church? As soon as we begin to understand the relative autonomy of each societal entity, this problem vanishes.

(b) Second, in an analogous way, the motif of the *Fall* can be turned into the starting point of one's idea of the state. The state is reduced here to a divinely instituted means to curb evil in society. This view reverberates in the Belgic Confession (Art. 36), which says that "because of the depravity of the human race, our good God has ordained kings, princes, and civil officers. God wants the world to be governed by laws and policies so that human lawlessness may be restrained and that everything may be conducted in good order among human beings." Such a statement does not necessarily exclude the idea of the state as a creation ordinance, but it does tend in the direction of doing so. The view that bases the state upon the motif of sin loves to refer to Romans 13, especially verse 4b ("if you do wrong, be afraid, for he [i.e., the ruler] does not bear the sword in vain"), whereas Romans 13 is about much more. Thus, the authorities praise those who do what is good (v. 3), they are God's servants for the good of the citizens (v. 4a), they collect taxes (vv. 6–7), with which many good things are done (such as constructing dams, parks, and roads), much more than just curbing evil.

(c) The third manner in which one can go astray is to link the state with *creation*, viewed as separated from re-creation, as we find in NL2K. Here, our cultural task is not considered as having to be fulfilled with a view to the new world to which we are en route, and thus it is *not* considered to stand in any relationship to the kingdom of God, whether in its present or in its future form.[43] Culture is viewed as part of the supposed common realm, and is linked to God's providential sustaining of our world for the benefit of the entire human race. Culture keeps the world going until re-creation breaks through; culture has *no relationship* to re-creation.

Thus, all three wrong pathways have been tried, and, in my view, have failed because of the ways in which they fractured God's cosmic reality. As I see it, only a coherent, encompassing Christian-philosophical view, in which creation, *and* the Fall, *and* redemption, *and* the consummation, *and* the new world are taken into account and interrelated, can sufficiently provide the full biblical picture. In short: if we do not view culture within the framework of the kingdom of God, we will go astray.

---

[43] See, e.g., VanDrunen (2010a, 26).

4.5 AGAIN, STRUCTURE AND DIRECTION

4.5.1 Anthropological Structure

For a proper understanding of NL2K and its errors, it is important to see the proper relationship between the consequences of the Fall, on the one hand, and the creation structures, on the other. I do not know how to describe this relationship more adequately than with the pair of concepts mentioned in §3.2.2: structure and direction.[44] Here, *structure* refers to the distinct normative structures that the Creator has laid down in reality. All things, plants, animals, people, societal entities, events, and states of affairs within created reality have their own, God-given structure. These structures are not arbitrarily determined by humans but have a normative character, that is, they stand under God's norms for cosmic reality. This prepared, normative blueprint is what, according to God's ordinances, makes a thing to be this or that concrete *thing*.

If we call the creation structures "horizontal," we may call the direction "vertical," for this entails the orientation of people and their societal relationships either toward God as Creator and Law-giver, to serve and honour him, or, as is usually the case since the Fall, away from God, in an apostate attitude. Let me explain this first by means of an anthropological example (§4.5), and then a social-philosophical example (next chapter). Both are relevant to our NL2K discussion.

There has been much debate about whether, since the Fall, the human will is still free.[45] This discussion about human free will (Latin: *liberum arbitrium*) began with Pelagius and Augustine,[46] and was repeated time and again: between Desiderius Erasmus and Martin Luther, and between Jacob Arminius and Francis Gomarus. In Eastern Orthodoxy, theologians since Irenaeus speak boldly of human free will, and Western Evangelicals do as well. However, in traditional Protestantism, with its strong emphasis on the total depravity of the human race, things are different. The more that people emphasize predestination and total dependence on God's sovereign grace, the more that human free will comes under pressure.

In my view, to a large extent this discussion is based upon not distinguishing between structure and direction. If we view the matter from the

---

[44] On this matter, see Mekkes (1961), and especially Wolters (1992).

[45] See extensively, Ouweneel (2016i, especially §4.1).

[46] See McGrath (2016, 443–45).

angle of the human creation structure, it is evident that humans continually make choices, both before and after the Fall. The fact that humans can be called "responsible" at all is because, also today, they can still make free choices. If these choices were not free, they would not need to be responsible for them. Therefore, Moses could say freely, "*Choose* life, that you and your offspring may live, loving the LORD your God, obeying his voice and holding fast to him" (Deut. 30:19–20). Joshua said, "*Choose* this day whom you will serve" (Josh. 24:15). And David said, "Who is the man who fears the LORD? Him will he instruct in the way that he should *choose*" (Ps. 25:12). "I have *chosen* the way of faithfulness; I set your rules before me.... I have *chosen* your precepts" (119:30, 173). On the one hand, the Lord gives instruction concerning the options from which humans may choose. On the other hand, humans themselves must make the choice.

In summary, also after the Fall, humans can still think logically, still have authentic emotions, can still deliberate, and can still make choices for which they are responsible. Their anthropological *structure* has not been affected. Neither Satan nor sin has the power to affect God's creation ordinances, God's law, that is, God's will. This is true with respect to natural laws, but also with respect to the functioning of human emotions and logic.

4.5.2 Anthropological Direction

When we turn now to consider the *direction* of the human heart, things are very different.[47] Thoughts, feelings, emotions, deliberations, and choices proceed from the human heart: "From within, out of the heart of man, come evil thoughts, sexual immorality, theft, murder, adultery, coveting, wickedness, deceit, sensuality, envy, slander, pride, foolishness. All these evil things come from within, and they defile a person" (Mark 7:21–23). Since the Fall, these thoughts, feelings, deliberations, and choices are, in the unregenerate, by definition sinful: "For although they knew God, they did not honor him as God or give thanks to him, but they became futile in their thinking, and their foolish hearts were darkened" (Rom. 1:21). "The god of this world has blinded the minds of the unbelievers, to keep them from seeing the light of the gospel of the glory of Christ, who is the image of God" (2 Cor. 4:4). "You must no longer walk as the Gentiles do, in the futility of their minds. They are darkened in their understanding, alienated from the life of God because of the ignorance that is in them, due to their hardness of heart" (Eph. 4:17–18).

---

[47] König (2006, 496–97) makes here the not very transparent distinction between "formal" and "material freedom."

Please note what this implies. As to its creaturely structure, the human will is still free; otherwise, humans could never make free choices, or even choose evil: "You did what was evil in my eyes and *chose* what I did not delight in" (Isa. 65:12; cf. 66:4). "These have *chosen* their own ways, and their soul delights in their abominations" (66:3). However, as to the heart's moral-religious direction, the will is *not* free: "The intention of man's heart is evil from his youth" (Gen. 8:21). People are no longer free to choose for God because they are "foolish, disobedient, led astray, *slaves* to various passions and pleasures, passing our days in malice and envy, hated by others and hating one another" (Titus 3:3); "the mind that is set on the flesh is hostile to God, for it does not submit to God's law; indeed, it *cannot*" (Rom. 8:7). What does it help if humans would have some "natural law written on their hearts"? They would be neither able nor willing to *live* according to this supposed law (see §4.1.2). "The natural person does not accept the things of the Spirit of God, for they are folly to him, and he is not able to understand them because they are spiritually discerned" (1 Cor. 2:14).

We ought to realize what this entails. Outside the kingdom of God (in the narrower sense of the term: the Christian world), there is not some "divinely-ordained common kingdom," as NL2K claims,[48] but only apostate individuals, apostate families, apostate marriages, apostate states, apostate schools, apostate companies, apostate associations, apostate political parties, and even apostate pseudo-Christian denominations. As to their exhibiting the God-given normative creation structure, certain secular families may be an example to certain Christian families, certain secular schools may be an example to certain Christian schools, certain secular parties may be an example to certain Christian parties, and so on. But when it comes to their orientation—which is either toward God or away from God (and often a mixture of the two)—they are *apostate* families, marriages, states, schools, companies, associations, and political parties all the same.

In the sense that the *direction* of the natural heart is corrupt, by nature no person has a free will; one is entirely dependent on the grace of God. In the sense that the *structure* of the human will has not been affected, the natural person remains entirely responsible for the wrong choices that one makes. As to the *direction* of one's heart, a person is totally corrupt, that is, full of egotism, full of immorality, full of arrogance and selfishness, full of wickedness, full of foolishness. As William Shedd put it, this state of affairs is demonstrated by the fact that, though the natural person has a conscience, there is no real battle within that person between sin and

---

[48] Cf. VanDrunen (2010a, 26).

holiness, as there is in the spiritual person. The apostasy was the fall of the human will, with no remnants of original human righteousness. Total depravity means the complete absence of holiness, rather than the highest intensity of sin. A totally depraved person is not as bad as he can be, but he has no holiness, that is, no highest love toward God.[49]

4.6 THE ERRONEOUS APPROACH OF NL2K

4.6.1 *Qodesh* and *Khol*

This is one of the problems of NL2K: it wishes to distinguish between two "divinely ordained" kingdoms: one that is holy, and one that is common: legitimate, but not holy.[50] This is very un-Reformed, or as I would prefer to say, very unscriptural. In the Bible, there is the holy and the *unholy*, but never the *non*-holy.

As a counter-argument, some might point here to Ezekiel 42:20, which speaks of a wall that makes "a separation between the holy [*qodesh*] and the common [*khol*]" (cf. 48:15).[51] However, the common is here that which is not consecrated to the Lord in a particular way, as is the case with the temple and the sacrifices (cf. Lev. 10:10; Ezek. 22:26; 44:23). Today, it is only our *heavenly* sanctuary that can be called "holy" in *this* sense of the term (cf. Heb. 10:19–23). All our earthly existence is *khol* in the sense that the word has in the passages mentioned. But what is identified in Ezekiel as *khol* is now, as part of the kingdom of God, *all consecrated to God*. Thus, Christian families are holy (1 Cor. 7:14), and not-yet-Christian families are unholy, apostate—but never common in the sense of neutral.

I would like to ask NL2K theologians to which of the two supposed kingdoms the Christian family belongs. Is it part of the church (which they mistakenly identify with the kingdom of God), or part of the common realm? The question poses a false dilemma, as we will see (§7.3.2): the family is a realm of its own, distinct from both the church and the state, just like marriage is a realm of its own, as well as the school, the company, the association, the party, and so on (cf. §§4.6.2 and 6.5.1). None of them functions either under the state or under the church. Only some superficial thinking may assume that the state encompasses churches, families, schools, companies, associations, political parties, and so on. It does

---

[49] Shedd (1889, 2:257).
[50] Cf. VanDrunen (2010a, 26).
[51] This is the kind of argument used by Horton (1995, 85).

definitely *not*. There is not only a separation between state and church, but also between state and family, state and school, state and company, state and association, and even state and party. Or more correctly, each of these societal relationships is autonomous within its own confines. The state exists only to administer public justice; it never interferes with the strictly internal affairs of churches, families, schools, companies, associations, political parties, and so on.

4.6.2 "Eight Kingdoms" Theology

If we definitely wish to divide things up, instead of a "two kingdoms" theology I would propose an "eight kingdoms" theology, in which we distinguish between churches, states, marriages, families, schools, companies, associations, and political parties. Of course, we must not attach too much value to the number eight. Some people may suggest even more societal relationships (clubs, unions, etc.), others will argue that parties, clubs and unions are nothing but specific forms of associations. What matters right now is the distinction of a number of societal relationships that are equally autonomous, and may be equally holy or unholy.

It is pure scholasticism to suggest that only churches are holy, and that the other societal relationships are common (secular, neutral, profane). Every *Christian* church, state, marriage, family, school, company, association, and political party is *in principle holy* (in practice not always so holy), and every *non*-Christian denomination, state, marriage, family, school, company, association, and party is by definition unholy, apostate. Every Christian church, state, marriage, family, school, company, association, and party is a part of the kingdom of God, and every non-Christian (unholy, apostate) denomination, state, marriage, family, school, company, association, and party is not yet part of the kingdom of God; in fact, it is still under the rule of the kingdom of Satan (Matt. 12:25–28).

It is the wind of the Spirit that blows within the kingdom of God. It blows throughout lives, marriages, families, churches, even through schools, companies, and states, and brings not only individuals but also entire societal relationships out of the kingdom of Satan under the blessed dominion of Jesus Christ. Jesus said that it is through "water and Spirit" that people enter the kingdom of God (John 3:5). Paul says that the kingdom of God is righteousness, peace, and joy in the Holy Spirit (Rom. 14:17). Because of this Spirit, it is a kingdom of power; as Paul says, "The kingdom is not a matter of talk [i.e., of idle words] but of power" (1 Cor. 4:20). In connection with the kingdom, Jesus told his disciples, "You will receive power when the Holy Spirit comes on you" (Acts 1:3, 8).

God's kingdom is a domain of power. Already during his earthly ministry, Jesus told his opponents, "If I cast out demons by the Spirit of God, surely the kingdom of God has come upon you" (Matt. 12:28 NKJV). That is, where the power of the kingdom is manifested, there apparently the kingdom itself has arrived. This power can manifest itself in *every* societal relationship in which people submit to the authority of Christ and to his Word and Spirit.

4.6.3 A Neutral No Man's Land?

Of course, NL2K might reply: But what about when we are in the streets? Is that not a neutral no man's land? What about shopping? Is it not unrealistic to identify every store as belonging to either the kingdom of Satan and the kingdom of God in a black-and-white way? What about working in a secular job, in a secular office? Is that not a neutral zone? Is every job within either the kingdom of Satan or the kingdom of God? What about our children playing in a park? Is every park within either the kingdom of Satan or the kingdom of God?

I can understand these objections, but they all presuppose the same mistaken thinking. Until now, we have spoken of societal relationships. According to NL2K, only the church belongs to the kingdom of God, and all other societal relationships belong to the "common kingdom." In opposition to this, I stated that both the kingdom of Satan and the kingdom of God can be manifested in *each* of these societal relationships ("church" taken in the immanent meaning of church denomination or local congregation). This is a matter of differentiating between structure and direction. Now do not suddenly begin talking about streets, stores, and parks, to make your point! Believers and unbelievers share the same earth, drive on the same streets, buy in the same stores, go to the same doctors and lawyers, have accounts at the same banks, and finally are buried in the same ground. However, that is not evidence of some "common kingdom."

The mistake in thinking is this: the fact that believers and unbelievers have so many things in common does not mean that *therefore* some specific "common *kingdom*" exists independently from the kingdom of God. Any common ground can become part of the kingdom of God. I repeat: both the kingdom of Satan and the kingdom of God can be manifested in every societal relationship, and I add now: even in each park, every street, each store. The kingship of Christ is manifested in every believer who is a fair and safe road user, in each Christian who is an honest and friendly buyer or seller, in every believer who is a witness (often even a silent witness) to the character of Christ at the bank, in his job, in a hotel or restaurant.

The mistake made by NL2K is trying to find some "domain" that nobody can deny is "neutral." But this error continues to confuse structure and direction. The point is not that certain domains are Christian, and others are neutral; the point is that both the kingdom of Satan and the kingdom of God can be manifested in every domain of life. No *structure* as such belongs to either the kingdom of Satan or the kingdom of God, or to some "common kingdom." The kingdom of *Satan* can be manifested even in a church denomination or a local congregation, and the kingdom of *God* can be manifested even in a political party, and on a street corner where the gospel is preached, in a park where hundreds of Christians sing to the glory of God, in a hotel that is rented for a Christian convention, in a bank where the managers are devoted Christians.

NL2K creates a "horizontal" dualism between structures, that is, on the one hand, the (visible) church (falsely identified with the kingdom of God) and, on the other hand, all the other societal relationships (not one common realm, but at least seven realms, each of which may be holy or unholy). What it should do is distinguish the "vertical" dualism, that is, the antithesis between the Godward orientation and the apostate orientation of societal relationships. I repeat: in *every* societal relationship, the kingdom of God can be, and is, manifested if this community is, in faith, brought under the rule of King Christ Jesus and under the authority of God's Word, temporarily (as in the rented hotel) or permanently. Similarly, in *every* societal relationship, the apostate rebellion of natural persons can be manifested. There is no such thing as a holy realm and a common realm. There are at least eight realms (none of which can be reduced to one of the other realms[52]), and in *each* of them the kingdom of God can be manifested (though always in a defective way because of the sinful nature of believers), but so too can the kingdom of Satan be manifested in them.

4.7 ADDITIONAL CONSIDERATIONS

4.7.1   Two Biblical Kingdoms

For the sake of completeness, I would like to add a few more thoughts on the distinction between structure and direction. First, if one insists on distinguishing between two kingdoms, that is fine with me. But then it should not be anything other than the only two (spiritual) kingdoms that the Bible distinguishes: "Every kingdom divided against itself is laid waste,

---

[52] Perhaps with the exception that one might call political parties nothing but a special kind of "association" (just like unions, leagues, etc.).

and no city or house divided against itself will stand. And if Satan casts out Satan, he is divided against himself. How then will *his kingdom* stand? … But if it is by the Spirit of God that I cast out demons, then the *kingdom of God* has come upon you" (Matt. 12:25–28).

Please note that this *biblical* distinction between the kingdom of Satan and the kingdom of God is, so to speak, "perpendicular" to the distinction advocated by NL2K. The latter's two kingdoms are based upon a scholastic ("horizontal") splitting of holy and common creation *structures*. The Bible's two kingdoms have to do with ("vertical") *direction*: in every societal relationship, anchored in God's creation order, it is either (primarily) the kingdom of God that is manifest, or the kingdom of Satan. Where this is properly understood, NL2K can be viewed as in principle refuted. In more direct terms: the kingdom of Satan can easily be manifested, and *has* often been manifested, within a church denomination, or a local congregation, while the kingdom of God is manifest in every Christian marriage, family, school, company, association, and political party—and vice versa, of course.

The kingdom of God can even be manifest in a nation state, in which government and population for a substantial part are Christians, who submit both their individual lives and the activities of the state to the authority of King Jesus and his Word, as best as they can. This does *not* just mean that they behave as good magistrates and citizens, as is fitting for Christians, but that they consecrate their magistracy and citizenship *as such* to the service of the great King. It is the King himself who, as it were, rules through the devoted Christian magistrate, just as he rules through devoted Christian parents in the family, through devoted Christian administrators and teachers in the school, through devoted Christian bosses in the company, through devoted Christian board members in associations and political parties.

4.7.2   The "First Man"

Second, when it comes to the *structure* of their being, we still admire in human beings the image of God:[53] their beauty, their intellectual and artistic capacities, their humanness, and even their altruism, their often high morals (Rom. 2:14–15). Looking at the rich young man, Jesus loved him (Mark 10:21), *not* because of what he saw in him of the (sinful) "old man" (Rom. 6:6; Eph. 4:22; Col. 3:9 KJV) but what he saw in him of (the honesty and sincerity of) the "first man," Adam (1 Cor. 15:45, 47). The contrast between the "old man" and the "new man" involves direction, whereas the splendour of the "first man" that can still be (dimly) seen involves structure.

---

[53] See extensively, Ouweneel (2008a, chapter 5, especially §5.1.2).

This splendour cannot be denied—but because of the apostate direction of the natural human heart, even "all our *righteous* deeds are like a polluted garment" (Isa. 64:6); "the mercy of the wicked is cruel" (Prov. 12:10). "The sacrifice of the wicked is an abomination to the Lord" (15:8; 21:27). "The splendor of the wicked is sin" (21:4), says a Dutch translation. Therefore, even the noblest deeds of the unregenerate are no more than "dead works" (§4.4.1). Because of the wrong direction of his heart, the rich young man did not get any further than his sincerity: his interest in Jesus remained a dead work, which did not bring him any closer to the kingdom of God.

In my view, all theories about the "intrinsic goodness" of the human nature (from Pelagius, via Jean-Jacques Rousseau, to Karl Barth)[54] are based upon overemphasizing the anthropological *structure* and ignoring the moral-religious *direction* of the heart. The reverse is true, as well: all hyper-Calvinist resistance against societal reformation ("improving the world," "polishing the brass on a sinking ship") with an appeal to the total depravity of humanity is based upon overemphasizing the moral-religious *direction* of the heart and ignoring the anthropological *structure*. It is true, if humanity were left to itself it might have perished long ago. The fact that this has not happened is ascribed by NL2K to God's providence, and by Kuyper & Co. to God's common grace.

If we eliminate any misplaced cultural optimism and triumphalism from the doctrine of common grace, the question is whether the doctrine of God's providence and that of God's common grace are that much different. Except in one respect: for NL2K, God's providence in the common realm does not function with any other purpose than keeping the world going until the second coming of Christ. But in the doctrine of common grace, God has a much better plan for what NL2K calls the common realm: God desires the kingdom of the glorified Man Christ Jesus to become manifest *in every domain of cosmic reality—already now.*

It may be true that, in Kuyper's expectations, there were too much cultural optimism and triumphalism. But this must be understood in terms of the time in which he lived, a time that was still characterized by cultural optimism everywhere. The first great change came with the First World War (1914–1918), and the Russian Revolution (1917). Western expectations turned around one hundred eighty degrees, and the decades after this were far more characterized by cultural pessimism, irrationalism, existentialism. No wonder that even we, as Christians, have become a little more realistic, more sober, and reluctant in our cultural expectations. But this does not

---

[54] Cf. Berkhof (1996, 233–35).

change the general issue: either we believe in a God who providentially keeps the non-church world just going *until* the return of Christ, or we believe in a God who desires the kingdom of Christ to become manifest in every domain of human life and society *with a view to* the return of Christ.

WORKING IT OUT: CHRISTIAN POLITICS, YES OR NO?
Is the idea of "Christian politics" in conflict with the separation of church and state?

It depends on what you understand by the "separation of church and state." In the United States, the notion found its origin with Thomas Jefferson, one of the American Founding Fathers and the principal author of the Declaration of Independence (1776). In his view—clearly influenced by the Enlightenment—the United States wished to avoid the situation in England, where the Church of England was the national church, or in various European countries, where either the church took authority over things of the state, or vice versa. Separation of church and state meant, and means, that any church denomination as such should not interfere with state matters, and that the state should not interfere with internal church matters. The state does administer public justice, however, so that churches cannot do anything they like; for instance, courts rightly refused polygamy to Mormons because this did not fit into our general ideas of justice (*Reynolds v. United States*, 1878).[55]

However, in the course of time many people, especially atheists and agnostics, surreptitiously changed this separation of church and state into a separation of religion and society, which is a totally different matter. It is an outright falsehood that separation of church and state would entail keeping religion out of every public domain of society. Incidentally, such a change of meaning was not so difficult because both the older and the newer view were nothing but products of Enlightenment thinking: religion is okay, but only for the "closet" (Matt. 6:6 KJV). It is all the more remarkable that NL2K is now trying to underpin this Enlightenment idea with a theological theory!

In fact, NL2K has joined the atheists and the agnostics in this attitude by its unholy endeavours to keep religion out of the public square as much as

---

[55] The court considered that, if polygamy were allowed, some people might eventually argue that human sacrifice was a necessary part of their religion, and "to permit this would be to make the professed doctrines of religious belief superior to the law of the land, and in effect to permit every citizen to become a law unto himself" (http://caselaw.findlaw.com/us-supreme-court/98/145.html).

they can. This was never the intention of early Reformational thinkers, no matter how much NL2K advocates try to read their ideas into Luther's and Calvin's writings. Therefore, for centuries it was no problem that there was public prayer at presidential inaugurations, or that the magistrate made payments to faith-based community projects, or that school teachers (moderately and modestly) witnessed to their religious beliefs in class-rooms, or that politicians did so in parliament.

The idea that "Christian politics" would be in conflict with the "sep-aration of church and state" is rooted in this awful confusion, as if such separation would mean that politicians are not allowed to witness to, or work out the implications of, their faith in the public square. Apparently, people advocating such ideas have never considered how it is possible that most European countries have a strict separation of church and state, yet at the same time have Christian-democratic parties, sometimes for over a century now. In none of these countries has this ever been seen as a problem because people correctly interpreted the separation of church and state. It means only that no church should meddle in state affairs, and no state should meddle in church affairs (except in matters of public jus-tice). A Christian political *party* is not a church. Even if a certain Christian party would in fact represent the members of only one particular church denomination, there would be no problem because it is not this church as such that is doing politics but only this party, and doing so entirely according to all the rules of the democratic game.

It is a very sad thing that NL2K has taken sides here with atheists and agnostics. Of course, the latter wish to extirpate religion altogether, and NL2K does not. But the effect is the same: religion should be kept out of the public square as much as possible. This is a disaster. Christians are called upon to witness to their faith in the public square (Matt. 10:18; Acts 1:8; 2 Tim. 4:1–2; 1 Pet. 3:15). This is not left to preachers within the churches, and to evangelists on the street corners or on the mission fields. On the con-trary, in a truly free country teachers (also at public schools) should have the right to witness to their pupils (without their beliefs *dominating* the curriculum), nurses should have the right to witness to the sick (without their beliefs *interfering* with their common duties), and politicians should have the right to witness to their beliefs in order to explain why they are for or against a certain matter. And let me hastily add that, in such a society, Muslims, Hindus, and atheists have the same rights!

What a sad thing it would be if religious members of parliament could declare themselves to be against abortion only by appealing to some "natural law"! I could very well imagine others to be *for* abortion with an appeal to their own type of "natural law," as we have seen. It would be the same with problems such as homosexual marriages, euthanasia, the death penalty, caring for the weak in society, a limited or an extended federal government, and so on. What a shame if the believing politician were not entitled to say: I am for A, or against B, because of my deepest religious convictions. Imagine a country with such strong Christian roots, and where there are still so many Christians, but where atheists and agnostics try to muzzle Christians in the public square by giving a false picture of what the separation of church and state entails. Imagine that now even some Reformed theologians have joined their company on totally mistaken grounds, as this book tries to show.

I am a warm supporter of the separation of church and state, and I am a warm supporter of Christian politics, if only the two are correctly understood. Those who see a conflict between the two have either falsely represented one or the other, or even both, of these elements.

KINGDOM THEOLOGY[1]

PREPARATORY PONDERINGS

1. What do you think: Is the kingdom of God "everywhere" in this world (and what exactly would this imply?), or is it, in the present age, limited to the "spiritual" (religious, sacred) domain of life?
2. Is the kingdom of God (mainly) limited to the church, or do *Christian* families, *Christian* schools, *Christian* companies, and so on, also belong to the kingdom of God? Try to defend your answer.
3. There are two kingdoms in the New Testament: that of Satan, and that of God. How does this distinction, in your opinion, relate to the two kingdoms being identified in today's two-kingdoms theology?
4. Try to define what the separation of church and state exactly involves. Does it mean, for instance, that outside the church life is lived in an a-religious or non-religious arena?

---

[1] See also Ouweneel (2016e) for a much wider treatment of this subject.

5.1 SOCIAL PHILOSOPHY

5.1.1   Where Is the Kingdom of God?

As I said in the previous chapter, "direction" means the religious orientation of people and their societal relationships. This direction is either toward God, to serve and honour him, or since the Fall, it is the apostate orientation away from God. For instance, in the latter case, the nation state is there only to serve itself (socialism), or the individual (liberalism, capitalism), or "the party" (communism), or "the people" (National Socialism, Nazism). I am not aware of any other possibilities than these.

If we properly understand "direction" and "structure" as two dimensions that, as it were, are perpendicular with respect to each other—that is, not as a dualism—we will understand immediately that sin can never be limited to certain domains of reality. This is what earlier Calvinists (and other Protestants) thought, with their lists of worldly places like brothels, casinos, bars, cinemas, theaters, and so on. What was overlooked is that sin is present also within the (visible) church, in the Christian family, the Christian school, the Christian association, and so on.[2] All the worldly places mentioned involve things that are good in themselves: sexuality, playing, moderate use of alcohol,[3] movies, theater. However, these things can easily be corrupted by sin. Please note again that this sinfulness is never inherent in the *structures*, in the things as such, but in the sinful *direction* of the people using these things (e.g., sexual immorality, gambling, drunkenness). And exactly these same, and many other, matters can be corrupted within the church, the Christian school, the Christian association, and so on, as well. The structures (things, plants, animals, people, societal relationships, events, states of affairs) as such belong to God's good creation gifts. It is the sinful direction of the human heart by which these structures are corrupted.

To use NL2K terminology: in the supposedly "holy" realm of the visible church, or the kingdom of God, the structures are just as good, God-ordained, as in the supposedly common (non-holy, secular) realm. And in the supposedly "holy" realm, things can be just as corrupted by sin as in the supposedly common realm. Sometimes, the Holy Spirit may work

---

[2] See extensively, Strauss (1991, 9–21).

[3] The Corinthian believers used alcohol at their meals (1 Cor. 11:21); Paul did not sympathize with those who forbade wine as a general rule (see Rom. 14:21 in context). Cf. also Deut. 14:23, 26; Prov. 31:6; 1 Tim. 5:23.

powerfully in dedicated families, schools, associations, and he may be quenched in the churches (cf. 1 Thess. 5:19).

In my view, we can express things much more accurately using different terminology. The all-governing starting point here is the insight that the kingdom of God cannot be identified with and restricted to one single societal relationship, namely, (especially) the (visible) church.[4] In the history of Christian thought, many examples of such mistaken identification and restriction can be pointed out; NL2K is just one in a long series of similar erroneous views. (No wonder it loves to emphasize how faithful it is to "the" Reformed tradition: both Lutheran and Reformed traditions have exhibited many such mistaken approaches, due to scholasticism.) NL2K loves to identify and restrict the kingdom of God especially to the (visible) church. Others have identified it with the state; we need think only of the "*Holy* Roman Empire" (800–1806),[5] but also of the Byzantine Empire (330–1453).[6] Still others have felt that the kingdom of God in the present age consists primarily of Christian families. All these views are mistaken; they all fail to distinguish between structure and direction. The kingdom of God does not involve certain societal relationships, to the exclusion of other such relationships. Rather, it involves the *direction* of *each* of the various *societal structures*.

The Psalms say prophetically, "God reigns over the *nations*," not just over his own people (Ps. 47:8). "The LORD reigns! Yes, the *world* [not just Israel, or the church] is established" (96:10; cf. 93:1). "The LORD reigns, let the *earth* rejoice" (97:1). "The LORD reigns; let the *peoples* tremble!" (99:1). These are not just references to God's general providence, because the same things are said of the glorified *Man* Christ Jesus. Revelation 19:6 says, in typically Old Testament language, "Hallelujah! For the Lord our God the Almighty reigns." But in the book of Revelation, the Almighty is explicitly identified with the glorified Man Jesus: "I am the Alpha and the Omega, …who is and who was and *who is to come*, the Almighty" (1:8; cf. 4:8) (see more extensively §§5.4.3 and 8.5.2).

---

[4] *Contra* VanDrunen (2010a, 131): "Though it resembles other earthly institutions in some outward ways, it is *not* just one earthly institution out of many."

[5] At its greatest extent (thirteenth century), it encompassed present-day Germany, the Netherlands, northern Poland, eastern France, Switzerland, Austria, Italy, and parts of Eastern Europe.

[6] At its greatest extent (about AD 555), under Justinian the Great, it encompassed the South of Spain, large parts of northern Africa, large parts of southern and southeastern Europe, present-day Turkey, and the Middle East.

5.1.2   What Is "the World"?

It would be an utter mistake to identify the kingdom of God specifically with the rule of Christian kings and heads of government. In this way, God's kingdom is associated with the ("Christianized") empires and nation states of this earth. It is equally erroneous to identify the kingdom of God especially with Christian families, which supposedly shine as bright lights amid a dark, wicked world.[7] They do so—but the positively Christian school, the explicitly Christian company, the Christian association, and the Christian political party are just as much bright lights of the kingdom of God in contrast with the realm of darkness: "The Father...has delivered us from the domain of darkness and transferred us to the kingdom of his beloved Son" (Col. 1:12–13).

The basic error here is the ancient and ineradicable Anabaptist-pietist mistake: identifying the "world" with "society." NL2K does not do this, but in my view, distinguishing the "holy" realm of God's kingdom (identified with the visible church) and the common (non-holy, secular, though supposedly God-ordained) realm is almost as bad. Of course, the difference is important: pietists call the world, and thus society, objectionable, whereas NL2K does not do so. But the distinction, if not separation, that is created here is basically the same.

Once again, the mistake consists in confusing structure and direction. *All* believers must avoid "the world" in the *vertical* sense (direction). This is the world of which Satan is the god and the ruler (2 Cor. 4:4; John 12:31; 14:30; 16:11), the domain where "the rulers, the authorities, the cosmic powers over this present darkness, the spiritual forces of evil in the heavenly places" are active (Eph. 6:12), the world that "lies in the power of the evil one" (1 John 5:19; cf. 2:15–17), and to which we should not be "conformed" (Rom. 12:2). "The world" in the biblical sense is not "society" or "culture," or—according to some—especially political life, the arts, the sciences, and various forms of social life. Society and culture are never neutral; but they are not intrinsically bad either. The moral-religious *direction* within the social *structures* is manifested either in apostasy ("the world"), or in consecration and obedience toward God ("the kingdom of God"). The structures are God-given; the direction is either carnal or Spirit-directed.

Of course, in practical life until the second coming of Christ, we will always be dealing with a mixture: "The desires of the flesh are against the Spirit, and the desires of the Spirit are against the flesh, for these are

---

7 Some have made a comparison with the "fires of Rohan" in J. R. R. Tolkien's *The Return of the King*.

opposed to each other, to keep you from doing the things you want to do" (Gal. 5:17). In every societal relationship, including the (visible) church, there is only "a small beginning of obedience,"[8] in other words, a limited manifestation of the kingdom of God. But this beginning is unspeakably more than nothing, just like the smallest ray of light means unspeakably more than darkness. One single candle may fill an entire room with light, even though it may be ever so dim.

In the New Testament, "world" is very often a *vertical* concept, which has to do with direction, and not with certain domains of society. "Society" is a *horizontal* concept, which has to do with structure. It is futile to try to avoid certain societal relationships, because in *every* societal relationship the evil world can be manifest. This is the same as saying that sin and Satan are manifest in it. Do pietists want to avoid the church? I ask this because even in the church, the world (that is, "the desires of the flesh and the desires of the eyes and the pride of life," 1 John 2:16) can be manifest.[9] Do pietists want to avoid the family? Because even the family is not safe from the influences of the world. No societal relationship or societal place is *by nature* more worldly than any other: *in itself* the cinema is no more worldly than any local church congregation, a sports club no more worldly than the family, a political party no more worldly than a Bible club.

This may sound a bit idealistic, but as a matter of *principle*, I wholeheartedly maintain this claim. In all of the relationships and places mentioned, either the kingdom of Satan or the kingdom of God can be manifest (or a mixture of the two). There is nothing wrong with them as such—although I have to admit that, *in practice*, the kingdom of God is more likely to be manifested in a Christian family than in any cinema or any nation state.

5.1.3   Theocracy and Democracy

A remarkable example of the confusion between structure and direction involves the discussion about theocracy and democracy. One example: Darryl Hart condemns the notion of an explicitly Christian state because this would imply a theocracy: "Either the state is God-honoring or it is God-denying. But seldom considered in this form of absolute dualism is that the most God-honoring state would at least be one that tolerates only

---

[8] Cf. the Heidelberg Catechism (Q/A 114): "Even the holiest men, while in this life, have only a small beginning of such obedience (1 John 1:8–10; Rom. 7:14–15; Eccl. 7:20)."

[9] This is clearly seen by Horton (1995, 85); although he (wrongly) says that "we live in the 'in-between' time, when the holy, the church, is separated from the common, the world," he rightly adds that the latter "is a battleground in which good and evil, truth and error, belief and unbelief struggle. But so is the church!"

the true faith, with theocracy being a distinct possibility."[10] As I see it, this indicates that Hart is confused about the relationship between notions like the Christian state, democracy, and theocracy. Part of the reason is that the United States has no experience with Christian political parties. As I said (§1.4.3), in the Netherlands, there have been Christian political parties since the beginning of parliamentary democracy (1848), and they have all been thoroughly democratic, while at the same time defending a certain ideal of theocracy, if only rightly understood.

I believe in both theocracy and democracy. To me, the two notions are not at all contradictory, or mutually exclusive. Theocracy and democracy relate to one another as *direction* relates to *structure*. Within the normative ground structure that, according to God's creational ordinances, makes a state to be a state, several different state *forms* are possible, of which democracy is only one. The great Dutch Reformed historian and politician, Guillaume Groen van Prinsterer (d. 1876), was for many years a member of the Dutch parliament. In his famous work, *Unbelief and Revolution*,[11] he argued that, for a Christian political science, what is decisive is not the state *form* as such— although some forms are definitely better than others—but the extent to which, within a given state form, God's commandments are observed.

In our terms, what is essential for a Christian political science is not primarily the *structure* of the state, but its *direction*, its spiritual orienta- tion, toward God or toward sin and Satan—that is, the extent to which the kingdom of God comes to manifestation in the state. If viewed this way, theocracy and democracy are not opposites. On the contrary, a theocratic, that is, theocratically oriented, democracy is quite conceivable, and in the present age, many Christians find it highly desirable. This is a democracy that is governed by a theocratic attitude, i.e., by the recognition that God is in charge, and by submission to his Word.[12]

In the sense in which I have circumscribed it here, the terms "theocracy" and "kingdom of God" are almost interchangeable. The only difference is that theocracy is a very general reference to God's universal government, in which the historical-eschatological dimension is lacking that is so char- acteristic of the term "kingdom of God." The latter phrase refers not only to the general dominion of God, but also to the way God is moving forward

---

[10] Hart (2006, 229–30); Stellman (2009, xiv–xxv) is equally confusing on "theocracy."

[11] Groen van Prinsterer (1975).

[12] Very helpful to me was Rouvoet (1992; 2000; 2006); the Reformed politician André Rouvoet (b. 1962), as a representative of the *ChristenUnie* (ChristianUnion), was a minister and deputy prime minister in the Dutch government from 2007–2010 under Reformed prime minister Jan Peter Balkenende (b. 1956).

toward the "end of the age" (Matt. 13:39–40, 49; 24:3; 28:20), the time when all enemies will be made a footstool for the feet of the glorified Man Jesus Christ (Heb. 1:13), the "world to come," which will be laid beneath the feet of the Son of Man (Heb. 2:5–8), the progress of Christ's dominion until God will be "all in all" (1 Cor. 15:24–28). Bible-believing Christians have many different views on eschatology; these differences are of no concern to us now (but see chapter 9). The only point that matters right now is that they all agree on this eschatological character of the "kingdom of Christ and God" (Eph. 5:5), the "kingdom of our Lord and of his Christ" (Rev. 11:15).

Of course, we do not want to speak naïvely of a "theocratic democracy," that is, a democracy with a theocratic attitude, or directed by theocratic norms. We do realize that to a great extent modern democracy is a product of Enlightenment humanism. Therefore, the question might arise as to whether a typically humanistic state structure harbours *a priori* the possibility of ever assuming a theocratic orientation. The answer is that modern Western democracy acquired its typically humanistic form for the first time in the nineteenth century. Before that time, Christian thinking influenced the development of democracy at least as much as humanism did.[13]

5.1.4 Ecclesiocracy?

In a certain sense, *every* democracy is necessarily a theocratic democracy because in every state, whatever its political form may be (its *structure*), the Lord reigns, whether the majority of the citizens acknowledge this or not (its *direction*). Theocracy is not a kind of ideal of God that should be realized by his believing children, just as the kingdom of God is not a kind of ideal that will be realized only at the second coming of Christ. Already now, the kingdom of God is "forcefully advancing" (see §5.5.3), namely, in all places where people and societal relationships explicitly put themselves under the dominion of Christ and his Word. To be sure, today sin is still reigning on this earth (Rom. 6:12), and Satan is still the god of this world (2 Cor. 4:4). But that does not alter the fact that the kingdom of God is pushing forward. Behind the scenes, it is Christ who is reigning. Even sin and Satan's work can occur only under his permission; willy-nilly they are instruments in his hand.

Some people have suggested that a so-called theocratic political form involves the church having supremacy over the state (cf. §10.3). This again is a regrettable confusion of structure and direction. The underlying error usually is that, in some way or another, the church is considered to be

---

[13] See, e.g., Rutherford (1998; orig.: 1644).

nearer to the kingdom of God than any of the other societal relationships; we find this error also in NL2K.[14] The latter does not distinguish between the church as the eternal-transcendent body of Christ (e.g., Eph. 1–3) and the church in its historical-immanent form as a denomination, or a set of denominations, on earth (what is sometimes inaccurately referred to as the "visible church"), or a local congregation (see §10.1).[15] However, it is insufficiently realized that, in this historical-immanent form, "the" church—more correctly, a certain church denomination, or a local congregation—is *nothing but one societal relationship among many others*: an association with members, rules, fees, administration, and people in charge.

The practical significance of this distinction between the church and the kingdom of God can be easily explained. One need only ask: Is the kingdom of God manifested in a certain church denomination, or in a local church congregation, in a better, higher, clearer way than in any other societal relationship? Is not the kingdom of God manifested more gloriously in many Christian marriages, families, schools, companies, associations, and political parties, than in certain (backsliding) church denominations or deteriorating local congregations? Sometimes, churches harbour evils that in other societal relationships would not be tolerated (cf. 1 Cor. 5:1)! Of course, to me, a local church congregation, because of its structural nature, has more spiritual substance than, for instance, a local Christian sports club or a Christian trade union. But I also know that some of these latter associations look after their own people better than certain church congregations do. In no way are we ever allowed to place "the church"—that is, in our experience, always a certain church denomination, or a local church congregation—above any of the other societal relationships or communities.

5.2 SIN IN SOCIETAL RELATIONSHIPS

5.2.1 Sin in the State

I would not trust anyone who believes he can shape the state according to some "natural law written on the hearts," or some "sound popular sentiment." The power of sin is too strong for that. First, there is sin on the subject side: many ideas of the state have been advocated, and many forms

---

[14] See, e.g., VanDrunen (2010a, 15, 26, 30–31).

[15] The distinction is not made clearly in the Belgic Confession, which, on the one hand, calls the church "a holy congregation of true Christian believers" (Art. 27; this is the body of Christ), and, on the other hand, says, "All men are in duty bound to join and unite themselves with it" (Art. 28), which refers to the church as denomination or local congregations.

of the state realized, which were not the product of some "natural law" but of sinful hearts. Examples are individualism (with Thomas Hobbes' idea of the state treaty)[16] and universalism (with its absolutization of certain societal entities, especially the church or the state). Other examples are state despotism, abuse of power, violence and suppression by the authorities, disobedience and rebellion by subjects, anarchy and revolution, restorationism and reactionism. *At times, unfortunately, each of these matters has been defended by certain Christians (or "Christians").* This is enough to distrust any "natural law," any "sound popular sentiment," any supposed natural awareness of what the state should be.

However, sin also operates on the law side of reality.[17] Not in the sense that sin could ever affect God's commandments as such; how could any power hostile to God change or annul God's own laws? It is true, however, that, in the normative structure of the state, elements have been added that without the Fall would not have been needed. Neither the state's historical shaping according to the creation mandate (§2.1), nor its leading principle of public justice (§§6.5 and 12.2.3), necessarily presupposes sin—but the power of the sword does (Rom. 13:4). The idea of a sword that disciplines, and even kills, evildoers, presupposes a sinful world. This means that apparently, after the Fall, the power of the sword was added to the creation structure of the state.

This thought is confirmed by the following element in the Noahic covenant: "Whoever sheds the blood of man, by man shall his blood be shed, for God made man in his own image" (Gen. 6:9). Thus, the power of the sword was entrusted to humanity not before the Fall, but only after the Flood. What was instituted here was not the *state*, or the principle of *human authority*, as has been claimed,[18] for this principle goes back to the creation order. It is rather the human power of the sword that is instituted here. In Genesis 9, this does not yet occur in a specified way: it is not the authorities that are mentioned, but the murderer must be executed "by man." Even in early Israel, we see that execution was not yet carried out by a regular government or judicial system, but by the "avenger of blood" (Num. 35; Deut. 19:1–13; Josh. 20). At the same time, however, we see in the Mosaic Law how this right of the avenger was considerably restricted, namely, by the elders of the cities of refuge, that is, by authorities. Interestingly, in later times we never

---

[16] Some wanted to reduce the entire notion of sin to the notions of individualism and rivalry; see Erickson (1998, 610–13).

[17] Ouweneel (1986, 336–37).

[18] E.g., Kelly (1894, 289); dispensationalism speaks of the post-Flood dispensation of "human government"; see Scofield (1967, ad loc.).

again hear of these avengers of blood; the power of the sword was exclusively in the hands of the authorities.

The operation of sin within the state comes to light in a striking way in the well-known comparison between Romans 13 and Revelation 13. On the one hand, although Paul addresses his letter to the Romans during the rule of the emperor Nero, he consciously presented the state in Romans 13 in its most ideal form. This is the state as God had intended it since, and in spite of, the Fall. We encounter here an implicit description of the normative structure of the state, with its law side, *not* with its concrete positivized form (on the subject side) that the state had under Nero; the apostle does not refer to this at all. On the other hand, Revelation 13 portrays the state according to its *subject side* in its most anti-normative form: blasphemy instead of submission, outright Satan service, abuse of power, violence, oppression of God's people.

5.2.2   Sin in Marriage

Also in marriage, sin is active on the subject side: bigamy and polygamy, gay marriages; think also of rape in marriage, and of adultery and fornication (which lives parasitically on what belongs exclusively to marriage). However, sin is also active on the law side, since here, too, we find the addition of certain elements because of sin. To be sure, the Mosaic Law did not explicitly "permit" divorce as such, but it did presuppose its possibility (Deut. 24:1–4). That is to say, the possibility of divorce was added to the creation ordinance of marriage since, and because of, the Fall.

When the Pharisees interrogated Jesus about this matter, he referred them back to the pure creation ordinance, as it had been given before the Fall: "Because of your hardness of heart [i.e., because of *sin*] Moses allowed you to divorce your wives, but *from the beginning it was not so*" (Matt. 19:8). "Have you not read that he who created them *from the beginning* made them male and female…? So they are no longer two but one flesh. What therefore God has joined together, let not man separate" (vv. 4, 6).[19] Here Jesus describes marriage as God had intended it "from the beginning," that is, from creation (Gen. 1:27–28; 2:18–25). In addition to this, Scripture gives various guidelines for dealing with these matters since the Fall (e.g., 1 Cor. 7).

The Christian ethics of marriage, sexuality, and divorce is a delicate and complicated matter. Various interpretations of the relevant Bible passages, 1 Corinthians 7 in particular, have given rise to many different practices. But at least we can start from Scripture here. Imagine the impossible situation

---

[19] See more extensively Ouweneel (2006, chapter 6).

of having to argue about marriage, sexuality, and divorce (e.g., in view of state legislation) purely on the basis of some "natural law written on the hearts," or some "sound popular sentiment"! We would be lost.

5.3   THE BIBLICAL TWO KINGDOMS[20]

5.3.1   The First and the Last Adam

It is my conviction that the notion of "Christian politics"—whatever that may be remains to been seen—cannot be separated from the notion of the kingdom of God. This kingdom is, first of all, very simply God's general government over all created things, from the foundation of the world until eternity (cf., e.g., Ex. 15:18, "The LORD reigns [or, is King] for ever and ever"). Secondly, and more specifically, it is God's intention to put this kingdom under the feet of Man, and entrust world dominion to his care (Gen. 1:28, "Fill the earth and subdue it. Rule over…every living creature"). The first Man, the "first Adam" (cf. 1 Cor. 15:45), utterly failed in this, for through his Fall Adam surrendered his rule to the power of sin, death, and Satan (Gen. 3). This aspect of the Fall is seldom emphasized but very important.

Indeed, Satan could truly say to Jesus that all the authority and splendour of the kingdoms of this world had been "given" to him (Luke 4:5–6)—and Jesus did not deny it. On the contrary, on another occasion, he recognized that there is something in this world that can be called the "kingdom" of Satan (Matt. 12:26). Three times Jesus called Satan "the ruler of this world" (John 12:31; 14:30; 16:11). But he could also say that, through his coming into this world and his manifestation of the power of God, apparently the kingdom of God had arrived (Matt. 12:28). Satan, since Calvary a sentenced rebel, will never be able to compete with this kingdom, no matter how much noise he continues to make, "prowling around like a roaring lion" (1 Pet. 5:8).

What the "first Adam" has ruined, the "last Adam" is restoring (cf. 1 Cor. 15:45–47; then vv. 24–28). In his hands is the "restoration of all things" (Acts 3:31 NKJV). If we look at Psalm 8 as explained by Hebrews 2, this transition from the first to the last Adam is beautifully brought to light: the Son of Man, under whose feet all created things are put, is no longer (the first) Adam, but: "we do see Jesus, who was made lower than the angels for a little while, now crowned with glory and honor because he suffered death, so that by the grace of God he might taste death for everyone" (v. 9).

---

[20] What now follows is an abbreviated, yet expanded and annotated, version of parts of Ouweneel (2014b). For a much more extensive treatment of the doctrine of God's kingdom see Ouweneel (2016e).

Please notice that Jesus' domain of power cannot possibly be smaller than Adam's. If the first Adam had dominion over the sea, the heavens, and the earth (Gen. 1:26, 28), the last Adam cannot do with less. Therefore he could say of himself, "All authority in heaven and on earth has been given to me" (Matt. 19:28; cf. Ps. 72:8 CEV: "Let his kingdom reach from sea to sea, from the Euphrates River across all the earth"). Please note: not *will be given*, as NL2K *de facto* wants to have it, but "*has been* given to me." In principle, every state, every marriage, every family, every school, and so on, stands under the kingship of Christ, whether these states, marriages, and so forth, wish to acknowledge it or not.

5.3.2 The Scope of the Kingdom

In the Old Testament, the coming of the kingdom of God in this new, Messianic form is announced many times (e.g., Isa. 9:6–7). Both John the Baptist and Jesus himself could say in their day that now the kingdom of God had come "near" (Matt. 3:2; 4:17). In the person of the King, the kingdom of God itself had arrived. As Jesus told his opponents, "Do not say, 'Here it is,' or 'There it is,' because the kingdom of God is *in your midst*" (Luke 17:21), namely, in his person. The natural-born Jew could not enter that kingdom automatically; he had to be born again—born "of water and the Spirit"—just like any Gentile who wishes to enter the kingdom of God. Without this new birth, one would not even be able to "see" (grasp, understand) the kingdom of God (John 3:1–6). Therefore, the "mysteries" of the kingdom are only for the true disciples of the King, who keep his royal laws (see Matt. 13:22; 28:19–20). This refers to the kingdom in its inward form.

At the same time, the parables in Matthew 13 make clear that, as long as the King has not returned, the kingdom in its outward form contains both true and false disciples (cf. also Matt. 25:1–30). The domain of operation of God's kingdom is the entire world, for Jesus says, "The kingdom of heaven may be compared to a man who sowed good seed in his field," and explains: "The field is the world" (Matt. 13:24, 38). We thus find three meanings of the kingdom of Christ as it is presented in the Gospels (cf. §6.3.2).[21]

(a) In its *most restricted* meaning, according to its inward form, the kingdom of God encompasses all the regenerated, and only the regenerated (John 3:3–5), *not* necessarily viewed in the collective sense of "church," but individually.[22]

---

[21] See Ouweneel (2016e, chapter 7).

[22] This distinction between the sum total (the church) and individual Christians is often blurred: the whole is not only *more* than the sum of its parts, but also *different*. Not only is it obvious that "the church" does not do cultural work, or politics, or science—Christian (and

(b) The *intermediate* meaning: the kingdom of God encompasses all the Christian confessors, both the wheat and the weeds (Matt. 13:24–30, 36–43), the good and the bad fishes (vv. 47–50), the good and the bad sons (21:28–32), the good and the bad wedding guests (22:1–14), the good and the bad servants (24:45–51; 25:14–30), the wise and the foolish virgins (25:1–13); in short, worldwide Christendom, which at present encompasses about one third of the present human race.

(c) The *most extended* meaning: the kingdom encompasses the entire world (13:38), "heaven and earth" (28:18), all that Satan could offer to Jesus, that is, "all the kingdoms of the world and their glory" (4:8). The kingdom is the field of operation of the Holy Spirit (cf. Matt. 12:28; John 3:5; 1 Cor. 4:20; Rom. 14:17): where the Spirit is active, there is the kingdom of God—and where is the Spirit not active?

5.3.3 Visible and Invisible

The kingdom as Jesus Christ announced it is "not of this world" (John 18:36). This does not mean, however, that it is not established here on earth. On the contrary. It means that it does not fit into the sinful, demonic, violent categories of "this world." The phrase "this world" refers, then, to those evil categories. The kingdom of Jesus Christ is established as the very opposite of these evil powers, and until the return of the King it exists in the midst of, and over against, these evil powers.

For his followers this may involve shame and persecution. Therefore, until the public return of the King, the kingdom exists largely in a hidden form because the King himself is still "hidden" (cf. Col. 3:3); he "went to a distant country" (Luke 19:12). The earth has not yet been filled with "justice and righteousness" (cf. Isa. 9:7), nor with the "knowledge of the glory of the LORD" (Hab. 2:14), and this will not, and cannot, happen as long as the King has not re-appeared.

On the other hand, the kingdom of God *is* clearly visible. We can perceive it *at all places* where we find people who have submitted their lives to the dominion of the Lord Jesus Christ. This involves not only their individual lives but also their marriages, their families, their churches, their schools, their companies, their associations, their political parties, and even their states (if they have a devoted majority in the latter). In this way, Jesus' followers form a kind of bridgehead for the King on this earth, until he

---

other) individuals do so—but the church as a collective does not even preach or evangelize; Christian individuals do so (see §6.3.1). I call this absolutizing of "the church" a form of churchism or ecclesiasticism (see chapter 10).

comes to utterly defeat his enemies.

The last thing the "world" has seen of the King is that he was laid in a tomb. But his disciples know his "secret:" they know of his resurrection and ascension, they know that all things have been put under his feet, and that "all authority in heaven and on earth" has been given to him (Matt. 28:18). Behind the curtain, Jesus Christ has the reins in his hands, not only in the church and in individual lives but in *all the domains of cosmic reality*. His disciples know this; therefore, they love him, they serve him, and they follow him with joy. Indeed, the kingdom is a realm of love: God "has delivered us from the power of darkness and conveyed us into the kingdom of the Son of His love" (Col. 1:13 NKJV).

5.4 SUBJECTS OF THE KING[23]

5.4.1 The Law of the Kingdom

NL2K advocates talk a lot about the kingdom of God, as contrasted with the "common kingdom," but I believe they could hardly make such a contrast if they really understood the true character of the kingdom of God. Or let me say: if they understood *discipleship*: being subjects, followers, trainees of the Master. Reformational thinkers have always been very aware of the gospel of God's grace for poor sinners (cf. Acts 20:24), but much less aware of the gospel of the kingdom (cf. v. 25).[24] However, in the end times it is especially *this* gospel of the kingdom that is being preached to all the nations (Matt. 24:14; cf. 4:23; 9:35). In the briefest form it is this: get out of the kingdom of Satan (cf. 12:25–28), and join the kingdom of God by surrendering your life, your service, your devotion to the lordship of Christ, and become his disciple.

Jesus said, "All authority in heaven and on earth has been given to me. Go therefore and make disciples of all nations, baptizing them in the name of the Father and of the Son and of the Holy Spirit, teaching them to observe all that I have commanded you" (Matt. 28:18–20). That is, (a) Jesus is King over the entire world, (b) people should become disciples (subjects, followers, trainees) of this King by baptism and instruction in his commandments. These commandments are the rules of the kingdom, but in essence they represent the image of Jesus himself. Jesus is the deepest

---

[23] See extensively, Ouweneel (2016e, chapter 6).

[24] *Contra* Schuyler English (1986, 44 note), who identifies the "gospel of the kingdom" with the "gospel of grace"; cf. Ouweneel (2016e, §7.5.2).

essence of his own teaching; therefore he said, "It is enough for the disciple to be like his teacher, and the servant like his master" (10:25). The great longing of the true disciple is to acquire the inner mind of his Master (cf. Phil. 2:5 NIV, "have the same mindset as Christ Jesus"): "Everyone when he is fully trained [Greek: *katērtismenos*] will be like his teacher" (Luke 6:40), who for his disciples is Jesus himself.

Self-evidently, the Torah of Christ (cf. 1 Cor. 9:21; Gal. 6:2) cannot be less exalted than the Torah of Moses. If the latter encompassed *all* aspects of life, then the former does too. The Mosaic Torah referred to marriage life, family life, education, citizen relationships, employers and employees, buyers and sellers, kings and subjects, and so on. The Law of Christ contains no less than this. If the kingdom of God coincided with Israel in the Old Testament, it coincides with the entire world in the New Testament. Can anyone imagine Jesus Christ at one time operating in the kingdom of God, and at another time operating in some "common kingdom"? As he was and is *always* the King, in whatever domain of life he has operated and still operates, so too the Christian is always a disciple of the King, in every domain of life.

Jesus submitted to the earthly authorities, but always in a kingly way (e.g., John 18:36–37; 19:10–11). He did not keep silent in any domain of life, and he taught his disciples the same: "You will be dragged before governors and kings for my sake, to bear witness before them and the Gentiles" (Matt. 10:18). There is no "common kingdom" where he told his disciples to keep silent and simply behave like unbelievers (though with a Christian *attitude*). You could not imagine Jesus anywhere in society keeping silent out of respect for some "common kingdom," and he expected the same of his followers: "Whoever believes in me will also do the works that I do" (John 14:12).

5.4.2 The Message of the Kingdom

Paul and Silas preached the gospel of the kingdom at Thessalonica, among many other places. Paul preached what Jesus had commanded in the Great Commission. This was not only "repentance and forgiveness of sins" (Luke 24:47), but also: "*All authority in heaven and on earth has been given to me.* Go therefore [i.e., in the light of this fact] and make disciples of all nations" (Matt. 28:18–20). In Thessalonica, the emphasis of Paul and his co-workers was indeed on this gospel of the kingdom. This is evident from the accusation that was leveled against them: "These men who have turned the world upside down have come here also…and they are all acting against the decrees of Caesar, saying that there is another king, Jesus" (Acts 17:6–7).

In verse 6, we find the same Greek word (*oikoumenē*) that we encounter in Revelation 12:9 as the power domain of Satan (cf. 16:13–14). The word *oikoumenē* (cf. "ecumenical," from Greek: *oikeō*, "to dwell, inhabit," thus: the "inhabited world") is usually a very general term, but in Luke 2:1 it is clearly a description of the then "inhabited world," namely, the Roman Empire, the power domain of the Roman emperor. On the Mount of Temptation, Satan showed Jesus all the kingdoms of the *oikoumenē*, in order that Jesus would accept them from his hands by worshiping him. Thus, in fact, Satan offered Jesus the imperial crown over the Roman Empire (4:5–6).[25] Jesus did not wish to obtain the power over the Roman Empire in this way, however, namely, by kneeling down before Satan and worshiping him; rather, he wished to do this through his death and resurrection and his ascension to God's right hand. There, in that position, he is invested with all authority in heaven and on earth (Matt. 28:18), including the Roman Empire.

In Acts 11:28 and 24:5, and in Revelation 3:10, the *oikoumenē* is the Roman Empire as well,[26] and this is what clearly is in view in Acts 17:6–7, just quoted. Paul turned the *oikoumenē*, that is, the Roman Empire, upside down by preaching that there was "another [Greek: *heteros*, not *allos*] King," that is, a King of a different kind than what people had been used to: Jesus. Paul preached the supreme kingship of Jesus, and in this way he challenged the Roman emperor, the *basileus* of the Greek world.

If NL2K advocates were right, Paul would not have had too many problems. He would have said something like this: I do preach another King to you, but don't worry. This King is no threat to the emperor of Rome. Our King is only King in his own kingdom, namely, the church; all the rest of life belongs to the "neutral" kingdom of the Roman *basileus*. So there is no reason for concern: by far the greatest part of the world is still under the rule of the "powers that be;" Jesus is King only of the [then still tiny] church. But no, Paul did not preach that; his opponents understood him far better than NL2K advocates do. They saw in Paul's message a direct threat to the empire, and rightly so: within three hundred years the Roman Empire *as such* had to bow down before the King of Kings. Who in Thessalonica, and who in fourth-century Rome, believed in some "common (neutral, secular) realm"? I am not saying that this Christianized Roman Empire did everything right; on the contrary. But the principle was correct: just as the Empire encompassed the entire lives of its subjects, so too does the kingdom of Christ.

---

[25] Ouweneel (2016c, 113–15, 127–28).

[26] Ibid., 43–44, 98.

5.4.3 The Dominion of Christ

We have discovered two things that are true: the kingdom is "hidden" because the King is still "hidden" (cf. Col. 3:1). But the kingdom is also manifest in that it comes to light at all places where the rule of Christ and his commandments are being recognized in individual hearts and lives, as well as in the societal relationships or communities, insofar as Christians can make their mark on them. I will give a few examples.

A Christian family is part of the kingdom of God, not necessarily because all the children have already committed their hearts and lives to the King, but because formally and practically the parents have sought to lead the family in a way that acknowledges the dominion of Christ. "In this family we recognize Jesus Christ as our King and Lord," is the confession of these believing parents.[27]

A Christian school is part of the kingdom of God, not necessarily because all its pupils have already committed their hearts and lives to the King, but because formally and practically its administrators and teachers have sought to provide education that acknowledges the dominion of Christ. They tell the pupils, as it were, "At this school we maintain—in all weakness—the rules of the King, we teach you the rules of the King, and we try to follow these rules ourselves." Within the safe boundaries of such a school, the pupils are not "in the world," but in the wonderful realm of Christ, that is, the kingdom of God.

A Christian company is part of the kingdom of God, not necessarily because all its employees have committed their hearts and lives to the King, but because the employers have sought to conduct business in a way that acknowledges the dominion of Christ. They tell the employees, "In this company, we endeavour to maintain Christian principles of fairness and stewardship." This is nothing else but telling the employees that they, the employers, want this company to be part of the kingdom of God.

Was there ever a truly Christian state? Perhaps the Dutch Republic was a fair approximation of it. The Republic of the Seven United Netherlands (Dutch: *Republiek der Zeven Verenigde Nederlanden*), existed from 1581, when part of the Netherlands cast off Spanish rule, until 1795 (French occupation). (In 1813, after the Napoleonic period, it was replaced with the Kingdom of the Netherlands.) Especially the period of Willem III (1650–1702), *stadtholder* of Holland and four other Dutch provinces from 1672, and king of England, Ireland, and Scotland from 1689, must be mentioned.

---

[27] Notice Mark 10:14 (NKJV), "Let the little children come to Me, and do not forbid them; for *of such* is the kingdom of God"—not *for* them, as if they did not yet share in it.

Many heralded him as a champion of Protestantism, someone whose faith influenced his rule.[28]

The Christian state respects the various views and liberties of all its citizens, but is nevertheless an expression of the kingdom of God. This is not necessarily because all its citizens are Christians, but because the authorities introduce and maintain biblical principles in this state, which become evident in their way of ruling and in legislation that accords with the principles of Scripture. Such a Christian government has the courage to oppose abortion, not because of some "natural law written on the hearts," or some "sound popular sentiment," but because the King opposes it. We will return to this idea of the Christian state, especially in chapter 12.

5.5 SEPARATION OF CHURCH AND STATE[29]

5.5.1 Utter Confusion

Let me say immediately that the things I described have nothing at all to do with the notion of the separation of church and state. There is a tremendous misunderstanding here. The separation of church and state is a great thing, for which we can all be very thankful. We know from the past what it means when "the" church—which is, of course, always one specific denomination out of many!—rules over the state. This is what the Roman Catholic Church did in the Middle Ages, for instance, by publicly and formally condemning heretics, and then hypocritically handing them over to the state authorities to be executed. The situation was similar to what we find today in Iran, where the ayatollahs hold the reins. We also know, by the way, what it means when the state rules over the church, and tells her what to believe and what not to believe, as in communist countries (North Korea) and Islamic countries. In a much milder form, it was the States General in the Netherlands, not the church, that convened the Synod of Dort (1618–19).[30]

---

[28] One of the finest descriptions of William's Christian significance is found in De Graaff (1977, 270–81): William "exalted Holland and England to instruments that were used to give Europe, and even a large part of the world, a Messianic revival and liberation" (270). "William III was allowed to renew Western culture by the new relationship with God. As a consequence, he could combat the empire of the Disturber.... He passed on the blessing of the Reformation, which granted humaneness and freedom, to the world.... For centuries hereafter, Europe and even the entire world have experience this blessing" (281). De Graaff refers to Pierre Bayle, who compared Willem to king David; De Graaff (279): "Both [David and William] are anointed ones of the God of Israel, who are called to liberate God's people."

[29] See "Working It Out" at the end of chapter 4.

[30] Cf. the Westminster Confession of Faith (23.3): "The civil magistrate...hath authority,

Later in this chapter I will explain in more detail that church and state—and each family, each school, each company, each association, and so on—is to be autonomous within its own sphere of influence. Christian denominations should not meddle in state matters (and family matters, and school matters, etc.), and states should not meddle in the business of churches, families, schools, companies, and so on, except when these touch matters of public justice.

Now the tremendous misunderstanding is this: *the separation of church and state has been turned into a separation between religion and society*, which is something totally different. I do not know whether this has happened on purpose, or unconsciously, but it is quite a malicious confusion that has been introduced here.[31] Again, it is a shocking confusion of structure and direction. The separation of church and state, if properly understood, is a "horizontal" matter of distinguishing between various societal relationships; in fact, we could speak of a separation of church, state, marriage, family, school, company, association, and political party. Each of them has its own autonomy within its own confines, and none should meddle with the affairs of any other. However, the supposed separation between religion and society is a "vertical' matter of *keeping Christianity (and Judaism, and Islam, etc.) out of every public sector.*

Since the time of the Enlightenment (eighteenth century), spiritual and political leaders have tried, ever more openly and actively, to ban religion entirely from the public square. This is what we call *secularization*: religion has been pushed back to the edge of society, that is, to the private lives of individuals. This is a great triumph for the kingdom of Satan, I must say, and a great setback for the kingdom of God. We are all responsible for this, since we have all let it happen. We ourselves have sometimes acquiesced to this confusion between, on the one hand, the separation of church and state, and on the other hand, the separation between religion and society. We ourselves have sometimes begun to believe that religion is a strictly

---

and it is his duty, to take order that unity and peace be preserved in the Church, that the truth of God be kept pure and entire.... For the better effecting whereof, *he hath power to call synods, to be present at them*, and to provide that whatsoever is transacted in them be according to the mind of God (2 Chron. 19:8-11; 2 Chron. 29-30; Matt. 2:4-5)" (Dennison [2008, 4:262]; italics added).

[31] An example of this misrepresentation is Hart (2006), to whom the distinctions made in this section seem completely foreign. His book may be somewhat useful for those interested in American religious history, but not at all useful for those living in countries accustomed to Christian democratic parties. Hart tries to give his book a (meager) theological foundation simply by superficially referring to the two kingdom theology of Luther and Calvin (2006, 244), and by referring to the biblical example of Daniel (253–57; but cf. my chapter 8 below).

private matter, and that society and the state are (supposedly) neutral.

I see the rise of NL2K as a consequence of this process of secularization. This is the issue: either God's Word has full authority over the entire cosmic reality, or only over a limited part of it: the church. If the latter, we may fear that this part will get smaller and smaller as time goes on. Either the glorified Man at God's right hand has full authority over the entire cosmic reality, or he has limited authority only over a small part of it. Again, if the latter, we may fear that this part will get smaller and smaller as secularization advances. Since the time of the Enlightenment, it was semi-Christians or apostate Christians who led this process of secularization. Today it is (North American) Christians who want to delude us into thinking that *this was the early Reformational view.*

I ask the reader, can you imagine Martin Luther telling the Saxonian elector Frederick the Wise (d. 1525), who was a devoted Catholic but liked Luther's ecclesiastical ideas, that he had to be "neutral," and that for his rule it did not matter whether he was a Christian as long as he was a good and wise ruler? Can you imagine John Calvin telling the city council of Geneva that they had to be "neutral," and that for their rule it did not matter whether they were Christians as long as they were good rulers? And much earlier, can you imagine Augustine telling the Roman emperor that he had to be "neutral," and that for his rule it did not matter whether he was a Christian as long as he was a good ruler? In the societies of Augustine, Luther, and Calvin, it made a world of difference that the rulers mentioned *were* Christians, and that, in their position of magistrates, they advanced the cause of Christians over against pagans and heretics.

NL2K is much more dangerous than the older schools of semi- and apostate Christians because it presents itself as thoroughly Reformed. Some of its advocates strongly imply that one is not classically Reformed if he does not accept their view! That is, if one wants to be faithful to early Reformational thinking, he understands today that *he must deny the universal authority of God's Word as well as the universal kingship of Christ.* No wonder many Christians have great difficulty believing that *this* is authentic Reformational thinking.

5.5.2 No Dominant Church

To be sure, I do not wish for a moment that *the church should control the state.* I would move abroad if that would happen in my own country—it does not matter what denomination it would be. Indeed, in practice this can only be one specific church *denomination* (out of a total of about 42,000), or an alliance of church denominations, for instance, the North American

Presbyterian and Reformed Council, or the World Alliance of Reformed Churches. I would never entrust civil government to church leaders as such;[32] moreover, it would not work: sooner or later they would be divided over theological matters, to the detriment of the population in such a country.

Yet, the Roman Catholic Church is still the state church in countries like Argentina, Bolivia, Liechtenstein, Monaco, Paraguay, and Peru. The Church of England is still the state church in England (but not in the rest of the United Kingdom), the Lutheran Church is still the state church in Denmark and Iceland (no longer in Sweden and Norway), and the Orthodox Church is still the state church in countries like Greece and Georgia. It is under-standable if people in such countries would view the kingdom of God as being manifested in their country especially in connection with their state church. But this would be wrong. The kingdom comes to manifestation—or should come to manifestation—in individual lives as well as in *all* societal relationships, in families, schools, companies, etc., just as much as in the state and the church.

None of these societal relationships is neutral—least of all the state. Where do we find any neutral authorities? Politicians almost always come from political parties, which obviously always have a definite ideological colour: they may be conservative, or liberal, or socialist, or social-democrat-ic, or Christian-democratic, or communist, or "green," or libertarian, you name it. Within such parties, politicians are recruited for office. These are conservative, or liberal, or socialist, or social-democratic, or Christian-democratic, or communist, or "green," or libertarian politicians—not to mention the distinction between positive Christian and atheist politicians. Where is the neutrality here?

Some American presidents were Baptists, others were Congregationalists, others Dutch Reformed (with good Dutch names: Van Buren,[33] Roosevelt), or Episcopalians, or Methodists, or Presbyterians, or Quakers, or Unitarians.[34] Either their religious affiliation had not the slightest influence on their presi-dency—but then they were weak Christians. Or their religious affiliation did influence their presidency—and then the illusion of neutrality evaporates.

---

[32] Which does not mean that clergymen might not become politicians, as has happened so many times: e.g., Rev. Abraham Kuyper was prime minister of the Netherlands (1901–1905), and the Dutch parliament has known several pastors as members; some of the best known were Rev. Henry Kersten (d. 1952), Rev. Pieter Zandt (d. 1961), and Rev. Hette Abma (d. 1992) (the latter two were Dutch Reformed). And think of the Presbyterian Rev. Ian Paisley (d. 2014), Ulster unionist, who was a member of the British and the European parliaments.

[33] Martin Van Buren (president 1837–1841) spoke Dutch, even in the White House, although he was a fifth-generation American.

[34] https://en.wikipedia.org/wiki/Religious_affiliations_of_Presidents_of_the_United_States.

Please note, my point is not that I advocate a greater role for religion in society; rather, I claim that society *is* religious (in the broad sense of the term) from top to bottom, from left to right. One can agree with a separation between church and state, and at the same time assert that the entire society is religious, and that therefore the notion of a separation of religion and society is nonsensical. Within the boundaries of the nation state, the battle between the kingdom of Satan and the kingdom of God is constantly raging. The same happens within so many families, schools, companies, and—unfortunately—even church denominations and local congregations. But in the state it is perhaps most conspicuous. As long as the King has not yet returned, we cannot escape this battle. But at least we can do our best to manifest the kingdom of God within our own families, and within the schools to which we send our children, and within the companies we found and direct, and within the associations, political parties, unions, and clubs we form—and, as far as possible, even in the state.

5.5.3   All Society Is Religious

Of course, we do keep "church and state" carefully apart. But at the same time, we recognize that "all of life is religion,"[35] that is, all of life is either apostate or Godward, is either under the dominion of sin and Satan, or under the dominion of Christ (or, as unfortunately is often the case, somewhat under both). We do not want any *church denomination* to rule our states, families, schools, and companies, but we definitely want *Christ* to rule our states, families, schools, and companies. *All things* have been put under his feet (Eph. 1:22; Heb. 2:8)—that includes all the societal relationships and communities we are involved in. What God already did objectively, we want to do ourselves subjectively as an act of faith and love: place all our societal relationships at the feet of Christ.

Even an NL2K advocate like Michael Horton says,

> Man is *homo religionis*—intrinsically religious. Even after the Fall, the constant urge to set up idols was an evidence of this intrinsic religious dimension: Man cannot live without gods, a sense of the transcendent. Every human activity was designed to be inherently religious, from the planting of crops (agriculture) to the naming of animals (zoology).[36]

---

[35] This statement was often made by Reformed philosopher H. Evan Runner (d. 2002); cf. the title of the essays published in honour of him (Vander Goot [1981]): *Life Is Religion*.

[36] Horton (1995, 145–46).

What a pity that Horton did not draw the proper conclusion from this, namely, that also after the Fall, every human activity is still inherently religious. After the Fall, the work of unbelievers is no longer "sacred,"[37] but it is still thoroughly religious; it is either Godward or apostate, and therefore never "common." The opposite of holy is not common, but unholy.

We do not believe in the illusion of "commonality" (see extensively §§7.1–7.3 on the universal lordship of Christ). A battle is going on, in which no individual and no institution can pretend to be neutral (or "common," if you like). An enemy who overtly presents himself as an enemy is to be preferred to an enemy presenting himself as common (which actually means "neutral"). We prefer to face the "roaring lion" (1 Pet. 5:8) rather than interact with the "angel of light" (2 Cor. 11:14). The former wears wooden shoes, as we would say in Dutch—one can hear him coming from afar—the latter wears slippers.

It is unthinkable that the kingdom of God, as some would have it, encompasses only a few domains of life: your private life, your family, and your church (see the next sections). That would ostensibly be the extent of God's kingdom. If this were true, it would mean that our schools, our companies, our associations, must be viewed as part of the kingdom of Satan because there are no other kingdoms. We cannot let that happen. It is unbiblical and irresponsible. The kingdom of God is being manifested in all domains of life. This comes to light when officials in these domains—parents, elders, bishops, teachers, professors, employers, administrators, magistrates, and so on—wield their authority in the concrete, explicit recognition that they themselves stand under the authority and commandments of Christ the Lord. This implies that those who are under these officials—children, church members, pupils, students, employees, citizens, and so on—recognize and obey this authority as the authority of the King himself.

In fact, at stake here is the essence of Christianity as such. Darryl Hart asserts, "Christianity is essentially a spiritual and eternal faith, one occupied with a world to come rather than the passing and temporal affairs of this world."[38] Apparently, Hart prefers Ephesians 1–3 ("spiritual blessings in the heavenly places," 1:3) to Ephesians 4–6, where we find that genuine Christians make better husbands and wives, better parents and children, better employers and employees—and I do not hesitate to add: better citizens, better school teachers and pupils, better professors and students, better chairmen and union members, and so forth. Any dualism of spiritual

---

[37] Cf. ibid., 147.
[38] Hart (2006, 12).

vs. material, eternal vs. temporal, salvation vs. politics, and so on, is nothing but ancient scholasticism; it is not biblical. God's grace is "training us…to live self-controlled, upright, and godly lives *in the present age*" (Titus 2:12), not only in the age to come.

It belongs to the essence of the "kingdom of heaven" that it is a kingdom *on earth*.[39] "All Scripture is breathed out by God and profitable for teaching, for reproof, for correction, and for training in righteousness, that the man of God may be complete, equipped for every good work" (2 Tim. 3:16–17)—not just for his "quiet time" and for church work. "So then, as we have opportunity, let us do good *to everyone*" (Gal. 6:10).

In summary: all Christians must behave as disciples of the King, who live, work, serve out of a burning love for him, whether in their marriages, their families, their churches, their schools, their companies, their associations, their political parties, and their nation states. This is what I find in Matthew 11:12,[40] where Jesus told his listeners: "From the days of John the Baptist until now the kingdom of heaven has suffered violence [note ESV: has been coming violently; Greek: *biazetai*], and the violent [Greek: *biastai*] take it by force" (Matt. 11:12–13). In the version of Luke 16:16, Jesus said, "The Law and the Prophets were until John; since then the good news of the kingdom of God is preached, and everyone forces his way into it [note ESV: everyone is forcefully urged into it; Greek: *biazetai*]."

The interpretation of Matthew 11:12 has been hotly debated.[41] We do not have to make a choice because for our argument the core of the matter suffices: the presence of God's kingdom in this world is linked with *violence* because there are both proponents and opponents of it.[42] Because of the opponents, the proponents have to use "violence," that is, make great efforts, to get into it, and to maintain it and push it forward. This explains Luke 13:24, where Jesus says, "Strive to enter through the narrow door. For many, I tell you, will seek to enter and will not be able" (cf. Matt. 7:13–14). It takes great effort to enter into God's kingdom because there are opposing forces, both from within the individual (weights that the human sinful nature would like to carry in; cf. Heb. 12:2) and from without: powers that

---

[39] Cf. Frame (2011, 256), in reply to NL2K.

[40] See Ouweneel (2016e, §5.1.2).

[41] See how, e.g., Carson (1984, 265–68) and France (2007, 429–31) deal with various interpretations.

[42] Flusser (2001, 52) chooses the notion of "breaking through," and links this with Micah 2:13 (CJB), "The one breaking through [i.e., Elijah? John the Baptist?] went up before them; they broke through, passed the gate and went out. Their king [i.e., the Messiah] passed on before them; *Adonai* was leading them." However, the Septuagint does not support such a rendering.

try to stop those who desire to come in. Satan does not surrender his prey easily. It is from Satan's domain of *power* (Acts 26:18), from the realm of *darkness* (Col. 1:13; 1 Pet. 2:9), that a person is transferred to the kingdom of God, and this always occurs under opposition on behalf of Satan's empire.

One possible rendering is that God's kingdom "forcefully advances" in the entire world. That is, it cannot be identified with any societal relationship or community in particular, but it breaks in everywhere. The kingdom of God "forcefully advances" in every possible societal relationship where righteousness is sought and maintained according to the principles of God's Word and Christ's dominion.

WORKING IT OUT: **MAKING PUBLIC STRUCTURES MORE BIBLICAL**
Can and should Christians aim at changing social structures, policies, and practices, such that they "fit" more clearly with the Bible?

I can immediately surmise the response of some Christians. God's kingdom is *in* this world, but it is not *of* this world. We are not here to improve society, but to preach the gospel. Jesus and the apostles did the same; they did not try to change the social structures as such. It is more important that the *hearts* of people are changed than that their outward circumstances are changed. What people need is the bread of life—far more than bread for their stomachs.

In principle, I fully agree with these last sentences. Some things are more important than others, and if I had to choose I would rather preach the gospel than help improve external societal structures. However, fortunately I do not have to choose. I think of Jesus' statement: "Woe to you, scribes and Pharisees, hypocrites! For you tithe mint and dill and cumin, and have neglected the weightier matters of the law: justice and mercy and faithfulness. *These you ought to have done, without neglecting the others*" (Matt. 23:23). That is, justice, mercy, and faithfulness are far more important than tithing mint, dill, and cumin—but that does not mean that we should neglect the latter things (figuratively speaking). The very first thing is to preach to the *hearts* of people; but wherever we *can*, we also *should* try to influence their external circumstances.

Imagine a land or a city where most inhabitants are affected by the gospel, and become Christians. On Sundays, you see them streaming by the thousands to their various churches. Now don't you think these people would like to see the effects of their faith from Monday through Saturday too? Don't you think they would like to have fully renewed schools, in which now all the lessons would be given in the light of the kingdom of God? How could believing teachers and believing pupils be together without their teaching and learning being directed by the principles of God's Word?

Don't you think that the atmosphere in the various shops, businesses, and companies would drastically change if both the bosses and most of their employees have become Christians? I believe that they would do business in a different way, and that their businesses would thrive as never before. It is not just that they have become more honest and fair; no, they develop different *principles* of doing business, in which the starting point is not profit-making and gaining wealth, but serving society.

Don't you think that in such a country or city, the atmosphere on the streets would become different? That the judicial system would change, not only because there would be far fewer criminals but also because different principles of justice would be applied? In the courts, judicial justice remains judicial justice; court sessions would not be turned into consistory meetings. But, for instance, punishment would have less the character of revenge, and more the character of education; it would be less directed at breaking the criminal, and more at his rehabilitation (after he has served his deserved years in jail).

Don't you think that in such a country or city, the atmosphere in parliament or city council would drastically change? People would not be ashamed anymore to publicly appeal to Scripture to explain why they wish these or those measures to be adopted, these or those changes to be made. They are so used to the fact that the Word of God encompasses people's entire lives that it would become self-evident to arrange every domain of life according to the principles of God's Word. All legislation would be scrutinized according to Christian principles. This would not be easy, because Christians often differ quite strongly about their Christian principles. But they would work this out in a Christian atmosphere, realizing that debates on Christian principles are always better than functioning without Christian principles at all.

At the same time, these Christians appreciate their Christian freedom so much that they would allow freedom to the Hindu and Muslim citizens as well, who might be living in this same country or city. They would naturally deal with them as they would wish to be dealt with if they lived in a Hindu or Muslim country or city: "Whatever you wish that others would do to you, do also to them, for this is the Law and the Prophets" (Matt. 7:12). At the same time, they would kindly present the gospel to such Hindus and Muslims, so that they may come to the knowledge of the truth. However, this preaching is not the duty of the (Christian) state as such, but of Christian individuals. The state exists to administer public justice for *all* its citizens.

Can Christians aim at changing societal structures according to the Bible? Sure; in many Western countries (and also South American and African countries) there are Christian-democratic parties that often have a chance to take part in coalition governments, and thus have the chance to change circumstances in their countries for the better.

Should Christians aim at changing societal structures according to the Bible? Sure; wherever they get the chance—that is, wherever enough Christian-democratic supporters are available—they should work for a better society, in which Christians can thrive, and non-Christians will be attracted by the Christian principles of such a society.

KINGDOM-CHURCH THEOLOGY[1]

PREPARATORY PONDERINGS

1. In your view, is the (institutional) church a unique phenomenon, or is it in principle just one of many societal relationships (marriage, family, state, school, company, association, political party) that can be just as Christian as the church? Why or why not?
2. Does the kingdom of God come to light more in the church than, e.g., in a Christian family, or in a Christian school, or in a Christian political party? Explain your answer.
3. Try to precisely define what it means that believers are "in the world," but not "of the world." To mention just one aspect: how *can* believers at all function *in* the world if they are not *of* the world?
4. What kind of authority does the church, as such, have over marriages, families, states, schools, companies, associations, political parties? Think, for example, of families within a certain church, or schools founded by certain denominations. Or are all these societal relationships autonomous?

---

[1] On the subject of this chapter, see the much broader treatment in Ouweneel (2016e).

6.1   CHURCH AND KINGDOM[2]

6.1.1   Introduction

The only New Testament writer who has thoroughly explained the church of God is the apostle Paul.[3] Among the letter writers, he is the only one (apart from Heb. 12:23) who uses the Greek term *ekklēsia* in reference to God's worldwide church. However, he is not the only one who has used the term; Matthew 16:18 and 18:17 are the first New Testament occurrences of it. We begin our investigation concerning the relationship between church and kingdom with these passages, and afterward return to Paul.

Sometimes the complaint has been heard: "Jesus preached the kingdom, but what came was the church."[4] The idea, then, is that the church came about when those who waited in vain for the coming of the kingdom unfortunately began organizing themselves into congregations and denominations.[5] If "organizing" means excessive structuring, and especially introversion, linked with a slackening attention to the kingdom of God, this indeed implied a measure of derailment. But at the same time, we realize that Jesus himself has announced his *ekklēsia*, not (only) as a product of an inevitable historical developmental process, and even less as a sign of inner degeneration, but as an organic, spiritual building, that is, distinct from human organizations and denominations. He himself would bring about this building within the framework of the history of God's kingdom.

This is the first reason why the claim is incorrect, not to say absurd, that the church originated out of disappointment among the early Christians. Jesus himself announced the church, and founded her. The second reason why we have to reject the thesis, "Jesus preached the kingdom, but what came was the church," is that it falsely suggests that the church originated out of a *diminished* eschatological expectation. Herman Ridderbos has unmasked this suggestion by emphasizing the permanent eschatological perspective, which on all sides surrounds the church in its expectation and ministry.[6] That is, the kingdom was not *replaced* by the church, nor was it

---

[2] This is an abridged version of parts of Ouweneel (2016e, chapter 7), applied to the problem of NL2K; as to the church, see also extensively, Ouweneel (2010b; 2011).

[3] See extensively, Ouweneel (2010b and 2010c).

[4] Quoted in Ridderbos (1962, 337; see references there; see the entire §36, 342–56). The quote goes back to Alfred Loisy; see Berger (2004, 495–96); Ratzinger (2008, 48).

[5] See Ouweneel (2007b, §13.3.3).

[6] Ridderbos (1962, 355); cf. Van Genderen (2008, 680).

ever *identified* with the church, as NL2K does;[7] on the contrary, the church is one of the glorious harbingers of the kingdom as it will one day arrive in glory and majesty, at the second coming of the King.

It is essential to see that church and kingdom do relate to each other as structure and direction. A church denomination or a local congregation—as fundamentally distinct from the universal, transcendent body of Christ!—is one of the many societal relationships, and as such belongs to the "horizontal" dimension of creation structures. The kingdom of God is a "vertical" matter of direction, which may manifest itself not only in the (visible) church but in any societal relationship, not only in the "age to come" and "world to come," but also in the present age.

6.1.2   "I Will Build My Church"

In the kingdom of God in its present form, the church consists of the true disciples of the glorified King, as opposed to the false confessors. The church could not have existed before the kingdom of Christ existed; and the kingdom of Christ could not have existed before the church existed.[8] Or, to be more precise, we may argue that the kingdom was actually established from the very moment the King had taken his place at the right hand of God (apart from anticipatory statements such as Matt. 12:28; 28:18; and Luke 17:21). The church existed from the moment the Holy Spirit was poured out, by whom the believers were forged together to be one body, one temple (cf. 1 Cor. 12:12–13). The latter event was only ten days after the former event (Acts 1–2).

Many believers do not clearly see the impact of the ascension and glorification of Christ. This is a problem with many studies on the kingdom of God. For instance, David VanDrunen recognizes scarcely any difference between (what he calls) the "redemptive kingdom" in the Old and in the New Testaments.[9] One source of this failure to distinguish is a Christological misunderstanding (see more extensively §8.5.2). People seem to think that Jesus came down from the Father, and simply returned to the Father, and after this forever was and is what he was before. In a sense, this is correct, of course (see, e.g., John 16:28, "I came from the Father and have come into the world, and now I am leaving the world and going to the Father"). Yet, there is an essential difference between his two dwellings in heaven.

---

[7] See, e.g., VanDrunen (2010a, 15, 26, 30–31, etc.).
[8] See extensively, Ouweneel (2010b, especially chapters 2–3).
[9] VanDrunen (2010a, especially Part I).

(a) From eternity, Jesus *had been* with the Father as *God the Son*, the *Logos asarkos* (the "not-[yet-]incarnate Word"): "No one has ever seen God; the only God [or, the only One, who is God], who is at the Father's side, he has made him known" (John 1:18).

(b) In the fullness of time (Gal. 4:4), this person descended as Man (at the same time remaining God the Son), the *Logos sarkos* ("incarnate Word"): "[T]he Word became flesh and dwelt among us, and we have seen his glory, glory as of the only Son from the Father, full of grace and truth" (John 1:14); he became the "man from/of heaven" (1 Cor. 15:47–49).

(c) After he had accomplished his work, he returned to the Father as both God and Man—the glorified Man at God's right hand, forever remaining the *Logos sarkos*: "In him the whole fullness of deity dwells [present tense!] *bodily*" (Col. 2:9). Since the incarnation, it is impossible any longer to speak of the *Logos asarkos*.[10]

We need clear discernment here. From eternity, God the *Son* was in the *bosom* of the Father (1:18 NKJV); in that eternity, there was not yet a Man at the right hand of God. There was only the kingdom of (the Triune) God in a very general, universal, providential sense. However, right now the Son is still in the bosom of the Father (John 1:18), but additionally he is the glorified *Man* on the *throne* of the Father (cf. Rev. 3:21).[11] It is the same person, but these two *states of affairs* are *not* the same. If we allow these matters to be blurred—as if they all amount to the same thing—we will definitely lose sight of the proper meaning of Christ's glorification and Christ's kingdom, with all that this involves.

A glorified Man at the right hand of God—*this* is the first and foremost characteristic of the kingdom of God in the present age. That is, all power has been given to this *Man* in glory: the Father "has given him [i.e., the Son of God] authority to execute judgment, *because he is the Son of Man*" (John 5:27), that is, in this quality. God "has fixed a day on which he will judge the world in righteousness by *a man* whom he has appointed; and of this he has given assurance to all by raising him from the dead" (Acts 17:31). The *Son of Man* is "seated at the right hand of the power of God" (Luke 22:69). And as the *Son of Man* he will one day return with the clouds of heaven to accept the visible dominion over the world (Matt. 24:30; 26:64; cf. 16:28).

---

[10] *Contra* Bolt (1983) and, e.g., VanDrunen (2010c, 153 note 28), who maintains that civil government proceeds from "the Son as Logos, through the work of common, preserving grace, rather than from the Son as Christ." For a response to VanDrunen, see Kloosterman (2012a, chapter 9; on the underlying Christology, see extensively, Ouweneel (2007b).

[11] Notice here the distinction: Christ *now* sits on the *Father's* throne, and the day is coming when he will sit on *his own* throne (i.e., the throne of David; cf. Isa. 9:7; Luke 1:32).

Just as there can be no "redemptive" kingdom of God in the New Testament sense without the Son of Man sitting on the throne of God, so too there can be no church in the New Testament sense—and that is the only sense of "church" that the Bible knows[12]—without the Son of Man sitting on the throne of God, for *as such*, in this quality, he is the head of the body (Eph. 1:20–23). No matter how different church and kingdom are, as we will explain later in this chapter, one thing is certain: in the coming age the one will never exist without the other. They began at virtually the same time (Acts 1–2), and they will both last forever, in clear association with each other.

6.1.3   Calvin's Two Kingdoms

In this connection, it is noteworthy to look at the preliminary title that Tuininga gave to his work: *Christ's Two Kingdoms*.[13] If I understand correctly, NL2K advocates usually speak of *God's* two kingdoms but never of *Christ's* two kingdoms, in which the title "Christ" (i.e., the Anointed One) obviously refers to him as the glorified *Man* at God's right hand (cf. Acts 2:36, "God has made him both Lord and Christ"). According to NL2K, the kingdom of God in the New Testament sense, as it is manifested within the church, is the kingdom of Christ. But the "common kingdom" is the "kingdom of God" only in the general, providential sense of the latter.

Tuininga's study pertains to the two kingdoms as Calvin speaks of them,[14] which is rather different from the way NL2K advocates speak. Before I explain this, let us remember that holding a "two kingdoms" view as such does not make a theologian an NL2K adherent. One may speak of two kingdoms in the sense of Matthew 12:25–28 (the kingdom of Satan and the kingdom of God), or of Augustine (the "two cities"), or of Luther (the "two regiments"), or of Calvin, and none of these different views is identical with that of the modern NL2K position. Thus, in Tuininga's description of Calvin's view, both kingdoms stand under the kingship of the glorified *Christ*, and are subject to his authority. But Christ exercises his kingship in two different ways: there is supposedly a *preservative* kingdom (the political order), and there is a *restorative* kingdom (the spiritual kingdom, which Calvin identifies with the church). Within the latter, Christians begin to experience the full eschatological riches of Christ's kingdom.

---

[12] See note 8.

[13] Tuininga (2016).

[14] See extensively, Tuininga (2016, chapter 4).

Tuininga writes:

At the same time, they [i.e., the Christians] continue to serve God in a fallen, temporal world, whose institutions and cultural phenomena, though governed by Christ's providence and law, are destined to pass away. Thus, in the spirit of self-sacrificial service that characterizes the love of Christ, Christians continue to submit themselves where necessary to temporal institutions, even where these institutions seem to contradict the kingdom's liberty, equality and peace. Some institutions are the expressions of the natural, created order, such as gender and marriage, while others are the products of the fall into sin, such as slavery and coercive civil government. Yet God uses all of these institutions as means of preserving outward or civil righteousness for the welfare of human society. Civil government in particular acts coercively according to the civil use of the law to preserve a modicum of piety, justice and peace. But only the kingdom of Christ restores humans to the spiritual use of the law so as to create inward, spiritual righteousness, the true forms of piety, justice and peace.[15]

I am not going to expand upon this, as Tuininga does, because the purpose of the present book is not to delve deeply into the thought of Luther and Calvin. I mention the point only to show how easily one can adopt and adapt the Reformers' views for one's own purposes. To a certain extent, I could defend the position that I am more on the side of Calvin than are NL2K advocates because Calvin maintains that Christ is Lord of the universe, and that the "preservative" kingdom is also part of *his* rule over humanity. At the same time, NL2K advocates stand with Calvin in agreeing with the latter's distinction between, on the one hand, Christ's rule over all things as divine Creator and Preserver, and on the other hand, Christ's renewal of all things as human Saviour.[16]

I cannot accept this distinction between Christ's sovereignty over all things as the Son of God, and his sovereignty over all things as the glorified Man. Of course, since the incarnation and glorification of Christ, we must still distinguish forever between his divine and his human nature. However, when it comes to his dominion, we cannot make a division within his

---

[15] Tuininga (2016).

[16] Therefore, C. S. Lewis (1973, 42) seems a little too optimistic when he, in the words of Horton (1995, 92), "stated that the transformative impulse in Calvin's thought and life 'sprang from his refusal to allow the Roman [i.e., scholastic] distinction between the life of "religion" and the life of the world.'"

being as if there could be things over which he only rules according to his divine nature, and other things over which he rules according to his human nature. I repeat (see §6.1.2): the Father has given *all* authority to Christ *because he is the Son of Man* (i.e., *in this quality*). God rules the world in righteousness by *a Man* whom he has appointed. The *Son of Man* is seated at the right hand of the power of God, and as the *Son of Man* he will one day return on the clouds of heaven to publicly receive dominion over the world. I see no basis in Scripture for assuming that Christ is presently exercising any dominion without his humanity being involved.

6.2   KINGDOM AND CHURCH

6.2.1   General Relationships

In summary, there can be no kingdom (in the New Testament sense of the term) without a glorified Man at God's right hand, and there can be no church (in the New Testament sense of the term) without a glorified Man at God's right hand. Therefore, in Matthew 16:18 Jesus is still speaking in the future tense about "*my* church," that is, the totality of all who would be followers and servants of Jesus, the true subjects of the kingdom of God.

Both the kingdom and the church are founded upon the very same work of Christ that he accomplished here on earth: the work of glorifying God (in Jesus' own words: John 17:4) and redeeming repentant sinners (Matt. 20:28). Thus, here church and kingdom are distinguished, but not separated. On the contrary, their coherence is clearly implied, especially in two respects. First, immediately after having mentioned his (future) church, Jesus speaks of the keys of the kingdom of heaven that he would give to Peter (Matt. 16:19). Second, in Matthew 18, Jesus' teaching about the (local) "church" (v. 17) stands between his kingdom teaching about "these little ones" (vv. 1–14) and his kingdom teaching about forgiveness (vv. 21–35).

Please note that, in these chapters, we are not yet ready for Paul's teaching on the church; in Matthew, *Jesus' teaching about the church is part of Jesus' teaching about the kingdom*. However, this should not lead us to commit the error of NL2K advocates, namely, that in the present age the church and the kingdom are more or less identical. This is a twofold mistake: on the one hand, it ignores the fact that the kingdom of Christ is also manifested in many other societal relationships in addition to church denominations and local congregations. On the other hand, we should notice that, in Paul's teaching, the church *extends beyond* the kingdom. To give an example: the kingdom of Christ is bound to time; it stands within a perspective that reaches *from* the "foundation of the world" (Matt. 13:35) until the moment that Christ delivers the kingdom to the Father (1 Cor. 15:24). However, the church is the object of God's "eternal purpose" (Eph. 3:11) and encompasses those who have been chosen "*before* the foundation of the world" (1:4), that is, since eternity, and extends into all eternity.

The way Jesus speaks of the "church" in Matthew 18:17 makes it more concrete than in 16:18, for here we encounter the "church" in its everyday form experienced by the common believer: the local, structured (institutionalized) "church" led by elders, in which the Word would be preached, the sacraments would be administered, and church discipline would be maintained. If the trespasser does not listen to the brothers calling him to account, "tell it to the church. And if he refuses to listen even to the church, let him be to you as a Gentile and a tax collector."

6.2.2 Societal Relationships

Perhaps, the local church could be called the most important orderly structured "concentration point" within the kingdom of God. However, we should not overlook the fact that Christian families constitute such "points" just as well. "Let the little children come to me and do not hinder them, for *to such belongs the kingdom of heaven*" (Matt. 19:14). Christian children are not part of the kingdom of God because they are part of the church—this claim is another form of "churchism"[17]—but because they are part of a Christian family. Children are "holy" (on holy ground), not because they have been baptized into the church, but because at least one of their parents is a believer (1 Cor. 7:14). Notice the title "Lord" (implying royal authority; see §§7.1–7.3) in Ephesians 6:4 ("Fathers, do not provoke your children to anger, but bring them up in the discipline and instruction of the Lord") and in Colossians 3:20 ("Children, obey your parents in everything, for this pleases the Lord"). Children in Christian families are living explicitly on the terrain of the kingdom of God. As it has been expressed, the church consists of individual believers, while the kingdom consists of families.

We could go one step further now, for in principle the same is true for Christian schools, companies, societies, political parties, and nation states.[18] The kingdom of God is manifested in many different Christian societal relationships, including the ones just mentioned. The only difference is this: marriages and families are explicitly based on God's creational order; God established them before the Fall (Gen. 1:28; 2:18–25). Christian

---

[17] See chapter 5 note 22; see further, chapter 10.
[18] See extensively, Ouweneel (2014b); cf. Noordegraaf (1980, chapter 7).

schools, companies, societies, political parties, and nation states are the products of humanity's cultural-historical activities. But even these cannot be severed from God's creational order,[19] for, as Kuyperian theology and philosophy emphasized,[20] they are the fruits of God's cultural mandate, given both before the Fall ("The LORD God took the man and put him in the garden of Eden to work it and keep it," 2:15) and after the Fall ("the LORD God sent him out from the garden of Eden to work the ground from which he was taken," 3:23).

No matter how this may be viewed, the kingdom of God does not only consist of Christian individuals, but also encompasses the societal relationships in which Christian individuals function, insofar as these relationships have been submitted to the commandments of Christ. I repeat, the *church* consists of individual believers—members of the body of Christ—but the *kingdom* consists of (or, if you like, is manifested in) marriages and families, schools and companies, and so on, insofar as they are "in the Lord" (cf. 1 Cor. 7:39; Col. 3:18–20), that is, submitted to his "lord"-ship (see again §§7.1–7.3). When, some time from now, the Sun of righteousness rises (Mal. 4:2; cf. Matt. 17:2; Acts 26:13; Rev. 1:16), the "day" of God's kingdom will rise over the earth in splendour and glory (Rom. 13:12; 1 Thess. 5:1–8; 2 Pet. 1:19). At present, it is still "night," in which, however, truly Christian marriages and families, truly Christian schools and companies, and so on, that is, societal relationships that are "in the Lord," will shine as bright lights (cf. Matt. 5:14–16; Phil. 2:16), harbingers of the coming glorious kingdom.

In the explanation just given, a church denomination or a (local) church—not the transcendent body of Christ!—has been mentioned as one of the many societal relationships in which Christians function. In this respect, this clearly differs from the kingdom of God: the (local) church is just one of these relationships, but the kingdom of God encompasses them all. In my view, every theology concerning the relationship between church and kingdom will fail if this distinction is not made. The (local) church is not more than one of an entire series of societal relationships that Christians form within the framework of God's kingdom as a result of God's creational command. From a purely phenomenological point of view, it is an association with members, leaders, membership fees, boards, a place of gathering, an agenda, a calendar, and so on, just like any other association. However, from a faith perspective, it is *the* immanent expression of the transcendent body of Christ.

---

[19] I emphasized this with regard to the state in §§4.4.2 and 5.2.1.

[20] For a standard work on this, see Kuyper's "Stone Lectures" (Kuyper [2009]).

6.2.3 The Church over against the Kingdom?

The kingdom exists and functions wherever the lordship of Christ is acknowledged and obeyed: in individual lives and in many societal relationships, of which the local church is only one. However, it cannot be denied that the church does play a pivotal role in the kingdom: it is *here* that the preaching of the Word occurs and sheds light on all the other societal relationships in which Christians function. Therefore, John Calvin saw the church as the centre from which God's dominion takes shape in the various relationships of our earthly lives.[21] To say it with Augustine: here in the church, something of the *civitas Dei*, the "city" or "state of God," is already becoming visible.

The view of, for instance, the Montanists (second/third century) and the Anabaptists (sixteenth century), that there is a *contrast* between the (established) church and the kingdom of God, has become a minority view, and rightly so. Of course, it is appropriate to protest all the secularization that has occurred in the established churches (Roman Catholic, Eastern Orthodox, Lutheran, Calvinist, Anglican, Baptist, etc.) as well as in Evangelical free churches. However, this does not constitute a contrast with the kingdom of God because, in the present age, this kingdom in its outward form, just like the "visible church," has become a mixture of good and evil as well, consisting of true and false worshipers. Protests against the established church(es) do not bring Christians any closer to the kingdom of God,[22] because by definition such Christians are, and remain, part of the Christian world, or the "visible church." Christians cannot leave the Christian world without ceasing to be Christians. They may try to form congregations of truly born-again and devoted believers, but they will not succeed; after a decade or so they will be like all the rest, as church history has proven many times. The body of Christ is holy; but in practice there are no purely holy (unmixed) congregations and denominations.

Both the church and the kingdom can be defined in a wider and in a narrower sense. In the wider sense, the "(visible) church" is the Christian world, which coincides with the kingdom of God in its wider sense. This is the "church" as it is portrayed, for instance, in the seven churches of Asia (Rev. 2 and 3), of which at least five were such unhappy mixtures of good and evil. In the narrower sense, the kingdom of God comprises only the regenerated (John 3:3, 5), and the church is the "holy gathering of the true believers in Christ" (see above). In this sense, the church stands in

---

[21] Graafland (1973, 52).
[22] Küng (2001, 88–96).

opposition to all false Christians ("false brothers," 2 Cor. 11:26; Gal. 2:4; cf. 1 Cor. 5:11), and all non-Christians. However, the kingdom's "field" is emphatically "the world" (Matt. 13:38; see §5.3.2 and following). To illustrate the point I am making, we need only think here of the Holy Spirit: the Spirit's present *dwelling place* on earth is the church of God (1 Cor. 3:16; Eph. 2:20–22), but his *field of operation* is the entire world. Where we find the kingdom of God (in its true, inward form), we find the Spirit working, and where the Spirit is working, we find the kingdom of God.

Essentially, the church comprises only true believers in Christ; the kingdom comprises all people who (truly or falsely) have accepted the dominion of Christ in their lives. One could call the church a *sign* of the kingdom:[23] what has become reality in the church will one day become reality in the entire world. Today, every knee in the church bows before Jesus, while soon *all* inhabitants of the earth will bow their knees before him (cf. Phil. 2:10; cf. Isa. 45:23; Matt. 27:29; Rom. 14:11). Because of its sign character, the church is continually oriented toward the world: the disciples of Christ are the "salt of the earth" and the "light of the world" (Matt. 5:13–14). This comes to light also in Christian families, Christian schools, Christian companies, Christian associations, Christian political parties, and so forth.

One could say the same thing in the following way. Today, the kingdom is on a small scale what one day it will be on a worldwide scale. Through the Holy Spirit, it is today a sphere of true divine *righteousness* in the midst of a world full of unrighteousness. It is a sphere of true divine *peace* in the midst of a world full of war and violence. It is a sphere of true divine *joy* in the midst of a world full of sadness and mourning (Rom. 14:17). One day, the entire world will be filled with true divine righteousness, peace, and joy (cf. Isa. 9:7; 32:17; 55:12).

6.3   THE CHURCH AND THE COMING KINGDOM

6.3.1   "*In* the World"

When we say that Jesus' disciples are the "salt of the earth" and the "light of the world" (see previous section), we do well to remember that, in practice, the church is rarely this salt and light *as church*. Again, we have to beware of churchism (ecclesiasticism) here. It is not "the church" (in its quality as church) that founds Christian schools, companies, societies, and political parties; the church does not do arts, or science, or politics; the church does

---

[23] Heyns (1988, 353–54).

not establish a judicial or economic order. It is always individual believers who do this kind of work.[24] They do so either individually, or they organize themselves in Christian cooperative associations (school boards, labour councils, boards of directors, etc.) to do Christian work.

It is not even "the church" (in its quality as church) that preaches and evangelizes,[25] that is, that extends the kingdom of God in this world, but individual believers do so, personally or (usually) collectively through gospel societies, missionary organizations, and so on (even if church *denominations* may found their own schools, gospel societies, etc.). More concretely, strictly speaking, individual Christians do not do such missionary work in their capacity as members of Christ's body but in their role as disciples in God's kingdom (cf. Matt. 28:18–20). Not every arbitrary group of Christians can be called "church,"[26] although they may all be members of the same congregation or of the same church denomination.

Reformed theologian Johan Heyns has well formulated this state of affairs by emphasizing that the Christian family, the Christian school, the Christian cultural association, the Christian state, Christian science and art are all manifestations of the kingdom. As such they are not "church," neither the church as "organism," nor the church as "organization" or "institution." There is an ecclesiastical manifestation of God's kingdom in the form of church denominations and local congregations, but there are also many non-ecclesiastical manifestations of God's kingdom.[27]

Jesus' disciples always perform their tasks under the tension mentioned earlier: as those who are *in* the world but not *of* the world (John 17:11, 14, 16, 18). The kingdom is "not of this world," as Jesus himself emphasized to Pilate (18:36); it is not from "below" but from "above." However, at the same time the world is a domain that is seasoned with the salt of this kingdom. Being "in the world" implies that believers take part in Christian, and even so-called neutral schools, companies, associations and political parties, and in (strongly secularized) politics, arts and sciences. It seems to me that, in principle, there is no function within ordered society that

---

[24] Cf. VanDrunen (2010a, 11–12, "…what responsibilities your church might have with respect to contemporary political controversies or economic development"; but also 117, "I distinguish between the work and life of *the church* and the work and life of *individual believers* (or group of believers) as they make their way in this world").

[25] Cf. Horton (1995, 13): "The institutional church has been given the unique commission to preach the Word and make disciples." The term "church" is mistaken here, but the phrase "institutional church" makes the statement even worse.

[26] Those who propagate "house churches" (or "home churches") may feel differently; cf. Ouweneel (2010b, §1.3).

[27] Heyns (1988, 354).

could not be fulfilled by a Christian. (I am not talking about the "under[!] world" of prostitution and crime.) But this is not the same as saying that "the church" fulfills these functions.

Please note: church consistories (councils of elders, etc.) do not fulfill the kingdom tasks of raising children, teaching, conducting business, pursuing politics, producing art, doing science. They are not even *called* to do such things. Individual Christians, or Christian organizations, are called to do these things. Not "the church" (or whatever church denomination) as such extends God's kingdom in this world—individual Christians, or Christian organizations, do so. They do so not in their capacity as members of Christ's body, but *in their capacity as disciples of Jesus*.[28] Of course we may not separate here; but we should certainly distinguish.

6.3.2 The Breadth of the Kingdom

In this context, it is of interest that Reformed theologian Herman Ridderbos has defined the kingdom as "not narrow but wide," as wide as the entire creation. Believers are free in Christ to take part in the entire life of eating and drinking, marrying, learning and teaching, buying and selling, painting and sculpting, reigning and being reigned, and so on. But, he argues, in this "Christian freedom" there lies a "Christian mission," for believers must be in the service of God, and thus of God's creation, humanity in particular.[29]

Reformed dogmatician Herman Bavinck emphasized that the kingdom is not "organized," at least not here on earth. In principle, the kingdom exists wherever the spiritual benefits of Christ have been granted, and nowhere on earth is the kingdom finished and completed. But the church is—Bavinck should have said: (individual) believers are—the means through which Christ distributes the benefits of the kingdom in the world, and prepares the completion of the kingdom.[30]

At any specific moment, the church is a "given," consisting of the total number of all true believers as known by God who are at that moment alive on earth. In such a sense, the kingdom is never a "given." It is a far more fluid concept. The kingdom is like "the Spirit of God hovering over the face of the waters" (Gen. 1:3), touching and driving people, all the time changing people and various societal relationships, "turning" the hearts of kings (presidents, prime ministers) as a "stream of water" (cf. Prov. 21:1), driving the "chariots" of the world powers between "mountains of bronze" (Zech.

---

[28] Discipleship is a highly neglected subject, and thus one that is little understood, especially by "ecclesiasticists"; see extensively, Ouweneel (2016e, especially chapter 6).

[29] Ridderbos (1995); cf. Spykman (1992, 479–80).

[30] Bavinck (*RD* 4:298).

6:1), reviving backsliding followers of Jesus, admonishing and encouraging them, constantly fighting the good fight against the powers of darkness.

Reformed theologian Geerhardus Vos emphasized that Jesus considered every normal and legitimate domain of human life as intended to form a part of God's kingdom.[31] This reminds us of Kuyper's earlier statement: "There is not a square inch in the whole domain of our human existence over which Christ, who is Sovereign over *all*, does not cry: 'Mine!'"[32] Therefore, the scope of God's kingdom must not be restricted in any way, says Reformed theologian Al Wolters, as would happen if we would divide the world up into a sacred part and a profane (secular, common) part, or if we would limit the kingdom to personal godliness, to the institutional church, to the eschatological future, or to humanitarian aspirations.[33]

There are indeed limitations to the church in its true New Testament sense: only genuine believers are part of it. However, there are no limitations to the kingdom: it may be defined as the totality of Christian confessors, but it may also be defined as encompassing God's entire creation. "The earth is the LORD's and the fullness thereof, the world and those who dwell therein" (Ps. 24:1; cf. 1 Cor. 10:26). "The earth shall be full of the knowledge of the LORD as the waters cover the sea" (Isa. 11:9; cf. Hab. 2:14). This will be completely true in the "age to come," but the present "age" is the prelude to it.

6.3.3 "Not *of* the World"

The kingdom of God is not merely "in the world," but it is *everywhere* in the world. At the same time, being "not *of* the world" means that the disciple of Jesus is always confronted with the activity of sin and Satan in the various societal relationships, and this always leads to tensions. As the apostle Paul puts it, believers are "children of God without blemish in the midst of a crooked and twisted generation, among whom you shine as lights in the world" (Phil. 2:15). Not *of* the world: that is, without blemish *in opposition* to the crooked and the twisted—but certainly *in* the world: without blemish *in the midst* of the crooked and the twisted, sometimes intermingled with them in an outwardly inextricable way, as iron particles may be mixed with grains of sand (cf. the metaphor of Dan. 2:43, though it is used here with a different meaning). Yet, the great difference comes to light when a strong magnet is moved above the mixture because it will attract the iron but not the sand.

---

[31] Vos (1903, 88).

[32] For the source reference, see chapter 2 note 40.

[33] Wolters (1985, 60–61, 65).

It is quite helpful to keep in mind here the distinction between the two "perpendicular" dimensions of *structure* and *direction*, which I have dealt with above (§§3.2.2 and 4.5).[34] The term *structure* has to do with the creational structures, the structural laws that God has instituted for the various creatures and cosmic modalities, and also for the societal relationships within creation. *Direction* is a dimension that is, so to speak, perpendicular to that of structure; it involves the directedness of any entity, event, or state of affairs. There are numerous structures, but there are only two directions: either the positive direction toward the Creator and his honour, or the apostate direction, away from the Creator, to his dishonour.

These two dimensions help us understand the position of Christians in the present world. They take part in *all* the structures of creation, without any exception. This is the universality of the kingdom. However, they do so in a dimension that is, despite considerable weakness, opposite to that of unbelievers. Believers are active *in* society, and also *for* society, but not for their, or its, own glory. They are active in view of that to which society is en route: the kingdom of God in power and glory. There are secular (and falsely-religious) families, secular (and falsely-religious) schools, secular (and falsely-religious) companies, secular (and falsely-religious) associations, and so forth, and there are truly Christian families, Christian schools, Christian companies, Christian associations, and so on. The former serve their own interests only; the latter—if they properly fulfill their duties—serve the interests of God and of Christ and his kingdom. The form of families, schools, companies, associations, and so on, has to do with *structure*; the orientation of secular (and falsely-religious) versus Christian has to do with *direction*.

In the church, society sees its own religious destination reflected, as it were (at least if it has enlightened eyes to perceive this, and if the church to some extent fulfills its duty).[35] That is, if unbelievers would only wish to see it—or would be able to see it—they would behold in (the bright and beautiful character of) the church what the entire world will look like one day. The Christian never accepts the world as it is, but only as it must become, and one day *will* become. He stands in the midst of the world, but with his heart he lives already in the "world to come" (Heb. 2:5) and in the "age to come" (Mark 10:30; Luke 18:30; Eph. 1:21; Heb. 6:5). He knows that, even in the power of the Spirit, he will never bring about this new world all on his own, not even with the help of millions of other Christians. But

---

[34] Cf. Ouweneel (2014b, chapter 4)
[35] Cf. Heyns (1988, 373).

he also knows that, in the power of the Spirit, he may endeavour to bring this world as close to its goal as he can. He knows that the end result will be one hundred percent the Lord's work. But he works as if the end result will be one hundred percent his responsibility. He knows that, in this age, he will never reach "the goal," yet he "presses on" as if he could (cf. Phil. 3:14).

6.4 VARIOUS VIEWS

6.4.1 Reformed

(a) Herman Bavinck claimed that the church is a notion of present-day (German: *diesseitige*, "this-worldly") significance, and the kingdom is especially an eschatological ("other-worldly") notion. Therefore, the church is "organized," and the kingdom is not.[36] The church consists of a definite number of people, but the kingdom is wherever Christ is working through his Spirit.

There is some truth in these descriptions, yet, in my view, they are not sufficiently accurate. First, the former is valid only for *organized* churches (denominations and local congregations), not for the body of Christ, the "holy gathering of true believers in Christ." Any organized church and this "holy gathering" at best overlap; there are many denominations but there is only one body of Christ. To make it even more complicated, I fear that almost all local churches do not contain only believers, whereas in most cases genuine believers in a certain locale are divided among several organized churches. And as far as the kingdom is concerned, to a certain extent it too is "definite" as either consisting of all Christian confessors, or as covering the entire world. As such, the kingdom is even more easily identifiable than the church as the "holy gathering of all true believers."

Second, I do not think the contrast between "present-day" ("this-worldly") and "eschatological" ("other-worldly") is felicitous. Both church and kingdom belong to both the "present world" and to the "world to come," that is, they are both "this-worldly" and "eschatological." In addition, the church should not be viewed too much as a static entity, in contrast with a dynamic (continually developing) kingdom.[37]

(b) Louis Berkhof believed that the operative sphere of God's kingdom is wider than that of the church because the kingdom strives to dominate life

---

[36] Bavinck (*RD* 4:297–98); cf. also chapter 7, "The Church's Spiritual Power" (4:389–440) on the power of the church in relation to the kingdom.

[37] Cf. Berkhof (1986, 415–17).

in all its manifestations.[38] He called the visible church the most important external organization of the kingdom, and the only one instituted by God. We have seen that the latter cannot be right: marriage, the family, and even the state have been instituted by God as well, in principle all three before the Fall.[39] In those situations where marriage, the family, and the state are manifested in their Christian character, they are all three just as much organized forms of God's kingdom as the institutional church. I leave aside here Christian schools, Christian companies, Christian associations, Christian political parties, and so on, which are not based on explicit institutions by God but are definitely fruits of God's "creation mandate" (see §3.1).

Moreover, Berkhof virtually identified the (invisible) church and the kingdom of God so much so that it seems as if "kingdom" is one of the special names of the church, just like body, house, and bride.[40] In this way, the relationship between the two is not properly presented, though. The kingdom of God is a wider notion than the church, which at best is the core of the kingdom, as Berkhof himself said.

(c) Johan Heyns called the church (a) a *sign* of the kingdom, (b) a *part* of the kingdom ("the fighting vanguard and a triumphant fragment of God's kingdom"), and (c) a hint of (harbinger of) the *fullness* of the kingdom.[41] This seems to me a succinct and, though not entirely accurate, yet appropriate approach to the matter.

6.4.2 Views other than Reformed

(d) George Ladd compared kingdom and church such that the kingdom is the rule of God, and the church the group of people living under this rule.[42] This description does not strike me as very accurate. It seems to me the notion of "kingdom," taken very generally, always involves more than a rule as such; it also involves a King, a territory, and a number of subjects. The laws of a kingdom never constitute that kingdom as such (in Dooyeweerdian language: it is a confusion of the law-side and the subject-side of the kingdom).

As we have seen, the "territory" of the kingdom is either (1) the totality of

---

[38] L. Berkhof (1996, 569); here is what he wrote: "The Kingdom may be said to be a broader concept than the Church, because it aims at nothing less than the complete control of all the manifestations of life. It represents the dominion of God in every sphere of human endeavor" (570).

[39] See Ouweneel (2014a).

[40] L. Berkhof (1996, 569); we say "virtually" because this is what he wrote: "While the Kingdom of God and the invisible Church are *in a measure identical*, they should nevertheless be carefully *distinguished*" (630; italics added).

[41] Heyns (1988, 353–55).

[42] Ladd (1964, 259–60); cf. Erickson (1998, 1051–52).

all the regenerated (John 3:5), or (2) the totality of all Christian confessors (wheat and weeds, wise and foolish virgins, etc.), or (3) the entire world: the "field" of the kingdom is the "world" (Matt. 13:38).

(e) Wolfhart Pannenberg pointed out that the church is not simply identical with the imperfect original form of the kingdom of God, because this would mean that church and kingdom in the end would coincide.[43] The church is a company of people who rejoice in the coming kingdom, and to whom the preaching of the kingdom has been entrusted.

Here, too, the description is inaccurate. First, recall that it is not "the church" that preaches but the teachers and preachers of the church, who not only address the world, but also the church itself. Second, the emphasis is here again on the eschatological character of the kingdom. In this way, it remains unclear how the church relates to the kingdom of God in its *present* form.

(f) The same holds for Hans Küng, who sees the church as a "fore-sign" of the (coming) kingdom of God.[44]

(g) Jürgen Moltmann sees the church as the "anticipation" of the (coming) kingdom.[45] This is acceptable as far as it goes; we cannot adequately emphasize the significance of the kingdom as it will one day be established in power and majesty. But it is equally important to emphasize the significance of the kingdom in its present form, as encompassing all those who have submitted their lives to the rule of Christ, the guidance of the Holy Spirit, and the authority of God's Word.

6.4.3   Summary of Kingdom Teaching

The kingdom of God in its present form is the dominion of Christ over the entire creation, hiding behind, but also being manifested in, all governing authorities in this world, who are therefore "servants" of God (Rom. 13:4; cf. Prov. 21:1). More specifically, the kingdom involves the rule of Christ over the hearts and lives of all those who confess to follow and serve him, whether they truly serve him or not. After all, there are true and false disciples, good and evil servants, good and bad fishes, there is wheat and weeds, obedient sons and disobedient sons, wise and foolish virgins.

---

[43] Pannenberg (2009, 30–32).

[44] See Küng (2001).

[45] Moltmann (1975); also see Zorn (1962); Pannenberg (2009, chapter 12); Saucy (1997, 239–47); Lohfink (1998); Eggenberg (2010).

This rule concerns individual believers, but also the societal relationships that they form: marriages, families, church denominations and local congregations, nation states, associations, schools, companies, political parties, unions, leagues, clubs, and so forth. That is, Christ is King of every Christian family, of every Christian state (if such a thing exists), of every Christian school, of every Christian company, and so on.

As we have seen, in its broadest sense the kingdom of God comprises the entire creation, or the entire human race. In a somewhat narrower sense it comprises all those who maintain a Christian confession, or the Christian world. In the narrowest sense, the kingdom of God is the totality of all disciples of Christ who are truly born again (John 3:5). Similarly, the church in its broadest sense comprises the entire Christian world, or at least the totality of all professing Christians who are members of local congregations (sometimes called the "visible church"); at present, this is about one third of the world population. In the narrower sense, it is the body of Christ, which contains only true believers, those who are born again and have been sealed with the Holy Spirit.[46]

Whatever description of God's kingdom we choose, we are dealing with categories that are very different from the church as the holy gathering of all true believers of Christ, the body of Christ, the house or temple of God on earth, the bride of the Lamb. In *Christian* families, schools, companies, political parties, societies, and so on, usually not everybody is a regenerated believer; in the body of Christ, by definition everybody is (cf. the Belgic Confession, Art. 27). Moreover, the Christian's *character* is different: in the kingdom of God, regenerated Christians are followers (disciples) and servants of Christ, in the church they are members of the body. To all intents and purposes, the differences are tremendous.[47] The kingdom of God in its present form consists of disciples of Christ, good and evil ones, whereas the body of Christ consists of Spirit-sealed believers. The latter may be spiritual but can also be carnal (Gal. 5:16–26). However, this is something essentially different from the wicked servant of the King, who in the end is cast into the "outer darkness," where there will be "weeping and gnashing of teeth" (Matt. 8:12; 22:13; 25:30), or the foolish virgins, who in the end find the door to the marriage feast shut (25:10–12).

---

[46] This is sometimes called the "invisible church," although, strictly speaking, this is an immanent notion, whereas the body of Christ is a transcendent notion; see Ouweneel (2010b).

[47] See again Ouweneel (2010b, chapter 6).

6.5 EIGHT SOCIETAL RELATIONSHIPS

6.5.1 Autonomy

As we have seen, each of the eight (?) types of societal relationships is relatively autonomous.[48] The state has the responsibility to administer *public justice* (see §6.6.1), and thus to create the outward conditions under which churches can operate. But the state does not meddle in the internal affairs of churches (or synagogues, or mosques, or temples). The same is true for marriages, families, schools, associations, political parties, and so on: each is relatively autonomous within its own boundaries, and should be free from interference from either the state or the church. Even a Roman Catholic or a Reformed Christian school is not to be run by Roman Catholic or Reformed church leaders *as such*, but by Roman Catholic or Reformed *school leaders*.

This is very important. The notion of a Christian state does *not* imply that Christian authorities enforce Christian values upon its citizens, but that they administer public justice in a Christian way. The notion of a Christian school does *not* imply that Christian teachers force Christian values down their pupils' throats, but that they teach and educate according to Christian principles. The notion of a Christian political party does not imply that Christian politicians derive the answers to political issues directly from the Bible—this would be possible only in a very limited number of cases—but that they do politics on the basis of a Christian worldview and its associated biblical principles, specifically a Christian view of the state and of politics.

Let us look a bit more closely at this notion of societal relationship autonomy. For instance, the state as such—Christian or not—has nothing to say about what goes on in people's bedrooms, or how parents educate their children,[49] about how schools teach pupils, about with whom companies will do business, about whether women are to be allowed to preach, and so on. But the state does administer *public justice*, so it does have something to say about husbands raping their wives, about killing infants in their mothers' wombs, about parents or teachers abusing the children entrusted to them, about the academic quality of education in schools, about companies that operate illegally, about churches having loud praise meetings in the middle of the night, and so on.

---

[48] This is what Kuyper (1880) called "sphere sovereignty;" personally, I prefer the term "autonomous" to "sovereign," mainly because I would like to reserve the latter term for God.

[49] Cf. VanDrunen (2010a, 198); he speaks of "limited government."

In the worst case scenario, a state ruling over its citizens' private lives, their marriages, their churches, the way they educate children, a state that in fact owns all the schools and all the companies, is a dictatorial, and often even terrorizing, system. This totalitarian system is found in communist countries, and also in Muslim countries ruled according to *Shari'ah* law. It is totally against the Christian notion of the state as a strictly juridical system. In the Christian view, the state creates the necessary legal preconditions for the optimal functioning of societal life, but at the same time guarantees the freedom and unique responsibility of its citizens, individually as well as in their religious organizations, families, schools, companies, associations, and so on.

The state can easily go wrong here. Socialism has ideological reasons for giving too much authority to the state, that is, for giving the state too many responsibilities that actually belong to the citizens. Classic liberalism (the foundation of libertarianism) does the opposite: it has ideological reasons for minimizing the state's authority, so that the state cares too little about those citizens who are hardly able to stand on their own feet (the weak, the sick, the aged, the disabled, etc.), or who have no other people to help them. In a Christian view of the state, both ideological pathways, commonly identified today as socialism and libertarianism, are fundamentally rejected. In such a Christian view of politics, the power of the state involves only "public justice" (see below), but this does include looking after the weak, as we will see later.

6.5.2 The Limits of the State

Darryl Hart[50] has not understood anything of this. In the words of John Frame: "Hart's main argument…against Christian politics, is that it inevitably leads to such unsoluble questions [e.g., may Catholics be permitted to hold office?]. Christianity is an exclusive, intolerant faith, and so it cannot support a general social policy which, by definition, must be open to all faiths and to secularists as well." [51] Frame rightly responds that such problems have developed throughout history, "but I don't believe that they are a *necessary* consequence of Christian social action."

I would say: on the contrary. It is one of the basic mistakes of Hart that he can imagine a "Christian" state only as a totalitarian state, and therefore opposes it. He does not discern that it is precisely a *Christian* ideal to strive for a state that is not totalitarian but that has understood where its

[50] Hart (2006, passim).
[51] Frame (2011, 263).

boundaries lie: it guarantees the freedom of its citizens by limiting itself to the maintenance of public justice, and nothing more. It may still be hard enough to define what public justice exactly entails (see §6.6.1)—but we honour this boundary.

Also when it comes to the church's sphere of influence and authority, it is important to emphasize the meaning of the autonomy of societal relationships. I said that the state should not rule over the church, but the opposite is also true: the church—that is, any church denomination—should not rule over the state. This happened in medieval Roman Catholic Europe, where the church could condemn someone for (alleged) heresy, and then hand him over to the state to be executed. Today, that would be unthinkable in any civilized country. Actually, the situation in Islamic Iran is largely like this. Here, the spiritual leaders, the *ayatollahs*, hold the real political power, and the president is subservient to them. Many Christians are afraid of the notion of a Christian state because they think that such a state will look very similar to such an Islamic state. This is one of the reasons why NL2K prefers the neutral (or secular, or common) state. This is because it has not grasped the notion of "public justice," and the specific way Christian authorities give shape to this "public justice" (see further §§6.6 and 12.2).

6.5.3 Other Societal Relationships

I trust it will be clear by now that the notion of the autonomy of societal relationships does not pertain only to churches and states. The entire debate about the separation of church and state has focused our attention too exclusively on these two institutions. In my view, this is one reason why NL2K speaks of two kingdoms, instead of distinguishing at least four divinely instituted realms: church, state, marriage, and family, all four of them autonomous with respect to each other. NL2K should at least have been a "four realms" theology, and actually an "eight realms" theology, because no civilized society is conceivable without schools, companies, associations, and political parties. It is totally unacceptable to lump all non-church societal relationships together into one "realm," the so-called "common kingdom." This is nothing but churchism (or ecclesiasticism: the absolutization of the church denomination or the local congregation over the other societal relationships).

In historical cases in which the state ruled over the church, the state in the Western world was usually considered to be a "Christian" state (just like Iran, where the *ayatollahs* are in charge, is a Muslim state).[52] In such

---

[52] I know of only two Jewish states in post-biblical times, before 1948. One was the Himyarite

a situation, no one considered either the state or the church to be neutral. But what about all the other societal relationships or communities, such as families, schools, associations, companies, and political parties (insofar as some of these relationships could exist in those days)? Could these ever be religiously neutral?

Here I have to emphasize again that there are no neutral people, or common societal relationships. The state ought not to be under the authority of any church. But that does not alter the fact that the people who exercise the state's authority are always *religious* people—in the broadest sense of the term, which includes even political ideologies and atheism—whether they like it or not. That is, they stand before God as his servants (Rom. 13), whether they acknowledge this or not. They will have to give an account to him. The church (or the synagogue, or the mosque, for that matter) does not have the monopoly on religion! *All* people are religious in the sense of being oriented toward some Ultimate Ground of certainty and confidence, whether this is God or particular idols and ideologies. Therefore, not only churches but also states, schools, companies, associations, and so on, are responsible to God, and have to give account to him.

In fact, in the United States, the two major parties, Republican and Democrat, have always implicitly recognized that politics is not religiously neutral. How else could we explain that, traditionally, the great majority of Protestants in the northeast have historically voted Republican, whereas the great majority of Roman Catholics, Jews, African-Americans, as well as Protestants in the south have historically voted Democrat? The reason for this is a fascinating subject in its own right; the discussion of it would carry us too far afield. Suffice it to say that religion obviously plays a role in American politics, as can be seen in the political choices people make, even if the Republican and Democrat parties are not explicitly Christian parties.

6.6 THE KINGDOM AND GOD'S RIGHTEOUSNESS

6.6.1 Public Justice

In order to explain the various aspects of this important subject in more detail, I believe that the following notions need to be discussed: (a) the notion of *public justice*, as a fundamental principle in Christian politics (which Thomas Aquinas sometimes referred to as the "common good,"

---

kingdom in ancient Yemen (c. AD 380–527), the other was the Khazar kingdom in the North Caucasus during the high Middle Ages.

Latin: *bonum commune*); (b) the notion of *theocracy*, one of the most mis-understood principles in Christian politics (cf. §5.1.3); (c) the notion of Christians being *exiles and pilgrims* in this world (Eph. 2:19; cf. 1 Pet. 1:1; see more extensively chapter 8); and (d) the Lutheran notion of the *two regiments* (cf. §7.4.2). This will be our agenda for some of the following sections in this book.

Public justice is a facet of biblical justice or righteousness, which is a vital element within the kingdom of God. When the Lord Jesus says, "Seek first his [i.e., God's] kingdom and his righteousness" (Matt. 6:33), he is apparently referring to righteousness, both public and private justice, as a matter that touches the essence of God's kingdom. It is said of the Messiah, "See, a king will reign in righteousness and rulers will rule with justice" (Isa. 32:1; cf. 9:7; 11:4–5). These terms, *righteousness* and *justice*, do not refer just to the future new heavens and new earth, although it is said that righteousness will dwell there (2 Pet. 3:13). If it were only a notion for the future, how then could the Christian be called to pursue God's kingdom and his righteousness—privately but also publicly—already today? Sure, there is a big difference: in the end, righteousness will rule when all unrighteousness will have been eradicated, and all powers of unrighteousness will have been destroyed. Today, we seek righteousness in the midst of, and in opposition to, a world full of unright-eousness; this is the "pursuing" of righteousness of which Solomon (Prov. 15:9), Isaiah (Isa. 51:1), and Paul (1 Tim. 6:11; 2 Tim. 2:22) speak.

When Paul refers in Romans 14:17 to the kingdom of God, he definitely speaks of it as a present reality, and yet as a kingdom that is "a matter of... righteousness and peace and joy in the Holy Spirit." He says this in spite of all unrighteousness, all disharmony and disorder, all the battles and conflicts, and all the sadness and emptiness still around us. In the midst of all this, Paul maintains, there *is* a realm of righteousness, peace, and joy, which are concretely realized in the power of the Holy Spirit. This is not the church, but the kingdom of God. And when Jesus speaks about the kingdom in *his* day, he sees it as an empire that is "forcefully advancing" (Matt. 11:12 NIV note; see §§5.1.4 and 5.5.3), that is, a kingdom that is introducing God's righteousness into this world, in opposition to all the "violent people raiding it," all powers of unrighteousness that seek to stop and overwhelm this kingdom.

6.6.2 Sharing in the Spirit

Of course, no nation state is identical with the kingdom of God, for this kingdom involves a kind of righteousness that reaches much farther than simply the domain of public justice. The kingdom of God "forcefully advances" in civic life wherever and whenever authorities and citizens bow before God's Word and the authority of Christ. It does so even when only some of the magistrates and citizens respect God's Word. In doing so, they still put the mark of God's kingdom—no matter how imperfectly—on the functioning of the state.

Similarly, the kingdom of God "forcefully advances" in marriages and families, wherever and whenever husband and wife, parents and children, bow before God's Word and the authority of Christ. Even if only one of the marriage partners bows before God's Word, this one person puts the mark of God's kingdom on that marriage and that entire family. This is, I presume, the sense of 1 Corinthians 7:14, where Paul argues—in my words—that the believing wife places the stamp of God's Word on her marriage or family in such a way that her husband and children are "sanctified" and "holy," respectively. Even if these children have an unregenerate heart, they still dwell in the hallowed atmosphere of the kingdom of God, where God's Word reverberates and the Holy Spirit is working.

Even pseudo-Christians, who eventually "fall away," have for a time "shared in the Holy Spirit" (Heb. 6:4; they have been "partakers of the Holy Spirit," ASV). This does not necessarily imply that the Holy Spirit has *dwelt* in these people—which is the case only for true believers (1 Cor. 6:19)—but that they have been in the atmosphere of the kingdom of God: that blessed domain where God's Word is preached and his Spirit is working. We often find it hard to imagine what the unfettered preaching of God's Word can do in a society. It is no wonder that Satan tries to push religion to the very edge of society (secularization)—he knows the power of that Word and that Spirit! In their spiritual battle, believers use "the sword of the Spirit, which is the word of God" (Eph. 6:17).

In a similar way, the kingdom of God is "forcefully advancing" in schools and companies, associations and political parties, wherever God's Word, the measuring-rod of God's righteousness, is maintained and observed, no matter how weakly. Perhaps only a few of the teachers, or the employers, or the administrators in such societal relationships, are followers and servants of the King. However, through their testimony and their obedience to the Word of God and the dominion of Christ—in education, management, and administration—they should be able to have an impact on such societal relationships or communities as a whole. In spite of all the opposing forces of Satan and sin, in such relationships something of the kingdom of God "forcefully advancing" would become visible.

That is why we need Christian schools, Christian companies, and Christian political structures, which reject the false illusion of neutrality, and maintain the righteousness, peace, and joy of God's kingdom in their respective domains. What a mistake if people seek or pursue God's kingdom and his righteousness only in their private life, and at best in their families and churches, but not in public society, not in their schools and companies, not in their associations and political parties. What a catastrophe it would be if we, in this way, would surrender the totality of public life to the evil powers. What a tragedy if the misunderstood separation of church and state, and the lie of the "privacy of religion," would lead people to such an attitude!

WORKING IT OUT: **CHRISTIANS PARTICIPATING IN SOCIETY**
How can we participate in society, even in culture, the arts, science, and politics, without being "of the world"?

Both in the past and in the present, this question has embarrassed many Christians. In my younger years, I was bothered by it myself. I was convinced that Christians should not vote, and that a "Christian" culture was nonsense. Satan is the ruler of the world (John 12:31; 14:30; 16:11). The apostle John said,

Do not love the world or the things in the world. If anyone loves the world, the love of the Father is not in him. For all that is in the world—the desires of the flesh and the desires of the eyes and pride of life—is not from the Father but is from the world. And the world is passing away along with its desires, but whoever does the will of God abides forever (1 John 2:15–17; cf. 5:4–5, 19).

The apostle Paul said that once,

you were dead in the trespasses and sins in which you once walked, following the course of this world, following the prince of the power of the air, the spirit that is now at work in the sons of disobedience— among whom we all once lived in the passions of our flesh, carrying out the desires of the body and the mind, and were by nature children of wrath, like the rest of mankind (Eph. 2:1–3).

I wanted to have nothing to do with this world of sin and Satan. "Our citizenship is in heaven, and from it we await a Savior, the Lord Jesus Christ" (Phil. 3:20). We are heavenly citizens in a foreign country; we do move around in earthly society—we cannot avoid it—but we try to be involved in it as little as possible. Non-Canadians may have permission to live in Canada, but they cannot vote in that country, and there are several other rights they do not have. They do have such citizen rights, but only in the countries to which they belong. Similarly, we are "strangers" in this world; we have nothing to do with it.

I was a boy when one day—it was election time—we got a folder in my parents' mailbox from an orthodox Reformed political party in the Netherlands (it was the Gereformeerd Politiek Verbond [Reformed Political Union], for those who wish to know). With large letters I read on the front page: "Our citizenship is in heaven." I was flabbergasted! This was *our* text, with which we defended why we did not vote! And now this verse was being quoted to tell orthodox Christians that they *should* vote, preferably for a radically Christian party!

It took some years before I came to see how I should understand these things. God "raised us up with him [i.e., Christ] and seated us with him in the heavenly places in Christ Jesus" (Eph. 2:6). We are seated in Christ *in heaven*! Yet, the same letter makes clear to us that this ought to have clear consequences in all our *earthly* relationships: as church members, as husbands and wives, as parents and children, as employers and employees (Eph. 5:22–6:9)—and today we may add: as teachers and pupils, as citizens and voters, as scientists and artists, as taxpayers and politicians, as bakers and butchers, as cooks and contractors. Paul shows us how *heavenly* people become better husbands and wives, fathers and mothers, teachers and pupils, party members and voters, and so on, that is, in all sorts of very *earthly* spheres.

Some time later, I began to understand the vital distinction between structure and direction, or the horizontal and the vertical dimension of cosmic reality (see §§3.2.2 and 4.5). I learned that "the world" is not a specific *domain* that must be shunned; that would be horizontal. Rather, "the world" represents an apostate orientation (vertical), away from God, an evil directedness that may be encountered in every domain of society. If people do not understand this, they will—consciously or unconsciously—leave a great deal of society to the evil powers that dominate it, and withdraw within their churches and Bible clubs. This is what hyper-Calvinists did for a long time, at least in the Netherlands (however, since 1922 they have been represented in parliament uninterruptedly; their party is the Staatkundig Gereformeerde Partij, the Reformed Political Party).

Instead of abandoning society to the evil powers, Reformed (and many other) Christians in the Netherlands have understood that, in God's power, they should further the kingdom of God in all of societal domains: culture, arts, science, politics, you name it. In every domain, "the world," that is, the kingdom of Satan, is manifested. It is our task that in each domain something of the kingdom of God may become manifest as well, and thus will make the kingdom of Satan retreat.

I realize that, in this regard, as long as Christ has not returned, we will not make as much progress as we might have hoped. But a little progress is infinitely better than no progress, or not even *trying* to make some progress. All talk about a so-called "common kingdom" means in the end that we allow the kingdom of Satan to prevail in the public square.

TWO-KINGDOMS THEOLOGY[1]

PREPARATORY PONDERINGS

1. Do you see a connection between Jesus' lordship and the kingdom of God? If so, what consequences might this have for your views on the church and on society?
2. Can you say that Jesus is the Lord and King over the president of the United States (or over the head of state of whatever country), whether the latter is a believer or not?
3. How could we maintain that Jesus has power over all the heavens and all the earth, and simultaneously hold the view that, alongside his kingdom, there is a common (neutral, secular) kingdom?
4. Is Jesus Mediator of the spiritual realm only, or Mediator of the entire world? What exactly does this entail? And what are your arguments for the one or the other view?

---

[1] For this chapter, see the much broader treatment of the subject in Ouweneel (2016e).

7.1   JESUS' LORDSHIP

7.1.1   The Lordship of the King

In this chapter, I am bringing together a few subjects that were already touched upon in previous chapters but must now be elaborated a little further.

The first thing I wish to discuss is the universal lordship of Christ in order to illustrate—in contrast to NL2K—the universality of the one kingdom of God in the present world. Actually, the number of times that the apostle Paul explicitly mentions the "kingdom" is limited (see Acts 14:22; 19:8; 20:25; 28:23, 31; Rom. 14:17; 1 Cor. 4:20; 6:9–10; 15:24, 50; Gal. 5:21; Eph. 5:5; Col. 1:13; 4:11; 1 Thess. 2:12; 2 Thess. 1:5; 2 Tim. 4:1, 18). The number of times that he implicitly hints at the truth of the kingdom is much larger. I think that wherever Paul emphasizes the lordship of Jesus Christ, whether his lordship over the world or over the believers, the truth of the kingdom is implied or included. The German theologian Karl L. Schmidt rightly said, "We can thus see why the apostolic and post-apostolic church of the NT did not much speak of the *basileia tou theou* [kingdom of God] explicitly, but always emphasized it implicitly by its reference to the *kyrios Iēsous Christos* [the Lord Jesus Christ]."[2] We need only recall the Day of Pentecost, where Peter said that God had "made him both Lord and Christ [i.e., Messiah, the Anointed One]" (Acts 2:36). That is, God anointed him to make him Lord and King over all things.

In some cases, it is immediately evident that Jesus' lordship refers to God's kingdom: "Therefore God has highly exalted him and bestowed on him the name that is above every name, so that at the name of Jesus every knee should bow, in heaven and on earth and under the earth, and every tongue confess that *Jesus Christ is Lord*, to the glory of God the Father" (Phil. 2:9–11). Similarly in 2 Timothy 4:18, "The *Lord* will rescue me from every evil deed and bring me safely into his heavenly *kingdom*." In my view, the latter means here, as at other places: a heavenly kingdom *on earth*. "Heaven rules," as in Daniel 4:26, that is, on earth (Nebuchadnezzar's kingdom). As Philip Towner puts it: the reference is to "the kingdom of Christ as presently real but yet future in its culmination, awaiting 'that day' when heavenly realities enter fully the earthly sphere (4:8)."[3]

---

[2] Schmidt (1964, 589).
[3] Towner (2006, 647).

Of special interest in this context is the expression "day of the Lord" in Paul's letters, and in the New Testament in general. Sometimes we are dealing here with an Old Testament expression, Hebrew *yom* YHWH, Greek *hēmera [tou] kyriou*. This may be a direct quotation, such as in Acts 2:20 ("the day of the Lord comes, the great and magnificent day," cf. Joel 2:31), or an indirect reference (e.g., 1 Thess. 5:2; 2 Thess. 2:2; cf. 2 Pet. 3:10).

An underlying Christological problem is that the Greek *kyrios* can have two very different meanings in the New Testament (apart from secular meanings such as in Acts 25:26, where *kyrios* refers to the Roman emperor). First, following the Septuagint, writers use it as a rendering of God's name, YHWH, especially in Old Testament quotations. But second, it refers to the *Man* Jesus Christ, sometimes before his death and resurrection (e.g., Matt. 21:3; Luke 7:13, 19), sometimes after his resurrection and before his ascension (Mark 16:19; Luke 24:3; Acts 1:21), but mostly after his ascension and glorification (so many times in the Acts and the letters). In the latter case, the "day of the Lord" may be the day of his appearance and the establishment of his kingdom (1 Cor. 1:8; 5:5; 2 Cor. 1:14; cf. "that day," Matt. 7:22; 24:36; 26:29; Luke 10:12; 21:34; Rom. 2:16; 1 Thess. 5:4; 2 Thess. 1:10; 2:3; 2 Tim. 1:12, 18; 2 Tim. 4:8; "day of [Jesus] Christ," Phil. 1:6, 10; 2:16).[4]

7.1.2   The Lord's Kingdom

We have seen in NL2K the failure to properly observe the distinction between the (universal, providential) kingdom of the Lord (that is, the triune God), from the beginning of creation, and the kingdom of the Lord Jesus, the *Man* Christ Jesus glorified at God's right hand. First, there is no hint in the Old Testament that the "redemptive kingdom" began under the Abrahamic covenant, as David VanDrunen asserts.[5] Apart from God's universal, providential rule, there is no "redemptive kingdom" that is established anywhere in the Old Testament, for the simple reason that the Redeemer had to appear first. That is, *redemption* occurred right from the beginning, with the converted Adam and Eve after their Fall, but that does not imply a "redemptive kingdom."

The Messianic kingdom—there is no other "redemptive kingdom"—is something that, since Genesis 3:15, is eagerly looked for, and that is typologically presented especially in David and Solomon. But it did not exist before the coming of Jesus. The whole idea that the Noahic covenant rules

---

[4] *Hē kyriakē hēmera* ("the Lord's day," Rev. 1:10) is a different expression; it has often been explained as referring to the first day of the week.
[5] VanDrunen (2010a, 29–30, 75–88, 97).

the common kingdom, and the Abrahamic covenant governs the "redemptive" kingdom,[6] is pure theological fantasy,[7] as we will see.

Second, there is no hint in the New Testament that, today, the (universal, providential) kingdom of the LORD (that is, the Triune God) and the
kingdom of the Lord Jesus would exist alongside each other, as two different
entities; this is another invention of NL2K. The only two kingdoms that exist
today are the kingdom of God and the kingdom of Satan (Matt. 12:25–28).
There are not *two* kingdoms in the sense of the "common" kingdom and
the "redemptive" kingdom, nor are there two kingdoms in the sense of the
(universal, providential) kingdom of the triune God and the kingdom of
the Lord Jesus.

We have to read carefully here. To the *Son of Man* has been "given
dominion and glory and a kingdom, that all peoples, nations, and languages
should serve him; his dominion is an everlasting dominion, which shall not
pass away, and his kingdom one that shall not be destroyed" (Dan. 7:13–14).
In addition to *this* kingdom, God did not keep some providential kingdom
for himself, one that would be essentially different from the Messianic
kingdom. There is only one kingdom today: God rules the world through
the glorified Man at his right hand. God has put *all things* under Jesus' feet
(1 Cor. 15:27; Eph. 1:22; Heb. 2:8); there are no exceptions, except God
himself (1 Cor. 15:27) and the body of Christ (Eph. 1:11). God did not keep
part of the kingdom for himself. "*All peoples, nations*, and languages should
serve him," for "*all* authority in heaven and on earth has been given" to him;
therefore the apostles are commanded to go out and "make disciples of *all
nations*, baptizing them in the name of the Father and of the Son and of
the Holy Spirit, teaching them to observe all that I have commanded you"
(Matt. 28:18–20).

In addition to this kingdom, there is no other divinely ordained kingdom in the present age. There is no biblical proof for the existence of

---

[6] The idea is not altogether new to NL2K; it finds its origin with Meredith Kline (see
especially 2006), predecessor at the same Westminster Seminary California where VanDrunen,
Clark, Hart, and Horton teach. For example, consider this statement by Kline (2006, 157):
"In the coexistence of the holy and common lies the peculiar character of the present world
aeon." Kline was one of the main instigators of NL2K in general (cf. Frame, 2011, 8–12); there
would be no NL2K advocacy by Scott Clark, Michael Horton, Darryl Hart, or David VanDrunen,
without Meredith Kline. They are "Klineans," as the term goes. It is shocking to see how little
Kline (2006, e.g. 170–71) understood his ("neo-Dooyeweerdian") opponents (the present
book may be proof of this); what then can we expect from his followers?

[7] Cf. Frame (2011, 136): "In my view, Van Drunen's treatment of Genesis 9...reads far too
much into the passage.... There is no specific reference in the passage to unbelievers, or a secular
state, or to 'temporal affairs,' or to some system of social organization beyond the family."

two different divinely ordained kingdoms in the present world. This is a conclusivist invention, that is, a conclusion based on conclusions from conclusions from conclusions. Such a kind of conclusivist theology must not only be thoroughly mistrusted, it is also in direct conflict with many explicit statements of Scripture, as I am trying to show. These are two reasons to call it *bad* theology, apart from the many dramatic practical consequences of this theology.

7.2 SUBMISSION TO THE LORD

7.2.1 Confessing the Lord

In Romans 10:9–10, Paul emphasizes that confessing Jesus as *Lord* is an essential condition to salvation: "If you confess with your mouth that *Jesus is Lord* and believe in your heart that God raised him from the dead, you will be saved. For with the heart one believes and is justified, and with the mouth one confesses and is saved." One cannot be saved if one accepts Jesus as Saviour only. In other words, one should accept not only the gospel of God's grace for sinners but—explicitly or implicitly—also the gospel of the kingdom of God (Matt. 4:23; 9:35; 24:14).[8] The former gospel brings a person into the *church* and takes him to *heaven*, the latter brings him into the *kingdom* and makes him a follower of Jesus on *earth*. I challenge the reader to ponder this distinction (not separation!) carefully. Without the latter, the former cannot become a reality (and, of course, the reverse is true as well). One's surrender in faith to Christ is necessarily to him as Saviour but also to him as Lord; the two cannot be separated.[9]

Naturally, the reference is not to some confession with the lips only. "No one can say 'Jesus is Lord' except in the Holy Spirit" (1 Cor. 12:3), but of course Paul speaks here of a sincere saying, a saying from the heart. In other words, truly acknowledging Jesus as Lord is expressed in concrete acts of obedience, surrender, devotion, dedication, discipleship.[10]

N. T. Wright emphasized that the calling to faith is also a calling to obedience.[11] This is because, said he, the One in whom we believe is the legitimate Lord and Master of the world. (The language that Paul used concerning Jesus will have reminded his hearers immediately of the language they were accustomed to hearing about the Roman emperor). This is

[8] Cf. Ouweneel (2016e, §7.5.2).
[9] Cf. Stott (1959, 37); Boice (1986, 10, 21).
[10] See Ouweneel (2010a, 126–29).
[11] Wright (2010, 208).

why Paul could speak of "the obedience of faith" (Rom. 1:5; 16:26; cf. 6:17; 10:16; 15:18; 16:19).[12] Wright points out that the Greek word that the early Christians used for "faith," *pistis*, can also mean "loyalty" or "faithfulness." Coming to faith is becoming faithful to Christ and his word. The message of the gospel is the good news that Jesus is the one, true "emperor," who rules the world under his own standard of self-sacrificing love.

Indeed, the emperor of Rome was venerated as (Lat.) *dominus et deus*, "Lord and God" (Greek: *kyrios kai theos*) (cf. Acts 12:22; 25:26). In opposition to this, Peter testified of Jesus that God had made him "both Lord and Christ [Messiah]" (2:36), and, "he is Lord of all" (10:36). The apostle Thomas made the tremendous confession that it was this very Man Jesus, freshly risen from the dead, and no one else, who was *kyrios kai theos* (John 20:28). Or more correctly, *ho kyrios mou kai ho theos mou*, "*my* Lord and *my* God." There can be no true faith without this very personal recognition of Jesus as "my" Lord (cf. Luke 1:43; John 20:13, 28; Phil. 3:8) and "my" God (John 20:28; Rom. 1:8; 1 Cor. 1:4; 2 Cor. 12:21; Phil. 1:3; 4:19; Philem. 1:4).

In the Roman Empire, the kingdom of Satan had been manifested (cf. Matt. 12:25–26). Satan himself had offered Jesus the dominion over the "kingdoms of the *oikoumenē*" (Luke 4:5), that is, the Roman Empire (cf. 2:1 NIV, ERV, GNT, etc.; Acts 11:28; 17:6; 19:27; 24:5). Indeed, Jesus did gain dominion over the Roman Empire; however, not by bowing down before Satan, but by breaking the latter's power at the cross (cf. Heb. 2:14). This means that, since his resurrection and ascension, Jesus was indeed King in the kingdom of God, but *this kingdom in principle also included the power over the Roman Empire*. This is why Paul preached not only forgiveness, but to the inhabitants of the Roman Empire he preached also "that there is another king, Jesus" (Acts 17:7; see §§5.4.2 and 7.3.3). He quietly suggested to these inhabitants that there might be an emperor (Greek: *basileus*, "king") sitting on a throne in Rome, but that beyond him there was another King over the Roman Empire, sitting on a throne in heaven. Within the Roman Empire, the kingdom of Satan was still powerfully evident, as appeared from the fact that Paul was taken captive after this preaching. However, every time an inhabitant of this Empire accepted Jesus, not only as his Saviour but also as his King, the power of the heavenly King was extended within the Roman Empire.

---

[12] Wright understands this "obedience of faith" as the obedience that comes from faith; on this, see Ouweneel (2010a, 141 note 6).

7.2.2   Living to the Lord

In Romans 14:4–9, Paul emphasizes again the fact that every Christian is under the lordship of Christ, and thus a subject of the kingdom of God. This time the emphasis is on the fact that every believer is personally responsible to his Lord:

> Who are you to pass judgment on the servant of another? It is before his own master that he stands or falls…. For none of us lives to himself, and none of us dies to himself. For if we live, we live to the Lord, and if we die, we die to the Lord. So then, whether we live or whether we die, we are the Lord's. For to this end Christ died and lived again, that he might be Lord both of the dead and of the living.

The same Jesus who one day will be Lord of the dead and the living is now the Lord of every individual follower of his. This same thought is found elsewhere: "He died for all, that those who live might no longer live for themselves but for him who for their sake died and was raised" (2 Cor. 5:15); and: "You are serving the Lord Christ" (Col. 3:24; cf. 4:1, "you have a Lord [*kyrios*] in heaven," WYC).

Thus, a few verses later, Paul uses different terminology to refer to the same subject: "So do not let what you regard as good be spoken of as evil. For the kingdom of God is not a matter of eating and drinking but of righteousness and peace and joy in the Holy Spirit. Whoever thus serves Christ is acceptable to God and approved by men" (Rom. 14:16–18). Being under the lordship of Christ is the same as being in the kingdom of God, and this is the same as "serving" Christ.

One could hardly imagine a person willing to *receive* everything from Jesus if he would not be willing to *give* everything to Jesus: his heart, his life, his possessions. The conversion of Saul of Tarsus began with the question, "Who are you, Lord?," immediately followed by the question, "What shall I do, Lord?" (Acts 22:8, 10). He became an "imitator" of Christ the Lord: "Be imitators of me, as I am of Christ" (1 Cor. 11:1; cf. 1 Thess. 1:6, "You became imitators of us and of the Lord:" cf. 1 Pet. 2:21; Rev. 14:4). This is why it has been said: *becoming* a Christian costs you nothing (the gospel is free), *being* a Christian costs you everything (with the addition that you receive everything back; Mark 10:29–30). This is expressed in the concept of discipleship (Luke 14:26–27, 33),[13] and also in James 2, where genuine faith is demonstrated through works of obedience (vv. 20–24).

---

[13] See Ouweneel (2010e, chapter 6); cf. MacArthur (1988, 21, 30).

7.2.3   Other Examples of Lordship

It is quite remarkable to see how often the title "Lord" is used at the Lord's Supper. Paul speaks of the cup of the Lord, the table of the Lord, the Lord's death, and the body and blood of the Lord (1 Cor. 10:21–22; 11:26–27; in 11:20 ["the Lord's supper"] the word is not the noun *kyriou* but the adjective *kyriakon*; only in 11:29 is the addition "of the Lord" uncertain[14]). In this way, the Lord's Supper is peculiarly linked with the kingdom of God; see especially 11:26, "you proclaim the Lord's death *until he comes.*" It reminds us of Jesus' own words: "Truly, I say to you, I will not drink again of the fruit of the vine until that day when I drink it new in the kingdom of God" (Mark 14:25). The Lord's Supper is celebrated in memory of the triumph of Christ. It is the testimony that Jesus is Lord, proclaimed in the presence of all the defeated powers; as David said, "You prepare a table before me in the presence of my enemies" (Ps. 23:5). In this way, it is also an expression of (renewed) dedication to him. As says Psalm 116, "What shall I *render* to the Lord for all his benefits to me? I will lift up the *cup of salvation* and call on the name of the Lord, I will pay my *vows* to the Lord in the presence of all his people" (vv. 12–14).

In the same remarkable way, Paul uses the word "Lord" five times in 1 Thessalonians 4:15–17,

> For this we declare to you by a word from the *Lord*, that we who are alive, who are left until the coming of the *Lord*, will not precede those who have fallen asleep. For the *Lord* himself will descend from heaven with a cry of command, with the voice of an archangel, and with the sound of the trumpet of God. And the dead in Christ will rise first. Then we who are alive, who are left, will be caught up together with them in the clouds to meet the *Lord* in the air, and so we will always be with the *Lord.*

The reference is not to some "rapture" of the "bride of Christ," that is, the church in this quality,[15] but to the warriors of the Lord who, with a military command (Greek: *keleusma*) and a trumpet (probably derived from Jewish apocalyptic),[16] will be released from their duties and will enter into their rest (*Oh, when the saints go marching in…* a bride does not march and is not

---

[14] See Metzger (1975, 562–63).

[15] So, e.g., Schuyler English (1986, 60); cf. Hoek (2004, 209).

[16] See the connection with the "archangel," i.e., Michael, who blows the trumpet to announce God's approach for judgment (*Apoc. Mosis* 22); Moffatt (1979, 38).

commanded). The battles and sufferings of Jesus' followers will then be over; the kingdom of God will arrive in power and majesty.

In 1 Corinthians 12:3 Paul says, "No one can say 'Jesus is Lord' except in the Holy Spirit." The confession of Jesus' lordship "counts" only if it comes from the heart, and this is possible only in the power of the Spirit. A confession merely with the lips is insufficient; a real surrender is demanded. As Jesus said,

> Not everyone who says to me, "*Lord, Lord*," will enter the kingdom of heaven, but the one who does the will of my Father who is in heaven. On that day many will say to me, "*Lord, Lord*, did we not prophesy in your name, and cast out demons in your name, and do many mighty works in your name?" And then will I declare to them, "I never knew you; depart from me, you workers of lawlessness" (Matt. 7:21–23).

"Afterward the other virgins came also, saying, '*Lord, Lord*, open to us.' But he answered, 'Truly, I say to you, I do not know you'" (25:11–12). "Why do you call me '*Lord, Lord*,' and not do what I tell you?" (Luke 6:46). In the New Testament, this double "*Lord, Lord*" is used only in a negative sense (cf. the "Martha, Martha" in Luke 10:41, and the "Saul, Saul" in Acts 9:4).

Finally, I refer to Ephesians 4:4–6, "There is one body and one Spirit—just as you were called to the one hope that belongs to your call—one Lord, one faith, one baptism, one God and Father of all, who is over all and through all and in all." There are seven "units" here, of which, in my view, the first three belong together, as well as the second group of three.[17] The first three, the one body, the one Spirit, and the one hope, may refer to the *inner* side of Christian unity, linked with the church as the body of Christ and the inner working of the Spirit. Then follows the *outer* side of Christian unity, the *external* testimony in this world, linked with the kingdom of God: one Lord (as the King in this kingdom), one faith (here faith refers not to the heart's act of believing, but to the believed truth: "the Christian faith," as the foundation of the kingdom), one baptism (as the introduction to the kingdom; cf. Matt. 28:18–20). After the *body* and the *kingdom* follows, thirdly, the *family* of God: "One God and Father of all, who is over all and through all and in all" (v. 6). In my view, this refers to God's Fatherhood with respect to believers.[18]

---

[17] So, e.g., Grant (1901, 340–41).
[18] Cf. the Annotations to the Dutch Statenvertaling; Wood (1978, ad loc.) (*contra* many expositors).

7.3   JESUS' LORDSHIP IN SOCIETAL RELATIONSHIPS

7.3.1   Marriage

Let us now examine how the New Testament connects Jesus' lordship to various societal relationships in such a way that the kingdom of God is clearly manifested in such relationships. The first example is *marriage*: "A wife is bound to her husband as long as he lives. But if her husband dies, she is free to be married to whom she wishes, *only in the Lord*" (1 Cor. 7:39). "Wives, submit to your husbands, as is fitting *in the Lord*" (Col. 3:18).

A believing man and a believing woman cannot marry just anyone, as though, for instance, marriage supposedly belongs to the common realm. They are to marry "in the Lord," that is, in the recognition of Jesus' lord- and kingship in their personal lives. They are disciples of the Lord, not only in the church, but also in their marriage. In this recognition of Jesus' lordship, the kingdom of Christ becomes manifest also within the sphere of their marriage. The wife respects her husband as is fitting *in the Lord*, but we may add: the husband loves his wife, gives himself up for her, nourishes and cherishes her, *in the Lord* (Eph. 5:22–31). That is, both fulfill their duties as personally standing under the authority of Christ. The wife serves the Lord, and *therefore*, out of this attitude, serves her husband; the husband serves the Lord, and *therefore*, out of this attitude, serves his wife.

It is not just that each of the two individually serves the Lord within their marriage, but their marriage is concluded "in the Lord," which also involves that they dedicate their marriage *to* the Lord. It is the smallest societal relationship in which the lordship of Christ, and thus the kingdom of God, comes to light.

7.3.2   The Family

"Children, obey your parents *in the Lord*, for this is right.... Fathers, do not provoke your children to anger, but bring them up in the discipline and instruction *of the Lord*" (Eph. 6:1, 4). "Children, obey your parents in everything, for *this pleases the Lord*" (Col. 1:20).

Children obey their parents' authority, but this is only derived authority: in obeying them they are acknowledging the lordship of Christ. As a general principle, we find this in other contexts: "Wives, submit to your own husbands, *as to the Lord*" (Eph. 5:22). "Bondservants, obey your earthly masters with fear and trembling, with a sincere heart, *as you would Christ*... rendering service with a good will *as to the Lord* and not to man" (6:5, 7).

One way that the kingdom of Christ manifests itself in the family is by the way children obey their parents "in the Lord," that is, "as pleases the Lord." Conversely, parents bring up their children not according to general principles of education in the "common realm" (i.e., according to some "natural law"), not even general *biblical* principles, but "in the discipline and instruction *of the Lord.*" That is, the principles they teach their children are the principles of the kingdom of Christ; they raise them to be disciples (followers) of Christ, conscious of Jesus' own word: "Let the children come to me, and do not hinder them, for to such belongs the kingdom of God" (Luke 18:16). The relationships between Christian parents and their children are not ruled by common principles but by kingdom principles.

Notice here the parallel with marriage: both parties, parents and children, fulfill their duties toward each other as personally standing under the authority of Christ. The parents serve the Lord, and *therefore*, out of this attitude, they serve their children; (believing) children serve the Lord, and *therefore*, out of this attitude, they serve their parents. The Christian family is never "common;" it is "holy ground" (1 Cor. 7:14; cf. Exod. 3:5). The Dutch rhymed version of the close of Psalm 133 says: "Where love dwells, the Lord commands his blessing; there he dwells himself, there his salvation is obtained, and life everlasting." The Christian family is *kingdom ground.*

7.3.3 The State

All "lordship" within a state (or a federation, or a province, or a municipality) is derived lordship, whether the people concerned wish to acknowledge it or not. When Festus referred to the Roman emperor as "my Lord" (Acts 25:26), he did not realize that his "lord's" authority was derived from that of *the* Lord: Jesus himself. Paul could have said to him what Jesus told Pilate: "You would have no authority over me at all unless it had been given you from above"—in Festus' case: from the glorified Christ (cf. John 19:11).

This is why Paul and the other apostles did not just preach forgiveness of sins. When the people of Thessalonica made Paul a prisoner, it was not because he preached forgiveness, but because he preached "that there is another king, Jesus" (Acts 17:7; see §§5.4.2 and 7.2.1). If he had believed in NL2K, I suppose he would have restricted himself to preaching God's grace for poor sinners, and he would not have bothered about the state, which supposedly belonged to the "common realm." Instead, he freely preached that the emperor of Rome was subject to "another king," who was the real ruler.

In fact he told the people (as I understand it): Whatever societal relationship there may be, each knowing its own authorities, know that there is One who always transcends these authorities: daddy is the king in the family, but know that there is another King in the family: Jesus, who surpasses your daddy. The emperor is the head of the empire, but know that there is another King in the empire: Jesus, who surpasses your emperor. Employees, the CEO is the head of your Christian company, but know that there is another King in your company: Jesus, who surpasses your CEO. Students, the headmaster or principal is the head of your Christian school (college, university), but know that there is another King in your school: Jesus, who surpasses your headmaster.

Notice again the parallel with marriage and the family: both parties, the believing magistrates and the believing citizens, fulfill their duties toward each other as personally standing under the authority of Christ. The magistrates, whether believers or not, are called to serve the Lord, and *therefore*, out of this attitude, to serve all their citizens; believing citizens serve the Lord, and *therefore*, out of this attitude, serve the magistrates.

7.3.4 Daily Work
This pattern pertains as well to all areas of people's daily work:

> Bondservants, obey your earthly masters with fear and trembling, with a sincere heart, *as you would Christ*, not by the way of eye-service, as people-pleasers, but as bondservants *of Christ*, doing the will of God from the heart, rendering service with a good will *as to the Lord* and not to man knowing that whatever good anyone does, this he will receive back from *the Lord*, whether he is a bondservant or is free. Masters, do the same to them, and stop your threatening, knowing that he who is *both their Master and yours is in heaven*, and that there is no partiality with him (Eph. 6:5–9).

> Bondservants, obey in everything those who are your earthly masters, not by way of eye-service, as people-pleasers, but with sincerity of heart, *fearing the Lord*. Whatever you do, work heartily, *as for the Lord* and not for men, knowing that from *the Lord* you will receive the inheritance as your reward. You are serving *the Lord Christ*.[19] For the wrongdoer will be paid back for the wrong he has done, and there is no partiality. Masters, treat your bondservants justly and fairly, knowing that *you also have a Master in heaven* (Col. 3:22–4:1).

---

[19] One Dutch translation says, *Gij dient Christus als Heer* ("you are serving Christ as Lord"), which is quite possible (cf. 1 Pet. 3:15 ESV: "Christ the Lord"; many others: "Christ as Lord").

The relationships between employers and employees (to use these modern expressions) are described in terms of the kingdom of Christ: servants, try to see in your master the Lord himself; serve him as you serve the Lord. Bosses, try to deal with your servants in the realization of your own servitude to the great Master in heaven. Again, the rules—not of some "common" kingdom, of which Scripture knows nothing, but—of the kingdom of God are the model for the rules in everyday labour. Christians do not serve the King only in church, but also in their marriages, families, states and municipalities, schools and companies, and so on. Believing school directors and teachers serve the Lord, and *therefore*, out of this attitude, serve their pupils and students. Believing pupils and students serve the Lord, and *therefore*, out of this attitude, serve their school directors and teachers.

7.4 THE HEART OF GOD'S KINGDOM

7.4.1 Two Realms

We have seen that, in Christian thinking, since the Christianization of the Roman empire,[20] repeatedly the question has arisen: Is Christ's government over the world to be associated primarily with the church, or primarily with the state? And if perhaps with both, which of the two has the primacy? In the fourth century, after the Roman emperor Constantine had accepted the Christian faith, the answer was *caesaropapism*: the Roman emperor practically functioned as the leader of the Christian commonwealth. For instance, he convened and formally presided at the Council of Nicea (325). In early Protestantism, it was in principle the same: Luther placed the Lutheran church explicitly under the protection of the German princes, in England the king became the head of the church—as he still is today, although he has no real power over the church—and in the Netherlands it was the States General that convened the Synod of Dort (1618–1619).

In the early thirteenth century, it was entirely the other way around: pope Innocent III (d. 1216) enjoyed supremacy not only in the church, but also in almost the entire Western world. He viewed all the kings and emperors in the Christian world as his vassals.[21] In those days, it was said that not only the bishops, but also the Holy Roman emperor and the kings

---

[20] In AD 313 emperor Constantine the Great converted to Christianity; in 380 emperor Theodosius I made Nicene Christianity the state religion of the Roman Empire.

[21] See extensively, Ouweneel (2016c, §6.3.3).

of the various Western countries, could not so much as lift their little finger without the pope's permission.

It is quite understandable that both situations occurred—at different times, of course—because seemingly convincing arguments can be adduced for both viewpoints. If we put the emphasis on the spiritual character of the Kingdom of God, we will give the primacy to the church (that is, to the pope), for the church is spiritual (sacred), and the state is worldly (profane, secular). This is also the perspective of NL2K (without the church *ruling* over the state). However, if we put the emphasis on God's government over the whole of humanity, we might give the primacy to the state. And if people refuse to choose between the pope and the emperor, they will construe some kind of *duplex ordo* ("double order"). This is a scheme in which the two, church and state, are arranged alongside each other like two parallel "realms," or, as in NL2K, two divinely ordained "kingdoms." NL2K is nothing but the latest form of the—essentially scholastic—notion of a *duplex ordo*.

In the Netherlands, since 1876, a *duplex order* has existed at the state universities as far as the study of theology is concerned: part of the theological study is organized by the government, part of this study falls under ecclesiastical authority. In the former case, theology is viewed as a "pure" (neutral, objective, unprejudiced) science of religion (*godsdienstwetenschap*); in the latter case, theology is rooted in a church's faith tradition (and therefore, according to many, cannot be "scientific"). It is again an example of the catastrophic scholastic nature-grace dualism, which separates "pure" (unprejudiced) science from the (prejudiced) domain of faith.

7.4.2   Realms or "Regiments"?

The two "realms," the sacred and the secular kingdoms, are considered to be two facets of God's universal providential government, which is to some extent identified with the kingdom of the glorified Man Christ Jesus. Most often we hear these identified as "two kingdoms," so this is the terminology we will use as well.

I must repeat here that speaking of "two kingdoms" may be quite confusing. The *only* two kingdoms that the New Testament speaks about are the "kingdom of Satan" and the "kingdom of God" (Matt. 12:25–28), and these correspond very generally to the two *civitates* ("cities," "realms") that Augustine discussed in his work, *De Civitate Dei*.[22] But this is not at all what NL2K means; it views *both* the kingdoms that it distinguishes as

---

[22] See on this VanDrunen (2010b, 22–32), but also VanDrunen (2010a, 14 note 3).

kingdoms ordained by God, both standing under his providential dominion. It reminds us of what Martin Luther—still under the strong influence
of scholasticism—called the two "regiments," that is, divine "regimes."
Luther used this term to express the idea that both in the church and in
the state (or wider, secular society) we are dealing with a divine regime,
a divine rule of government. With the former regime, the church, also
called the regime of the gospel, God leads people to faith. With the other
regime, the state, also called the regime of the law, God keeps a check on
the unrighteous. In the former kingdom we are dealing with the *iustitia
fidei*, "the justice (or, righteousness) of faith" (cf. Rom. 4:11, 13). In the
latter kingdom we are supposedly dealing with the *iustitia civilis* or *politica*,
the "civil (or, political) justice (or, righteousness)," that is, the outward
righteousness of societal life.

In line with the nature-grace model, scholastic dualism identifies two
"realms," "regiments," or "kingdoms" which are clearly distinguished, and
are thought to be fundamentally irreducible and independent of each other.
This corresponds with the just mentioned Lutheran dualism of *law and
gospel*: the law is the norm for the former, the gospel is the norm for the
latter kingdom. In Lutheran terminology, they are the kingdom of God's
left hand and the realm of his right hand, respectively. The one domain is
that of nature: the domain of temporal, earthly, natural, rational, secular,
profane life, which also includes the state. The other domain is that of
grace: the domain of the eternal, spiritual, supernatural, divine, sacred life,
which also includes the church. It is the ancient scholastic nature-grace
dualism all over.

Please note: for Luther himself, the former domain, that of the state,
or more broadly, society (often the two are not properly distinguished),
was not at all viewed as being separated from God, for the authority of the
worldly kings and presidents is also God-given authority (Rom. 13:1–7; 1
Pet. 2:13–17), not to mention the role of the husband as the head in marriage, and the role of the parents in the family. In this respect, this domain,
too, is thought to be a divine "realm" or "regiment," in which God realizes
certain purposes, namely, maintaining order and peace in temporal, earthly
life, and constraining the unrighteous. The magistrates were even *urged* to
take their responsibility before God in this sense. Yet, NL2K thinks that this
realm is far removed from the actual kingdom of God, the spiritual kingdom
of his Christ, which realizes itself virtually exclusively within the church.

In his publication *An den christlichen Adel deutscher Nation (To the*

Christian Nobility of the German Nation, 1520),[23] Luther urged the German princes to pursue the Reformation of the church because, as he said, the bishops had failed in this respect. It shows how far NL2K theologians are removed from Luther because they would be implacably opposed to such appeals to any secular governments.

7.4.3   Secularization

In fact, the most striking characteristic of whatever type of two-kingdoms doctrine we may encounter is always the secularization of the state, or more broadly, society. Sacred (spiritual) life, the life of faith, is found in the church, as well as in the private, inner life of faith. For the rest, the entire life of the believer is secularized, or considered to be neutral, or "common," as NL2K likes to put it. According to this scheme of thinking, apart from church life and the inner life of faith, the Christian's life is just as secular as that of non-Christians, of course apart from the obvious fact that the good Christian is led by general moral principles in everything he undertakes.

Professional life, science, schooling, business, the arts, politics, and so on, are all considered to be neutral, or "common." Some advocates of this view who deny that they are defending neutrality,[24] nevertheless see no place for faith affecting societal relationships and structures, but have room only for faith-directed private, individual relationships in the world. A Christian state is viewed as a fundamental impossibility, and at best, Christian schools are tolerated as long as they are entirely financed by the parents.[25] A Christian school is understood in terms of individual Christians providing education that is, with the exception of a Bible class, just as secular and neutral as that of the state schools. People committed to this view, including NL2K, often assert, for example, that there is no such thing as Christian mathematics, Christian chemistry, Christian agriculture, Christian medicine, or even Christian psychotherapy.[26] So then, only the church is thought to represent the kingdom of God on earth: the state can

---

[23] See https://librivox.org/search?title=To+the+Christian+Nobility+of+the+German+Nationandauthor=LUTHERandreader=andkeywords=andgenre_id=0andstatus=allandproject_type=eitherandrecorded_language=andsort_order=catalog_dateandsearch_page=1andsearch_form=advanced.

[24] See chapter 1 note 15.

[25] I suppose that, for NL2K, a situation that has obtained in the Netherlands since 1917—Christian schools (governed by state-independent boards), if approved by the authorities, receive the same financial support from the government as state schools—would be unacceptable.

[26] On this latter subject, cf. Ouweneel (2015).

at best serve the kingdom of God by helping, supporting, and defending the church.

A number of years ago, in South-Africa, I heard a highly respected Nigerian theologian, Dr. Tokunboh Adeyemo (d. 2010),[27] defend the two-kingdoms doctrine in such strong terms that he even rejected the *principle* of a Christian state.[28] He explained that, in a certain African country, where more than ninety percent of the people confess the Christian faith, he had pleaded very strongly with the government *not* to establish, under any circumstances, a Christian state! To him, a Christian state necessarily implied the oppression of non-Christians within that state. Therefore, the state definitely had to be neutral! This is what happens when you leave philosophy and politicology to the theologians, even Bible-believing theologians (see extensively chapter 10). They may think they can adduce biblical arguments, but in reality they are caught in the age-old scholastic two-kingdoms doctrine.

Dr. Adeyemo, though with the best of intentions, had not even grasped the notion of a state that has *no other* task than maintaining public justice in a Christian way, without interfering with the beliefs of individual persons. In this sense, the Christian state will never force Christian beliefs on its citizens. Apparently, my African colleague could imagine the Christian state as being only a totalitarian state.

One practical example: a Christian government does not prohibit the building of mosques by Muslims. This is not because this government is pro-Islam—it is not—but because it does not meddle in the religious convictions of its citizens. A Christian government must guarantee to all its citizens the same religious freedom that Christians would like to enjoy. Please note again: this has nothing to do with the state being neutral. The state is never neutral. The authorities always have their own personal beliefs; they may be pro- or anti-Christian, pro- or anti-Islam. That is not the point. The point is that *the power of any government ought never to go any further than maintaining public justice.* Therefore, the state has a say about the external conditions under which mosques (synagogues, temples) are built, not about the buildings as such, and even less about the things that happen inside (as long as there is no question of criminal activities, as determined by the law).

---

[27] I respect him, e.g., as the editor of the *Africa Bible Commentary* (Adeyemo, 2010).
[28] His position would accord very well with that of Darryl Hart (2006).

7.5   THE MEDIATORSHIP OF CHRIST

7.5.1   Cosmological or Soteriological?

NL2K's standpoint is closely related to what some people suppose to be the meaning of the cosmological and/or soteriological mediatorship and kingship of Christ.[29] Is Jesus Christ the centre, the focal point, of the new creation only, or also of the first creation?

Karl Barth wrote that, when the Old and the New Testaments speak of what older theology called the divine decree they are speaking directly or indirectly about Jesus Christ.[30] In his view, the one reality of the counsel of God becomes visible in Christ. Nothing of what belongs to God's counsel could be viewed apart from Jesus Christ. Everything that God wills is enclosed in this person. According to Barth, the entire *counsel* of God, also when dealing with purely cosmological aspects, is thoroughly Christocentric. There are many things on which I do not agree with Barth, but on this point I believe he is right. As Paul says, God made "known to us the mystery of his will, according to his purpose, which he set forth in Christ as a plan for the fullness of time, to unite all things in him, things in heaven and things on earth" (Eph. 1:9–10).

Herman Bavinck had no difficulty acknowledging that, according to numerous biblical passages, already at the first creation, Christ "has both soteriological and cosmological significance. He is the mediator not only of re-creation but also of creation."[31] Thus, in his view, the plan of salvation was already included in the plan of creation. As he said, "The foundations of creation and redemption are the same. The Logos who became flesh [John 1:14] is the same by whom all things were made [v. 3]. The first-born from the dead [Col. 1:18] is also the first-born of every creature [v. 15]."[32]

Especially the Colossians passage is of fundamental importance here: Jesus Christ

> is the image of the invisible God, the firstborn of all creation. For in him all things were created, in heaven and on earth, visible and

---

[29] Cf. Ouweneel (2016i, §2.4).

[30] Barth (1936, II/1:521–22; cf. II/2:91–93).

[31] Bavinck (*RD* 2:423).

[32] Bavinck (1909, 27). *Caveat lector*: the English translation of Bavinck's *Wijsbegeerte der openbaring* that is available at https://www.ccel.org/ccel/bavinck/revelation.ii.html is incomplete and defective at this point, lacking material at the conclusion of chapter 1.

invisible, whether thrones or dominions or rulers or authorities—all things were created through him and for him. And he is before all things, and in him all things hold together. And he is the head of the body, the church. He is the beginning, the firstborn from the dead, that in everything he might be preeminent (Col. 1:15–18).

"In" the Second Person of the Godhead all things were created, but since his incarnation this person is identical with the *Man* Christ Jesus. Please note, I am not saying that the divine and the human natures of Christ are identical, but I emphasize, in line with Chalcedon, that the *person* in and through whom all things were created is identical with the *person* who is now glorified at God's right hand.

Similarly, we read elsewhere: "In these last days he [i.e., God] has spoken to us by his Son, whom he appointed the heir of all things, through whom also he created the world" (Heb. 1:2). "By his Son" is more literally "in [the] Son," that is, *God* spoke to us, and the person who spoke was (God the) Son. But this is the same *person* as the *Man* who made "purification for sins," and "sat down at the right hand of the Majesty on high" (v. 3). It is this *one* person (God and Man in one) who is both the cosmological and the soteriological centre of the universe, *not* of a redemptive realm only. The latter corresponds with Paul's statement: "For *all* the promises of God find their Yes in him. That is why it is through him that we utter our Amen to God for his glory" (2 Cor. 1:20). I see no reason to think in this verse of soteriological promises only, and not also of cosmological promises, as the word "all" clearly suggests.

7.5.2 Power over All Flesh

This discussion is directly connected to whether only redeeming grace, or also common grace—God's providential care for his creation (see §4.4.1)—is Christocentric, and a result of *salvation* in Christ. It is typical of hyper-Calvinist author Henry Kersten that he deliberately seeks to separate common grace from Christ's work of atonement. I presume that this is because he cannot agree that the work of Christ could bestow any good on the reprobate, even if this included only temporal blessings.[33] He fears that such an idea could lead to the doctrine of universal atonement, that is, the theory that Christ bore the sins of all people.[34] However, such an inference is not at all required. *All* promises, *all* manifestations of common grace, are

---

[33] Kersten (1980, 1:76–77).
[34] See Ouweneel (2009a, §12.2).

not only "in Christ," but to some extent could not be separated from his work of redemption without leading inevitably to universal atonement.

Jesus himself said concerning this that the Father had given him "authority over *all* flesh," because "I glorified you on earth, having accomplished the work that you gave me to do…. And now, Father, glorify me in your own presence with the glory that I had with you before the world existed" (John 17:1–4). The class of believers (cf. v. 3) does not include *all* people; they are only part of the human race. The Father has given all judgment to the Son, which the Son uses to bring, on the one hand, "those who have done good to the resurrection of life, and," on the other hand, "those who have done evil to the resurrection of judgment" (5:22–29).

The glorified Man at God's right hand has authority over "all flesh" because of the work that he has accomplished here on earth. There is no king or president, no husband or parent, no school principal, chairman or CEO, who is not under the authority of the glorified Man Christ Jesus, whether these persons in power wish to acknowledge it or not. This is not simply because he is the Second Person of the Godhead, but because, as the Man Christ Jesus, he has accomplished the work, and is now seated at God's right hand in glory. He has authority over all states, marriages, families, schools, and so on, of the world—which is the same as saying that *in principle* all these relationships are under his royal authority, to which they *practically* must submit, and one day shall do so.

It is not only *in spite of* his work that Jesus condemns the wicked, but also *on the basis of* his work that he has the power to do so (cf. 2 Cor. 5:10; Rev. 22:12). The eternal Father has given all judgment to the eternal Son because this Son has become the "Son *of Man*" (without ceasing to be the Son of God) (cf. John 5:22, 27). It is as the Son *of Man* that he has accomplished the work of redemption (Matt. 20:28), and on the basis of this work he will execute judgment upon *all humanity*, whether in view of eternal life or of eternal death. Since Jesus' finished work, no dealings of God with humanity can be viewed apart from the Man Christ Jesus and his work. God "has fixed a day on which he will judge the world in righteousness by a *man* whom he has appointed; and of this he has given assurance to all by raising him from the dead" (Acts 17:31).

As we heard Bavinck say, he who is the "firstborn from the dead" (Col. 1:18; cf. Rev. 1:5) is also the "firstborn of all creation" (Col. 1:15). "In" Christ, "through" him, and "for" him *all things* were created (v. 16). In the eternal purpose of God, it was decreed "to unite *all things* in him [i.e., Christ], *things in heaven and things on earth*" (Eph. 1:10). Not only do believers find their final destination "in Christ," but unbelievers do as well (although their destination is very different), because the entire world is Christ's domain of power. Also the apostate belong to those whom "the Master bought" (2 Pet. 2:1)—not for their salvation (it says "bought," not "saved") but in order to obtain through his work on the cross a right to exercise authority over *all* people, either to save them or to condemn them.[35]

7.6 THE NOAHIC COVENANT

7.6.1 Noah's Burnt Offering

Let me give an example of the point mentioned above: a decree that seems to be typically connected with God's general providential rule over the world, but disconnected from redemption, is God's promise to Noah after the flood: "While the earth remains, seedtime and harvest, cold and heat, summer and winter, day and night, shall not cease" (Gen. 8:22). However, it would be a fundamental mistake to view this promise apart from the "pleasing aroma" of Noah's burnt offering (v. 21), which, as is the case with all bloody sacrifices, pointed to the sacrifice of Christ (cf. the burnt offering in Lev. 1:4, which is for atonement, and the application of this sacrifice in Heb. 10:4–10, where Christ is presented as the true burnt offering).

Meredith Kline, who wrote extensively about the Noahic covenant, limited himself to saying: "In the token form of representative animals offered on the altar as burnt offerings (v.20b), Noah consecrated to God the consummated kingdom in the ark. By this offering the priest-kings of the theocratic ark-kingdom consecrated themselves to God, making doxological confession that they were servant-kings in the kingdom-house of the Lord and that their Creator-Vindicator was King of kings. This perfecting of human kingship in the ritual of priestly consecration pointed to the priestly act of the coming royal Son, who, when all things have been subjected to him, will deliver up the kingdom to God."[36] Note carefully what is being said here: the burnt offering was nothing but an act of consecration of the supposed "priest-king" that Noah was!

One of Kline's disciples at WSC, David VanDrunen, wrote extensively about the Noahic covenant as well. However, he hardly mentioned Noah's burnt offering, and where he did, he attached hardly any meaning to it, perhaps only as an act of worship. He apodictically stated that this sacrifice does not "mean that the Noahic covenant is redemptive rather than common,"

---

[35] Also see Ouweneel (2016i, §5.8.2).
[36] Kline (2006, 229–30).

and his sacrifice "appears to be a sacrifice of consecration [echoing Kline] rather than of expiation for sins."[37] His only reason for these presumptions was that, apparently, the opposite conclusion did not fit into his model. He drew far-reaching conclusions from the Noahic covenant,[38] except this one: *Noah's sacrifice places anticipatively and typologically the post-Flood world on the foundation of the sacrifice of Christ.* Since the Fall, there can be no other foundation; there is no neutral or common realm. The entire world constitutes the kingdom of God, that is, stands on the foundation of redemption, even if this does not mean that all individual people will be saved (cf. the "all things made new" *and* the eternal condemnation of the wicked in Rev. 21:5 and 8).

Please note this statement from before the Flood—"The LORD saw that the wickedness of man was great in the earth, and that every intention of the thoughts of his heart was only evil continually" (Gen. 6:5)—and this one from after the Flood: "the intention of man's heart is evil from his youth" (8:21). The correspondence is obvious. Why did God destroy the world with the argument that "the intention of man's heart" was evil if after the Flood this "intention" was just as evil as it was before? Did God intend to destroy the post-Flood world again? On the contrary, he promised that he would *not* do this (same v. 21). How can this be? The answer is of essential importance: *because of Noah's burnt offering,* that is typologically, because of the atoning work of Christ.

We must carefully follow the logic of the passage:

When the Lord smelled the pleasing aroma, the Lord said in his heart, "I will never again curse the ground because of man, for [NKJV: although] the intention of man's heart is evil from his youth. Neither will I ever again strike down every living creature as I have done. While the earth remains, seedtime and harvest, cold and heat, summer and winter, day and night, shall not cease" (vv. 21–22).

In my view, it is most obvious to read this as follows: the human heart has not changed through the Flood, but henceforth God will be dealing with the world *on a different footing,* namely, on the basis of Noah's burnt offering, which is an anticipation of Christ's burnt offering. This is not only an excellent description of what has been called "common grace," but it shows

---

[37] VanDrunen (2010a, 80–81 note 2; 135).
[38] VanDrunen (2010a, 78–81).

moreover that neither this common grace, nor any "common kingdom" one might postulate, *can ever be separated from the redemptive work of Christ.* There is no neutral or common or secular ground here.

This finding has implications for our understanding of all those passages that speak of God's universal providence, such as: "In past generations he [i.e., God] allowed all the nations to walk in their own ways. Yet he did not leave himself without witness, for he did good by giving you rains from heaven and fruitful seasons, satisfying your hearts with food and gladness" (Acts 14:16–17). Or, God

> made from one man every nation of mankind to live on all the face of the earth, having determined allotted periods and the boundaries of their dwelling place, that they should seek God, and perhaps feel their way toward him and find him. Yet he is actually not far from each one of us, for "in him we live and move and have our being"; as even some of your own poets have said, "For we are indeed his offspring"(17:26–28).

None of this can be viewed apart from Christ and his work of atonement, even if this does not mean that in the end all human beings will be saved.[39]

As Reformed theologian Cornelis Van der Waal put it:

> It is not so that redemption rests on creation—nature does not form the first floor and grace the second. In God's gracious dealings with his people, all creation is involved. The "world sacrifice" Noah made foreshadowed the work of Jesus Christ. His unique and perfect sacrifice brings the restoration of all things, also the salvation of the eagerly longing creation…. We may not think of categories like "general" and "special" as if the covenant with Noah was a general covenant and that with Abraham a "special one." It is all or nothing. The whole of creation is for God's people and hence its use was given to Noah and his seed. But not to them as "general people" but as participants in the covenant. Those who disassociate themselves from the covenant, waive the right to re-creation.[40]

---

[39] Cf. Frame (2011, 137): "God's covenant with Noah is an administration of God's redemptive grace, religious through and through, just as those with Abraham, Moses, David, and Christ."

[40] Van der Waal (1990, 28–29).

7.6.2   The Noahic Covenant Is Redemptive [41]

The Noahic covenant was a covenant with the entire human race after the Flood, and even with "every living creature of all flesh that is on the earth" (Gen. 6:18; 9:9–17). God promised that he would never again destroy his creatures through a worldwide flood. It was an "everlasting covenant" (v. 16), that is, a covenant that would remain valid as long as the present earth would exist, that is (on a pre- or postmillennial standpoint), including the future Messianic kingdom.

The primary partner in this covenant was Noah, and in him, secondarily, all living creatures; it is a universal covenant. Some expositors have presumed that this is the same as "the covenant that I had made with all the peoples" (Zech. 11:10).[42] Others have thought here of God's "covenant of security and restraint, by which he had been apparently holding back the nations from his people (cf. Ezek. 34:25; Hos. 2:18)."[43]

I repeat: it is quite amazing that the argument that God used to bring a water flood over humanity (Gen. 6:5) was virtually the same as the argument he used after the Flood to henceforth spare humanity (8:21). In his (justified) anger, he brought judgment; but in his love, he spared humanity on the basis of Noah's sacrifice (see §7.6.1). This is why this sacrifice is so crucial—a point entirely overlooked by Kline and VanDrunen, as we have seen. The burnt offering that Noah brought from all clean animals, and whose "pleasing aroma" was smelled by God (Gen. 8:20–21), shows that the Noahic covenant was not at all some covenant pertaining to a supposed "common kingdom." It was not even a covenant of *common* grace, as has sometimes been asserted,[44] but of redemptive grace.[45] Since the Flood, God deals with the earth, not according to humanity's sinful works but according to the sacrifice of Christ that is anticipated here. Note well: common grace is based on the cross; that is to say, those temporal favours bestowed upon unbelieving humanity are due to Christ's atoning work (cf. Matt. 5:45; Acts 14:17).

The sign of the Noahic covenant is the rainbow: "This is the sign of the covenant that I make between me and you and every living creature that is

---

[41] See Ouweneel (2016g, §2.2.3).

[42] So Ridderbos (1935, 158).

[43] Barker (1985, 677); rejected by Ridderbos (see previous note).

[44] Cf. Bavinck (*RD* 3:218–19); Van der Waal (1990, 28); Brown and Keele (2012, 74–75).

[45] Though he hardly referred to the sacrifice, Gentry (2012, 175) underscored the redemptive nature of this covenant: "The unmerited favor and kindness of God in preserving his world in the covenant with Noah creates a firm stage of history where God can work out his plan for rescuing his fallen world. It also points ahead to the coming deliverance in Jesus Christ."

with you, for all future generations: I have set my bow in the cloud, and it shall be a sign of the covenant between me and the earth" (Gen. 9:12–13). We must compare this with Ezekiel 1:28, Revelation 4:3 and 10:1, where the rainbow is connected with the glory of God, and stands in the framework of God's redemptive dealings with his people. Again, the Noahic covenant cannot be separated from the redemptive kingdom of God.

Another argument for the direct relationship of the Noahic covenant to the redemptive kingdom of God is the fact that there are *two* promises here (VanDrunen underscores only the first promise): (a) the promise that God will not again destroy the earth through a flood (Gen. 9:14–15); *and* (b) the promise of blessing for the "Japhethites" (read: the western Gentiles) in the "tents of Shem" (read: Israel, Shem's most significant offspring; v. 27). The blessings that Noah pronounced upon his sons cannot be separated from the Noahic covenant; they supply its historical and eschatological perspective. God is no longer dealing with the human race in its totality, as he had done before the Flood. The redemptive line, which had begun with Noah and his sons, is now being continued with only one of the three: Shem, although the Japhethites, too, would find blessing in the "tents of Shem." After this, among the descendants of Shem the line is continued with Eber, and eventually with Abr(ah)am (Gen. 10).

Please note, there is no question of two different kingdoms that supposedly are being delineated by means of the Noahic covenant; that notion is mere theological fantasy. The Noahic covenant eventually narrows to the line of Abraham and his descendants. Both promises just mentioned are anticipatorily rooted in the cross of Christ, and both point forward to the kingdom of the Man Jesus Christ.

7.6.3 Cultural Homogeneity?

Perhaps the most disturbing aspect of NL2K's view of the Noahic covenant is the idea that this covenant would be the basis for cultural homogeneity throughout history and throughout the world.[46] Brian Mattson, in his sharp attack on NL2K, rightly said,

> Few suggestions can be more historically ignorant and empirically false. To state the blindingly obvious: the history of the human race is not a history of cultural homogeneity. It is nothing but the record of cultures in conflict, most often resulting in warfare, bloodshed, persecution and slavery. Very simply, if God's promises cannot fail and

---

[46] Cf. VanDrunen (2010a, 31, 78–81, 168–69).

yet human history displays to us cultural conflict instead of homogeneity, we should entertain the notion that God never promised cultural homogeneity. And, in fact, he never did. There is nothing whatsoever in the Noahic covenant that promises such a thing.[47]

Joseph Boot rightly remarked:

Where in the Genesis text [Gen. 6–9] is to be found a promise of shared cultural values and norms throughout time? Crucially, if this idea were explicit or implicit in this text then we should expect, without fail, widespread homogeneity of cultural values and norms amongst the human race across all civilizations since the time of Noah. Since God's promises cannot fail VanDrunen and company must argue that there has been such homogeneity.... It is plain to any serious observer of human life and culture that we have anything but a history of cultural sameness. The obvious choice then is [that] either is God a liar or the 2K view of Noah's covenant is wrong. History is the record of radical conflict of norms and values. Even today in the West alone we might consider issues like abortion, human sexuality, marriage, criminal law, political doctrine, and far-reaching philosophical ideas that shape every field of education like evolution to show the complete lack of homogeneity in the things that matter most. The *evolutionary paradigm*, for example, has increasingly generated an intellectual climate and culture hostile to Christianity at almost every point in the West. And just in the last century, where was the cultural hegemony in Europe [and Asia] with the rise of Hitler's Germany, Stalin's Russia, Mao's China, Pol Pot's Cambodia, Mussolini's Italy or the Ayatollah's Iran? Today where is our commonality with the West's death cult manifest in its wanton destruction of human life and the family?[48]

Boot added that the main reason why the Western world has had such high ethical values—I would say: despite its wars, fascism and communism, human trafficking and enslavement[49] and a resulting civil war—is not

---

[47] Mattson (2011).

[48] Boot (2016).

[49] Cf. Mattson (2011): "Why is there widespread denunciation of slavery in the world today? Because cultures uninfluenced by Christianity, with no contact with God's special revelation, reflecting merely on the created order decided to reverse millennia of slave-trading practice? Hardly. It took a persevering Christian culture-warrior named William Wilberforce to infuse Western culture with its abhorrence of slavery."

because of Noah's covenant but *because of the Judeo-Christian tradition.* It is simply impossible to derive evidence for a "common kingdom" from our present-day Western societies because everything that is still so valued and valuable about these societies is the earlier effect of the gospel. Notice how absurd this whole argument is: proving a "common kingdom," as distinguished from the "kingdom of God," *on the basis of a society that was once thoroughly Christian!* As Mattson put it: insofar as there is cultural homogeneity at certain places it is because "Christians have historically been effective in transforming cultural norms and expectations."[50]

WORKING IT OUT: BEING UNDER CHRIST'S LORDSHIP IN YOUR JOB
How can I show in my daily job that I am under the lordship of Christ?

In my view, there is a more superficial, and a deeper answer to this question. On the superficial level, we can easily understand that Jesus is the Lord of every believer, that is, the Master over the believer's life in everything he does. As Paul says, "If you confess with your mouth that Jesus is Lord and believe in your heart that God raised him from the dead, you will be saved" (Rom. 10:9). "For if we live, we live to the Lord, and if we die, we die to the Lord. So then, whether we live or whether we die, we are the Lord's" (14:8). "In your hearts revere Christ as Lord" (1 Pet. 3:15 NIV). Whether I am a church member, a husband or a wife, a parent or a child, a citizen, a teacher or a pupil, an employer or employee, in all these capacities I am under the authority of the Lord, and I must behave accordingly.

A few biblical examples are:

Children, obey your parents *in the Lord,* for this is right.... Fathers, do not provoke your children to anger, but bring them up in the discipline and instruction *of the Lord.* Bondservants, obey your earthly masters with fear and trembling, with a sincere heart, as you would Christ..., rendering service with a good will as to *the Lord* and not to man, knowing that whatever good anyone does, this he will receive back from *the Lord,* whether he is a bondservant or is free. Masters, do the same to them, and stop your threatening, knowing that he who is both *their Master and yours* is in heaven, and that there is no partiality with him (Eph. 6:1–9).

---

[50] Mattson (2011).

Wives, submit to your husbands, as is fitting *in the Lord* [cf. Eph. 5:22] .... Children, obey your parents in everything, for this pleases *the Lord*.... Bondservants, obey in everything those who are your earthly masters, not by way of eye-service, as people-pleasers, but with sincerity of heart, *fearing the Lord*. Whatever you do, work heartily, *as for the Lord* and not for men, knowing that from *the Lord* you will receive the inheritance as your reward. You are serving *the Lord Christ*. Masters, treat your bondservants justly and fairly, knowing that you also have a *Master* in heaven" (Col. 3:18–4:1).

However, having said this, we must realize that this, in itself, does not prove that marriage, our family, our businesses and companies, our schools and associations, *as such* stand under the lordship of Christ, which is the same as saying that they are part of the kingdom of God. This brings us to the deeper answer: in our daily jobs we are under the lordship of Christ, not just because we *individually* are servants of the Lord but because the societal relationships in which we function *as such* are objectively, and must subjectively be brought, under the lordship of Christ.

Take a person's family. In my view, it is untenable that father and mother, as well as all the believing children, are *individually* under the lordship of Christ, that is, are subjects of the kingdom, whereas the family *as such* would belong to the supposed "common kingdom." In reality, the parents may say something like this: in this family, Christ is our King. This family as a family stands under his rules, and mom and dad try to establish and maintain these rules as well as they can. There are basically only two kingdoms in this world. I am not referring to God's kingdom and some "common kingdom," but to the kingdom of God as opposed to the kingdom of Satan (Matt. 12:25–28). A family is basically either under the rule of Satan, or under the rule of Christ. There is no middle position, and certainly no "common," "neutral," or "secular" position. It is either sin and Satan that dominate any family, or (in spite of all weakness in the family) King Jesus. It is either the kingdom of Satan that is primarily manifested in any family, or it is the kingdom of God. There is no neutral ground.

In principle, it is the same in a Christian school. If the term "Christian" has not been debased, if it still means something, the school leaders may say something like this: in this school, Christ is our King. This school as a school stands under his rules, and the school leaders and teachers try to establish and maintain these rules as well as they can. A school is basically either under the rule of Satan, or under the rule of Christ (although often it is a bit of both). It is either sin and Satan that dominate any school, or (in spite of all weakness in the school) King Jesus. It is either the kingdom of Satan that is primarily manifested in any school, or it is the kingdom of God. Again, there is no neutral ground here.

The same holds in principle for any Christian business or company, that is, a company of which the directors are sincere and convinced Christians, and, of course, part of their employees as well. Perhaps the directors will not put it in these words; yet, they might implicitly argue: in this company, Christ is our King (formulated more modestly: we try to follow Christian principles). This company as a company stands under his rules, and the directors try to establish and maintain these rules as well as they can.

Do you see my point? As a matter of principle, it is the same in any Christian association and in any Christian political party: *here, at this place, we basically follow the commandments of the King* (in spite of all the weaknesses that we encounter in ourselves).

So we see that, in all their societal relationships, Christians are under the lordship of Christ. At the very least, this is the case individually: a Christian in an unbelieving family, or at a "neutral" school, or in a "neutral" company, or in a "neutral" political party, is still personally a follower and servant of the Lord. However, wherever Christians get a chance, they endeavour to bring the entire family, school, company, or political party under the lordship of Christ, that is, under the rules of the kingdom of God. Of course, in such societal relationships, the rights, freedom, and dignity of non-Christians are always respected. The Christian family, school, or company does not coerce its non-Christian members to become Christians too. The only thing that is asked of them is to respect the fact that they are in a domain where the rules of Christ are supreme.

SOJOURNER THEOLOGY[1]

PREPARATORY PONDERINGS

1. What does it mean to say that we are "strangers and sojourners" in this world?
2. Are certain domains of society more wicked than others? Or can wickedness—as well as God's power!—be manifested equally intensely in every domain of life (including even the church)? Explain your answer.
3. Does our present Christian situation in society resemble that of Israel in Canaan, or that of Israel in Babylon? Why?
4. Does our present Christian situation in society resemble that of Israel under kings David and Solomon (prefiguring Christ)? What are the similarities, and what are the dissimilarities?

---

[1] See also the much wider treatment of this subject in Ouweneel (2016e).

8.1 STRANGERS AND SOJOURNERS

8.1.1   Four Meanings

The biblical notion of a Christian living as a "stranger" and "sojourner" plays an important role in NL2K thought,[2] although conclusions have been drawn from this notion that, in my opinion, cannot be theologically sustained. For starters, with regard to God's people (i.e., apart from the foreigners living in the midst of Israel; see Lev. 25:35, 47; Num. 9:14; 15:15; 35:15), this notion has at least four different meanings in the Bible.

(a) *Israel in Canaan.* In the Mosaic Torah, God told the people of Israel, "The land is mine. For you are strangers and sojourners with me" (Lev. 25:23). David VanDrunen makes a great distinction between Israel's living in the promised land and Israel dwelling in Babylon,[3] which in itself is correct, of course. However, it is good to realize that, from a certain point of view, the Israelites were also "strangers and sojourners" *in their own land,* because basically the land was not theirs at all, but the Lord's. This point is entirely overlooked by VanDrunen (see §8.4.3).[4] Even when living under kings David and Solomon, the Israelites were "strangers and sojourners" with God. Similarly, we are "strangers and sojourners" in the present world, while at the same time the entire world is the kingdom of Jesus Christ (see §8.5.3). David himself expressed this as follows: "But who am I, and what is my people, that we should be able thus to offer willingly? For all things come from you, and of your own have we given you. *For we are strangers before you and sojourners,* as all our fathers were" (1 Chron. 29:14–15). Elsewhere he sings, "I am a sojourner with you, a guest, like all my fathers" (Ps. 39:12).

(b) *Israel in exile.* Interestingly, the expression "strangers and sojourners" is never used for the Israelites who lived in exile. However, Ezra 1:4 does speak of Israelites "sojourning" at certain places in the Persian Empire, and God speaks of Israelites whom he would lead "out of the land where they sojourn" (Ezek. 29:38). They were "in a land that was not theirs," and "they were servants there" (cf. Gen. 15:13). Even after their return from the Babylonian Empire, the Israelites were still "slaves" of the Persian king (Neh. 9:36) because the land of Israel was still part of the Persian Empire.

---

[2] See, e.g., VanDrunen (2010a, Part II; 2014, chapter 6); cf. also Hart (2006, 253–57); Stellman (2009, xxiii–xxv).

[3] VanDrunen (2010a, 69, 75–97).

[4] Ibid., 89–90.

(c) *Unconverted Gentiles.* The apostle Paul tells Gentile Christians, "Remember that you were at that time separated from Christ, alienated from the commonwealth of Israel and strangers to the covenants of promise, having no hope and without God in the world.... So then you are no longer strangers and sojourners, but you are fellow citizens with the saints and members of the household of God" (Eph. 2:12, 19 ESV note). Verse 12 describes what these Gentile believers were before their conversion, in relation to the believers from Israel. If we wish to emphasize that Christians are "strangers and sojourners," we have to realize that, from a different point of view, they are *no longer* strangers and sojourners today, after having become part of the body of Christ and the temple of the Holy Spirit.

(d) *Christians.* Peter writes to his addressees, "Beloved, I urge you as sojourners and exiles to abstain from the passions of the flesh, which wage war against your soul" (1 Pet. 2:11; cf. 1:1, "To those who are elect exiles of the Dispersion..."). And the letter to the Hebrews presents to the believers the example of the patriarchs, who recognized "that they were strangers and exiles on the earth.... For people who speak thus make it clear that they are seeking a homeland...they desire a better country, that is, a heavenly one" (Heb. 11:13–16).

8.1.2 The "World"

The believer is a foreigner, an exile, a stranger in the present world, or, as some would say, a pilgrim,[5] that is, someone travelling through a foreign country to some holy place (cf. the important parallel in Exod. 15:13, 17).[6] This means that the regenerated, believing person realizes that he finds himself in the midst of, and in opposition to, a world that is strongly dominated by sin, Satan, and death (see §5.1.2). According to his new nature, the believer is "foreign" to this evil world, whereas at the same time he stands right in the middle of this world. This is not a contradiction, for "world" in the latter meaning has to do with society (horizontal: *structure*), whereas "world" in the former meaning has to do with Godward versus apostate living (vertical: *direction*; see again §§3.2.2 and 4.5). The Christian has a calling that he must fulfill in the world (i.e., society) in the horizontal sense,

---

[5] We find the notion already with Augustine, *Confessiones* IX.13: "...in the eternal Jerusalem, to which go out the sighs of your people of pilgrims, from their exodus until their return to there" (www9.georgetown.edu/faculty/jod/latinconf/9.html). Cf. also Bunyan's masterpiece (written during the 1660s; repr. 2007), and many Puritan and pietistic hymns.

[6] To Horton (2011), the notion is so important that the subtitle of his book is: *A Systematic Theology for Pilgrims on the Way*; interestingly, though, the word "pilgrim" does not appear anywhere in the book's Subject Index.

but he does so in an "unworldly" way ("world" in the vertical sense).[7] As a pilgrim, the Christian is on his way, travelling through the present world, to another, better world, the holy world of God and his Christ, the Messianic kingdom as it will be displayed in glory and righteousness at the second coming of Jesus.

Some scholastic (including pietistic) Christians have used this very notion of pilgrimage to reject the whole idea of Christian politics—"we have nothing to seek in this world"[8]—or to reject any Christian participation in politics. "Foreigners don't vote in the country where they sojourn." This is certainly not the attitude of NL2K.[9] However, the theology of NL2K does use the notion of "strangers and sojourners" as an argument for their distinction of two realms: the kingdom of God and the common kingdom. This is a categorical mistake. The notion of "strangers and sojourners" has to do with the vertical dimension of our existence in the present world: we are foreign to everything that in the present world is of sin and Satan. However, the distinction between the kingdom of God and the common kingdom is an (inherently erroneous) division of a horizontal nature: it creates a gap between the church (in its immanent meaning) and the rest of society.

The Christian notion of being strangers and sojourners may indeed help us to get a clearer idea of the position of Christians in society, and of their proper attitude towards politics, but there are at least two conditions. First, the horizontal and the vertical dimensions must be carefully distinguished, as I just explained. Second, pictures like this one always fail in certain respects. For instance, the Israelites were servants/slaves of foreign kings in the lands of their exiles (§8.1.1 point [b]), but we Christians are definitely not. We may still sin, but we are no longer slaves of sin, Satan, and death (Rom. 6:20–22; Heb. 2:14–15). We are servants/slaves of Christ (1 Cor. 4:1; 2 Cor. 11:23; Phil. 1:1; Col. 4:12; 1 Tim. 4:6) in all that we undertake. We are not slaves of the world, like the Israelites were slaves of the kings of Egypt, Babylon, and Persia, respectively.

Sometimes, the word "world" has quite a neutral meaning in the Bible. In these cases, it means the totality of creation (e.g., Matt. 4:8; Rom. 1:20), or the entire human race (e.g., John 3:16; Mark 14:9). In many other cases,

---

[7] Horton does not clearly distinguish between the two dimensions: he recommends that we be "worldly Christians" (1995, 15–34), but avoid "the virus of worldliness" (1995, 179; cf. 176). Stellman (2009, 127–28) is not very clear on this point, either.

[8] Cf., e.g., this hymn by John N. Darby (d. 1882): "This world is a wilderness wide! / We have nothing to seek or to choose; / We've no thought in the waste to abide; / We've naught to regret nor to lose.... 'Tis the treasure we've found in His love / That has made us now pilgrims below."

[9] Cf. VanDrunen (2010a, 194–205).

the word has a negative meaning: it is the system of sin and Satan (in addition to the verses quoted earlier in §5.1.2, see Rom. 3:19; 1 Cor. 3:19; Gal. 1:4; 6:14; 2 Tim. 4:10). *But never are we viewed as slaves of this world.* To be more precise: we are in the world in its first meaning, but in fact we are not at all in the world in its second meaning. We have nothing to do with the spiritual kings of Egypt, Babylon, and Persia, so to speak; much less are we their slaves.

When Jesus says that his followers are still "in the world" (John 17:11), the word may still have more or less the neutral, horizontal meaning. But when he adds that they are not "of the world" (vv. 14–16), then "world" refers to this negative realm of sin and Satan to which believers no longer belong. It is very important to distinguish between the two meanings. Christians are "in the world," that is, they not only live on the same planet as the wicked, but they are part of the same society. They participate in it as employers and employees, as buyers and sellers, as citizens and taxpayers, they participate in all forms of traffic, in business life, in the world of science, in cultural life, and so on. All of this has to do with the divinely ordained structures of society, including all the societal relationships.

However, "world" in the other, negative meaning has to do with direction: with the kingdom of God versus the kingdom of Satan. In the former, horizontal sense, we are definitely *not* foreigners and exiles: we may be proud of our earthly country, we may be happy with the place we occupy in society. We may participate in it fully, and derive great satisfaction from it, for which we are thankful to the Lord. In the latter, vertical sense, however, we realize that we *are* foreigners and exiles: we do not want to have anything to do with the world as the kingdom of Satan (although, unfortunately, we cannot always avoid it). Taking the two dimensions together, we might say, there is nothing we have to fear in society except sin and Satan. The kingdom of God is realized and manifested in *every* sector of society (*contra* NL2K), but in constant conflict with the kingdom of Satan, which is manifested in *every* sector of society as well.

8.1.3 World Flight

It is quite understandable that, in church history, the notion of Christians being "strangers and sojourners" has often led to what the Dutch call *wereldmijding*, that is, "avoiding the world" through world flight, separatism, quietism.[10] In this way, the two meanings of *world* were totally confused,

---

[10] In this connection, Horton (1995, 141–45, 175–76) speaks of "pietism" and a "Christian ghetto"; see also Stellman (2009, 80–83).

that is, structure and direction were mixed up. There is no single domain in this world (read: society) that is inherently unworthy of our participation, as long as its direction is Godward.

Those who misunderstood this began to avoid certain *domains* in society, as if these domains in themselves were unworthy of our participation: politics, universities, sports clubs, trade unions, the arts, music, science, etc. They did not see that *any* of these domains—without exception—could indeed become subservient to sin and Satan, but could also be consecrated to God within the kingdom of God. None of these domains are wrong in themselves—it is only their direction that may be very problematic. This observation pertains to *every* societal domain, including marriage, the family, and even the church (in its immanent meaning)—they all can become apostate.

The power of sin and Satan is not by definition stronger in one societal relationship than in any other. If people want to "avoid the world" in the sense I have just described, they would be consistent only if they would withdraw from *all* societal relationships and communities (cf. 1 Cor. 5:10). In this context, it may strike us that, when Paul wants to illustrate the practical significance of the "new man" in the domains of life (Eph. 4:25–6:9), he devotes some verses to servants and masters (five), and to the family (four), and to marriage (twelve), but most to the believers' functioning together, say, in their churches (twenty-nine verses; part of these concern more the believers' personal behaviour, though). In other words, Paul does not assume that the atmosphere within the church is by definition more holy than in the family and at work!

The church is not a safe haven when it comes to avoiding sin, Satan, and world. The most devoted church denomination, the most dedicated local church congregation, would not be safe because they are "open vessels;" sin and Satan may manifest themselves there no less than in any other societal relationship. We need only compare Christ's own complaints against five of the seven churches in Revelation 2 and 3 (no "first love" anymore, heretical teaching, idolatry, sexual immorality, spiritual death, tepidity, self-conceitedness).

Therefore, even withdrawing into a convent (monastery, nunnery, or a sacred Protestant community) would not help because the convent, too, is a societal community in which sin and Satan can be manifested. This is because in every societal institution there are people who live in terms of the "flesh" (their sinful nature). Anyone wanting to withdraw from the world would, as it were, have to withdraw from *himself*, for the world is manifested also in our own hearts (Rom. 12:2). It is not just an enemy out there, but it is an enemy that finds an ally, so to speak, a "fifth column," within ourselves.

8.1.4 The Options

NL2K does not follow the pietistic road (see previous section); it follows what I call the "neutrality road." In this connection, I see three options.

(a) The *pietistic* (within the Reformed world: hyper-Calvinist) option: society is in principle bad; stay away from it as much as you can.

(b) The NL2K option: it makes the same objectionable horizontal division between the church and (the rest of) society. However, it does not declare the world bad, but common; it distinguishes between the two as the kingdom of God and the divinely ordained common kingdom.

(c) I see this as the *biblical* option: there is *no* division between church and (the rest of) society. Instead, there are two distinctions to be made. One is the *horizontal* distinction between the church (in its immanent meaning, i.e., a church denomination or a local congregation), the state, marriage, the family, the school, and so forth. The other distinction is the *vertical* one between the kingdom of God and the kingdom of Satan; both are manifested in *both the (visible) church and in all other societal relationships.*

In other words, the Holy Spirit manifests himself primarily in the hearts and lives of individual believers, and subsequently in all the societal relationships and communities to which these believers belong. No societal relationships are inherently evil or worldly because each of them is rooted in God's creational ordinances. Therefore, if some societal relationships would be inherently evil, we would have to blame God's creational law for these relationships! No, it is not the God-given structures that are bad; it is only their direction that can be bad because of sinful people functioning in them. To these structures belong faithful, dedicated churches, as well as apostate cultural and scientific associations—to state the matter in black-and-white—*just as there are also corrupt, apostate churches as well as cultural and scientific associations dedicated to God.* The structures are never inherently bad—it is their direction that can be very bad.

8.2 "SACRED" AND "PROFANE"

8.2.1 Wrong Distinctions

The entire effort to connect our pilgrimage to some form of "avoiding the world," in the sense of avoiding (parts of) society or avoiding (parts of) culture, is mistaken *a priori*. (This is what I say to pietists, not to NL2K advocates.) The basic error is identifying what is sinful, evil, and unholy with certain areas in life and in society that are to be avoided. This is a relic of medieval scholastic thinking, in which nature—the allegedly profane domain—is viewed apart from grace, the sacred domain.

There are many examples of this error. It occurred in strict Roman Catholic circles with their various forms of asceticism, especially in convents. It occurred in very conservative (hyper-)Calvinist circles, as during the *Nadere Reformatie* ("Second Reformation") in the Netherlands (seventeenth and eighteenth centuries), where almost the whole society seemed taboo and was left to the enemy. It occurred in Anabaptist circles where, in its most extreme form, the German city of Münster at a certain moment was considered to be the safe haven for God's true people, led by John of Leiden (1535). It occurred in neo-Calvinist circles with their strong emphasis on their own entirely independent Christian organizations in virtually every domain of life.[11] These are very different religious denominations, but with one common error: the idea that there are sacred domains, and there are profane domains. To such Christians, "Do not be conformed to this world" (Rom. 12:2), mainly meant, and means, "Stay away from the 'profane' areas," ranging from politics to entertainment.

Note well: the difference between this "world avoidance" attitude and that of NL2K, which reduces these "profane areas" to a supposed "common kingdom," is only one of degree. In the former case, the "profane areas" are bad, while in the latter case they are "divinely ordained." To be sure, that itself is an enormous difference. However, the important (and objectionable) similarity is this: *in both cases these domains are carefully kept separate from the kingdom of God.*

The entire distinction between sacred and profane domains, as a horizontal distinction between structures, has to be utterly rejected, whether the distinction roots in a worldview that is pietistic or a NL2K type. *Every* societal relationship, including politics and entertainment, can become sacred if it is dedicated to God and his kingdom. And *every* societal relationship, including churches and Bible clubs, can become profane if it actually—consciously or unconsciously—turns its back on God and his kingdom. In principle, there are (or have been) apostate and sacred families, apostate and sacred churches, apostate and sacred states, apostate and sacred schools, apostate and sacred companies, apostate and sacred cultural activities, apostate and sacred universities. In the apostate relationships, the kingdom of Satan is manifested, in the sacred relationships the kingdom of God is manifested. I say "in principle," because too often we are dealing with some mixture of good and evil. No single earthly domain

---

[11] Cf. the slogan of Dutch Reformed historian and politician Guillaume Groen van Prinsterer (d. 1876), viewed as one of the forerunners of neo-Calvinism: "In isolation lies our strength."

is totally wicked, and no single earthly domain is totally sacred and safe. There is no institution in which the kingdom of God is manifested perfectly, not "even" the church.

The pilgrim metaphor is helpful: far too often the path travelled by the Christ-believing pilgrim goes through a wilderness with an oasis here and there. That is, it goes through very unsafe, wicked areas, with a few sacred rest areas along the way (not only churches, but any company of Christians, individually or within societal relationships). But if the pilgrim's heart has been taken captive by God's Word and Spirit, he will spread the light of God's kingdom in *any* of the societal relationships in which he participates, no matter how defectively.

8.2.2 Wicked Societal Relationships?

Some might argue here that it cannot be true that any societal relationship or community as such could become sacred. They may mention examples such as a pack of thieves, or a brothel, or a "church" of Satan. Are these not societal relationships that as such are wicked? My answer is that this is the wrong question. A pack of thieves and a brothel are, according to their law structure, profit-making enterprises, and neither profit-making nor enterprises as such are wrong.

However, on the subject side, or factual side,[12] we are dealing with an absolutely anti-normative realization of the entrepreneurial structure. The pack of thieves lives parasitically in violation of the eighth commandment ("You shall not steal"), and the brothel lives parasitically in violation of the seventh commandment ("You shall not commit adultery," or more generally, "fornication") (Exod. 20:14–15). Thus, the "church" of Satan, too, according to its law structure, is a church in the sense of a religious community (if it is not, instead, just another profit-making enterprise), and there is nothing wrong with respect to this law structure as such. However, with respect to the subject side, the "church" of Satan is the most anti-normative realization of a church structure one could imagine. It is an outright rebellion against the first commandment: "You shall have no other gods before [or, besides] me" (Exod. 20:3; cf. 2 Cor. 4:4).

Again I must emphasize that there are no sinful creation structures as such. Not being conformed to the world does not simply mean avoiding certain "bad" places. We need good Christian entrepreneurs, and politicians, and musicians, and scientists, and social workers, and so on—and don't forget the plumbers! If somebody asks whether Christian entrepreneurs,

---

[12] See Ouweneel (2014a) for these terms.

politicians, musicians, scientists, social workers, and plumbers do their job in a way essentially different than non-Christians, we reply: as to horizontal creational structures, the answer is no. A Christian businessman, or mayor, or pianist, or plumber, does not do his job (leading a firm, leading a municipality, making piano music, doing plumbing) necessarily in a qualitatively better, or even different, way than the non-Christian. But when it comes to the vertical direction, the answer is an emphatic yes! Christian entrepreneurs, politicians, musicians, scientists, social workers, and plumbers consecrate their jobs, or ought to do so, to the service of the kingdom of Christ, and to the honour of the King. (For more discussion of "Christian plumbing," see §11.4.2.)

Let me put it this way: in a non-Christian environment, Christians play their harps to possessed king Saul (cf. 1 Sam. 16:14–23); in a Christian environment, they play their harps to Christ-presenting king David. They play the same notes—yet, the music sounds different to anyone who can hear. It is like the music that you play for a person you don't like, or the music that you play for your beloved. Or, to modify an illustration used by Reformed theologian Klaas Schilder: some unbelievers are quarrying marble to build a fancy brothel, some believers to build a cathedral. They use the same marble-quarrying techniques, but in service to an antithetical agenda.[13]

8.3 HEAVENLY CITIZENS

8.3.1 Heaven versus the Earth

From the foregoing, we can now easily see how the notions of pilgrimage and exile are to be understood, and how they can be linked with the notion of the kingdom of God. Does the fact that we are foreigners, exiles, and pilgrims (1 Pet. 2:11) mean that we have nothing to do with earthly society? Longing for a heavenly country (Heb. 11:13–16)—does that imply that we want nothing to do with our earthly country? Not at all—and here we can agree with NL2K over against pietism or hyper-Calvinism. I can easily demonstrate why the attitude of the latter is wrong. Peter makes clear that our being foreigners does *not* imply that we no longer have anything to do with earthly relationships. On the contrary, he gives us several exhortations as to the earthly relationships or communities to which we certainly do belong: the state (vv. 13–17), work (vv. 18–25), and marriage (3:1–7).

---

[13] Schilder (2016, 32).

Our pilgrimage and exile do not imply that we abstain from politics, from business, from marriage (horizontal), but that we "abstain from the passions of the flesh, which wage war against your soul" (2:11) (vertical)! Not politics, nor business, nor marriage, nor the arts—the horizontal structures as such—are wrong, but all "passions of the flesh" in politics, business, marriage, and the arts (the vertical dimension). The structures are not wrong, but the apostate direction within these structures, or within individual life, is wrong. This holds both for non-believers and for believers whose lives and drives are taken up with these structures. All Christians who lose sight of the vertical dimension are forgetting their pilgrimage, and fall prey to "passions of the flesh," just like non-Christians do.

Similarly, the heavenly country in Hebrews 11 is not contrasted with the earthly country, as if we no longer have anything to do with the latter. Abraham, Isaac, and Jacob were foreigners and pilgrims in Canaan, but they were very much involved with the affairs of the country they lived in.[14] They even formed alliances and treaties with the people in the land (Gen. 14:13; 21:22–24; 26:28–31). We too participate in all kinds of earthly relationships, but our lives in them, and the tasks and responsibilities that we have within them, are governed by our longing for the heavenly country. The essential *difference* between NL2K and this point of view is that NL2K secularizes what it calls the "common kingdom," whereas we insist that the kingdom of God can be manifested in all societal relationships. In this sense a common kingdom simply does not exist at all.

This may help us understand Philippians 3:20, "our citizenship is in heaven," that is, we are citizens of heaven; we possess a heavenly citizenship. Being "strangers and sojourners" as well as being citizens belong together as two sides of the same coin: strangers and sojourners here below, citizens there above. However, we are *not* yet there above. Our actual *position* is there, in Christ (Eph. 2:6), our actual life is there, hidden with Christ in God (Col. 3:3), but *personally* we are still on earth, with all concomitant offices, tasks, and responsibilities. Moreover, the kingdom of God is explicitly a kingdom *on earth*. In our capacity as heavenly citizens, we endeavour to bring to light the kingdom of God in every domain of our earthly lives.

With reference to G. K. Chesterton, Jason Stellman put it this way:

A true saint has his hands in the dirt rather than his head in the clouds. Saints can afford to get themselves dirty as they roll up their sleeves and "do earth," engaging in the stuff of life. The gnostic and

[14] Cf. VanDrunen (2010a, Part II).

sanctimonious pretender to true piety, on the other hand, must keep his hands clean from such dirt (not so much because it is *earthy*, but because it is *earthly*). Of course, pilgrim theology's insistence on the tension between the already and the not yet demands that a saint be *both* otherworldly and worldly. "Head in heaven, fingers in the mire," in the words of one poet.[15]

Although Stellman represents NL2K, he correctly describes here how the heavenly citizen is called to function in every earthly relationship.

8.3.2 "The Earth Is the LORD's"

This earth, not heaven (in the sense of God's dwelling place), is the very domain of the kingdom of God: "The earth is the LORD's" (Exod. 9:29; Ps. 24:1; 1 Cor. 10:26). To be sure, in the Gospel according to Matthew, this kingdom is usually called the "kingdom of heaven," but in no passage is it a kingdom *in* heaven, as, for instance, Luther sometimes seems to suggest (his rendering *Himmelreich*, which can be understood as "heavenly realm," also tends in this direction). Entering the kingdom, as in Matthew 19:23–24 or 2 Peter 1:11, is then understood as entering heaven.[16] Among the church fathers, some believed in a *regnum caelorum terrestre* ("earthly kingdom of heaven") and others believed in a *regnum caelorum caeleste* ("heavenly kingdom of heaven").[17]

If we compare passages concerning the "kingdom of heaven" in Matthew with similar passages in Mark and Luke, we will soon discover that the "kingdom of heaven" is the same as the "kingdom of God" (see, e.g., Matt. 19:14; Mark 10:14; Luke 18:16). In Matthew, the word heaven is nothing but a euphemism for "God" (cf. Luke 15:21, "sinned against heaven;" Matt. 5:34, "swearing by heaven"). The "kingdom of heaven" is a kingdom in which "heaven," that is, the heavenly Man Christ, reigns over the earth. Compare here what Daniel told Nebuchadnezzar, "Heaven rules," that is, the Most High God rules over the earth (Dan. 4:26). Living believers are citizens of a "heavenly" kingdom *on earth*.

The heavenly citizenship of Christians is not just something to look forward to, as something that will be realized at death, or at the second coming of Christ. Rather, it is something to be realized in a preliminary form here and now, in *all* societal relationships to which Christians belong.

---

[15] Stellman (2009, 134–35).
[16] Thus, e.g., Matthew Henry (bible.cc/matthew/19-23.htm en bible.cc/2_peter/1-11.htm).
[17] See Hill (2001).

Christians have the calling to demonstrate in every earthly relationship the way that heavenly citizens behave in them. What kind of husbands and wives, parents and children, civil authorities and citizens, church leaders and church members, administrators, teachers and pupils, employers and employees, and so on, are heavenly citizens supposed to be? How do *heavenly* people behave in such *earthly* relationships? That way is different from that of the "earth dwellers," that is, people who not only live on this earth, but who find their whole existence there, clinging to it because they have nothing else (cf. Rev. 3:10; 6:10; 8:13; 11:10; 13:8–14; 14:6).

What the apostle Paul says about believing slaves can basically be said of all believers, in whatever societal position they live: in the heavenly manner in which they behave in all their earthly relationships and communities they "adorn the doctrine of our God and Savior in all things" (Titus 2:10 NKJV). Paul says this about slaves because for them, behaving this way poses the greatest challenge.

The Philippian Christians understood Paul's imagery very well because they lived in Philippi, which at that time had the status of a Roman colony. This meant that its inhabitants were considered to be citizens of Rome, although they lived in Philippi, far away from Rome. As citizens of Rome, the inhabitants were to take pride in showing to the whole Macedonian environment how a Roman citizen lives and works in Macedonia. Similarly, this earth is the "colony" where heavenly citizens are to show to their neighbours how a heavenly citizen lives and works on this earth.

We find parallel imagery in the letters to the Ephesians and the Colossians. They emphasize that our actual position, our actual life, exists in and with Christ in heaven. But this does not mean that these epistles encourage us to walk with our heads in the clouds. On the contrary, in the second half of both letters, our feet are given firm footing on the ground by showing us how a heavenly citizen glorifies God, and serves his neighbour, in such very earthly relationships as the local congregation, marriage, family, and work (Eph. 4:17–6:9; Col. 3:9–4:1). Therefore, the Christian is not only a heavenly citizen, but also a citizen of the kingdom of God, and this is on earth. (I even wonder if these two qualities are not basically the same.) The believer enjoys his position in the heavenly realms in Christ (Eph. 2:6), but he also possesses his "inheritance in the kingdom of Christ and God" (5:5). The believer's life is "hidden with Christ in God" (Col. 3:3), but he has also been "transferred...to the kingdom of his [i.e., the Father's] beloved Son" (1:13), and has been made a fellow worker for the kingdom of God (cf. 4:11).

8.4 BABYLON AND CANAAN

8.4.1   Schuurman on Babylon

In NL2K, as represented by David VanDrunen, the Babylon theme plays a considerable role.[18] In his battle against neo-Calvinism, or "transformation-alism," as it is sometimes called, it may be interesting to see that a typical neo-Calvinist like Egbert Schuurman has extensively made use of the very same theme. Schuurman is a Reformational philosopher, specializing in issues involving technology (his early training was in engineering), and was professor of Reformational philosophy at three Dutch universities. Moreover he was a member of the Senate of the Dutch Parliament for almost twenty-eight years (1983–2011), first representing the *Reformatorische Politieke Federatie* (Reformational Political Federation), and after the latter's fusion with the *Gereformeerd Politiek Verbond* (Reformed Political Alliance), the newly formed *ChristenUnie* (ChristianUnion). He has written many books, at least two of which have appeared in English translation.[19]

Regarding the scope of God's decree and Christ's kingdom, Schuurman wrote that God's "decree includes both the believer and the unbeliever, and it unfolds towards the coming of His Kingdom [at Christ's return]. In his Christian faith, hope and expectation, the Christian is called to serve that Kingdom, a service that *includes his scientific work and technical achievements.*"[20]

He describes the warrant for responsible Christian activity in today's culture this way:

> We cannot, in good faith, avoid the world. The Babel culture is a perversion of the Kingdom of God, a perversion which feeds off the forces of God's Kingdom. The Bible calls this culture the culture of darkness, and yet this darkness cannot extinguish the light that has burst upon this world with the coming of Christ (John 1:5). Through the coming of the Kingdom of God the Babel culture will be judged. The perspective of renewal, signified by Christ's glorification, is the perspective of responsible thought and action.[21]

---

[18] VanDrunen (2010a, 29–30, 92–97).
[19] Schuurman (1987; 2003).
[20] Schuurman (1987, 27); italics added.
[21] Schuurman (1987, 45).

Schuurman wrote about the kingdom of God especially according to its eschatological perspective. He saw no reason to speak any longer of a "Christian" culture, not because he adhered to the doctrine of the "two kingdoms," but because of the present "decline and doom of culture."[22] He called it "Babylonian:" "Here man worships various gods as he builds whatever his science and technology enable him to build," and described the position of Christians in it as "exiles:" "Exiles yearn to return to the living God. We must reject the false deities of our society and continue to fight the good fight."[23] To Schuurman, "Babylon" is not the kind of "common kingdom" that NL2K makes of it, where the Daniels and the heathen work together harmoniously. On the contrary, it is a demonically deteriorating culture.

At the end of this little book he wrote:

> I conclude that we should first of all learn not to see the Kingdom of God as the final goal of history and of our cultural endeavors. We must constantly remind ourselves that the Kingdom of God is a gift that has been given, is also truly given now, and, finally, will be given to us again in the future. The final renewal will show us the real meaning of our cultural endeavors. Then even Babylon will become Jerusalem. This divine mystery, given to us throughout history, cannot be comprehended, yet it is a life-giving dynamic deserving our respect, devotion, gratitude and sense of responsibility.[24]

8.4.2   The Use of Old Testament Examples

I find Schuurman interesting because, as a Christian philosopher, he clearly stands in the neo-Calvinist tradition of Abraham Kuyper and Herman Dooyeweerd. Yet, we do not find in his work the ideas that VanDrunen ascribes to neo-Calvinists, such as transformationalism ("we have to transform our world into the kingdom of God") and cultural optimism or triumphalism ("our cultural activities help to usher in the kingdom of God in all its God-intended splendor"). Rather, Schuurman is a cultural pessimist;[25] his hope is focused upon the Messianic kingdom as it will arrive at the second coming of Christ. Yet, Schuurman clearly sees that all our Christian activities, *including our scientific work and technical achievements*, belong to our kingdom task. In my words, in every domain of life, the kingdom of God represents the upward orientation toward Love, Light, and Life, and

---

[22] Schuurman (1987, 7).
[23] Schuurman (1987, 8).
[24] Schuurman (1987, 53).
[25] Cf. here the French Christian philosopher Jacques Ellul (1967; 1980).

Babel represents the downward orientation toward the Devil, Darkness, and Death. This is the cosmic contest of "3L versus 3D." These are not two domains (the structural dimension) but two different orientations within every cultural domain (the directional dimension).

VanDrunen, on the one hand, and Schuurman, on the other, illustrate that interpreters can use and apply Old Testament motifs like "Babylon" to "demonstrate" quite opposite conclusions. The illustrative meaning and power of such motifs are placed in service to a previously adopted view of society and culture; by themselves, these motifs prove nothing. VanDrunen says, "The experiences of...the Israelite exiles in Babylon (though not of Israel in the Promised Land) especially exemplify the two-kingdoms way of life in the Old Testament."[26] What this really means is this: if you already believe in NL2K, you might find the Babylon theme helpful to underpin this thought system. However, if you believe in a neo-Calvinist approach, you might find the Babylon theme equally helpful, but then applied in a rather different way.

Let me give one example of the intricacies of the Babylon theme. Israel had no choice: as long as the LORD did not lead them back to their own country they had to stay in Babylon. Similarly, we live in a world in which we are strangers and sojourners. However, at the same time we hear the following appeal: "Come out of her [i.e., the Great Babylon], my people, lest you take part in her sins, lest you share in her plagues; for her sins are heaped high as heaven, and God has remembered her iniquities" (Rev. 18:4–5). This is an implicit reference to Isaiah 48:20, 52:11, and Jeremiah 51:6, 45, where Israel was called to leave Babylon after the seventy years of exile. However, in Revelation 18 the appeal comes directly to us, right now, and not simply at Christ's return: get out of Babylon, as soon as you can! Have nothing to do with the culture system that it represents.

Again, this is another way to use the Babylon motif, comparable to Paul's statement: "Do not be conformed to this world" (Rom. 12:2), and John's statement:

Do not love the world or the things in the world. If anyone loves the world, the love of the Father is not in him. For all that is in the world—the desires of the flesh and the desires of the eyes and pride of life—is not from the Father but is from the world. And the world is passing away along with its desires, but whoever does the will of God abides forever (1 John 2:15–17).

_____

[26] VanDrunen (2010a, 29).

In terms of John 17, we are "in the world" but not "of the world" (vv. 11, 16). Or to put it this way: we are surrounded by the Babylon culture, but this should not pull us down; Christ's kingdom should pull us up. In other words, the Babylon motif fits very clearly illustrates the "structure and direction" distinction that forms the heart of biblical neo-Calvinism.

8.4.3 The Canaan Motif

VanDrunen says, "Israel's experience under the law of Moses in the Promised Land of Canaan was *not* meant to exemplify life under the *two* kingdoms. The cultural commonality among believers and unbelievers ordained in the Noahic covenant was suspended for Israel within the borders of the Promised Land."[27] Now first we wonder how VanDrunen knows all this. The Bible doesn't say anywhere that there is some common kingdom, and even less that such a kingdom was ordained under the Noahic covenant, and even less that such "cultural commonality" was "suspended" for Israel in Canaan. All these suppositions exist only within the framework of VanDrunen's theory; they are *his* conclusions drawn from conclusions drawn from conclusions.

This problem is not all that uncommon, because it belongs to how things often work in theology, and even in every science. Hypotheses are launched, they are tested, sometimes they are supported by newer evidence, sometimes they must be discarded. However, VanDrunen exhibits hardly any awareness of the fact that he is *merely presenting a theological model* (and not a very good one at that). Like all scholastic theologians, he presents his model as the ultimate biblical truth, and even as "the" Reformed truth. I will return to this important methodological point in §11.3.

In addition to these considerations, notice carefully what VanDrunen is saying. *In Canaan the two-kingdoms model was not applicable.* There was only one kingdom (I may add, specifically as viewed under the kingship of the Davidic kings), in which the Israelites were not "strangers and sojourners" (VanDrunen has apparently forgotten Lev. 25:23 here [see §8.1.1]). There was no common kingdom in Canaan, but only the one kingdom of God. But VanDrunen fails to see that this is *a perfect type of the present Christian's position.* Just as the Babylon motif can be applied to Christian living in the world, viewed from one angle, the Canaan motif can be applied as well, viewed from another angle. I view Canaan as a type or model of the "heavenly places" mentioned in the letter to the Ephesians: our position is in Christ, who is seated in the heavenly places (Eph. 2:6; cf. 1:20, and

---

[27] Ibid., 89.

also v. 2; 3:10). Our spiritual warfare is in the heavenly places (6:12), and is typologically represented by Israel's conflicts with the Canaanites and neighbouring nations. The Davidic kingdom in which we dwell, in the spiritual sense of the term, is that "of Christ and God" (5:5). There is no "commonality" here because everything we do is necessarily in the sphere of "David's" (read: Christ's) kingdom.

If VanDrunen seeks to underpin his two-kingdoms model with a one-sided appeal to the Babylon motif, we must provide needed balance by appealing to his own Canaan motif. We are living in the heavenly places, and as such we are church members, husbands and wives, parents and children, employers and employees (Eph. 4:1–6:9). None of this belongs to any "common realm," because all these functions are within the sphere of our dedication and obedience toward our great David. Under king David's rule, anything that his adherents did was for the glory of their king and his kingdom. They could all say what Amasai enthusiastically told David: "*We are yours, O David*, and with you, O son of Jesse! Peace, peace to you, and peace to your helpers! For your God helps you" (1 Chron. 12:18). No Israelite in those days could ever have said, "This or that part of my life is none of the king's business"—unless he had something evil in mind! Nothing was "common," everything was for David.

8.5 THE "REDEMPTIVE KINGDOM"

8.5.1   Not in the Old Testament

In addition to all that I have said so far, we must realize that the use of the Babylon motif may be rather far-fetched. Repeatedly, VanDrunen tells us that he finds the "redemptive kingdom" as well as the "common kingdom" in the Old Testament: in the Noahic covenant, in the patriarchs living in Canaan, in the Israelites living in Babylon.[28] However, the essence of the matter is being entirely overlooked here: *there was no redemptive kingdom of God in the Old Testament in the first place.* Of course, there was redemption, from Genesis 3 onward; but redemption as such does not imply a redemptive kingdom. And of course, there was the universal, providential kingdom of the Triune God, but this was basically the same kingdom before and after the Fall. And of course, there were typological anticipations of the redemptive kingdom under kings David and Solomon. *But there was as yet no Messianic kingdom.*

---

[28] E.g., VanDrunen (2006, 16, 27–32; 2010a, 75–97; 2014, 95–132, 263–81).

There is no other redemptive kingdom than this Messianic kingdom. This is beautifully expressed, for instance, in the words of the priest Zechariah, father of John the Baptist:

Blessed be the Lord God of Israel, for he has visited and redeemed his people and has raised up a *horn of salvation* for us in the house of his servant David…that we should be *saved from our enemies* and from the hand of all who hate us… to grant us that we, *being delivered from the hand of our enemies*, might serve him without fear, in holiness and righteousness before him all our days. And you, child [i.e., John the Baptist], will be called the prophet of the Most High; for you will go before the Lord to prepare his ways, to give *knowledge of salvation* to his people in the forgiveness of their sins (Luke 1:68–77).

Compare this with Isaiah:

For to us a child is born, to us a son is given; and the government shall be upon his shoulder, and his name shall be called Wonderful Counselor, Mighty God, Everlasting Father, Prince of Peace. Of the increase of his government and of peace there will be no end, *on the throne of David* and over his kingdom, to establish it and to uphold it with justice and with righteousness from this time forth and forevermore (Isa. 9:6–7; cf. Luke 1:32).

VanDrunen fails to appreciate the essential difference between the universal, providential kingdom of the triune God, which exists throughout history, and the specific form of this kingdom in the present age, that is, in the time since the glorification of Christ, the true David. There is a *Man* on the throne of God, and he makes all the difference. And God cannot be satisfied with this Man having authority over anything less than *all* the heavens and *all* the earth. Thus, since the New Testament, there *is* a redemptive kingdom (if we should even call it that), but there is no common realm, because the glorified Messiah has received dominion over *all* the domains of the world.

VanDrunen's perspective suffers from overemphasizing the continuity between the Old and the New Testaments, overlooking their essential differences. I have encountered this problem with many Calvinist thinkers, and have discussed it extensively.[29] I know that some go too far to the

---

[29] See, e.g., Ouweneel (2010b; 2012a; 2016e; 2016g).

other extreme, especially classical dispensationalists, and I have dealt with
this too, in the same publications. Yet, we should realize the enormous
significance of the post-Ascension and post-Pentecost situation: we have
a glorified Man at the right hand of God in heaven, and we have God the
Holy Spirit dwelling on earth in the church, which is the temple of God
and the body of Christ. No theological model of such scope as VanDrunen's
can be very helpful if it fails to integrate meaningfully these two great
soteriological, ecclesiological, and eschatological facts.

8.5.2 Christology

The hint was given earlier that part of the problem with NL2K is in fact a
Christological problem.[30] The church has always confessed—usually in
opposition to all kinds of heresies—that (a) there first was the *Logos asarkos*
(God the Son, not yet a Man), (b) since the incarnation the *Logos (en)
sarkos* (Jesus Christ, completely God and completely Man), and (c) since
his glorification he is still completely God and completely Man, this time
the glorified Man at God's right hand. In the practical thinking of many
Christians, especially if they are not theologically educated, there is no
essential difference between the *Logos asarkos* and the glorified Christ: he
was God before his incarnation, and he remains God in his glorification.
As the Second Person of the Godhead he ruled over the universe before
his incarnation, and since his ascension he again rules over the universe.

In itself, this is entirely correct. But there is an enormous difference:
since his incarnation, he is also completely Man, *and he is this forever.* God
"has fixed a day on which he will judge the world in righteousness by *a man*
whom he has appointed; and of this he has given assurance to all by raising
him from the dead" (Acts 17:31). The Father "has given him [i.e., his Son]
authority to execute judgment, because he is the *Son of Man*" (John 5:27).
Jesus was a Man on earth with a "lowly" body, since his resurrection he is a
Man with a risen body, and since his ascension he is a Man with a glorious
body (Phil. 3:21). "In him [i.e., the glorified Christ] the whole fullness of
deity dwells [present tense!] *bodily*" (Col. 2:9); that is, at the present time
the Triune God dwells in Christ's glorified body. With the enlightened eyes
of our hearts, we see in the glorified *Man* Christ Jesus all the glory of the
Triune God—Father, Son, and Holy Spirit—shining (cf. John 14:9). And
at the same time, this Man *is* and remains in his own person God the Son.

The "redemptive" kingdom is not simply the "kingdom of God" but,
since Jesus' glorification, it is more specifically the kingdom of the *Son of*

---

[30] See extensively, Ouweneel (2007b, chapters 7–9); cf. Kloosterman (2012a, 71–77).

Man (Matt. 13:41; 16:28). It is said of the Son of Man, "To him was given dominion and glory and a kingdom, that all peoples, nations, and languages should serve him; *his dominion* is an everlasting dominion, which shall not pass away, and *his kingdom* one that shall not be destroyed" (Dan. 7:14). This is the kingdom of the Father's "beloved Son" (Col. 1:13), the "kingdom of Christ and God" (Eph. 5:5), "the kingdom of our God and the authority of his Christ" (Rev. 12:10). Just as his typological forerunner David, Jesus can say, "I and *my kingdom*" (2 Sam. 3:28); he said to his disciples, "I assign to you, as my Father assigned to me, a kingdom, that you may eat and drink at my table in *my kingdom*" (Luke 22:29–30). And he said to Pilate, "*My kingdom* is not of this world." The angel Gabriel said about him, "He will be great and will be called the Son of the Most High. And the Lord God will give to him the throne of his father David, and he will reign over the house of Jacob forever, and of *his kingdom* there will be no end" (Luke 1:32–33). And Paul speaks of "Christ Jesus, who is to judge the living and the dead, and by his appearing and *his kingdom*" (2 Tim. 4:1).

8.5.3 The Davidic Rule

Let us return for a moment to the "Canaan motif" (§8.4.3). I believe that at Christ's return the Davidic kingdom will appear in full power and right- eousness: "I will rescue my flock; they shall no longer be a prey. And I will judge between sheep and sheep. And I will set up over them one shepherd, my servant David, and he shall feed them: he shall feed them and be their shepherd. And I, the LORD, will be their God, and *my servant David* shall be prince among them" (Ezek. 34:22–24). "*My servant David* shall be king over them, and they shall all have one shepherd. They shall walk in my rules and be careful to obey my statutes. They shall dwell in the land that I gave to my servant Jacob, where your fathers lived. They and their children and their children's children shall dwell there forever, and David my servant shall be their prince forever" (37:24–25).

Pre- and postmillennialists will apply this to the glorious Messianic king- dom to which they look forward; amillennialists will apply this either to the present time, or to the new heavens and new earth. But on one thing they all agree: the passages can be *applied* to the present age. In the kingdom of God in its present form, Christians live already under the blessed rule of "David" (in Ezek. 34 and 37, as well as in Hos. 3:5, this is the name of the Messiah). In this kingdom there is no common realm, as even VanDrunen recognizes (§8.4.3). That is, there is no domain in life that does not fall under the direct authority, dominion, and power of our glorified Lord. By the Spirit of God, we say—as church leaders and church members, as matrimonial partners, as parents and children, as school leaders and pupils/students, and so forth—"*We are yours, O David*, and with you, O son of Jesse!" (see again 1 Chron. 12:18).

During David's wanderings, when he had already been anointed king over Israel (1 Sam. 16:13), we read of him: "Everyone who was in distress, and everyone who was in debt, and everyone who was bitter in soul, gathered to him. And he became commander over them" (22:2). This is a marvelous picture of the redemptive force of David's kingship! And when it comes to determining whether our daily tasks—our cultural work—may help to usher in the Messianic kingdom in splendour and peace, I refer to "the chiefs of David's mighty warriors—they, together with all Israel, *gave his kingship strong support to extend it over the whole land*, as the LORD had promised" (1 Chron. 11:10 NIV). None of their tasks was common—all their tasks were devoted to nothing but the furtherance of David's kingdom, including the meals they cooked. This was not true for individual men only; their families were just as much involved in this tremendous task (cf. 1 Sam. 27:3; 30:3).

In one respect, VanDrunen is basically right: in Canaan—I add, under the Davidic rule—there was no "common kingdom." But how regrettable that he fails to grasp the obvious conclusion: this state of affairs means that, in the kingdom of God, under the dominion of the true David, there is no "common kingdom" either: there is only the kingdom of the glorified Christ on the throne of God. All our tasks are devoted to nothing but the furtherance of Christ's kingdom, including the meals we cook, the schools and businesses we run, the political parties and other associations we are involved in, the music we compose, the scientific models we develop. It may be correct to say that our "first kingdom task is to build churches which live by kingdom principles."[31] But if we leave it there, we fail. If *your* talents and calling point in another, equally sacred direction, it may well be *your* primary "kingdom task" to become a good artist, a good scientist, a good politician, for the glory of the King and the furtherance of his kingdom.

---

[31] Snyder (2001, 95); this book contains much sound practical advice for kingdom builders.

WORKING IT OUT: PILGRIMS, YET NO QUIETISTS
Why does the Bible's notion of pilgrimage *not* necessarily mean quietism, passivity, or "abandoning the world to the devil"?

You may not play off one metaphor against another.[32] We must remember that being pilgrims is a metaphor that covers only certain aspects of our Christian lives. It underscores the fact that we are en route to another world, which will be far better than our present world. It will be the kingdom of God manifested in glory and power. It will be a holy place, and we long to reach it one day. The Bible calls it the "world to come" (Heb. 2:5); it will be the world of the "age to come" (Matt. 12:32; Mark 10:30; Eph. 1:21; Heb. 6:5). As far as the "present world" (2 Tim. 4:10) is concerned, we are only passing through. In this chapter, we have seen that here we are strangers and sojourners.

However, that is only part of the story. There are other metaphors, which shed light on other aspects of our Christian lives in the present world. Think here especially of the kingdom parables. For instance, we are labourers in the vineyard of the Lord to produce fruit for him, for his pleasure (Matt. 20:1–16; cf. Isa. 5:1–2; see also Matt. 21:28–32, 33–44). We are household servants of the Master to look after his other servants, to give them food at the proper time (24:45–51). We are businessmen in the service of the King, to engage in commerce for him until he comes again (25:14–30; cf. Luke 19:11–27). All these parables refer to our vocations in the present world. To be sure, the parables speak of spiritual labourers in a metaphorical vineyard, and of spiritual businessmen with metaphorical treasures—but the point is that their tasks concern the present world. Whatever we do, it is for the pleasure and the glory of the Master, because all our work, all our service, all our vocations, move within the sphere of the kingdom of God.

However, note that this refers *not only* to spiritual tasks, such as those of apostles and prophets, evangelists, shepherds, and teachers (cf. Eph. 4:11). In *every* domain of life we would like to produce fruit for the Lord, for his pleasure: "Whether you eat or drink, or *whatever you do*, do all to the glory of God" (1 Cor. 10:31). "*Whatever you do*, in word or deed, do everything in

---

[32] Therefore, Seerveld (2014a, 373–79) should not be afraid to use the pilgrim metaphor, because it does not necessarily detract at all from our duties within the worldwide kingdom of God, which are described with different metaphors.

the name of the Lord Jesus, giving thanks to God the Father through him.... *Whatever you* [i.e., bondservants] *do*, work heartily, as for the Lord and not for men" (Col. 3:17, 23). Note the three "whatevers" in these passages: in whatever domain you may be active—in the family, at school, in the company, in the association, in politics, in science, in art, etc.—remember that you are under the lordship of Christ, within the kingdom of God, and that you work for his pleasure and to his honour.

You work so that the Master one day will say to you, "Well done, good and faithful servant!" (Matt. 25:21, 23; cf. Luke 19:17). This is what we would love to hear from his mouth: "As my subject, my servant within my kingdom, you have been a good husband/wife, father/mother, principal/ teacher, employer/employee, party member, politician, scientist, artist, and so on, because you did it all for me, with the best of your strength and your talents, for my sake, for my pleasure, to further my kingdom in this world. *Enter into the joy of your master*" (Matt. 25:21, 23). This refers not to entering into heaven, but to entering into the *kingdom* of heaven as one day, at Christ's return, it will be established in splendour and glory.

In summary, I see three possible views here:

(a) *Quietism, passivity, pietism, "abandoning the world to the devil."* Adherents of this view keep telling us that we should not "polish the brass of a sinking ship." They love to quote: "The world lies in the power of the evil one" and is "passing away along with its desires" (1 John 5:19; 2:17). So why should we care about the present world? Let "those who deal with the world [live] as though they had no dealings with it. For the present form of this world is passing away" (1 Cor. 7:31). This is perfectly true. But adherents of this view fail to distinguish between the horizontal and the vertical dimensions of society (what we have called structure and direction). We do not work to further the kingdom of Satan that is manifested in society, for this kingdom will soon pass away. But we certainly endeavour to further the kingdom of God as it becomes manifest in every domain of our daily lives.

(b) *The NL2K position.* The adherents to this view (like the adherents of position [c]) do see a task for Christians within society, but they assign this task to what they call the "common kingdom," which, despite God's providential rule over this kingdom, remains neutral and secular. In fact, we are dealing here with the same problem of failing to distinguish between structure and direction. This failure leads to dividing society (in its horizontal dimension) into two kingdoms: the kingdom of God (which is identified with the visible church) and the common kingdom. Instead, in my view, NL2K should make the biblical distinction between the kingdom of God and the kingdom of Satan (Matt. 12:25–28), properly identifying them and distinguishing between their horizontal and vertical dimensions. That is, both God's kingdom and Satan's kingdom can be manifested in every domain of life. To make this a bit more explicit: the kingdom of God can be manifested even within the most "secular" domain, and the kingdom of Satan can be manifested even within the most "sacred" domain (as it often has).

(c) *The biblical view*, as I see it, easily follows from my criticisms under (a) and (b). It is *not* true that *part* of earthly reality belongs to the kingdom of God (namely, the visible church), and *part* of it belongs to the evil world that is passing away (as position [a] claims), or to the supposed "common kingdom" (as position [b] claims). The evil world can be manifested in *every* domain of life, even within the visible church (think of all cases of apostasy or fundamental heresy within church denominations). Similarly, the kingdom of God can be manifested in *every* domain of life, even within families, schools, companies, associations, and political parties.

Position (a) says, as it were: Withdraw *in angulo cum libello* ("with a [good] book in a [quiet] nook,"[33] far away from the evil world).

Position (b) says, as it were: During by far the greatest part of your life (at least from Monday to Saturday) you are *not* living and labouring in the kingdom of God, but in the common kingdom.

Position (c) says: We do not want to withdraw to a little corner, and we do not want to spend most of our time outside the kingdom of God, either. We are in the kingdom of God *all the time*, and this means concretely that, in the power of the Holy Spirit, we constantly endeavour to manifest the kingdom of God in every domain of our daily lives: in church, but also in our marriage, in the family, at school, in our business, in our clubs and associations, and in the political party to which we belong.

When we think here of Richard Niebuhr's famous and highly influential book *Christ and Culture*,[34] with its five models concerning the relationship between Christ and culture, it seems to me that his first type: "Christ against culture," corresponds with what I called position (a) (pietism). Niebuhr's second type, "Christ above culture," referring to Aquinas' dualism of nature and grace, clearly seems to correspond with what I called position (b) (NL2K). The third type, "Christ transforming culture," is represented by neo-Calvinism, at least by the more optimistic (Kuyperian) version of it. The fourth type, "Christ and culture in paradox," is perhaps the one that I would feel most comfortable with. And the fifth one, "Christ of culture,"

---

33 This expression has been ascribed to Thomas à Kempis (d. 1471).
34 Niebuhr (2001).

represents a more liberal Christian approach to culture, as was found, for instance, in the *Kulturprotestantismus* ("cultural Protestantism") of Alfred Ritschl in Germany (first half of the twentieth century).

These are only rough parallels. Niebuhr's fourth type, which is the least lucid in his presentation, only vaguely reminds me of the model that I myself would advocate. Yet, I appreciate the description of this position given by John G. Stackhouse:

> The fifth [read: fourth] option in Niebuhr's scheme is the one that he has the most trouble making clear. He calls it "Christ and culture in paradox," and associates it with Martin Luther, Ernst Troeltsch, and (in "Types of Christian Ethics"[35]) his brother Reinhold. In this type, Christians live within a strong tension. They believe that God has ordained worldly institutions, and that they must work within those institutions as best they can. At the same time, however, they affirm that God's kingdom has penetrated the world here and now. Thus, under God's providence, they tread a path that can seem crooked and unclear, trying to honor what is divinely ordained in culture (such as family bonds, the rule of law, and deference to legitimate authority) while also living out the distinct values of the kingdom of God as best they can without compromise.[36]

---

[35] Stackhouse appears to be referring here to Reinhold Niebuhr's work, *An Interpretation of Christian Ethics* (1979).

[36] Stackhouse (2002).

RE-CREATION THEOLOGY[1]

PREPARATORY PONDERINGS

1. What is the "new creation" (the new heavens and new earth): a replacement or a repair of the present world? Defend your answer. What are some practical or theological consequences of your answer?
2. Is your "secular" vocation only a way of living in the present world (a pastime until the second coming of Christ), or could it have significance for the new world? If not, why not? If so, what significance?
3. Are you an amillennialist, a postmillennialist, or a premillennialist? Try to imagine what possible significance your own viewpoint, as well as the other two viewpoints, might have for the entire discussion in the present book.
4. Do you believe there can be such a thing as a "theology of the state"? Or a "theology of culture"? Or a "theology of politics"? Or a "theology of science"? Or a "theology of art"? Explain your answer.

---

[1] For this chapter, see the much broader treatment of the subject in Ouweneel (2012a, chapter 14; 2016e).

9.1 THE NEW CREATION

9.1.1 Replacement or Repair?

As we have seen (especially in chapter 2), NL2K is governed by the age-old (medieval and early Protestant) scholastic dualism of nature and grace, in NL2K called the "common kingdom" and the "kingdom of God," respectively. In one variety of this dualism, the natural realm of the earthly and human realities is thought to belong to the first creation, while the supernatural (spiritual) realm of the kingdom of God in Christ is associated in particular with the coming re-creation. As far as this kingdom is manifested in the present world, it is seen as concentrated in the church (which is part of the "new creation"), and in contrast with the common societal relationships (which are part of the "old creation"). The church consists (ideally) of believers, whereas the common societal relationships do not only contain believers and unbelievers, but are also *meant* for both believers and unbelievers as long as the new heavens and new earth have not yet arrived. The believers' activities supposedly occur partly in the "new creation" (the church), partly in the "old creation" (the common societal relationships).

Lurking behind the various views here is the problem of the precise relationship between the present creation and the new creation. "Heaven and earth" have been polluted by sin: even "the heavens are not pure in his sight" (Job 15:15).[2] Therefore, not only must humanity be renewed in view of eternity (see the "new creation" in 2 Cor. 5:17; Gal. 6:15; cf. the "new man" in Eph. 2:15; 4:24; Col. 3:10 NKJV), but also the creation as a whole. Sin must be eradicated from the entire *cosmos* (John 1:29), that is, the totality of created reality. In Christ "all the fullness of God was pleased to dwell, and through him to reconcile to himself *all things, whether on earth or in heaven*, making peace by the blood of his cross" (Col. 1:19–20). "Thus it was necessary for the copies of the heavenly things [i.e., the tabernacle] to be purified with these rites [i.e., Mosaic sacrifices], but the heavenly things themselves with better sacrifices than these" (Heb. 9:23), namely, with the sacrifice of Christ.

What exactly does a "new" creation involve: either a *substitution* (replacement) or a *restoration* (repair) of the old creation? Or, as Gerrit Berkouwer put it, either annihilation or renewal of the old creation?

---

[2] Perhaps the angelic world (the inhabitants of the heavens) is here included; cf. Job 4:18; 25:5.

Either discontinuity or continuity between the old and the new creation?[3] He described extensively how Lutheran theologians adhered especially to the former view, whereas Reformed theologians adhered especially to the latter—even though Reformed theologians have often corrupted the discussion by advocating scholastic speculations about a *substantia* that would remain the same, and a *qualitas* that would change.[4] Herman Bavinck also used similar scholastic terminology.[5]

Dispensationalist Walter Scott refused to speak of a new creation in the sense of substitution (replacement), for this would imply creating new, not yet existing material.[6] Indeed, the Bible does not speak of a genuine *disappearance* of the old heaven and earth,[7] in spite of the strong language of 2 Peter 3:10 ("the heavens will pass away with a roar") and Revelation 21:1 ("the first heaven and the first earth had passed away"). If the new creation were to involve a replacement of the old creation, supposedly because this old creation was irreparably corrupted, Satan would ultimately have gained a certain victory: he would have destroyed the old creation effectively and completely. Supposedly, the only thing God could do after this defeat is simply create a *replacement* for this old creation. Almost like the potter in Jeremiah 18, he would be using the clay of a spoiled vessel to make a new one. In this way, God would have to admit that Satan had indeed achieved a certain success: he had spoiled the vessel.

Is *this* God's great plan of salvation: Satan has corrupted the old world, and thus God ultimately creates an entirely new replacement world? Dispensationalist John Walvoord tended to this viewpoint as well, without sufficiently considering the continuity with the preceding creation.[8] George Caird and Alan Johnson thought that only the religious-political order of heaven and earth would pass away,[9] and George Beasley-Murray thought here only of cosmic signs: signs that accompany the last judgment, analogous to Revelation 6:12–14 and Matthew 24:29.[10]

Thus, the authors can be classified as those who tend toward replacement, and those who tend to repair. However, in fact the latter view is just as humiliating for God as the notion of replacement. This view would

---

[3] Berkouwer (1972, 219–25).
[4] See already Calvin, *Comm. 2 Peter*, on 2 Pet. 3:10.
[5] Bavinck (*RD* 4:720, 722); cf. the doctrine of transubstantiation; see Ouweneel (2011, 273–79).
[6] Scott (1920, 416-18); cf. Heyns (1988, 391).
[7] Cf. Smith (1961, 281).
[8] Walvoord (1966, ad loc.).
[9] Caird (1966, ad loc.); Johnson (1981, ad loc.).
[10] Beasley-Murray (1987, ad loc.).

imply that in a brief moment the first humans managed to corrupt the old world, and subsequently it took God thousands of years to repair the world. Is *this* God's great plan of salvation: a simple restoration of what was corrupted, that is, by means of a great detour, we return to the Paradise that was lost in Genesis 3? Is salvation simply this: back to the beginning? In both cases—replacement and repair—God's omnipotence and honour are at stake. In the former case, he apparently is not mighty enough to put creation back in order, and thus he replaces it with another one. In the latter case, he apparently could not prevent the Fall, or at least it took him a long time to repair what went wrong in the beginning.

Where does David VanDrunen stand when it comes to the question of replacement or repair? He protests against the (supposedly neo-Calvinist) idea that the Christ-wrought redemption "is essentially *restoration* or *re-creation*."[11] I suppose that, here, the term "re-creation" is a synonym for "restoration," whereas the term as such could just as well have been a synonym for the "replacement" idea. VanDrunen's novelty is:[12] "Redemption is not 'creation regained'[13] but 're-creation gained.'" Apparently, he is against the restoration idea and for the replacement idea. However, a minute ago we got the impression that, in his thinking, restoration and re-creation are the same (and are both objectionable), whereas he now tells us that redemption is re-creation. Has he become a victim of the ambiguous term "re-creation"?

9.1.2   Exaltation

Let me explain a third option, in addition to replacement and repair. Reformed theologian Jan Hoek tried to find a third way by speaking of *re-creation*, but not of a *nova creatio* ("new creation").[14] There is no question of a destruction of the old world. God does not say, "Behold, I am making all kinds of new things," but: "Behold, I am making all things new" (Rev. 21:5). The assumption of a creation of new things goes too far, but *restoration* or *restitution* says too little: we are dealing with *re-creation*. The new world will represent a different, entirely new order of things, but at the same time guarantee the continuation and restoration of the old heaven and earth. One of the entirely new elements will be—even though Scripture never explicitly says so—that in this new world a new Fall will be impossible.

---

[11] VanDrunen (2010a, 18).

[12] Ibid., 26; cf. 36.

[13] This is an allusion to Wolters (2005), which itself is an allusion to *Paradise Regain'd*, the poem by John Milton (1671).

[14] Hoek (2004, 271–75); cf. Bakker (2009, book title: *From Creation to Re-Creation*).

Let me put it this way: if we compare redemptive history with the creation week (Gen. 1), the *status aeternus* ("eternal state") will not be a "first day," as if everything starts anew, but an "eighth day;" this is the first day of a new "week," which will contain all the experiences and achievements of the preceding "week." In my view, this renewal is prefigured by the eighth day of the Feast of Booths (Lev. 23:36, 39) and by the day of circumcision (Acts 7:8); also compare Luke 9:28 (Jesus' transfiguration) and John 20:26 (Jesus' new appearance to his disciples).

The new creation is not the mere restoration of the old one, nor the replacement of the old one. It is the thorough *exaltation* or *elevation* of the old creation. Redemptive history is not a circle but a spiral: it leads upward to a perfect world in which humanity will *both* have knowledge of good and evil, *and* will never again fall into evil. In this respect, Dutch dogmatician Bram Van de Beek is correct:[15] in the beginning there *was* no Paradise, no idyllic living together of man, woman, and animals; there was only a shadow of what will become reality only at the consummation.[16] VanDrunen is correct, too: the road of salvation is not a road leading straight from a *Paradise Lost* to a *Paradise Regain'd* (John Milton, d. 1674).[17] All the beautiful things that pious fantasy has dreamed up concerning the Paradise in Genesis 2 may be not much more than a backward extrapolation of what Scripture teaches us about the consummation.

The new world will be infinitely more than what was lost in Genesis 3. And in one respect it will be less: there will be no tree of the knowledge of good and evil, and no serpent that might seduce humanity (cf. Gen. 2–3; Rev. 12:9; 20:2). Instead, the new Garden of Eden will be filled with the Lamb (cf. about the New Jerusalem: "Its lamp is the Lamb," Rev. 21:23). As Jan Hoek says, "Like Adam in Paradise, we will still serve God with our free will. But this freedom will no longer contain any risk. We will have lost the taste for sinning."[18]

9.1.3 *Nova Creatio*

The more that the newness of the new creation is emphasized at the expense of the old creation, the more the two are placed in dialectical opposition to each other. The kingdom of God is no longer seen as a realm that is realized within *this* creation; that is, it is *this* creation that God wants to restore and renew. NL2K argues that in the church, as (the germ of) the kingdom

---

[15] Van de Beek (1996, 178; 2005, 188).
[16] Cf. Isa. 11:6–8; 65:17–25; Hos. 2:17; Rev. 21:9–22:5.
[17] Cf. VanDrunen (2010a, 26).
[18] Hoek (2004, 274).

of God, the beginning of the re-creation can be seen, which is supposed to stand dialectically over against the old creation. In this view, the nation state, as we know it today, is only part of the common kingdom, a temporary arrangement by God to create and maintain order among humanity until the last day, that is, as long as the old creation continues.

With regard to the relationship between church and state, a lot of varieties may be, and have been, invented. For instance, it makes a lot of difference whether one sees the state as the domain of Satan or a "realm" ("regiment") of God, though one that is sharply distinguished from the kingdom of God. The most drastic separation between church and state occurs where religion is excluded from public life altogether. Here we are no longer dealing with just a separation of church and state, but with a separation of religion and society, which, as I have argued above (§5.5), are very different matters. In such a situation, the illusion of the religiously neutral state—and in its wake, the illusion of the neutral school, neutral companies, neutral political parties, neutral politics—is defended and implemented most vigorously.

In the Lutheran view of the state, we find a similar separation between church and state as in the traditional view, but it is less strong.[19] It is true that, as the spiritual and the temporal realms, respectively, church and state have no inner connection, according to this view. However, the state is not neutral but sacred, for the king, prince, duke, or count receives his authority from God, and is responsible to him, not to the church. At best, there is a relationship with the church to the extent that the church, in addition to being a spiritual realm, is an earthly institution as well, which as such falls under the jurisdiction of the state. However, the state does not meddle in church affairs, just as the church does not meddle in state affairs.

The disastrous consequences of Luther's views in sixteenth-century Germany are well known. On behalf of the newly begun "Evangelical" (Lutheran) church, Luther sought the support of the German princes who had become Protestants, or at least sympathized with Protestantism; in Saxony this was the elector, Frederick the Wise (d. 1525).[20] Luther vehemently opposed the oppressed and very poor German peasants in the Peasant's War (1524–1526), because in his opinion the peasants' rebellion against the rulers was outright rebellion against God. (This is why Thomas Müntzer, the peasants' leader, called Luther a *Fürstenknecht*, "servant of

---

[19] See especially Luther, *On Secular Authority* (http://ollc.org/wp-content/uploads/2013/11/Secular-Authority-To-What-Extent-It-Should-Be-Obeyed.pdf); see Höpfl (1991).

[20] Formally, Frederick remained a Roman Catholic, although as time went on, he became more amenable to Luther's views.

princes.") At the Peace of Augsburg (1555, after Luther's death), Catholics and Lutherans agreed on the famous slogan, *Cuius regio, eius religio*, "Whose realm, his religion" (the phrase itself was coined in 1582). That is, the religion of the prince dictated the religion of his subjects, either Catholic or Lutheran. (Interestingly, the principle did not hold for Calvinist [Reformed] princes, or for Anabaptist regions.) Inhabitants who could not conform to their prince's religion were allowed to leave his realm. Imagine: the ruler determining what would be the favoured church denomination in his domain! Worst of all: the Lutheran position explains to a significant extent the docile character of the majority of the German nation at the rise of Hitler's Nazism. The "prince" must be obeyed at all costs!

9.2 AN ESSENTIALLY NEW APPROACH

9.2.1 Augustine

Desperately needed by early Lutheran, early Anglican, and early Reformed thinking—as well as Catholic thinking, for that matter—was an entirely new Christian view of cosmic reality, in which the power of the traditional nature-grace dualism would be fundamentally broken. Elsewhere I have discussed some elements of such a new way of thinking, such as the plurality of offices and responsibilities (cf. §6.5), the notion of theocracy (cf. §5.1.3), and the elements of structure and direction (cf. §§3.2.2 and 4.5).[21]

It is of the utmost importance to distinguish between the medieval and early-Protestant nature-grace dualism, on the one hand, and the more recent Christian view of the state, on the other hand. In scholastic dualism, the directional antithesis between God and Satan, or between the Spirit and the flesh (cf. Gal. 5:16–18), is replaced by a supposed antithesis that, as I have expressed it, is perpendicular to the one just mentioned: an artificial structural antithesis within created reality, namely, between church and state. In such a view, the kingdom of God is supposedly realized through the church, and in spite of, *or* with the help of, the allegedly neutral state. This view is totally mistaken because the directional antithesis between Spirit and flesh runs right through what is allegedly natural, such as the state, as well as what is allegedly supernatural, such as the church. That is, it runs right through the two supposed realms or kingdoms. In other words, this antithesis of God and Satan, of Spirit and flesh, is manifested both in the church and in the state, and similarly in every other societal relationship,

---

[21] Ouweneel (2014b, chapters 3–5).

that is, within both the "sacred" and the "secular" domains, within both the domain of faith and that of reason (if we may still use these misleading distinctions for the sake of the argument).

In his *De civitate Dei*, "The City of God" (written between AD 413 and 426), the great church father Augustine discerned very well that the *civitas Dei*, the commonwealth (or city) of God—let us say, the kingdom of God—cannot simply be equated with the church, and the *civitas terrena*, the earthly realm (in which both good and evil powers are at work), cannot simply be equated with the state. Of course not; in Augustine's time there were Christian (or "Christian") emperors on the thrones of Rome and Constantinople![22] In Augustine's view, there was also something of the *civitas Dei* in the state, and something of the *civitas terrena* in the church. But in the end, Augustine, too, erroneously associated the *directional* antithesis of the two "cities" particularly with the *structural* antithesis between church and state.

In my opinion, the terms *civitas Dei* ("city of God") and *civitas terrena* ("earthly city") as such are quite appropriate, but only if they are used as a *directional* antithesis. This antithesis is manifested equally in *every* societal relationship, both within the church and within the state, as well as within marriage, the family, the school, the company, the political party, the association, etc. Instead of this, unfortunately, scholasticism has abused the two terms time and again to draw a dividing-line within created reality—between church and state, or between the church and the rest of society—thus blurring the distinction between structure and direction.

9.2.2 Again: Exaltation

Radical Christian thinking has fundamentally broken with all these false contrasts and dualisms. It is firmly based on both the biblical notions of creation and re-creation. These two can never be considered apart from each other because, as I said, it is the re-creation (renewal, restoration, elevation, exaltation) of *this* creation that God has in mind. *Creation* is going to be delivered (Rom. 8:18–22), but *we* are not going to be delivered from creation. It is impossible to separate creation and the kingdom of God because this is what the kingdom of God is all about: the elevation of *this* creation by Jesus Christ, through the Holy Spirit, for the glory of God the Father. It will be a *new* world, in the sense not of a replacement but of a renewal and elevation of this creation.

---

[22] I mention Theodosius I (reigned 379–395) and his sons, Arcadius (reigned 383–408) and Honorius (reigned 393–423).

In his *Enchiridion*, Augustine spoke of *felix culpa*, the "fortunate fall:" "God judged it better to bring good out of evil than not to permit any evil to exist."[23] His teacher, Ambrose, also spoke of the "fortunate ruin" of Adam in the Garden of Eden, in that his sin brought more good to humanity than if he had stayed perfectly innocent.[24] The elevation of God's creation occurs through fall and redemption. But it will still be this creation. Therefore, the creational ordinances remain most highly relevant.

As an example of how we can go astray, consider Oepke Noordmans, one of the best known Dutch Reformed theologians of the twentieth century. He claimed that only Genesis 1 and 2 speak about creation, and the rest of the Bible speaks about re-creation.[25] Other Reformed theologians have rejected such a formulation, and rightly so. The *entire* Bible is about *this* creation, about *its* redemption and *its* renewal in and through Jesus Christ. Such a statement seems to indicate how much Noordmans' thinking—and that of many Reformed theologians in his wake—still presupposed the scholastic nature-grace dualism. I repeat: re-creation always concerns the redemption and renewal of *this* creation.

Conversely, although we focus on *this* creation, this does not mean that we view it only in its present form, as being "in the pains of childbirth" as a consequence of the Fall. Rather, we learn to view it from the perspective of the re-creation, that is, of the kingdom of God. In unmasking scholastic dualism, we will no longer separate creation and re-creation, or even juxtapose them. This is what NL2K does by exempting part of creation from re-creation: the "common realm," which will supposedly come to an end at Christ's return. On the contrary, creation and re-creation are integrated within a single redemptive perspective, so that no part of creation can be isolated from re-creation.

What a blessing it would be if Bible-believing Christians would preach not only the gospel of God's grace for poor sinners, but also the gospel of the kingdom, as the Lord asked us to do (Matt. 28:18–20; cf. 24:14). Is our only message the gospel for the salvation of souls, without any message for the *totality* of Christian life? What is the Christians' contribution to science, to the arts, to culture, to society, to politics? In the last centuries, there have been countries in Northern Africa where, through intensive missionary work, the majority of people were won for Christ, at least

---

[23] *Enchiridion* viii; quoted by Thomas Aquinas, *Summa Theologica* III.1.3 ad 3; cf. also the Paschal Vigil Mass Exsultet: *O felix culpa quae talem et tantum meruit habere redemptorem* ("O fortunate guilt, which earned us such a, and so great a, Redeemer").

[24] See extensively, Haines (1982).

[25] Noordmans (2009).

outwardly. But soon after this, we saw the looming prospect that, if the gospel affects only souls, and not culture, society, politics—because these belong to the common kingdom only—then within a few generations many of these people will turn to Islam. This happens because it is *not* true that the redemptive renewal of people automatically affects and renews society, nor is it true that the gospel of the kingdom transforms only the church and the individual lives of Christians.

Here we see one of the bad consequences of the NL2K position: the common (neutral, secular) realm that this position advocates will be filled all too quickly by Islam, by Marxism, by secular capitalism (based on greed), you name it. *They* supply what many Christians fail to do: an Islamic, a Marxist, a capitalist view of the world—but certainly not a "common" view, inspired by some "natural law." Let NL2K keep propagating the error of the "common realm," and soon Christians in North America will be defenseless as they come to live in a totally secularized part of the world, where Christianity is restricted to what happens within church walls. It is most painful to see how Luther and Calvin are adduced to defend such a disastrous development.

9.3 KINGDOM THEOLOGY

9.3.1 The Christian Ground Motive

Indeed, it was not such a good idea that some neo-Calvinists wished to summarize the entire message of Scripture in these three words: Creation–Fall–Redemption. In the words of Herman Dooyeweerd: "creation, fall, and redemption through Jesus Christ in the communion of the Holy Spirit."[26] Others have added "consummation" to this triplet: Creation–Fall–Redemption–Consummation,[27] but my objections remain: the formula puts too much emphasis on the negative, namely, the problem of sin and its solution,[28] instead of putting it on the positive: God's plan of introducing the kingdom of God into the world.[29] This kingdom will become full reality, in power and majesty, at the second coming of Christ. But already now, the kingdom of God is a spiritual reality in this world because Christ is on the

---

[26] Dooyeweerd (1979, 28); cf. Plantinga (2002, xv); Wolters (2005, 10–11).

[27] E.g., Kloosterman (2012a, 7).

[28] A well-known Reformed church leader in the Netherlands once asked me during a Dutch radio program whether I did not believe that the entire biblical message could be summarized in two words: sin and grace. I answered with an emphatic: No!

[29] See extensively, Ouweneel (2016e).

throne. The kingdom is manifested wherever the Holy Spirit is working, and wherever we find people who—though in weakness—submit their lives and their societal institutions to the authority of the King in the power of the Holy Spirit (cf. Rom. 14:17–18; 1 Cor. 4:20; Col. 1:13).

Apart from the Bible's teaching about the divine persons of the blessed Trinity, I would say that the kingdom of God is arguably the most universal and concise summary of the contents of Scripture. It was the core of Jesus' message here on earth (from Matt. 4:17 to Acts 1:3), and also a main point in Paul's teaching: "…you among whom I have gone about proclaiming the kingdom" (Acts 20:25). "From morning till evening he [i.e., Paul] expounded to them, testifying to the kingdom of God.… [He] welcomed all who came to him, proclaiming the kingdom of God and teaching about the Lord Jesus Christ with all boldness and without hindrance" (28:23, 30–31).

David VanDrunen registers his own complaints against the threefold summary of Scripture (Creation–Fall–Redemption),[30] which are very different from mine, as we see from these words:

> The earlier Reformed view of cultural activity as a temporal task of the civil kingdom, theoretically a common endeavor among believers and unbelievers, governed primarily th[r]ough a natural law to which all people had access and insight, has thus been significantly redirected. For the neo-Calvinists considered here, there are no independent purposes of common grace or a civil kingdom, but all is subsumed under the purpose of redemption and eschatological consummation.[31]

In sum: the traditional Reformed view paid attention to the common kingdom, which is part of *this* creation, whereas neo-Calvinism is too much focused on *re*-creation.

I leave aside here the historical question whether the ideas of natural law and the common kingdom indeed represent "the" original Reformed view. But I do object to presenting the eschatological view of the neo-Calvinists as focused too much on re-creation. Remember: in the previous section I emphasized the fact that re-creation is about *this* creation being renewed. The neo-Calvinist rejection of the idea of a common realm, along with its acceptance of a view of God's kingdom being present everywhere is still concerned with *this* world, *this* creation. In no way may the present creation and the future re-creation be viewed as standing in dualistic opposition to

---

[30] VanDrunen (2010a, 17–18, 23).
[31] VanDrunen (2010b, 385).

each other. If VanDrunen's plea for the common kingdom is fundamentally a demand that we pay attention to *this* creation, he should listen to neo-Calvinists telling him that their focus upon the new world does not at all contradict this demand: re-creation *is* about *this* creation.

9.3.2 Transformationalism

One notion that seems to highly irritate advocates of NL2K is the (supposedly neo-Calvinist) idea of "redeeming" and "transforming" our present culture, and the idea that this would contribute to the realization of God's kingdom: "Many contemporary voices assert that God is *redeeming* all legitimate cultural activities and institutions and that Christians are therefore called to transform them accordingly and to build the kingdom of God through this work."[32] A similar (supposedly neo-Calvinist) idea is that "their cultural achievements will adorn the new heaven and new earth."[33]

Now I do indeed think that all Christian cultural activity contributes to extending and building the kingdom of God. First, we must consider the fact that *even preaching and evangelizing are cultural activities*. Cultural work is not something that is done outside the church only, but it includes all church work. I would even venture to say that no church denomination is beyond time but that each denomination as such is the product of a certain cultural process. For instance, Reformed and Presbyterian denominations could never have existed in antiquity or in the Middle Ages, and in North America they are quite different from those in Europe. Not the body of Christ, but certainly concrete church denominations and local congregations are always cultural products (no matter how much one believes the Holy Spirit to have been involved in this).

Second, not only good Christian sermons, but also certain scientific discoveries by Christians, certain decisions by Christian politicians, and even Christian novels, Christian music, and Christian paintings do advance the kingdom of God. How could it be otherwise? The music of Johann Sebastian Bach is Christian, not because he used different notes or techniques than non-Christians do, but because his music was firmly embedded in a thoroughly Christian (Lutheran) culture, which it helped to spread and advance. The paintings of Rembrandt van Rijn are Christian, not because he used different paints or techniques than non-Christians do, but because his art was firmly embedded in a thoroughly Christian (Reformed) culture, which it helped to spread and advance.

---

[32] VanDrunen (2010a, 13; cf. 15, 25, 51, 164, 166, 170–71, 194–95).

[33] VanDrunen (2010a, 34; cf. 51; also see 2014, 529). Interestingly, Stellman's (2009, 58) main argument against transformationalism is that it is not 2K!

I also sympathize with the idea that these cultural products will retain their value in the new world, even though NL2K advocates fiercely reject this idea. Three Bible passages come to mind here. The first is 1 Corinthians 15:58, "Therefore, my beloved brothers, be steadfast, immovable, always abounding in the work of the Lord, knowing that in the Lord your labor is not in vain [MSG nothing you do for him is a waste of time or effort]." I take this to mean that any labour that is in the Lord—and this is what all true kingdom work by definition is—has lasting value.[34] I maintain this despite the complaints of NL2K advocates.[35]

The second passage is 2 Peter 3:10, "The day of the Lord will come like a thief, and then the heavens will pass away with a roar, and the heavenly bodies will be burned up and dissolved, and the earth and the works that are done on it will be exposed." With regard to the last verb, most textual linguists agree today that the Greek verb *heurethēsetai* (lit., "will be found," cf. dnlt) is the better reading, to be preferred to *katakaēsetai* ("will be burned up"). The verb *heurethēsetai* is usually taken in the sense of "will be found out" (NABRE, OJB), or "laid bare" (NIV, net), or "exposed" (ESV, CEB, etc.).

This is the way VanDrunen interprets the verse.[36] However, such a negative explanation is not the only possibility. Reformed author Wim Rietkerk has extensively argued for a positive explanation: "exposed" means "brought to light, manifested." All works done on this earth for the honour and glory of God will be "found" in the new world in all their splendor.[37] Of course, we cannot prove that this is the true meaning of the phrase, but this interpretation is no less plausible than VanDrunen's.

9.3.3 Millennialism

The third passage is Revelation 21:24–26, "By its light will the nations walk, and the kings of the earth will bring their glory into it…. They will bring into it the glory and the honor of the nations." Amillennialist Anthony Hoekema interpreted this passage to mean that worthy cultural products of this world will be preserved to adorn the new world.[38] VanDrunen rejects this explanation, apparently for no other reason than that it does not fit into his model.[39]

---

[34] Cf. Wright (2008, 193, 208–209).
[35] Cf. VanDrunen (2010a, 22).
[36] Ibid., 67.
[37] Rietkerk (2009); see http://www.wimrietkerk.nl/?page_id=48.
[38] Hoekema (1994, 285–86).
[39] VanDrunen (2010a, 70).

On a premillennialist standpoint, the text, and especially Isaiah 60:3 to which it refers, becomes so much simpler.[40] According to this point of view, the Jerusalem of Isaiah 60 is the literal Jerusalem of the Messianic kingdom as it will appear at Christ's return. The city is distinguished from the nations, who bring their literal cultural products as gifts to the city. In Revelation 21, the Isaiah passage is applied to the New Jerusalem, which is not simply the "new world" or the "new creation," but the bride of the Lamb, that is, the true church (vv. 9–10). The nations and kings of verses 24 and 26 are those who will be allowed into the Messianic kingdom (cf. Matt. 25:34). Just as the cultural products of the Great Babylon (the false church)[41] will be destroyed (Rev. 18), those that are worthy of the kingdom will be preserved.

I do not wish to press the issue of (a)millennialism here, since I really need not do so to make my argument. Yet, I would like to emphasize that, according to millennialism, the coming Messianic kingdom is so much more similar to our present world, whereas both the present world and the Messianic world together differ as strongly from the new heavens and new earth as our present bodies differ from our future resurrection bodies (cf. 1 Cor. 15:35–44). Thus, from the millennialist position it is so much easier to see how cultural products of the present age will retain their significance in the "world to come," which is not at all the new creation but the Messianic kingdom (cf. Heb. 2:5; also cf. the concomitant "age to come," Matt. 12:32; Mark 10:30; Heb. 6:5).[42] By way of contrast, NL2K can easily underscore the difference between the present world and the new creation to underpin its thesis that our present cultural work will have no significance for the new heaven and new earth.[43] It can do so by ignoring the coming Messianic kingdom as we have just described it, about which pre-Augustinian eschatology was still so convinced, before supersessionism invaded theology.[44]

To me, the cavalier manner with which VanDrunen discards the whole notion of this Messianic kingdom is quite shocking.[45] It is simply nonsense to claim that the passages he mentions (e.g., 1 Cor. 15:22–24; 1 Thess.

[40] See extensively, Ouweneel (2012a, especially chapters 13–14).

[41] Carefully compare Rev. 17:1–3 and 21:9–11 to see the similarities and dissimilarities between the false church and the true church; cf. Ouweneel (2012a, chapter 11).

[42] The "world to come" is neither the present world, nor the new heavens and new earth (contra VanDrunen, 2010a, 100). There will be families in the "world to come" (contra ibid., 120): see the prophetic import of Ps. 22:31; 48:13–14; 78:6; Isa. 54:13; 59:21; Zech. 8:4–5.

[43] Cf., e.g., ibid., 15, 40.

[44] Cf. Ouweneel (2010b, chapters 2–3).

[45] VanDrunen (2010a, 63).

4:13–5:3; 2 Thess. 1:4–10) show that the return of Christ and the arrival of the new heaven and new earth are simultaneous.[46] Why does he not refer to Revelation 19–21, where we clearly find this order: the second coming of Christ, followed by the establishment of the millennial kingdom, followed by the judgment of the dead, followed by the new heavens and new earth? Of course, I know that, according to amillennialists, there is no chronological order here; they *must* make this unwarranted claim that VanDrunen defends. But it is simply not true that the New Testament shows that Christ's return is immediately followed by the new creation. This is nowhere the case, not even in the passages referred to by VanDrunen.

9.3.4 Three Millennial Views

Again, I do not wish to press this aspect, but from a millennialist position it is so much easier to see the parallel and continuity between the cultural task of the first Adam in the first world, and the cultural task of the last Adam in the world to come. It is the last Adam who ushers in the Messianic kingdom, and afterward the new heaven and new earth, but in the present age believers are God's "fellow workers" (1 Cor. 3:9).[47] We are *not* fellow workers in the work of redemption; Christ has accomplished this alone. But we are definitely fellow workers in extending and building the kingdom of God (cf. John 14:12). Compare this with what I mentioned earlier: it was God who made David king over Israel, and in due time put him on the throne. Yet, the Bible speaks of "David's mighty warriors," who "gave his kingship strong support to extend it over the whole land" (1 Chron. 11:10 NIV). They were his fellow workers, who—humanly speaking—helped him reach his royal goal.

It would go too far to enter any further into the subject of millennialism. Let me mention, by way of summary, only the following:

(a) Theonomy, or Christian reconstructionism, seems to be invariably connected with postmillennialism. This millennial view has always been a substantial part of the Reformed tradition.[48] In nineteenth-century America it was defended at Princeton Theological Seminary by Charles Hodge (d. 1878), Archibald A. Hodge (d. 1886), and Benjamin B. Warfield (d. 1921). In postmillennialism, it is essential to believe in notions such as Christian culture, Christian politics, and the Christian state.

(b) In spite of all their differences, NL2K theologians and Kuyperians (neo-Calvinists) usually have one important thing in common, and this is

---

[46] See again Ouweneel (2012a, especially chapters 9, 12–14).

[47] *Contra* VanDrunen (2010a, 28, 65, 100, 164).

[48] See extensively, Boettner (1984); Mathison (1999); Gentry (2003); cf. also Van Campen (2007).

amillennialism. That is, Christians must not expect some future millennial kingdom; Christ's return will be the beginning of the new heavens and new earth. Both parties have the full right to be amillennialists. But, although Luther and Calvin held this position as well, neither NL2K advocates nor neo-Calvinists have the right to claim that only amillennialists can be truly Reformed/Presbyterian.[49]

(c) In the non-Reformed and non-Lutheran part of the Evangelical world, premillennialism has slain its millions. Best known is the dispensational form of premillennialism, often linked with the doctrine of the "sacred rapture" (pretribulationalism). However, there is also a form called historical premillennialism, that is, holding to the premillennialism of many pre-Constantine church fathers. This form was defended by some faculty members of Covenant Theological Seminary in St. Louis (a Reformed institution), such as J. Barton Payne (d. 1935), J. Oliver Buswell (d. 1977), and R. Laird Harris (d. 2008); I am not aware of Reformed successors holding the same form of premillennialism.[50] Of course, some critics have called them non-Reformed because, in their view, Reformed thought and premillennialism are incompatible. However, I would not know why, for instance, the Five Points of Calvinism (TULIP) and premillennialism could not be compatible. I do not wish to press this matter any further, however, because my own presentation does not require or depend on resolving this issue.

9.4 "CHRISTIAN" POLITICS

9.4.1 Scholastic Prejudices

NL2K advocates appear to be afraid of every substantive modified with the adjective "Christian," except perhaps in expressions such as "Christian church" and "Christian lifestyle" (and probably "Christian theological seminaries"). NL2K advocates reject the idea of Christian politics, Christian education (except in church), Christian philosophy. (They do not at all clearly endorse or defend the reality of "Christian" families.) Their main argument is that such things as Christian plumbing, Christian calculus, and Christian grammar do not exist. As VanDrunen says, "Christ's resurrection, ascension, and establishment of the church have not changed the truths of calculus or the way that water flows. The fact that a plumber is converted to Christianity does not change his objective obligations as a plumber (even

---

49 Cf. Frame (2011, 5–6).
50 Cf. http://www.reformedreader.org/mchart.htm.

though he now has new motivation for being industrious and honest as he pursues his vocation)."[51] To my mind, this argument belongs to this category: there are no black flowers, so there cannot be black people either. There are no Christian plumbers, so there can be no Christian philosophers either.

In the next chapters I will enter more specifically into the problems underlying this claim (see especially §11.4.2). Two of these problems are what I call *churchism* (or *ecclesiasticism*; the typically scholastic absolutizing of "the" church, even the church as an immanent phenomenon, at the expense of other societal relationships) and *theologism* (the typically scholastic absolutizing of theology, at the expense of the other special sciences as well as philosophy). Apparently, VanDrunen and other NL2K advocates have not the slightest idea of the special philosophy of theology, that is, that part of philosophy that is occupied with the external prolegomena of theology.[52] I am going to defend the thesis that, if NL2K advocates do not accept the notion of a *Christian* philosophy, then they cannot know what theology is, let alone *Christian* theology. Here I am returning to the thesis with which I opened in chapter 1: NL2K *is entirely trapped in the bonds of scholastic thinking* with its nature-grace dualism. I do not care very much about the question whether NL2K is more Reformed than its opponents, or vice versa, because too much of the debate is, as early Reformational thinking was too, caught in precisely the same scholasticism. NL2K advocates will not enjoy hearing this, but if there was any merit in Kuyper-Dooyeweerdian thinking it was not transformationalism, but especially this: *liberating Reformed (and other Protestant) thinking from scholasticism.*

Take the matter of the "Christian" state and "Christian" politics. What *tools* do NL2K theologians have to assess this problem? Is theology as such qualified to make any statements on such issues? Of course not. How can theologians (*qualitate qua*) assess whether a state, or politics, can be Christian or not if they do not subscribe to a *Christian-philosophical view* of cosmic reality? Some Christian epistemology—Dooyeweerdian, Van Tilian, Plantingian, Wolterstorffian, it matters not which—must tell us what knowledge and science are, whether they can be neutral or not, whether it is true that all knowledge is fundamentally religious, what is the difference between practical and theoretical knowledge (including the difference between biblical and theological knowledge), in what way reliable theological knowledge is collected, how theology relates to the other special sciences, in what view of cosmic reality it is rooted, etc. I

---

[51] VanDrunen (2010a, 170; cf. 191).
[52] Cf. Ouweneel (2013, chapters 6–14; 2014c).

can guarantee you that the answers to such questions are very different, depending on whether it is a scholastic, a Marxist, a positivist, a post-modernist, a biblicist, or a radical-Christian philosopher who answers them. And I can guarantee you as well that, if the answer is not a radical-Christian-philosophical one, it will invariably be a scholastic, a Marxist, a positivist, a post-modernist, a biblicist, or any other philosophical (or pseudo-philosophical) answer. Theology as such is not equipped to decide between different *philosophical* models.

9.4.2 Theologism

Now ask NL2K advocates how they can know whether there is such a thing as "Christian" politics, and if so, what it should look like. I have some idea about what their answer will be. It is the answer that scholastic thinkers have always given: *theology must do the job*, and nothing else. This is what I call theologism, which Merriam-Webster defines as "excessive extension of theological presuppositions or authority." If I were simply a philosopher loudly protesting such theologism, people would say, "Well, you see, he is only a philosopher; he is jealous of the theologians." But no, I am both a doctored philosopher (from a largely Reformed faculty) and a doctored theologian (from a thoroughly Reformed faculty). The philosopher in me has no reason to be jealous of the theologian in me. I am thankful to be both, and that I became both in the sequence mentioned. I have written simple, popular introductions to both philosophy and theology, which, among many other things, explain the relationship between the two.[53] I have done this much more extensively and thoroughly in Dutch.[54] Any readers who really want to understand how I view the relationship between theology and philosophy should turn to the two books mentioned in note 53.

Now look what happens when scholastic theologians assess the matter. VanDrunen audaciously speaks of a "faithful biblical theology of Christianity and culture,"[55] whereas theology *as theology* knows nothing at all about culture (theologians are supposed to interpret the Bible, but the Bible does not say anything about the phenomenon of culture as such). VanDrunen accuses Kuyper and Dooyeweerd of offering "a distorted theology of Christian cultural engagement"[56]—whereas especially Dooyeweerd would have abhorred the idea of a *theology* of culture (as do I). One must be very poorly acquainted with Dooyeweerdian thinking to come up with

53 Ouweneel (2014a; 2014c).
54 Ouweneel (1995; 2013, chapters 6–14).
55 VanDrunen (2010a, 12).
56 Ibid., 16.

such an absurd suggestion. Dooyeweerd would also have been appalled at the idea that it is *the church* that must "teach ideas that have broad relevance for all the academic disciplines."[57] Not even theology (which in fact would be wrong too), but *the church*! This is incredible!

In the light of such thinking, I suppose *theology* must also make clear whether there can be such things as a Christian state and Christian politics. But in reality, theology is totally unqualified to do so. Even Abraham Kuyper did not properly grasp this. When he founded the Free University of Amsterdam (1880), he stipulated that each department of study had to be built on the foundation of the *gereformeerde beginselen* ("Reformed principles")—principles that had to be worked out by the *theological* faculty! NL2K advocates may well be vigorously opposed to Kuyper's thinking, but in this respect their views seem to be perfectly identical. Of course this could never work, and it did not work. Instead, various departments of study at the Free University, having no Christian philosophy as their foundation, began to look around in society, and began to adopt all kinds of current philosophies that conflicted very much with those celebrated "Reformed principles." This was not primarily *their* fault; it was the fault of a wrong starting point, namely, the overestimation of theology—*the very same overestimation seen today among VanDrunen & Co.*

Almost two generations later, in the thirties, two young professors at the Free University, the brothers-in-law Dirk H. Th. Vollenhoven (d. 1978) and Herman Dooyeweerd (d. 1977), understood that only a radical (that is, anti-scholastic, anti-humanistic, and anti-biblicistic) Christian philosophy could do the job. They developed such a philosophy, but unfortunately it was too late to turn the tide at the Free University. Theology was still trapped in scholasticism; the Reformed dogmatician Valentijn Hepp (d. 1950) blamed Dooyeweerd for teaching things "that even the pagans [Plato, Aristotle] had understood better." In the sixties, theology at the Free University underwent a rapid transition to liberal theology. It is painful that theologians who themselves are still scholastics have sometimes blamed Dooyeweerd for having developed his thought at such a "deteriorated" school as the Free University. They do not see that it was this same scholasticism that had caused its very problems.

9.4.3 A "Theology of the State"

A theology like that of NL2K, which believes in a "theology of culture," a "theology of the state," a "theology of politics," and all of this within a

_____

[57] Ibid., 175.

scholastic framework, has disqualified itself *a priori* from speaking about the Christian state and Christian politics. It is the same nature-grace dualism again, this time called the "common kingdom" and the "redemptive kingdom." If the redemptive kingdom comprises only the church, then *all the rest of life and society* belongs to the common (neutral, secular) realm, including the state, the schools, the companies, and of course the political parties. And what their status, their character is—well, it is up to theology to decide this.

A typically scholastic example is what VanDrunen calls a "theology of law," with reference to Thomas Aquinas.[58] Thomas called his masterwork *Summa Theologiae*, but this work is as much a philosophical as a theological work. It was called *theologia* because of the supposed superiority of Christian thinking (called "theology") to neutral thinking (called "philosophy"). Thomas' "Treatise on Law" in his *Summa* (questions 90–108) is really a work of legal philosophy, not of theology in any ancient or modern sense of the word. Yet, VanDrunen calls it Thomas' *theology* of law, entirely according to scholastic tradition. Similarly, there must be a "theology of the state," a "theology of culture," a "theology of politics," of course—and why not a "theology of science," and a "theology of art"?

What does such a "theology of the state" look like? VanDrunen gives us some idea.[59] Of course we hear about Romans 13—and let me openly declare that it is the theologians, and not the philosophers, who must do the exegesis of this chapter. No doubt about it. But this is very different from developing a *Christian view of the state*. Romans 13 tells us how Christians must behave very practically in a pagan state. Theologians can explain this to us. But Romans 13 does not tell us what a state is, and correspondingly, theologians cannot supply us with a theoretical view of what the ideal state—that is, the state as God intended it—should look like. What the Bible does not tell us, theologians (in their capacity as theologians) cannot tell us. The New Testament arose in a time when Christians did not have to *think* about what might be the God-intended ideal state.

I have experienced this supposed supremacy of theology several times. I know of a Christian university where, for instance, the department of the visual arts felt a bit guilty because they had no Christian view of the visual arts. So what did they do? *They invited a theologian to tell them, of course.* He gave a nice speech on the beauty of the tabernacle, and their conscience was set at ease. The psychology department, the economics department, the law department, they all could have done the same: invite a theologian to tell

---

[58] VanDrunen (2003, 30).
[59] VanDrunen (2010a, 197–98).

them what the "Christian" version of their discipline should look like, in order to quiet their consciences. In the end, they would not have made any progress at all. Theologians are qualified to expound Scripture, including what Scripture has to say about spirit and soul, or about the economics of ancient Israel, or about the judicial relationships in ancient Israel. *But theologians are not qualified to develop a Christian-philosophical anthropology,*[60] *or a Christian view of economics,*[61] *or a Christian view of civil justice.*[62]

Of course, the reply of NL2K advocates will be that we do not at all need a *Christian* anthropology, a *Christian* view of economics, or a *Christian* view of civil justice. These domains ostensibly belong to the common kingdom. But this is one of the core errors of NL2K. Let these advocates simply answer this question: Where do we find a neutral philosophical anthropology, that is, one that is *not* steeped in either scholasticism or humanism (or biblicism, for that matter)? I venture to say that it does not exist.[63] Where do we find a *Christian* view of economics, that is, one that is not plagued either by (extreme) capitalism or by socialism? NL2K advocates offer us only two options: ask theology (read: scholastic theology) for the explicit biblical data, and ask "common" (read: non-, and often anti-Christian), secular economics to interpret all the non-biblical data.[64] We know the results. In the United States, the Republican Party has often tended toward capitalism, and the Democratic Party has often leaned toward socialism. Or, as far as psychological and sociological matters are concerned, it cannot be a coincidence that Republicans tend more to *nature* ("what a person is, is due largely to his genes"), and Democrats more to *nurture* ("what a person is, is due largely to his environment"). Neither party has a *Christian* view of such things because they are not *Christian* parties.

Don't blame them. What they lack is a coherent, radical Christian-philosophical view of cosmic reality to help avoid such errors. Rather blame the (scholastic) theologians: it is they who have deluded people into believing that such a radical Christian-philosophical view of reality is completely unnecessary, or even fundamentally mistaken: you have theology, and you have "common" science—that will do. It is as if we are still living in the thirteenth century! Thomas Aquinas was dead set against the idea of a "Christian" philosophy, and NL2K advocates are too. Aquinas would rather have (Plato or) Aristotle tell us what the ideal state looks like, and NL2K

---

[60] Cf. Ouweneel (2015).
[61] Cf. Keizer (1986).
[62] Cf. Van Eikema Hommes (1979).
[63] On anthropology, for example, see extensively, Ouweneel (1986).
[64] Thus explicitly VanDrunen (2010a, 174–77, 183).

advocates have their own neutral, secular (perhaps not "pagan," but very probably apostate Jewish or Christian) philosophers to tell us. In their eyes, anything seems to be better than a "Christian"-philosophical view of reality. In the next chapter we will consider in more detail what is going on here.

WORKING IT OUT: **CONFESSIONAL DIRECTIONS FOR CHRISTIAN POLITICIANS**

Imagine a politician who is a Christian. Should (and if so, how should) his/her Christian convictions direct how he/she votes on a bill to legalize "civil unions" or "civil partnerships" (which are designed as a legal equivalent for "homosexual marriage")?

There are two possibilities: either this politician is a member of a Christian party—think of the Christian Democratic parties in many European countries, which partly involve orthodox Christians—or this politician is a member of a party that is religiously unaffiliated. In the Netherlands, we have orthodox Christians in Christian parties, but also in most other parties. In the United States, there are orthodox Christians in both the Republican and the Democratic parties. Within a Christian party, things are much easier. Members can openly declare that they are for or against a certain bill because of their Christian convictions. Of course, they respect the rules of democracy: it is the majority that decides. If a Christian party is part of a governing coalition, then also within this coalition they respect the rules. If they absolutely cannot live with the majority decision, they must withdraw from this coalition, or even from politics.

In a democracy, it is the majority that decides. But this should not prevent Christians from declaring why, because of their convictions, they are for or against a certain bill. Within a non-Christian party, things are in principle the same, except that Christians do have an additional challenge here: they must try to convince their fellow members within their own party.

Christians should never be intimidated by people who shout: Leave religion out of politics—perhaps even with an appeal to the "separation of church and state" (see §5.5). That is nonsense. We cannot leave religion out of our lives for even one second, and we do not want to be silent about it either. Moreover, those who shout things like this should look at themselves: what would they say if people urged them to leave out their ideological (liberal, socialist, humanist, post-modern, etc.) convictions? What is the principal difference between a religion or an ideology, when it comes to (accounting for) the deepest convictions of our hearts? Atheists, agnostics, and NL2K advocates may think that we should keep our religious mouths shut in public life. We might agree with this only if *they* would agree to keep their ideological mouths shut.

This is our guideline: "In your hearts honor Christ the Lord as holy, always being prepared to make a defense to *anyone* who asks you for a reason for the hope that is in you; yet do it with gentleness and respect" (1 Pet. 3:15; italics added). The last phrase may help show us how to express our opinions: never in a conceited, noisy, intrusive, pushy, authoritarian, self-assured way, but always in modesty, with gentleness, and with respect for the opinion of others.

Modesty will also help us remember that being a Christian does not automatically decide what your political position will be on a certain subject. Take, for instance, the subject of adultery. Every orthodox Christian will be, or ought to be, vigorously opposed to it (cf., e.g., Exod. 20:14; Lev. 20:10; Matt. 5:27–28; 15:19; 1 Cor. 6:9–10). Yet we have no civil laws that forbid adultery. This is because the only task of the state is to deal with *public justice*. It does not have authority over what happens behind bedroom doors (unless husbands rape their own wives, and are denounced by them), or behind school doors (as long as the quality of education is guaranteed), or behind company doors (unless there is tax evasion or criminal trading, etc.). Thus, Christians must certainly oppose adultery, and the church must certainly preach against it, but the *state* is not obligated to criminalize it. Similarly, in some countries the state often does not criminalize prostitution as such, unless matters of public justice are at stake (trafficking women, oppression by pimps, spreading diseases, etc.).

Most orthodox Christians are against so-called "homosexual marriages" because throughout the history of the human race, a marriage has been defined as a relationship between a man and a woman, in order to regulate procreation (children have a right to know who their parents are). A man and a man cannot procreate, nor can a woman and a woman; so it is absurd to call their legal relationship a "marriage." We are only waiting for those who, one day, will advocate polygamy again. Why allow a man and a man to "marry," and not a man and two women? Or a woman and two men? One day people will shout: *What discrimination is this!?* The floodgate is open: we can wait for new legal combinations simply because our culture has denied what a "marriage" actually is.

However, with a "civil union" (or "civil partnership") it is different. This is not a marriage, not only because the word "marriage" is not used for it, but also because this is not connected to people making vows of fidelity and allegiance to each other. In such a legal relationship, the word "homosexual" is not being used, either. The state does not come and check whether the partners in this arrangement are sleeping in the same bed, or in two beds. The main reason for such a relationship is purely financial. If two people— whatever their sexual orientation may be—wish to form a bond of friend- ship that includes the possibility of having a common purse, and of the one inheriting from the other, I do not see much objection to this from a purely political point of view. I can very well imagine two unmarried friends (two males or two females) making such a legal contract without seeking thereby to legitimize immoral sexual behaviour.

Now everyone may disagree with me on this matter. That is fine. I ask only two things. First, please make a clear distinction between your person- al convictions about sexual morals and the duty of the state (which is called to deal only with matters of public justice). Second, accept the humbling fact that not only Christians and non-Christians, but also Christians and Christians, may have different opinions on matters like these. Orthodox Christians differ on the death penalty (or on the practical implementation of it), on the size of the government (from liberal to socialist), on the exten- sion of social welfare, on the possession of private weapons, even on certain forms of abortion and euthanasia. Let's not demonize each other over such matters: "Who are you to pass judgment on the servant of another? It is before his own master that he stands or falls. And he will be upheld, for the Lord is able to make him stand.... Each one should be fully convinced in his own mind" (Rom. 14:4–5).

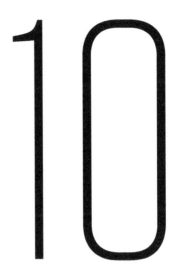

ECCLESIOLOGY[1]

PREPARATORY PONDERINGS

1. The Bible speaks in many ways about the notion of the church. Try to formulate what "the church" means concretely *for you*, and what authority you think it has over you.
2. Can you imagine in what way "the church" could be absolutized at the expense of other societal relationships that God has instituted? How would you explain such a development?
3. Can you imagine how theology could be absolutized at the expense of other academic disciplines? How would you explain such a development?
4. Describe how much authority Christian parents have in educating their children concerning God's Word (and Christian school teachers in teaching their pupils or students concerning God's Word), and how much of it should be left to the church.

---

[1] For this chapter, see the much broader treatment of the subject in Ouweneel (2010b and 2011).

10.1 WHAT IS THE CHURCH?

10.1.1   Five Meanings

NL2K advocates have a strong tendency to speak of "the church" as a specific "institution," which in practice is always a certain denomination out of the about 42,000 Christian denominations that we find today worldwide. Of course, NL2K formally recognizes the difference between the church as an organism and the church as an institute. But in practice it ignores the church as an organism, and refers only to the church as an institute. In the New Testament, we find at least *five* different meanings for the Christian church, which I briefly summarize here.[2]

1. The *worldwide, transcendent church*, that is, the church from its origin (either in Genesis, or in Acts 2, depending on one's ecclesiology) until Christ's second coming (see especially Eph. 3:9–11; 5:23–24, 32). This church, the body of Christ, the house of God, the bride of the Lamb,[3] in its ideal meaning, transcends time and history; the Latin phrase for it is *ecclesia universalis*.[4] By the way, this meaning must not be separated from the following four meanings; Hans Küng distinguishes between the former and the latter as between "being" (German: *Wesen*) and "form" (*Gestalt*).[5]

2. The *worldwide, immanent-historical church*, that is, the church that, here on earth, traverses a certain history, a process of growth and development, of failure and restoration, of ruin and renewal. As such it is a "building" that "grows into a holy temple in the Lord" (Eph. 2:21 NKJV), a "body" that "grows" to full maturity (4:13, 16; Col. 2:19). This church is catholic in the sense of comprising all true believers of all places and times, and also: the church that has spread over all the earth. Catholicity is a qualitative notion expressing unity and fullness.[6] Following Augustine, the Reformers began speaking of the "invisible" (ideal) church and of the "visible" church, which may be a mixture of good and bad elements (cf. Rev. 2–3).[7] Meanings 1,

---

[2] See extensively, Ouweneel (2010b, §1.3).

[3] Ibid., chapters 4–5.

[4] Cf. Calvin, *Institutes* 4.1.2; see also 4.1.9; cf. Graafland (1989, 60–61).

[5] Küng (2001, [13]).

[6] Van Genderen (2008, 719–20); Wentsel (1998, 335–38).

[7] Augustine, *De doctr. chr.* III.32.450 (implicitly also in *De civ. Dei* X.6; *De baptisma* V.38, VI.3, VII.99); cf. John Wycliffe in his *De Ecclesia*, Luther in his *Preface to Revelation*, and Calvin (*Institutes* 4.1.70); see Graafland (1989, chapter 2). Cf. the comments by Berkhof (1986, 398–99); Van Genderen (2008, 705–707); McGrath (2016, 483–84); Erickson (1998, 1054–58); König (2006, 346–47).

2, and 3 have more to do with the invisible church, whereas meanings 4 and 5 more with the visible church. In some sense, the term "invisible" is a little unfortunate:[8] in the midst of all confusion and division, *something of God's church always* becomes visible, if only in the love and fellowship of believers beyond church walls.[9]

3. The *worldwide concretely actual church*, that is, the totality of all believers who, at a given moment, are on earth. Throughout the ages, many members of the church in meanings 1 and 2 have passed away, others have not yet come to faith, or perhaps are not even born yet. Various practical admonitions, such as maintaining "the unity of the Spirit in the bond of peace" (Eph. 4:3), refer to the worldwide church as it exists right now actually on earth. If the Lord's Supper is an expression of the unity and fellowship of the body of Christ (1 Cor. 10:16–17), then this is the body as it concretely functions on earth at this moment. When Paul "persecuted the church of God" (Gal. 1:13), this referred to the entire church of *that* moment.

4. The *local church*, that is, the totality of all believers in a certain city or village (cf. Acts 8:1; 11:22, 25–26; 13:1; 14:21–23, 27; 15:4, 22; 18:22; 20:17; Rom. 16:1; 1 Cor. 1:2; 2 Cor. 1:1; Col. 4:16; 1 Thess. 1:1; 2 Thess. 1:1; Rev. 2–3). In this sense, the word *ekklēsia* can also be used in the plural (1 Cor. 16:1, 19; 2 Cor. 8:1; Gal. 1:2, 22; Rev. 1:4). The word *ekklēsia* can also refer to the *meeting* of the local church (1 Cor. 11:18; 14:19, 28, 34–35; Eph. 3:21; Col. 4:16). Incidentally, the local meaning of *ekklēsia* has gradually been pushed to the background. In the *Martyrium Polycarpi* ("Martyrdom of Polycarp," c. AD 160), *ekklēsia*, that is, the episcopal church in the broader sense, is distinguished from the *paroikia* (which in English has become "parish"), the local church, led by a presbyter (which in English has become "priest"). Roman Catholics still speak of the worldwide (catholic) church and the many local parishes. Only during the Reformation, and later in the free church movements, was the notion of the local *ekklēsia* taken seriously again.[10]

5. A church as a *part* of the local church, a term used when a local church meets at various places in a city or village ("house churches" or "home

---

[8] Küng (2001, [44–45]) says, "outdated'; "the one church is in its being as well as in its form always at the same time visible and invisible" ([49]).

[9] Cf. B. Hindmarsh in Stackhouse (2003, 33–34); cf. the comments on Hindmarsh by D. G. Hart in Husbands and Treier (2005, 26–28, 38); J. Webster in Husbands and Treier (2005, 96–113).

[10] Berkhof (1986, 405–406). Notice the difference, for example between the (Dutch or Christian) Reformed *Church* in North America, and the (United or Free) Reformed *Churches* in North America.

churches") (Acts 2:46; 3:1, 8; 4:4; 5:14; 6:6; 12:12, 17; Rom. 16:3–5, 10–11, 14–15, 23; 1 Cor. 1:11; 16:19; Col. 4:9–17; Phlm. 1–2, 10, 12, 23–24).

10.1.2 The Present Practice

Today, the term "church" is often used in quite different ways, which can be rather confusing. This matter is important for us to understand the way NL2K uses the term. Besides being used for a church *building*, in Reformational Protestantism the word has no global meaning anymore (such as the Roman Catholic Church), but only regional meaning: the Protestant Church in the Netherlands, the Church of England, the Evangelical (read: Lutheran-Reformed) Church of Germany, the Presbyterian Church in America (or in Canada), the Christian Reformed Church in North America, etc. Sometimes, the meaning is purely local, for instance, the Bible Church of this or that city or town. In such cases, there are often no formal (at best friendly) bonds with other similar churches.

In the course of church history, many different church *denominations* have originated, each consisting of a number of local congregations, united under a common name and creed, and usually under a single administrative and legal hierarchy. It is important to realize that, when we speak, for instance, of the Episcopal Church in the United States, we use the word "church" in a way that does not correspond with *any* of the five meanings mentioned in §10.1.1.[11] It is a *new* meaning that, in the post-New Testament period, has developed over time. However, for most Christians this is the most common way in which they use the word, together with the meaning "church building." Think of questions like: "To what church [i.e., building] do you go?," or: "To what church [i.e., denomination] to you belong?"

Now if NL2K advocates say, "The church teaches..." or "the church does not meddle in political affairs," or they speak of "the task of the church," with what meaning is the word "church" being used? It is "the church this," and "the church that," and unfortunately it is very common to speak like this. But as an academic theologian, I prefer clear-cut language. Which of the five meanings mentioned in §10.1.1 is intended? Preferably it should be meaning (3), but the worldwide church at this moment is far too divided to speak with one voice. It cannot be the local congregation, either, for either that is an independent congregation, and then what authority would it have, except over its own members? Or if it is part of a larger denomination, how could this denomination—one out of 42,000—ever be called "the church"?

---

[11] Sometimes, the term "church" is avoided in such general appellations, as in "Southern Baptist Convention."

So what church is this, which preaches and teaches, evangelizes and disciples, and supposedly has so many other tasks? In practice, it can never be anything other than a particular denomination. Is it the Orthodox Presbyterian Church to which Darryl Hart and David VanDrunen belong, and to which Meredith Kline belonged? Or is it the United Reformed Churches to which Michael Horton and Scott Clark belong? Or is it any other of the almost seventy Reformed and Presbyterian denominations in North America? Or is "the church" a reference only to those denominations that fulfill the criteria for being genuinely Reformed as defined by the confessionalist Scott Clark?[12]

Please note that I am not trying to be cynical. I simply want to show in the present chapter what "churchism" is (I mentioned this term already several times in previous chapters). Churchism is not only a bad thing, but it is also a main feature of NL2K.[13] Before we enter into this matter more deeply, I simply wish to expose the careless way in which we are told that "the church takes this or that position" on a certain matter. I am going to show that "churches" *as such* do not teach or educate or take positions at all; it is always individual Christians or individual church denominations who do so. But before entering more deeply into this matter, I must draw the reader's attention to the way NL2K advocates talk about "the church." I honestly do not know what they mean, and they never care to tell me. But I am terribly afraid that they secretly mean their own denomination—one out of about 42,000, or at least one out of almost seventy North American Reformed and Presbyterian denominations. If that were so, then I would also be concerned about the amount of authority they ascribe to this single denomination.

10.2 THE CHURCH'S AUTHORITY

10.2.1 The Church and Other Institutions

Let me give an example. VanDrunen says, "The church attends to the business of the redemptive kingdom and does not trample on the authority of common kingdom institutions [read: other societal relationships]. Unlike these other institutions, its authority derives from the Scriptures alone."[14]

Now this is a rather inaccurate way of describing societal reality. First, after having told us earlier that the church is "the present manifestation

---

[12] See Clark (2008).
[13] In this connection, Boot (2016) speaks of an "ecclesiasticization of the gospel."
[14] VanDrunen (2010a, 31).

of the redemptive kingdom"[15]—which is utterly wrong if taken in any exclusive sense—VanDrunen now tells us that the church "attends to the business of the redemptive kingdom." Not only is this wrong as well, but it also seems to suggest that the church and the redemptive kingdom are two different things after all. I do not see how A can be a manifestation of B, and simultaneously can attend to the business of B.

Second, what does it actually mean that the church attends to the business of the redemptive kingdom? I cannot find in Scripture that "the church" as such attends to the business of anything. It is *elders* who attend to the business of *the church*, and of nothing else (Acts 20:28). Try to discover in the New Testament anything churches "do" except coming together (1 Cor. 14:23), praying (Acts 12:5), giving thanks (Rom. 16:4), greeting (v. 5), submitting (Eph. 5:24), giving (Phil. 4:15), taking care of its widows (1 Tim. 5:16). "The" church—whatever that may be—does not teach, it *is* being taught (1 Cor. 4:17; 7:17; 12:28; Eph. 4:11). "The" church does not strengthen, it *is* being strengthened (Acts 15:41; 16:5). "The" church does not build up, it *is* being built up (Acts 9:31; 1 Cor. 14:4–5, 12). "The" church does not direct anything, it *is* being directed (1 Cor. 16:1). "The" church does not speak, it *is* being spoken to (Rev. 2:7, 11, etc.). "Through the church the manifold wisdom of God" is "now made known to the rulers and authorities in the heavenly places" (Eph. 3:10), *not* in the sense that the church preaches but through her very existence; the text says *dia* ("through"), not *hupo* ("by"; the KJV and other translations are misleading here).

Third, what does it mean that the church "derives its authority from the Scriptures"? What authority does "the" church—whatever that may be—have apart from singing, praying, celebrating the Lord's Supper? As we just saw, the church as such has no authority to teach; the church's teachers teach *the church*. If we could say at all that "the" church has authority, then this authority applies at most to *itself*, its own members, and this through its elders. There is no such thing in the Bible as "the" church exercising authority over other societal relationships, over families, over society, even over the state, as we will see. This is pure scholasticism, a certain Protestant denomination now usurping a position that the Roman Catholic Church had during the Middle Ages.

10.2.2 Objections Continued

Fourth, it is not correct to say that the church "derives its authority from the Scriptures alone." This is a subtle form of biblicism. Church denominations

---

[15] Ibid., 30.

are always products of cultural-historical development. They derive part of their authority from their own history, from which they must prove that they are either *the* faithful continuation of "the" church of God, or at least the *most* faithful continuation. What use is it to speak of "the" church's authority if the members of a given church cannot point out to us by means of historical arguments that they deserve the name "church" at all? Any group of Christians might have the audacity to call themselves "church," or even "*the* church," but are they entitled to do so?

In addition, churches derive their authority also from the laws of the country; they do not have more authority than the state allows them. It is the state that tells them where they can build church buildings, and what rules they have to observe with respect to their neighbourhood. They have no authority to rule the municipality, or to meddle in local politics. They have no authority over the other churches in town, nor over the mosques and synagogues.

I would venture to say that the church derives part of its authority from what NL2K itself calls "natural law"! In my terminology, a church has to respect the creation ordinances for all the different societal relationships, including itself. Do not conclude that the church is *not* one of the many societal relationships by referring to the meaning 1, 2, and 3 in §10.1.1.[16] This only confuses the discussion. As an immanent community of people, an association with rulers and regulations, church councils and church fees, every church denomination is, from a purely structural point of view, a societal relationship like any other. But it is a very *specific* societal relationship (like they all are, for that matter), with its own specific and autonomous characteristics, which must be observed by its members.

Fifth, in what respect does "the" church differ from "common kingdom institutions" (as VanDrunen calls them) when it comes to authority? From where do marriages and families derive their authority? Basically from the same authorities just mentioned: (a) from Scripture—it is the Bible, and the Bible alone, that tells us what genuine marriages and families are in God's eyes, (b) from the laws of the country (it is the state that has the monopoly on defining a legal marriage, and putting this definition in laws), (c) from history (it is historical development that has given our

---

[16] As does VanDrunen (ibid., 147): "Families, governments, schools, and businesses are natural institutions.... But the church is anything but natural. By a *supernatural* divine act Christ announced the establishment of the church." This statement not only expresses the scholastic dualism (nature-supernature), but it also confuses the church in meanings 1, 2, or 3 (§10.1.1) and the church as a human institution with official members, rulers, and regulations like any other association.

Western, present-day marriages and families their specific forms), and (d) from the creation ordinances, as laid down in God's natural revelation. So what remains of the specific authority of "the" church, that is supposedly "derived from the Scriptures alone"?

10.2.3 Why Important?

Why are the things just described so important? Because, if you begin with a scholastic two-kingdoms theology, you will invariably raise the significance of "the" church in an unwarranted way. Please don't misunderstand me: in the meanings 1, 2, and 3 (see §10.1.1), there is nothing more important on earth than the Christian church. But we cannot simply transfer this significance to any of the 42,000 church denominations, or to any local congregation! In living my Christian life, my marriage, my family, my local congregation, and even my Christian schools and Christian associations, are equally important, as autonomous expressions of the one kingdom of God. In each of these societal relationships, I am under the lordship of Christ. As such, my membership of the local congregation is *not* more important than my being a Christian husband, parent, professor, business-man, and party member.

However, this can never be true for NL2K advocates. In their two-king-doms model, you have "the" church on one side, and all the "common king-dom institutions" (marriage, family, state, school, company, association, political party) on the other side. In my view, the kingdom of God on earth encompasses all these societal associations. Not so in NL2K! The kingdom of God is *limited* to just one of these societal associations: "the" church, which is elevated above all the "common institutions" as grace is elevated above nature. So we can understand how important this church must be in this model; in a moment, we will see some striking examples of this.

I repeat—and this is very important—I am *not* referring to meanings 1, 2, or 3 (§10.1.1). Of course not: my marriage, family, school, business, country, party, and so on, will *not* last forever, but I will eternally be a member of the body of Christ. However, my denomination and my local congregation will not last forever. Moreover, what practical sense would it make to say that the worldwide church, the body of Christ, has authority over my life? No, it is my own church denomination, or my own local congregation, that, through its elders, has authority over me. One might say that my church denomination, or my own local congregation, *represents* the worldwide church for me. However, I am not sure whether the worldwide church is very pleased with my specific church denomination (one out of 42,000), or my local congregation. Are these two really so representative?

Any church denomination, and any local congregation, is a societal relationship just like all the others. I am not saying this in order to belittle denominations or congregations, but to *elevate* the *Christian* marriage (please don't tell me it is *not* Christian!), the *Christian* family, even those *Christian* schools where I have studied and taught, and those *Christian* associations (including my *Christian* political party) of which I am, or have been, a member.

It is incorrect to claim that my denomination or congregation exercises any authority over my marriage as such. They have authority over me only when I become an adulterer; then I come under church discipline. They have no authority over my family, unless I torture my children. They have no authority over my school, unless I teach fundamental heresy there. Each of these societal relationships is autonomous within its own boundaries, that is, is under the lordship of Christ, independent of the other relationships. I would venture to say that each of them "derives its authority from the Scriptures alone" (as well as from the laws of the country, from history, and from the creation ordinances, as explained in §10.2.2).

10.3 NOT THE CHURCH

10.3.1 Darryl Hart

Now let us see how this functions in NL2K. It has become very common to say "the church," where we actually mean individual Christians. "The church evangelizes"—no, the church never does this. It is individual *evangelists* who evangelize, and this is also the way it should be. "The church teaches"—no, the church never does this. It is individual *teachers* who teach (Eph. 4:11); the church does not teach, it *is* being taught. Note how Darryl Hart speaks of "the church" when his claims apply only to individual believers. For instance, he agrees with documents of the Lutheran Church, Missouri Synod, which state that the church's religious task involves "no specific design for society" and "no social policy."[17] What a strange argument! First, what is the "religious task" of *the church* at all, other than tasks like worshipping and celebrating the Lord's Supper? By speaking about "the church" instead of speaking about the responsibilities of individual Christians, Hart goes astray from the outset. *Of course*, "the church" has "no specific design for society"—but some individual Christians do, and they pursue this design explicitly in their capacity as Christians. Their church has nothing to do with this.

---

[17] Hart (2006, 233).

Indeed, it is my firm conviction that certain individual Christians, who have a calling from the Lord for this, *do have the task of designing what a Christian-shaped society should look like.* As long as we do not see the difference between the calling of the church and the calling of individual Christians, we will not make any progress in these things. For instance, Hart tells us that the Bible "is the guide for church life," and not "for political life."[18] This is a fundamental mistake. The Bible is the guide for *Christian life*, which is a far wider notion than just church life. Would Hart deny that the Bible is a guide for *Christian* husbands and *Christian* wives, and for *Christian* parents and *Christian* children? And why not for *Christian* employers and for *Christian* employees (cf. Eph. 5:25–6:9)? And why not for *Christian* politicians, or *Christian* businesspersons? The Bible does not teach me how to run a factory, or a municipality. But it does teach me how to behave as a Christian in a factory or in a municipal administration. However, there is more to it: the Bible is our starting point for developing a *Christian worldview* in which we investigate the creation ordinances for marriages, families, schools, companies, and so on. I am glad that Hart is utterly wrong: for non-church life, we do not rely only on reason and prudence, as he (following good scholastic traditions) asserts (see note 17), but on Scripture, as well as a Christian worldview rooted in Scripture. Thank God for that!

10.3.2 David VanDrunen (I)

VanDrunen makes a point of emphasizing that Paul addresses the churches of Galatia (1:2), not the (Christian) families, (Christian) schools, (Christian) companies, or (Christian) provinces of Galatia.[19] Of course not; there *were* no Christian schools, companies, and provinces in Galatia at that time. VanDrunen should rather be impressed by the fact that we read "churches" here—so very different from his constant talking of "the church," which in fact is nothing but a certain church denomination. Paul addresses local congregations, which should look out for heresies. Interestingly, he never writes to elders or overseers as such (they are included only in Phil. 1:1), but always to a local church, or local churches, that is, to *all* the members in such churches (except in the pastoral epistles, where he addresses one specific overseer: Timothy and Titus, respectively). This is because churches do not rule over their members, but each individual Christian in these churches is personally responsible for everything that Paul has to tell them.

---

[18] Ibid., 232; cf. 118; cf. Frame (2011, 258–59).
[19] VanDrunen (2010a, 103).

Indeed, VanDrunen should have been impressed by the fact that in many cases Paul does *not* address a church, or churches, but *individual Christians*: "To all those in Rome who are loved by God and called to be saints" (Rom. 1:7). "To the saints who are in Ephesus, and are faithful in Christ Jesus" (Eph. 1:1). "To all the saints in Christ Jesus who are at Philippi, with the overseers and deacons" (Phil. 1:1). "To the saints and faithful brothers in Christ at Colossae" (Col. 1:2). Only in the case of the Corinthians and the Thessalonians does Paul address their respective "churches" explicitly. The Romans, Ephesians, Philippians, and Colossians are addressed as individual Christians, and as such they are not only church members, but also Christian husbands and wives, Christian parents and children, Christian employers and employees (Eph. 5:22–6:9; Col. 3:18–4:1; cf. 1 Pet. 3:1–7).

Another expression of VanDrunen's churchism is this: "Though the New Testament does not create the family, it acknowledges its existence, confirms the authority structures within it, and speaks of how Christ and the church make special use of the family in bestowing saving blessing."[20] Now where does the New Testament speak of *the church* making use of the family? The answer, of course, is: nowhere. It is VanDrunen's churchism coming out here. *God*, or the glorified *Christ*, makes use of the family "in bestowing saving blessing." Think of the couple, Priscilla and Aquila, and how the Lord used them to enlighten Apollos (Acts 18:24–26). Such speaking of "the church" borders on Roman Catholicism. No wonder: both the Roman Catholic view of the church and the NL2K view of the church are firmly rooted in the medieval scholastic dualism of church and society.

Or consider this statement: "The church is primary for the Christian life. Every other institution—the family, the school, the business corporation, the state—is secondary in the practice of the Christian religion. The church is where the chief action of the Christian life takes place."[21] I think I understand the good intentions behind such a statement, yet it is dead wrong. It is nothing but the worn scholastic view of the religious realm and the common realm. The *entire life* of the Christian is *Christian* life! He is just as much a Christian in church as he is in the family, at school, and in his business. Views like VanDrunen's just enhance the catastrophic division of Christian living into a Sunday Christianity and a Monday-to-Saturday Christianity, which is often hardly any Christianity at all.

Indeed, I worship in church. However, I also worship in my family and in my work: "So, whether you eat or drink, or whatever you do, do *all* to

---

[20] Ibid., 119.
[21] Ibid., 132.

the glory of God" (1 Cor. 10:31); "*whatever* you do, in word or deed, do everything in the name of the Lord Jesus, *giving thanks* to God the Father through him.... *Whatever* you do, work heartily, as for the Lord and not for men" (Col. 3:17, 23). "Rejoice *always*, pray *without ceasing*, give thanks *in all circumstances*; for this is the will of God in Christ Jesus for you" (1 Thess. 5:16–18). The church is *not* the "special community that renders *worship* to God."[22] *Christians* render worship to God at all times, in all circumstances.[23] Notice again the churchism here: individual Christians are replaced here by the term "the church."[24]

10.3.3 David VanDrunen (II)

Here is another example of NL2K confusion: "When Jesus came, he did not establish a family, a state, a school, or a business, but the church alone."[25] I would rather put it this way: when Jesus came he created the *church* in the sense of meaning 1 (§10.11), and he left it to his followers to develop the *kingdom* of God, throughout the ages and by the power of the Holy Spirit, into a true Christian commonwealth containing Christian church denominations, Christian families, Christian schools, Christian businesses, and here and there even Christian states, no matter how weak. Please note carefully that Christian families, Christian schools, Christian businesses, and Christian political parties *are just as much the work of Christians* as Christian church denominations and local congregations. Or, if you prefer: the founding of Christian families, Christian schools, Christian businesses, even Christian states *is just as much the work of the Holy Spirit* through humans (in spite of all human weaknesses) as the founding of Christian church denominations and local congregations.

Another example of NL2K confusion is this: "Parents have primary authority for educating their children in the nontheological academic disciplines, but only *secondary* jurisdiction for educating them in theology (and in whatever else Scripture teaches).... [Parents] should undertake their children's biblical and theological education ultimately under the authority of their church's ministers and elders."[26] I don't believe what I'm

---

[22] Cf. ibid., 134.

[23] This is partly recognized by VanDrunen (2010a, 134–35), but he does not draw the proper consequences.

[24] Part of the problem is that, in English, "worship" has often become a synonym for "church service." "Where do you worship?" means for many people: "What church do you go to?" But when Jesus said that the Father looks for "worshipers" (John 4:23), he did *not* (just) mean "churchgoers."

[25] VanDrunen (2010a, 150).

[26] Ibid., 176; cf. 176–78.

reading! First, I did not know that parents have *any* authority at all for teaching any academic disciplines, including or not including theology. Sensible parents leave this to academic teachers (I am not referring to non-academic disciplines, taught by non-academic teachers or, in home schooling, by parents). But this is probably another scholastic confusion, namely, between the theoretical sciences on the one hand, and the practical education in the things of life on the other hand. So let us assume that VanDrunen simply means that parents have only secondary jurisdiction for educating their children in biblical things.

But, second, even this is absurd. I read in the Bible that *fathers*—not the church—must bring up their children in the discipline and instruction of the Lord (Eph. 6:4). I repeat what I said before: "the church" does not teach at all. So is VanDrunen in fact saying that the teachers of the church have more authority to teach the believers' children than the parents themselves? Only a radical churchism could come up with such ideas. The teachers in the church may help, just as the teachers at the Christian school may help. But teaching God's Word to the children is first and foremost the responsibility of the parents. This was already the case in the Old Testament (Exod. 12:26–27; 13:14–15; Deut. 6:20–25; Prov. 1–7 etc.). Although priests and other Levites were called to teach God's Word (Deut. 33:10; 2 Chron. 17:8–9; Neh. 7:7–8; Hag. 2:12; Mal. 2:7), it is nowhere said that teaching God's Word to children had to be left to them.

There is no hint in the Bible that teaching God's Word must "ultimately" occur "under the authority of their church's ministers and elders." Such an idea can be produced only by a churchism in which the *entire* Christian life is identified with "the" church. It borders on Roman Catholicism again:[27] "Parents and schools… do not have an authoritative office to interpret and minister God's Word in the name of Christ. Christian parents should be teaching their children the Bible as they reinforce the church's biblical education, but even parents have no right to *preach* the Word."

Again, this is absurd. How can fathers bring up their children in the discipline and instruction of the Lord without "interpreting and ministering God's Word in the name of Christ"? Who says that they are not *entitled* to do so? Perhaps the regulations in VanDrunen's denomination prohibit this, but my Bible does not. Priscilla and Aquila "explained" to Apollos (a servant of the Lord!) "the way of God more accurately" (Acts 18:26), and they were fully entitled to do so, whether officially appointed or not. "And there arose on that day a great persecution against the church in Jerusalem,

[27] Ibid., 177–78.

and they were all scattered throughout the regions of Judea and Samaria, except the apostles.... Now those who were scattered went about *preaching the word*" (Acts 8:1–4). They *preached*! And they were not even apostles, or official teachers—just common church members (see further in §10.6.1).

10.4 CHURCHISM LEADS TO THEOLOGISM

10.4.1 A "Theology of Culture"?

Given the scholastic background of NL2K, we may expect *a priori* the presence not only of churchism, but also of theologism. In the scholastic dualism of nature and grace (or supernature), the church as well as theology belong to the sacred domain of grace,[28] whereas the common societal relationships as well as the common sciences and humanities belong to the profane (neutral, secular) domain of nature." Everybody understands that the sacred is more exalted than the profane, so everybody is given to understand that "the" church—whatever this may be—is more exalted than the family, the school, the state, and so forth. And similarly, everybody must understand that theology, as the only sacred science, is more exalted than any of the other sciences, which by definition are neutral, secular, common. Actually, theology is the only science that is entitled to speak with some authority about the Scriptures.

In the next chapter we will enter more deeply into the background of this erroneous thinking. Let us now continue our investigation into how NL2K deals with these things. Back in chapter 9, we found some disastrous examples of theologism: VanDrunen spoke of a "biblical theology of Christianity and culture."[29] Now I have heard of the theology of Christ (Christology), of salvation (soteriology), of the church (ecclesiology), or of the last things (eschatology), and I can understand that: Christ, salvation, the church, and the last things are explicit subjects in the Bible. However, culture is not. The Bible speaks about many cultures (though not using this term), but not of the phenomenon of culture as such. Thus, "culture" cannot be a subject of theology—it is a subject of (Christian or non-Christian) *philosophy*. German-American theologian and philosopher Paul Tillich (d. 1965) may have spoken of a "theology of culture,"[30] but that does not make it right.

---

[28] Cf. ibid., 190–91): "The work of the ministry is truly a holy vocation. To say that other vocations are secular or common is not to insult them, but simply to respect proper biblical distinctions."

[29] Ibid., 12.

[30] Tillich (1964, *Theology of Culture*).

It is one of the examples in which a scholastic way of thinking assumes that anything that is sacred, such as "Christian culture," or a "Christian approach to culture," automatically belongs to the church or to theology.

In §9.4.3 I described the dangers of a "theology of culture," a "theology of the state," a "theology of politics," a "theology of economics," and this all within a scholastic framework. I tried to explain what happens if theologians in their capacity as theologians believe that *they* have to teach the other sciences the Christian principles of these various sciences. I know several Christian universities that have tried this, but it has never worked. The only way it *could* and *would* work is if at such universities a *Christian-philosophical* view of cosmic reality would be developed, which can serve as a foundation for the various sciences. Such a view was developed at the Free University of Amsterdam, but it came too late; secularization on a massive scale had already set in.

Apparently, NL2K believes it can still follow the scholastic way, and let theology do the job. With this enormous difference: NL2K does not believe in Christian philosophy, Christian psychology, Christian historical sciences, Christian sociology, Christian economics, Christian jurisprudence, and so on. Therefore, actually theology does not supply the sciences with a Christian foundation at all. It seeks only to protect itself: Christian psychologists, historians, sociologists, economists, lawyers, etc., should not dare to integrate any biblical data pertaining to their respective fields into their disciplines, for this job supposedly belongs exclusively to theologians!

10.4.2 Three Errors

Let me give an example. VanDrunen suggests "that Scripture says crucial things about the *big picture* of all the academic disciplines," but he continues:

> The discipline of theology, whose primary purpose is to interpret and communicate the Scriptures, is under the primary jurisdiction of the church. The church must teach the theological truths of Scripture. Second, the church must also teach ideas that have broad relevance for all the academic disciplines, that is, the big-picture concerns about which Scripture speaks. Since the church is to proclaim *all* that the Scriptures say, then the church should teach something (directly or indirectly) about every discipline.[31]

---

[31] VanDrunen (2010a, 175-76).

I find three major errors here.

(a) Preachers, pastors, ministers are indeed "under the primary jurisdiction of the church" (to be more precise: of the consistory or presbytery), *but not theologians as such*. Elsewhere I have argued extensively that the academy and the church are each autonomous in their own field, though each is subject to the Word of God. Of course, ministers *are* usually theologically trained, and theologians *are* often ministers, but the two things should be carefully distinguished (see further in §10.5). Preaching is always under the authority of the elders, but academic investigation as such must be perfectly free, apart from being subject to God's Word and Spirit.[32] Is a theological department a center of scholarly theological investigation, or is it a training center for certain (church) offices? Can the two be combined in one school in a reasonable and credible way, without one of the two, or perhaps even both, suffering under this combination? Can you tell the students what they later will have to teach to the members of their particular denomination, and at the same time guarantee academic freedom? Is true academic freedom even possible at such an institution, given the fact that the school and the professors and lecturers are subsidized by the denomination concerned, and are evaluated by representatives of that denomination?

(b) The *church as such* does not teach at all, as I have argued above.[33] It is the church itself that is taught, namely, by the preachers of the Word. To this end, God has given shepherds and teachers to the church (1 Cor. 12:28; Eph. 4:11). Through them, it is the Holy Spirit who speaks to the churches (Rev. 2:7, 11, 17, 29, etc.). Don't think the difference is a trifle. If we carefully consider the matter, it would be disastrous if "the church"—as an institution—were to teach, because who will teach *the church* if the church itself were to act as the teacher? To make it worse, VanDrunen tells us that it is *the church*—not even the theologians—that must "teach ideas that have broad relevance for all the academic disciplines." Can you imagine? We are not allowed to call any non-theological discipline a *Christian* discipline, and there is no Christian plumbing, either. However, if a scholar wants to perform his job well, he first has to listen to the theological teaching of *the church*, because it is *the church* that teaches the "big picture" for every discipline. This is scholasticism in spades: the non-theological sciences belong

---

[32] See extensively, Ouweneel (2013, chapter 10; 2014c, chapter 5). On this vital point, see also Popma (1946, 28–37); Dooyeweerd (1958, 13–14); Ott (1972, 60–67); Hasenhüttl (1979, 15); Wentsel (1981, 22-24); Lategan (1989, 115–16); Troost (2004, 179–80, 289–91, 340 note 1); Caputo (2006, 51–52).

[33] Another counter-example: "The church should teach these things" (on civil government and political involvement) (VanDrunen, 2010a, 198).

to the common realm, so by definition they cannot be Christian. However, the common realm is subordinate to the sacred realm, so, scholars working in the common realm, you must listen to what *the church*—not simply the theologians, but *the church!*—teaches you about your own discipline!

(c) Even if VanDrunen had insisted that "the theologians" "should teach something (directly or indirectly) about every discipline," he would still have been mistaken. Theologians may tell us the theological meaning of the expression "after its kind" in Genesis 1, but *as theologians* they cannot tell us the biological meaning of this expression. They may tell us the theological meaning of "soul" and "spirit" in the Bible, but *as theologians* they cannot tell us the psychological meaning of these terms. They may tell us the theological meaning of the year of jubilee in Leviticus 25, but *as theologians* they cannot tell us the economic consequences of the regulation. They might have some layman's wisdom about these things, but theologians are not qualified to make psychological, biological, sociological, economic, judicial, or esthetic statements, *even when such statements involve biblical data*. The only contribution that theologians may make is to assist with the precise grammatical-historical exegesis of certain biblical statements.

10.5 CHURCH AND ACADEMY

10.5.1 Church Seminaries?
In the previous section, I mentioned academic freedom. This brings me to a serious question that I must pose to NL2K advocates. If the kingdom of God is more or less identical with "the church" (read: the visible church, more specifically in fact a certain church denomination), and the rest of society belongs to the common kingdom, then *to which kingdom does a theological seminary belong*? From the NL2K viewpoint, only two possibilities exist: either a theological seminary is nothing but an extension of a certain church denomination, or it is a school like any other school, and thus part of the common kingdom.

Let us look a little more closely at these two options. The first one is this: a theological seminary may be an extension of the church, but then it definitely is not a genuinely academic institution. It is little more than a school for socializing students from a certain church denomination not only in general Christian truths, but also in the theological idiosyncrasies of that specific denomination. Teachers and students are strictly bound by the confessions (e.g., the Three Forms of Unity, the Westminster Standards) of that denomination. Many theologians have argued (see §10.4.2) that there can never be genuine academic freedom at such a school. At my ideal theological seminary, teachers and students are strictly subject to God's Word, but for the rest there is academic freedom to express any innovative idea, or test any new view, in terms of the Word of God. The test for such a school is not whether it is truly Reformed (or Presbyterian, or Lutheran, or Roman Catholic, or Baptist, etc.) but whether it is faithful to God's Word, and to God's Word alone[34] (or if people insist: faithful to the Nicene-Constantinopolitan Creed).

It is my experience that theology professors can become quite upset if one is skeptical about the academic standards of their ecclesiastical seminary, and (humanly speaking) understandably so. But it is also my experience that many theology professors have only vague ideas about what makes their school a genuinely *academic* institution, in contrast with many so-called Bible schools. A seminary administrator once told me that their education was scholarly because they taught the original Bible languages! But even some Bible schools do this. In the next chapter I hope to show what makes theology a scholarly enterprise, in contrast to ordinary Bible study. I also hope to show why such questions usually embarrass theologians; this is because, in fact, these are not theological questions at all, but philosophical questions.[35] The theologian *in his or her capacity as theologian* (I am not speaking of theologians with a philosophical training) cannot tell us what theology is, in distinction from other special sciences, and how academic theology can be distinguished from ordinary Bible study. If they have not been properly trained, their intuitive answers invariably turn out to be scholastic, humanistic, or biblicistic.

10.5.2 Are Seminaries Part of the Common Kingdom?

In principle, there is nothing wrong with a church denomination that wishes to found its own schools in order to train its own pastors. My only problem is that people should not call this a *theological* seminary (school, academy, university, college).[36] As a scholarly (academic) enterprise, theology requires complete academic freedom. A theological seminary (academy, university, college) is not run by church leaders as such (in their capacity as church leaders) but by qualified theologians. Such a school nominates professors,

---

34 See Ouweneel (2014c, chapter 1).

35 Again, I refer here to Ouweneel (2013, chapters 6–14), where the premises of academic theology are extensively dealt with.

36 I fully realize that the term "theology" has been rather significantly debased and distorted. Anyone can call his Bible school "theological" (the term is not legally protected), and nowadays certain Jewish and Muslim groups also call their schools "theological."

not because they are members of the "right" church denomination but strictly because of their academic qualifications. At such schools, theological
publications, including doctoral dissertations, are evaluated not according
to confessional standards, but according to academic standards. They may
be called "good," not (only) because they are confessionally correct but
(especially) because they are of high academic quality.[37]

However, another problem arises at this point. According to NL2K, *my
ideal seminary would automatically belong to the common kingdom.* A theological seminary is either under the roof of a certain church denomination,
or it is part of the common (neutral, secular) realm. In the latter case, we
preferably should not call such a school "Christian." In this case, theology
must be pursued as a common (read: neutral, secular) enterprise, just like
all other special sciences. But this, of course, is the last thing NL2K advocates
would accept. As good scholastics, these theologians dig an unbridgeable
canyon between sacred theology and the profane sciences (see the next
chapter). A theological seminary must be thoroughly ecclesiastical-con-
fessional. And here, NL2K advocates run stuck. They must view theology
either as a strictly confessional/denominational enterprise, in which case
it cannot be genuinely academic, or as a genuinely academic enterprise, in
which case it can belong only to the common kingdom.

Fortunately, my position does not suffer from this dilemma. First, I do
not believe in the existence of that common kingdom; it is unbiblical and
unrealistic. Second, I do not believe in church-run theological seminaries
because these can never be academically free. I need only remind the reader of the disaster involving Professor Norman Shepherd at Westminster
Theological Seminary (Philadelphia, PA), who in 1981 was dismissed from
the school because his teaching was alleged not to be entirely in accord
with the Westminster Standards. It is completely irrelevant whether I agree
with Shepherd;[38] the point is that he had no academic freedom to interpret
Scripture as he saw appropriate. (I must add, though, that God is to be
thanked that Shepherd's dismissal was condemned by many Reformed
theologians and church leaders.)

Third, in my view, *Christian* church denominations and *Christian* schools
(including theological seminaries), as well as *Christian* families, companies,
associations, and political parties, are bound together by the same Word
of God, yet each are autonomous within their own confines. Christian

[37] The term "good" is a dangerously slippery term here. When, e.g., Horton (1995, 77; cf.
109) speaks of "good" and "bad art," he should have explained whether he meant "good" and
"bad" according to aesthetic standards (structure), or standards of faith (direction).
[38] For this, see Ouweneel (2016h, chapter 4).

theological seminaries are subject to God's Word as well as to academic standards—never to church leaders as such. The latter would spell the end of academic theology. The Shepherd case showed how Reformed/ Presbyterian theology can walk down the dead alley of ever increasing introvertedness and intellectual inbreeding. The automatic consequence of this is continually new church splits, leaving us today with almost seventy Reformed and Presbyterian denominations in North America!

Let me add here a word of encouragement to the opponents of NL2K. I am thoroughly opposed to combating NL2K with purely confessional arguments. This would be nothing but putting the cart before the horse. NL2K must be combated with the Bible, and with academic (theological, and especially philosophical) arguments. I myself combated NL2K with appeals to the Three Forms of Unity (§1.3), not because I attach much value to confessional arguments as such, but to show NL2K theologians that they are not as Reformed as they pretend to be.

10.5.3 The Nature of Theology

What plays a role in NL2K's type of thinking is the fact that scholastic theologians never make a distinction between biblical facts and theological facts, that is, between practical, existential ("suprarational") faith knowledge and theoretical, rational academic knowledge. For instance, VanDrunen tells us that families have "only *secondary* jurisdiction for educating them [i.e., their children] in theology (and in whatever else Scripture teaches)."[39] Here again we encounter a threefold error. First, the Bible does not teach theology at all. Theology is an academic discipline practiced by theologians when they are rationally-analytically elaborating the biblical data. There is not a droplet of theology in the Bible, if we understand theology to be an academic discipline. I emphatically refer to what I have said about this elsewhere.[40]

Second, parents *never* teach their children theology (except perhaps when the parents are theologians, and their children are theology students); they teach them the contents of Scripture in a very practical way.[41] It is another painful example of theologism, namely, to theologize these contents of Scripture, that is, to call any practical Bible education "theology." Again, this is not a trifle. Theologians wish to be called doctors and professors, that is, to be treated as scholars (academicians)—but in the same breath they tell us that theology is nothing more than an exalted form

---

[39] VanDrunen (2010a, 176).

[40] See extensively, Ouweneel (2013, chapters 6–14; 2014c).

[41] Strangely, VanDrunen (2010a, 176) speaks of the "children's biblical *and* theological education" (italics added). One wonders where, in his view, the difference lies.

of Bible study; teaching the Bible is teaching theology. They want to play on both sides, and that does not work. You can't have your cake and eat it too.

Third, teaching the Bible is not at all the prerogative that belongs solely to the church. Such an idea is another example of churchism. The Bible passages that VanDrunen mentions do not prove his point at all: Jesus did not give the keys of the kingdom of heaven to "the church" but to Peter (Matt. 16:19) (no matter how one wishes to interpret this). Giving teachers *to* the church is very different from calling "the church" to be a teaching institution (cf. Eph. 4:7–16; Acts 20:27–28). This endless talking about "the church" when it is teachers or elders who are meant, or this restriction of any Bible teaching to "the church," is unbiblical churchism. Parents instruct their children, religion teachers instruct their pupils and students, and preachers instruct the members of their churches concerning the Word of God.

One reason NL2K advocates are afraid of Christian politics is that Christian politicians might quote and apply the Scriptures in the public square without being qualified clergymen. Therefore, NL2K advocates are also afraid of the Christian school because here the same "danger" is even greater:

> Christian schools should be mindful not to usurp the church's responsibility as their own. Many Christian schools devote significant time to service/mission projects, chapel and prayer services, and spiritual emphasis weeks. It is worthwhile for administrators and teachers to ponder why their schools would spend time on such things. Do they believe that Christ has insufficiently equipped his church for missions, worship, and the spiritual growth of their members?[42]

Again, this leaves me flabbergasted. It is churchism all over. *All* those who have been placed by the Lord in positions of authority should teach the Word of God, whether they are clergymen or not: parents in their families, believing teachers in schools, missionaries on the mission fields, Christian businessmen in their companies (when a word from Scripture is appropriate), chairpersons of Christian organizations, members of Christian political parties, believing politicians. Imagine how silly the following scenario would be: your not-yet-believing neighbour, or your colleague at work, or your golf buddy is interested in the Bible, and asks you all kinds of questions about the Bible. But you answer: "It is not my prerogative to answer biblical questions; only my pastor is allowed to do that; so please go to him."

---

[42] Ibid., 178.

10.6 BIBLICAL COUNTER-EXAMPLES

10.6.1 "Lay Preachers"

How differently the Bible speaks! Stephen's only authorization was to "serve tables," that is, to help with supplying for the needs of the poor. Yet, this did not prevent Stephen from preaching (Acts 6:1–11). A little later we read: "And there arose on that day a great persecution against the church in Jerusalem, and they were all scattered throughout the regions of Judea and Samaria, except the apostles.... Now those who were scattered went about preaching the word" (Acts 8:1, 4). None of them were qualified to do so, according to NL2K standards, for only "the church" is allowed to teach and preach. But fortunately these people did not know about NL2K. They simply did what the Holy Spirit urged them to do: *preach the Word.*

The story continues with Philip, *not* the apostle Philip but, like Stephen, one of those who were "serving tables" (Acts 6:5). A humble church member, we might say. Yet we read:

> Philip went down to the city of Samaria and proclaimed to them the Christ. And the crowds with one accord paid attention to what was being said by Philip when they heard him and saw the signs that he did. For unclean spirits, crying out with a loud voice, came out of many who had them, and many who were paralyzed or lame were healed. So there was much joy in that city.... Philip found himself at Azotus, and as he passed through he preached the gospel to all the towns (vv. 5–8, 40; in 21:8 he is called "the evangelist").

Now tell me: What would "the church," as it functions in the NL2K paradigm, think of such insubordinate behaviour?

Of the apostle Paul we read that he was called by the Lord entirely independently of what one in those days could call "the church" (cf. Gal. 1:11–24). None of the other apostles was involved in the preparation for his ministry. Yet he did his job, and was encouraged by others to do so. His calling from the Lord was sufficient. Apollos was not connected with, or commissioned by, any church, but he was

> competent in the Scriptures [and] had been instructed in the way of the Lord. And being fervent in spirit [or, in the Spirit] he spoke

and taught accurately the things concerning Jesus, though he knew only the baptism of John. He began to speak boldly in the synagogue, but when Priscilla and Aquila heard him, they took him aside and explained to him the way of God more accurately (Acts 18:24–26).

Now not only Apollo, but also Priscilla (she is even mentioned first, according to the best manuscripts) and Aquila were not commissioned by any church; even less did they represent "the church" (whatever that may be). Yet, they taught the Scriptures with boldness. And this is the way it should be today as well. As long as you do not preach fundamental heresy, your church has nothing to do with your preaching.

I think I do not commit the error of biblicism here. NL2K advocates might reply: This was only the time of the beginning; now we do it differently. I am aware of that. But do you necessarily do it better? Gradually, the charismatic ministries of the beginning have been replaced with the hierarchical-institutional offices as we know them today: episcopalian, presbyterian, congregationalist, what have you. Can these developments stand the test of Scripture? Do we do it *better* than Christians did it in the book of Acts? Can the Holy Spirit work better through our present-day offices than he did through the lay preachers' *charismata* in the time of the beginning?[43] Let NL2K tell me.

10.6.2 The Present Situation

It is not fair to stress that this was "only" at the beginning of church history. I understand very well that the church has undergone a certain development, and that we now have (rigid and not so rigid) institutions, where preaching and teaching are usually restricted to those who have received their authority from their respective denominations. After a while, people begin to think that *this* is how the Bible prescribes it: a multitude of denominations, each with its own hierarchical structure. In the Roman Catholic world, "the" church has become everything. Churchism and theologism dominate the Christian scene. God supposedly wants only academic theologians to teach and preach. And *thus*, God does want parents and school teachers to have only very limited authority to expound the Scriptures because they are only lay people. We do it thus, and therefore God wants it thus. But in the end, do you yourself still believe this?

---

[43] Many have discussed this problem, such as Brockhaus (1972); Noordegraaf (1980, chapter 6); Van Bruggen (1984, chapter 7); Burtchael (1992); Campbell (1994); Graafland (1999, 304–331); Liebelt (2000); Sullivan (2001).

"Fathers, do not provoke your children to anger, but bring them up in the discipline and instruction of the Lord" (Eph. 6:4), *but be careful!* Your authority in this field is very limited, because actually it is *the church* that must bring your children up in the discipline and instruction of the Lord.

Perhaps we may call it a natural development that the early church moved from a more charismatic to a more official structure (a structure dominated by church offices). In the New Testament, words for "office," such as Greek *archē* (cf. Titus 3:1) and *timē* (cf. Heb. 5:4), are never used with respect to church leaders. "Office" in Acts 1:20 and in 1 Timothy 3:1 ("office of overseer" is one word) is Greek *episkopē*, "oversight, overseer-ship." Therefore, Emil Brunner said that matters like church law and office belonged to the second generation of the Christian church (to the date of which he, incidentally, also assigned the pastoral letters, 1 and 2 Timothy and Titus), not to the original "charismatic" form of the church.[44] James Burtchaell, however, argued that the church officials as we know them were present from the beginning, though in the first century they were still dominated by the "charismatics."[45] This is mainly a question of semantics. Let us put it this way: during the early centuries, the offices of overseer and deacon were particularly charismatic ones, whereas in later centuries they became more and more a formal-hierarchical (clerical) matter.

Hans Küng argued that the New Testament avoided secular words like "office" because they express *Herrschaftsverhältnisse* ("dominating rela-tions") that the church did not wish to adopt from the surrounding world. Instead, the New Testament prefers a term that expresses the opposite, namely, *diakonia*, "service, ministry."[46] However, this does not change the fact that, because of the development of the *clergy*, the early church soon began to think in terms of (secular, or even worldly) domination.[47] The church began to reign, that is to say, in practice, its clergy began to reign, and to usurp all kinds of authority that it did not originally possess.

10.6.3 Summary

Strictly speaking, "the church" as such has no authority at all. Its elders have ruling authority over *her members*, her teachers have pedagogical authority over *her members*, and this *only in their capacity as members*. They have not the slightest authority over them in their capacity as parents, or schoolteachers, or scientists, or citizens, or party members, or politicians,

---

[44] Quoted in Lekkerkerker (1971, 79).
[45] Burtchaell (1992); cf. Brockhaus (1972, 7–46); Wentsel (1998, 556–61, 566–69).
[46] Küng (2001, 20).
[47] Cf. Ouweneel (2010b, §§7.1.2 and 7.3.2).

and so on. They have no authority to tell parents and schoolteachers what to teach—not even concerning the Bible—*unless parents or teachers are communicating fundamental heresy*. They have no authority to tell their members how to vote or what associations or political parties to join, etc. All Christians are servants of the Lord:

> Who are you to pass judgment on the servant of another? It is before his own master [or, lord] that he stands or falls. And he will be upheld, for the Lord is able to make him stand.... Why do you pass judgment on your brother? Or you, why do you despise your brother? For we will all stand before the judgment seat of God; for it is written, "As I live, says the Lord, every knee shall bow to me, and every tongue shall confess to God." So then each of us will give an account of himself to God (Rom. 14:4, 10–12).

This is the core of the matter: each individual Christian, but also *every societal relationship stands directly under the lordship of Christ*, independently of other societal relationships, including the church: "For if anyone thinks he is something, when he is nothing, he deceives himself. But let each one test his own work, and then his reason to boast will be in himself alone and not in his neighbor. For each will have to bear his own load" (Gal. 6:3–4). Christian parents, school teachers, scientists, citizens, party members, politicians, etc., *in these capacities*, are not at all responsible to their church leaders. The latter have authority over their members only if these openly communicate fundamental heresy, or live in serious sin (Matt. 18:17; Rom. 16:17–18; 1 Cor. 5; 2 Thess. 3:6; 1 Tim. 1:3–4; 4:6–7; 6:20–21; 2 Tim. 2:15–18; 3:5; Titus 1:13–14; 3:9–11). Parents are entirely autonomous within their families, schoolteachers within their schools, businesspersons within their companies, committees within their associations and political parties—and elders within their churches.

Only scholastic theologians, with their dualism of the sacred church versus common institutions, in which the church is superior to the latter, could ever have invented the idea that it could be otherwise. As we have seen, they can do so only by confusing the body of Christ as it exists in the counsel of God with church denominations, which are always man-made, and thus defective, products of human cultural history. In *this* sense, church denominations and local congregations are themselves nothing but societal relationships. There is nothing wrong with this, for that matter.

Let me conclude by citing two statements of Jesus:

You are not to be called rabbi, for you have one teacher, and you are all brothers. And call no man your father on earth, for you have one Father, who is in heaven. Neither be called instructors, for you have one instructor, the Christ. The greatest among you shall be your servant [Greek: *diakonos*]. Whoever exalts himself will be humbled, and whoever humbles himself will be exalted (Matt. 23:8–12).

The kings of the Gentiles exercise lordship over them, and those in authority over them are called benefactors. But not so with you. Rather, let the greatest among you become as the youngest, and the leader as one who serves. For who is the greater, one who reclines at table or one who serves? Is it not the one who reclines at table? But I am among you as the one who serves (Luke 22:25–27).

WORKING IT OUT: **CHURCH ANSWERS TO SOCIETAL PROBLEMS**
Should the church in its preaching and teaching stipulate answers to the kind of questions that were asked in previous chapters?

What do you mean by "the church"? The global church of God, divided into many different Christian denominations? Or do you mean one of these many denominations, which happens to be *your* denomination? Or your local congregation? How can any denomination speak with any formal divine authority, given the fact that there are so many other (orthodox) denominations, which might express quite different opinions on a lot of matters? So where is "the church" that might "in its preaching and teaching stipulate answers" to the various questions we have dealt with?

Moreover, I have never seen "churches" preach and teach, neither in Scripture, nor in practical reality. It is always preachers and teachers speaking *to the church* (and evangelizing to the world as well). These preachers and teachers may "stipulate answers," and they should certainly do so, as long as we keep in mind that they never speak with any *formal* authority but with the *moral* authority that is part of their vocation, and that is always to be evaluated by the listeners: is this in accordance with the Word of God? Is this from the Holy Spirit? "He who has an ear, let him hear what the Spirit says to the churches" (Rev. 2:7, 11, 29; 3:6, 13, 22). "The Helper, the Holy Spirit, whom the Father will send in my name, he will teach you all things" (John 14:26). "When the Spirit of truth comes, he will guide you into all the truth, for he will not speak on his own authority, but whatever he hears he will speak" (16:13). The Berean believers-to-be "were more noble than those in Thessalonica; they received the word with all eagerness, examining the Scriptures daily to see if these things were so" (Acts 17:11).

Let us now reformulate the question: Should the teachers of the church in their preaching and teaching stipulate answers to the kind of questions that were asked in previous chapters? The answer is primarily this: *the teachers of the church must interpret the Scriptures*:

> Preach the Word of God. Preach it when it is easy and people want to listen and when it is hard and people do not want to listen. Preach it all the time. Use the Word of God to show people they are wrong. Use the Word of God to help them do right. You must be willing to wait for people to understand what you teach as you teach them (2 Tim. 4:2 NLV).

The only thing that teachers of Scripture should *not* do in their capacity as teachers is go *beyond* the Scriptures. That is, they must be very careful in the application of the Word to all kinds of practical situations, especially situations that were not even known in New Testament times.

Let me give a number of examples.

(a) The teachers of Scripture must teach that, if killing a child outside its mother's womb is murder, then killing a child inside its mother's womb is also murder. However, from this fact, the road to concrete policy legislation is not easily paved. For instance, what about women who have been raped: should you give them the "morning after pill" or not? Or if you forbid abortion, what are you going to do for women who will have their babies, but for economic or psychological reasons are not able to care for them? These are problems that Christian politicians must address with concrete policies. They have no direct biblical indications for such matters, so they must follow their Christian-political instinct. At any rate, theologians in their capacity as theologians can in no way formally command them what they must do, or must not do. Christian politicians are under God's Word and Spirit; they are not under the theologians. They should be able to say: "My conscience bears me witness in the Holy Spirit" (Rom. 9:1) to all those who ask them to account for their views—even to the theologians, if necessary.

(b) The teachers of Scripture must teach that God forbids homosexual intercourse, as he, incidentally, forbids *all* sexual intercourse outside the husband-wife union. But these teachers must also explain that Scripture nowhere deals with the (possibly innate) homosexual *orientation* as such. Nor does the Bible tell us how we must deal with young people in our congregations who discover this orientation within themselves. In this respect, Christian psychologists can help us much more than theologians. However, because NL2K advocates do not recognize the legitimacy of Christian psychology, you can imagine that the only alternative to which they always turn is "the church" (that is, the teachers of the church).

(c) The teachers of Scripture must teach what few things the Bible has to say about culture, about the state, about economics. NL2K advocates recognize that these are indeed only a few things,[48] but then they leave it to *neutral* scientists to work out a view of culture, of the state, of the economic order. This is disastrous. Instead, they should point out that it is now up to *Christian philosophers* to work out a Christian philosophy of culture, a Christian philosophy of the state, a Christian philosophy of economics, a Christian philosophy of jurisprudence, and even a Christian philosophy of religion, in close interaction with Christian cultural anthropologists, Christian political scientists, Christian economists, Christian jurists, Christian religion scientists, respectively. In the next chapter, I will explain why this is so difficult for NL2K advocates, and where they go astray.

(d) The teachers of Scripture must expound what few things the Bible has to say about education. But as Bible teachers they can make no statements about schools in general, or about homeschooling, or about public schools, or about Christian schools, because Scripture does not speak about schools. The authority that they have as teachers of Scripture must not be confused with the wisdom they, as lay people, might have in non-theological fields. They should rather call upon *Christian philosophers* to develop a Christian philosophy of education, in close interaction with Christian education scientists and Christian developmental psychologists. (Of course, in rare cases the philosopher, theologian and pastor may be one and the same person.)

(e) The teachers of Scripture must expound what few things the Bible has to say about our being pilgrims, strangers, and sojourners here on earth, as long as they also explain that we are called to be active labourers in the vineyard of the Lord at the same time. But they should *not* apply these things to *your* personal situation by telling you what *the Bible* supposedly says you must do. *They* should develop the biblical framework, but *you* must apply the specifics to your own vocation, according to your own conscience, carefully listening to God's Word and God's Spirit.

I repeat: the teachers of the church must expound *Scripture*. In this capacity they have nothing to say about homosexual orientation, or about schooling, or about where to shop (and especially where not to shop), or

---

[48] See, e.g., VanDrunen (2010a, 175–78).

about what political candidate one must endorse, or what vocations are acceptable and what are not. Please note: a wise and prudent pastor may have so much practical wisdom and experience that you are happy to listen to his advice. You may thank God for such pastors! But they can never *command* you to do this or not to do that. If you fall into gross sin, you come under the discipline of the elders. But as long as you stay within the biblical framework, no preacher, teacher, or pastor can tell you what you *must* do.

PART III
PHILOSOPHICAL TOPICS

11

PHILOSOPHY AND THEOLOGY[1]

PREPARATORY PONDERINGS

1. What is your instinctive response to the idea of a Christian philosophy? Do you see room for it? Why? Or if not, what are your objections against it?
2. Some people claim that theology needs philosophy, and others strongly deny this. What do you think about this?
3. Is theology a special science, or do you think that basically it is just one out of many disciplines that study God's reality? Give the reasons for your answer.
4. In what sense might all these considerations be significant for our discussion about NL2K?

---

[1] For this chapter, see the much broader treatment of the subject in Ouweneel (2013, chapters 6–14; 2014a; 2014c).

11.1   WHAT IS PHILOSOPHY?

11.1.1   Christian Philosophy?

I am convinced that we can resolve many problems with the NL2K view only if we first get a clearer picture of the relationships between theology and philosophy.[2] As long as NL2K remains mired in its scholastic (Roman Catholic and early Protestant) past, it will stay mired in the ancient nature-grace dualism. That is, it will, on the one hand, exalt theology to the science of Christianity, and, on the other hand, categorically deny that there can be such things as Christian philosophy and Christian special sciences. Theology supposedly belongs to the domain of grace, or the kingdom of God, and the other sciences belong to the domain of nature, that is, the so-called "common kingdom." Within the latter kingdom, we can supposedly pursue biology or economics just like anybody else does, because such sciences are neutral and objective.

As long as we think that there can be some kind of neutral science—this belief is shared by scholastic and humanistic thinkers—we will indeed never accept the notion of Christian philosophy and of Christian special sciences (except theology, of course). However, many twentieth-century philosophers of science have pointed out that science can never be neutral (objective, unbiased).[3] Science is always rooted in pre-scientific beliefs, and, in my works mentioned in note 1, I have tried to show extensively that such beliefs are basically always rooted in faith, which by definition is religious because it always refers to people's deepest heart convictions.

Now if it is true that all philosophy, at its deepest level, is always rooted in some faith, then philosophy, too, ultimately has a religious nature. In its broadest, philosophical sense, religion is a person's transcendent, existential confidence in some Ultimate Ground for his being and knowing. In this sense, all philosophy is, at its deepest level, religious in nature. If this is right, then the choice is not between common, secular, neutral philosophy or some religiously biased philosophy, but *between philosophy*

---

[2]   This chapter consists of elaborated excerpts from Ouweneel (2014a; 2014c); I emphatically point to these works because they explain in far more depth my thinking on this subject. Far more extensive is Ouweneel (2013, chapters 6–14). See also the excellent introduction by Troost (2004).

[3]   See, e.g., De Vleeschauwer (1952); Stegmüller (1969); Lakatos and Musgrave (1970); Planck (1973); Polanyi (1974); Popper (1979; 1992; 2002a; 2002b); Lakatos (1980); Putnam (1981; 1985; 1992); Kuhn (1996; 2000); Gadamer (1998); Caputo (2006); Feyerabend (2010).

based on false religion or philosophy based on true religion. If there is no such thing as a neutral philosophy, then I am fully entitled to prefer a Christian philosophy. I truly believe that such a philosophy is not only possible, but also highly desirable, even indispensible.

Unfortunately, many Christians—especially theologians!—argue that we do not need any Christian philosophy because we already have theology. They forget that theology attempts to answer only *theological* questions, that is, questions related to the interpretation of Scripture.[4] It has no answers to, and does not even deal with, typically *philosophical* questions, such as: What is knowledge? What is theoretical knowledge? What is being? What is reality? What is science? What is nature? What is culture? What is history? What is language? What is society? What is politics? This is why I said that a "theology of law" or a "theology of Christianity and culture," as David VanDrunen calls it,[5] is nonsense. Theologians must expound the Bible, including those passages that we feel are of judicial or cultural significance. But the Bible does not deal with the question what is law, or what is culture, so these cannot be theological questions. They are philosophical questions. Therefore, there is such a thing as a "philosophy of culture" (German: *Kulturphilosophie*; Dutch: *cultuurfilosofie*) but not a "theology of culture" (except in NL2K and related thought).

Theology certainly does have *theological* things to say about cultural activity, but the things theology says are not foundational for all other sciences. Theology does not have, and never had, the task of functioning as a foundational science for all the special sciences, from mathematics to the humanities. In fact, theology itself is nothing but one of many special sciences, which has its own basic philosophical questions, such as: What kind of thing is theology? Is it nothing but extended Bible study, or is it an academic science, and if so, according to what criteria? And if so, what kind of science? How does it relate to the other special sciences? As a theoretical enterprise, how does it relate to practical faith knowledge that all believers have in common? What are its specific scientific methods? None of these questions can be answered by theology itself because the Bible does not speak about them. They are not *theological* but *philosophical* questions; they belong to the philosophical premises of theology as an academic discipline.[6]

---

[4] I am speaking here of the core of theology: exegesis and dogmatics, that is, apart from historical theology and practical theology, which belong to the periphery.

[5] VanDrunen (2003, 30; 2010a, 12).

[6] Like so many handbooks of systematic theology, Horton's (2011, 35–219) does not exhibit any sensitivity to this. Nearly all the philosophers mentioned in this book are pagans or humanists.

11.1.2   The Scholastic Approach

In the thirteenth century, Thomas Aquinas argued: philosophy is not the true theology (as, e.g., the Greek philosopher Xenophanes [d. *c.* 478 BC] had asserted), and theology is not the true philosophy (as, e.g., church father Augustine had claimed). No, the two must be clearly distinguished. For this reason, he strongly opposed the notion of a *Christian* philosophy, that is, a philosophy based on a Christian worldview, inspired by Scripture. On the contrary, he claimed that philosophy is an autonomous science belonging to the realm of nature. This means that philosophy is a science independent of any foundation outside itself, based exclusively upon human reason *severed from faith*. He considered Christian theology to be some supernatural, even sacred science, highly exalted above natural philosophy and all special sciences. Supernatural theology is done by the light of divine revelation, and is therefore sacred, whereas natural philosophy, as well as all the special sciences, are done by the light of autonomous reason. Again, this view is still quite dominant among those theologians who never shed their scholastic feathers.

Perhaps one of the greatest rediscoveries of the Reformers was the notion that God's Word has authority over *all* domains of cosmic reality, including philosophy and the special sciences, and *all* human thought. They did away with the separation between faith and science. What a great idea: a Reformational philosophy founded upon the Word of God! Alas, nothing really changed in practice. No Christian starting points for the various special sciences were developed. I do not blame the Reformers; probably, it was simply too early for that. The Reformers, Martin Luther and John Calvin, preached a clear gospel about God's Word having sway over all of human life. To a large extent, they pushed medieval philosophy out through the front door. But their successors, Philipp Melanchthon (d. 1560) and Theodore Beza (d. 1605), reintroduced medieval philosophy through the back door. Again, do not blame them too severely: they simply did so because they had nothing better to work with.

In spite of the efforts of the Reformers, the separation between faith and reason, between faith and philosophy, was maintained. Reason, along with rationalism, dominated Christian thinking. This rationalism was so strong that, as the Enlightenment began (seventeenth and eighteenth centuries), Christian thinking had no real defense against it. "Dare to use your own intellect," was the slogan of the great German philosopher, Immanuel Kant (d. 1804), with which he described what he saw as the essence of the Enlightenment. This did not mean that Kant removed God from his thinking. Rather, one of his noble motives was to rescue the Christian faith from the claws of the natural sciences. He did so by assigning faith its own safe corner. But, according to him, the whole of natural life belonged to the domain of pure reason. Many of the Enlightenment thinkers allowed God and religion their own little place—but only within the domain of religious life, the life of prayer, praise, and preaching. From the domain of philosophy, from the special sciences, and from societal life, religion was banned forever. This is what we call "secularization."

So we see that Kant basically worked with the same scholastic dualism, which we found with Thomas Aquinas, and which we still find with NL2K. For instance, note the interesting circular argument by VanDrunen: "The fact that pursuing these disciplines [e.g., physics, historical science] are activities of the common kingdom indicates that believers should be cautious and modest about claiming their academic work and conclusions as 'Christian.'"[7] But this is the very core of the matter: *are* they indeed activities of some common kingdom? *Does* something like a common kingdom really exist? As soon as we begin to understand that all Christian activities occur within the sphere of the kingdom of God, we begin to see that there is also room for a *Christian* pursuit and practice of science. Christian philosophers do not suggest that this Christian character comes to light in the methods and techniques of science, as VanDrunen falsely suggests,[8] but in the *Christian-philosophical foundations of every science*.

To be sure, VanDrunen admits: "Christians scholars and teachers may never pursue their work independent of or divorced from their Christian faith. *Study and teaching are never religiously neutral*. In this sense we can speak of a general Christian view of the various academic disciplines."[9] But the import of this statement is not very clear, and I am not sure that VanDrunen himself is very clear about it. If I read his statement carefully, I conclude that the author is not saying anything more than (a) there are biblical data that believing scientists cannot ignore, and (b) they have to do their work with a Christian attitude. Both points are true. However, every insight into the (Christian-)philosophical roots of both theology and the other special sciences seems to be totally lacking, which by now we have come to expect from a scholastic approach.

11.1.3   Theological and Philosophical Culpability

Remarkably enough, the relationships between philosophy and theology have always been rather strained, to say the least. In a famous lecture, Kant

---

7 VanDrunen (2010a, 180).
8 Ibid., 182.
9 Ibid., 179; italics original.

spoke of "The Contest of Faculties" (orig. 1798),[10] especially the conflict between the theological and the philosophical faculties. In my opinion, both theologians and philosophers were culpable for this conflict. Let us look at some of their mistakes.

Theology is not "the true philosophy," and philosophy is not "the true theology." Although both may be Christian, they have very different callings and objectives, just like Christian psychology, Christian sociology, Christian ethics, and so on.

Both Catholic and Protestant theologians have often claimed theology to be a supernatural, or sacred, science in contrast with other sciences, because the former works by the light of divine revelation, whereas the latter work with the light of natural reason alone. This is a mistake. First, *every* science works by the light of divine revelation[11]—although they may not recognize it—because God reveals himself not only in Scripture but also in nature, especially in the law-order for nature (cf. chapter 4). God reveals himself in cultural products as well, because they too always presuppose the divine law order. Science can be defined as the attempt to unveil the law-order that is valid for reality, and in this law-order God reveals himself.

Second, *every* science, including theology, necessarily works by the light of human reason because science is a logical-analytical type of human activity. Even if many theologians claim to have a supernatural *starting point*, theological work as such is of a fully rational nature. That is, theologians discuss, reason, argue, analyze, try to persuade and convince, like all other scientists.

Third, theology is as much an empirical science as any other science. It cannot make an academic investigation of God as such, in spite of its name: "theology," that is, science about God. Strictly speaking, it can study only what people have said and written about God. Theologians study certain written sources, namely, the Bible and thousands of Jewish and Christian writings. Literary scientists do the same with literature, and historians do the same with historical sources that are relevant to their work. In this sense, theology has sometimes been called a literary science, a set of theories concerning a specific type of literature, namely, Jewish and Christian literature, the Bible in particular. God cannot be laid on the dissection table of theological science, but writings about God can. In this sense, theology is an empirical science, just like every other science.

---

[10] See Kant (1991); cf. more recently Holzmüller and Ihmig (1997); Caputo (2006, 7–9).

[11] Interestingly, this is recognized by VanDrunen (2010a, 174), although he does not appear to see the consequences of this insight.

Fourth, *every* science, including theology, has not only internal but also external, that is, philosophical, premises (often called *prolegomena*). These include the following: (a) Determining whether theology is a science depends on philosophical considerations concerning the differences between scientific and non-scientific knowledge. (b) The comparison between theology and other special sciences is based on a philosophical totality view of cosmic reality. (c) Defining the study object of theology again presupposes a philosophical totality view of cosmic reality, in which this study object is delineated with respect to the study objects of other special sciences. (d) Defining the proper methodology of theology presupposes general criteria for scientific methodology, a topic that belongs to the subject matter of philosophy.[12]

Michael Horton wrote: the Reformers "did liberate Christian theology from philosophy, while affirming both, and gave each room in which to breathe."[13] But first, it is intrinsically impossible to separate theology from its philosophical premises. Second, theology should not even *wish* to be liberated from philosophy, as long as this philosophy is rooted in the same Christian faith as theology itself. Third, Horton can mean only that the Reformers perpetrated the medieval separation between Christian theology and neutral (common, secular) philosophy. There was nothing new, nothing liberating, in this. Fourth, we find Horton apparently praising the Reformers for this continuation of scholastic dualism, instead of regretting that they never designed a *Christian* philosophy, which might have prevented European culture from falling into the snares of the Enlightenment.

11.2 THE NECESSITY OF PHILOSOPHICAL PREMISES FOR THEOLOGY

11.2.1 No Theology without Prolegomena

Many past philosophical errors of theologians result from refusing to investigate critically the philosophical premises of their science. From a historical point of view, this is quite understandable when you look at the many harmful influences of *secular* philosophy, ancient or modern, within theology. However, the desire to get rid of all secular philosophy usually results in getting rid of all philosophy as such. The consequence is a lack of philosophical reflection upon the premises of theology. This leads to the

---

[12] All of these points are discussed extensively in Ouweneel (2013; 2014c).
[13] Horton (1995, 176).

inevitable result of theology falling into the very snare it wanted to avoid, that is, secular philosophy.

The reason is simple: theology cannot work without philosophical prolegomena. If it rejects the notion of a Christian philosophy, the first option involves falling into the arms of ancient scholasticism, that is, the semi-Aristotelian philosophy of the Middle Ages and of early Protestantism. The second option is buying into one of the modern or postmodern humanistic worldviews: (neo)positivism, existentialism, analytical philosophy, postmodernism, etc. The third option lands us in biblicist fundamentalism, which is itself a strange mixture of scholasticism and (neo)positivism without fundamentalists realizing it.[14] Remarkably enough, both those who plead for a separation between theology and (Christian or secular) philosophy, and those who plead for a kind of interaction between theology and (secular!) philosophy,[15] usually fall into one of these three snares.

Let me provide a remarkably revealing example of what happens when a person refuses a Christian philosophical basis for his theology. This example involves the relationship between rationalism and irrationalism. First, notice that these are not theological but philosophical terms, and that they involve a strictly philosophical problem. No theological investigation as such can ever teach you what rationalism or irrationalism is, or the difference between them, because this is not a matter of biblical investigation. Knowing such terms, and their problems, belongs to a person's philosophical baggage, whether he realizes it or not. If he is a theologian who refuses to study some necessary philosophy, he can hardly be aware of all the theoretical intricacies surrounding these terms. As a consequence, he can easily get lost. In Christian philosophy, the terms *rational* and *irrational* are carefully balanced against the terms *non-rational* and *suprarational*. If you do not do that, the only alternative you can see for the rational and rationalism are the irrational and irrationalism. However, irrational and non-rational are not the same, and suprarational and irrational are not either.

Here is a striking example: Reformed thinker Cornelius Van Til accused Reformed thinker Herman Dooyeweerd of irrationalism,[16] to which the latter answered that this was understandable for someone who knew only the choice between the rational and the irrational, and had no idea of the *supra*rational starting point of all thinking.[17] We encounter the same

---

[14] See extensively, Ouweneel (2012b, chapter 9).
[15] Cf. Heering (1944, 43–50).
[16] Van Til (1962).
[17] Dooyeweerd (1971, 83).

problem with, for instance, Millard Erickson.[18] When attempts to reconcile difficult Bible passages with each other were described by opponents as "rationalism," Erickson was quick to point out that this objection was due to the usual existentialist (!) emphasis on the paradoxical nature of reality and the absurdity of the universe! We find here the same defense against the reproach of rationalism, namely, accusing the opponent of irrationalism.

In this way, traditional theology remains caught in rationalism because it knows no alternative, and this is because it has no philosophical framework in which the rational and the irrational, as well as the non-rational and the suprarational, are assigned their appropriate places. As long as theology works without a Christian philosophy that is concomitant[19] with it, it will keep falling into the snare either of (scholastic or Enlightenment) rationalism, or of irrationalist mysticism, or of biblicism.

To say this in other words, as long as a theologian is caught in NL2K, he has no room for any Christian philosophy in his thinking, which leads to the dramatic consequences just mentioned. First, we discover that NL2K is nothing but a variety of ancient scholasticism. Second, undergirding the manner in which it seeks to discover "big pictures"[20] for the sciences we discover biblicism. Third, in the way it speaks of the common kingdom, we discover the danger of surrendering the entire world outside the church and theology into the hands of humanist thinking. *Thus, in refusing any Christian philosophy, NL2K ultimately falls into all three of the traps we have repeatedly identified: scholasticism, biblicism, and humanism.*

11.2.2 The Origin of Theology's Philosophical Premises
At least I hope to have shown that the problems involved are, by definition, philosophical problems, such as the relationship between the rational and the irrational, or between faith knowledge and theological knowledge, or between heart and reason, or the problem of the so-called object of theology's investigation, or of the presuppositions of theological hermeneutics (the science of interpretation), or the problem of theological methodology in relation to, and in possible contrast with, the methodology of other special sciences, or the foundations of anthropology, or the problem of time and eternity, of immanence and transcendence, and so forth. The fact that, just as in other special sciences, these are *philosophical* problems implies that theology needs its own philosophical prolegomena, grounded in a coherent Christian cosmology and epistemology.

---

[18] Erickson (1982, 391).
[19] Or, as Reformed theologian Spykman (1988, 141; 1992, 101) put it: "of one piece."
[20] Cf. VanDrunen (2010a, 175).

Similarly—and here we encounter our problems with NL2K again—scholastic theologians will present us with such nonsense as a "theology of culture," a "theology of law," a "theology of the state," etc. This is because they are clearly aware of the fact that Christians do have something to say as Christians about culture, law, the state, and so on. This is perfectly correct. However, because they reject the notion of a Christian philosophy they feel that theology is the only discipline that is able to speak of these things. Poor theology. It is like demanding of a man that he give birth to a baby.

In the present time, many theologians have realized that they cannot do without philosophical presuppositions. The only remaining question is: *From where do they get them?* I see only three possible sources.

(1) *These philosophical prolegomena are derived from the Bible.* An example of this is the American theologian Norman L. Geisler.[21] He did accept a philosophical foundation for his hermeneutics, and found it in theism, supernaturalism, and metaphysical realism. According to him, these "-isms" are taught, or at least presupposed, by Scripture. This is a theoreticalizing of Scripture, as if the latter would at all teach, or even presuppose, any scientific or philosophical theory. Scripture neither contains nor presupposes theories or "-isms." Geisler did not seem to recognize the fundamental difference between the non-theoretical faith language of Scripture and the theoretical language of philosophy and theology. That is because he lacked a Christian philosophy in which such distinctions are analyzed.

(2) *The necessary philosophical prolegomena are found in current philosophical tradition.* But what is this tradition? This is either medieval scholasticism, which has survived until now in the bosom of traditional Roman Catholic and Protestant theology—as NL2K illustrates—or, since the last five centuries, in the humanistic tradition with its many ramifications. The correspondence between the two is that scholasticism ties in with *ancient* (Greek-Roman) paganism (Plato, Aristotle, Stoics), and humanism with *modern* paganism (which, in fact, is nothing but apostate Judeo-Christianity). Both are foreign to a theology that is grounded in the self-testimony of Scripture.[22]

This certainly does not mean that humanistic philosophy is useless to the Christian and to Christian theology. Every scientific enterprise, no

---

[21] Geisler (1981, 333–34).

[22] Reformed counsellor Jay E. Adams speaks in VanDrunen (2004, 266) of "the now bankrupt Dooyeweerdian philosophy that stressed the theoretical over the practical." This is not only absurd, but if Adams (see, e.g., 1986) had better understood Dooyeweerd, his own "Christian" psychology would not have been a mixture of biblicist and humanist elements; cf. Ouweneel (2015).

matter how much it is grounded in an apostate ultimate commitment, contains important truth elements. The perspicuity of divine truth shines through even the darkest philosophies.[23] However, such truth elements are no excuse for also adopting the humanistic framework in which they are contained. Only a Christian philosophy can help us sift the truth elements from the dross of such philosophies.

11.2.3 "Of One Piece"

(3) The only option left is a philosophy that *is founded on the same biblical ground motive as theology itself,* and not on some scholastic or humanistic philosophy. In the words of Reformed theologian Gordon Spykman:

> Prolegomena must be of one piece with dogmatics proper. Such integration is possible only if philosophical prolegomena and dogmatic theology are viewed as sharing a common footing. Though differentiated in function, prolegomena and dogmatics must be perspectivally unified. The major thesis at this point is therefore that the most fitting prolegomena to a Reformed dogmatics is a Christian philosophy. The noetic point of departure for both is Scripture. It provides the revelational pointers, the guidelines, the "control beliefs" (Nicholas Wolterstorff[24]) for shaping a biblically directed philosophy as well as a Christian theology.[25]

In 1950s, the well-known German Reformed dogmatician Otto Weber (d. 1966) acknowledged the importance of a Christian concept of science, also for theology.[26] He stated that such a Christian approach indeed existed, and pointed to the (at that time) "recent" attempts in the Netherlands to develop this. He quoted several works by Reformed philosophers Dirk H. Th. Vollenhoven and Herman Dooyeweerd.[27] Other outstanding theologians did not refer to this philosophical school, but did—perhaps independently of it—develop strongly related ideas, such as Gustav Aulén and Paul Tillich,[28] and to a lesser extent Paul Althaus, Helmut Thielicke, Wolfgang Trillhaas, and Gerhard Sauter.[29]

---

[23] Cf. Holmes (1977): *All Truth Is God's Truth.* The expression goes back to Augustine (*De Doctrina Christiana* II.18.28).

[24] See Wolterstorff (1988).

[25] Spykman (1992, 101–102).

[26] Weber (1981, 13).

[27] Especially Dooyeweerd's main work (1984).

[28] Aulén (1960); Tillich (1968).

[29] Althaus (1952); Thielicke (1974); Trillhaas (1972); Sauter (1998).

Elsewhere I have set forth the thoughts of these theologians in great detail.[30] One can only regret that their elementary views have penetrated North American Reformed thinking far too little. This was partly because many North American theologians do not read German, and partly because some of these German theologians were quickly put into the category of "liberal" theology—as if this would mean that they might not have anything useful to say on the prolegomena of theology.

11.3 THEOLOGICAL THEORY BUILDING

11.3.1 Bacon and Popper

Let me add here a few observations about how scientific theories in general, and theological theories in particular, originate and are further developed. I do this in order to make some remarks on NL2K as a theological theory or model. I must be very brief here; I would refer those who read Dutch to my extensive elaboration of this subject elsewhere.[31]

I have always been thankful that I first finished my studies in the natural sciences (specialty: developmental biology) and in philosophy (including epistemology and the philosophy of science)—and dabbled in psychology—before I finished theology. This historical sequence gave me a certain awareness of what theology is as a special science, how it relates to other special sciences, and especially how its theories and models arise. There is more correspondence in the way biological, psychological, and theological theories develop than people realize, especially theologians. All three are *empirical* sciences, like *all* sciences (see §11.1.3): theology is not the "study of God" (although the term "theology" may suggest this)—God cannot be academically analyzed—but a study of *statements* about God and divine things, as we find them in the Bible, and in writings on the Bible.

Moreover, biology, psychology, and theology are *logical-analytical* enterprises, in that they consist of the rational elaboration of empirical data (found in nature and in the Bible, respectively). All three are founded in certain presuppositions concerning reality, such as the orderly structure of reality, and the reliability of our senses, and thus of our empirical observations. We have observed that all presuppositions of science are basically of a religious nature, if religion is taken in the broad sense of the existential,

---

[30] Ouweneel (2013, chapters 6–14).
[31] See extensively, Ouweneel (2013, chapters 6–14; in brief form: 2014a).

transcendent confidence in what people hold as the ultimate ground for their beliefs and their very existence.

Sciences like biology, psychology, and theology do not *begin* with empirical observations, as scientists since British philosopher Francis Bacon (d. 1626) have often thought. The reason is that we would not know where to start observing, and what data to collect: we need a leading idea. Especially Austrian-British philosopher Karl Popper (d. 1994) has pointed out that, indeed, scientists always begin with an idea, a presumption, a guess, a working hypothesis, which they test by making specific observations and conducting specific experiments.[32] Moreover, Popper emphasized that it is a snare for scientists to look for verification of their idea by collecting data supporting it, and neglecting data that contradict it. Instead, scientists should energetically try to *falsify* their own theories, that is, develop specific tests for their theory such that the results thereof, if they contradict the theory, would falsify the theory, that is, prove it to be wrong. In Popper's view, an academically good theory can be described, first, as being falsifiable in principle, and second, as having successfully survived a number of falsification tests.

11.3.4   Again: Theologism

In my experience, theologians belong to those scientists who, in general, are least aware of the premises of their science. First, this is because of their scholastic bias: they dismiss comparisons between their sacred discipline and those other sciences belonging to the secular realm (as they see it), for instance, because the former supposedly works by the light of God's revelation, and the latter by the light of human reason. This totally false contradiction is rooted in medieval scholasticism; *all* scholars are investigating God's (special or general) revelation, whether they wish to acknowledge this or not. (Remember, there are also unbelieving theologians.) And *all* scholars work by the light of human reason, which preferably is enlightened by the Holy Spirit, whether one is a theologian or a biologist or a psychologist.

Second, knowing hardly anything about the modern philosophy of science, such theologians still live by the outdated Baconian view: their theology is nothing but a "parroting" (Dutch: *naspreken*; German: *nachsprechen*) of what Scripture says.[33] This is one reason why so many theologians dislike

---

[32] See especially Popper (2002a).

[33] See, e.g., Bavinck (*RD* 1:38, 54); Brunner (1949, 84); Douma (1987, 19); Van der Merwe (1991, 66). Troost (2004, 262): "The idea that [theology]...needs only to 'parrot' Scripture... is very unrealistic, and in principle annuls scientific theology as such."

such relativizing terms as "theory" or "model" for what they are doing, because they really believe that their views have been adopted directly from Scripture. (They hardly ever seem to wonder why then so many *contradictory* models have been adopted from the same Scriptural data; of course, this must be because all the others are erring.) The tragic result is that such theologians think that, when their theories are attacked, Scripture itself is being attacked. History has shown that such theologians are prepared to create church splits for their theological theories! Most, if not virtually all, Reformed and Presbyterian church splits were caused by assigning the theological issue under debate to the redemptive foundations of faith (encapsulated in the judgment that "if you think otherwise, you cannot be saved").[34]

Third, many theologians are completely uninterested in trying to falsify their own theories. They find their ideas confirmed everywhere in the Bible, as well as in the works of venerated theologians of the past. Elsewhere, I have tried to explain how, in Reformed theology, the covenant was gradually "discovered" to be *the* central principle of Scripture[35] (something the other 87% of worldwide Christianity never saw). Similarly, the "imputation" model became the cornerstone of the Reformed doctrine of justification, although 83% of Christianity (that is, all Christians except Lutherans and Calvinists) knows nothing of it.[36] These ideas were read into the Bible for no other reason than that they ever more strongly appealed to successive generations of theologians within the confines of Calvinist (sometimes also Lutheran) thought. If people had better understood how theology in particular, and science in general, works, they would not have been so impressed with this result.

Not only as a theologian, but also as a philosopher with great interest in the philosophy of science, I find such developments highly fascinating, especially now that I see the same process occurring all over again in NL2K. Everybody can see that natural law is not found in the Bible; not only is the term not found in the Bible, but the contents of the term—a law that is written in the hearts of all people, and that can objectively be appealed to—is lacking as well (see §4.1). Everybody can see, too, that the Bible knows nothing of the modern "two kingdoms" (except the two kingdoms of Matt. 12:25–28, which are of a very different nature); there is no common kingdom in the Bible, least of all in the Noahic covenant (see §7.5). But as

---

[34] I do not wish to judge divisions in North America, but in my opinion, *none* of the Reformed church divisions in the Netherlands from 1900 until now (1907, 1926, 1944, 1953, 1967, 1980, 2004) was about a truly vital issue.

[35] See extensively, Ouweneel (2016g, chapters 4–5).

[36] See extensively, Ouweneel (2016h, chapter 4).

happens so often, so too now: theologians, steeped in scholastic dualism, begin to see these ideas (they think) everywhere in the Bible and in ancient theological literature. Moreover, NL2K is a view that comes in very handy in our present secularized Western society because it acquits us of the duty to testify to our Christian principles in the public square. And lo and behold, all of a sudden it is now being "found" everywhere in the Bible! No, it is not found there; it is read into the Bible, by theologians who have a vested interest (conscious or unconscious) in doing so.

Every person who knows a little of the history of science should notice what is going on here. *L'histoire se répète* ("History repeats itself"). This current NL2K debate has little to do with genuine theology, or with genuine scholarship in general. It is an example of Baconian and positivist wishful thinking. It is the fruit of an academic theology that greatly overestimates itself, as if its ideas have been directly inspired from Above, or at least by Augustine, Luther, and Calvin. Don't believe it. Whether it is in Augustine, Luther, and Calvin does not interest me very much—at least this ideology is not in the Bible. NL2K exists only in the minds of those who desperately want it to be true. It is not biblical, nor is it good science.

11.4 THEOLOGY AND THE OTHER SCIENCES

11.4.1 Again: the Scholastic View

It is really no wonder that Christians, including NL2K advocates, have always felt that theology occupies a very special place among the various sciences. Theology is about God and his Word, it was argued, whereas the other sciences had to do with more profane subjects such as mathematics, nature, history, literature, society, economy, the arts, law. These are all very mundane subjects, at any rate not on equal footing with the lofty Word of God. One need only look at the history of our universities to notice the special place of theology. The earliest universities (Bologna, 1088; Paris, c. 1150; Oxford, 1167; etc.) always viewed theology as the mother of the whole academic community, entirely according to the scholastic tradition.

Incidentally, interestingly enough, even in the Enlightenment, the same old scholastic sacred-profane dualism was still presupposed. The great difference was that the epithet "sacred" no longer assigned theology a place at the *top* of the pyramid of sciences, but at the *bottom*. The dualism as such, however, was still taken for granted. It seems to be extremely difficult to eliminate this scheme as such, assuming that scholars are at all interested in doing so. NL2K is one of the recent demonstrations of this truth. Scholastic dualism is like a staph infection: once you have it, it is virtually impossible to get rid of it.

Radical Christian thinking ought to reject the dualism of nature and supernature, and thus also of reason and faith, of philosophy (and the other special sciences) and theology, as totally against the spirit of Scripture. In opposition to this, Christian thinking states that, from a *structural* point of view, human reason is not autonomous at all but dependent on the spiritual attitude of the transcendent, existential human heart. It is from this (either apostate or God-oriented) heart that all immanent human functions, including the logical thinking function, proceed (cf. Prov. 4:23). As a consequence, all human thinking is basically apostate or God-oriented. The laws of logic as such have not changed—but Christians and non-Christians apply these laws in a God-oriented or in an apostate way.

Unfortunately, the scholastic dualism lives on, to this very day, not only in traditional Roman Catholic theology, but also in traditional Protestant (Lutheran, Reformed, Evangelical, etc.) theology—as NL2K proves. For instance, there is still a Christian apologetics that really seems to believe that people can be convinced of the truth of Christianity through purely rational arguments. American theologian and philosopher, Francis A. Schaeffer (d. 1984), was a great advocate of this rational—if not rationalistic—approach.[37] As a consequence of a lack of explicit reflection upon its philosophical prolegomena, this kind of theology has shown itself incapable of liberating itself from the effects of scholastic dualism, although Schaeffer in particular did expose the errors of the nature-grace dualism.

11.4.2 "Christian Plumbing"

NL2K advocates love to make statements to the effect that neither the Fall, nor redemption in Christ, has changed the laws of logic or the laws of physics. It is thought to be characteristic of the supposed "common kingdom" that the laws in this realm are valid for both believers and unbelievers. I fail to see the logic of this, for the laws of logic are valid for both believers and unbelievers also within the discipline of theology, and thus within the kingdom of God. Does this then prove that, after all, theology belongs to the common kingdom as well?

In a conference speech, VanDrunen argued that there is no Christian way to change diapers or to pilot a plane.[38] A favourite in these circles is what

---

[37] See, e.g., Schaeffer (1968).
[38] *Christian Renewal*, Nov. 18 (2015), 7.

I call the "no Christian plumbing argument." It is used by VanDrunen,[39] and also by Michael Horton:[40] "A Christian plumber does not have to install 'Christian' pipes," and "There is no 'Christian politics' or 'Christian art' or 'Christian literature,' any more than there is 'Christian plumbing.'"[41] According to this type of irrational logic, there can be no "Christian church" or "Christian theology" any more than there is "Christian plumbing." This is like saying: there are no fishes with feet, so there cannot be ferrets with feet.

Such arguments may perhaps impress the general public, but of course they do not hold water. For example, take the "no Christian diaper changing" argument. Joseph Boot spoke of

> well-circulated, catchy one-liners from David VanDrunen and Michael Horton like, "*there is no Christian way to change a diaper*" or "*there is no such thing as Christian stir fry.*"[42] These somewhat sardonic adages seem obviously true, until you observe that the cogency of these "defeater" arguments (i.e. allegedly demonstrating that there is no distinctly Christian view of most of life) rely on the hearer not giving them careful thought. For example, in Islam, Sharia law *does* actually govern how you go to the toilet; there is an Islamic way to use the washroom. The Greek cynics thought nothing of defecating in public to show their contempt for propriety. Or regarding the possibility of a "Christian" stir fry, this would depend on whether in fact you are a seventeenth or eighteenth-century cannibal (like the Carib Indians, from which the term "cannibal" is derived) who periodically enjoyed stir-fried man-flesh, or a Jewish or Muslim individual observing clean food preparation laws. Indeed there are many Christians who take biblical dietary laws seriously (as Jesus himself did) and would not stir fry pork or rodents, dog, cat, or any unclean animal—including those popular sea creatures eaten in vast quantities today that feed on the bottom of the ocean. In short, the issues of hygiene and ablutions, or questions of food preparation, are not as obviously "non-religious" as they first appear to many when hearing these populist and super-ficial arguments–there are in fact Christian and non-Christian ways to engage in all these activities.[43]

---

[39] VanDrunen (2010a, 169–70, 191).
[40] Horton (1995, 194).
[41] Horton (2006).
[42] See Horton (2002a, 196).
[43] Boot (2016); cf. the similar response by Mattson (2011).

I would add that plumbing and piloting planes are technical activities that are always embedded within a certain view of technology as a cultural phenomenon. Listen to Brian Mattson:

> But what about those bridges and buildings? Surely there is widespread homogeneity about the normative standards governing engineering, right? Ask yourself: why is it that when massive earthquakes hit the United States of America, we speak of casualties (when and if there are any) in the single digits? Yet, in 1999, Turkey suffered an estimated 45,000 dead from a single earthquake. This happened in a highly industrialized part of the country where one would think good engineering would be a priority. An official Turkish investigation showed the death toll to be due primarily to poor engineering and construction. How can this be, if everyone agrees to the norms, standards, and ethics of engineering and construction? Or how about the 2010 earthquake in Haiti, which leveled the entire country and left a staggering 300,000 people dead? Where were the homogenous, generally-understood principles of engineering then? Somehow (again, perhaps just coincidentally) the quality of the standards of engineering seems to greatly improve the closer you get to the leafy suburbs of the modern Western world. "The odds are good," are they, that my unbelieving neighbor shares my concerns when it comes to building safety [cf. §1.4.3]? Again, it behooves us to ask: my neighbor where and when?[44]

11.4.3 "Supernatural" Theology

Just as traditional Protestant theology accepts the notion of a "natural theology" (cf. chapter 4), it also accepts the idea of a "supernatural" theology—and, as Reformed theologian and philosopher in the Netherlands, Andree Troost, has put it, both are equally *un*natural.[45] Usually, scholastic theology does not speak of "supernatural," but of "sacred" theology; however, this amounts to the same thing. The notion of "sacred" theology goes back to the *sacra theologia*, or *sacra doctrina*, of medieval thought. One need only think, for instance, of the ancient title *sanctae theologiae doctor* ("doctor in sacred theology"). The expression "sacred theology" is found in the title of Herman Bavinck's inaugural address, and in that of Abraham Kuyper's *Encyclopaedie*

---

[44] Mattson (2011).
[45] Troost (1977, 180; 1982, 183; see especially 2004).

der Heilige Godgeleerdheid (*Encyclopedia of Sacred Theology*).[46] Of course, we also find the phrase in the titles of many older Reformed works, such as the *Theses de sancta theologia* (*Theses on Sacred Theology*) by Paul Madrat and Abraham Ramburtius (1661), or the *Katechismus der heilige godgeleerdheid* (*Catechism of Sacred Theology*) by Samuel van Emdre (1781/2).

Kuyper fully accepted the idea of a *theologia naturalis* ("natural theology"), along with its opposite, *theologia revelata* ("revealed theology").[47] The latter term is quite misleading because it suggests that the content of theology has been revealed by God.[48] Such an idea can easily arise when the content of Scripture and that of theology are more or less identified. According to Kuyper, the theorem of theology was traditionally this: *Principium Theologiae est Sacra Scriptura* ("The principle [or, starting point] of theology is Holy Scripture").[49] Just prior to making this statement, he extensively defended the notion of a "sacred" theology.[50] Elsewhere in his work, we encounter the traditional distinction between a *principium speciale* ("special principle") and a *principium naturale* ("natural principle")—yet another of the many after-effects of the nature-grace dualism.[51]

The Evangelical theologian Lewis Sperry Chafer is an American example of a similar line of thinking. He called systematic theology "the greatest of the sciences," and transferred the notion that theology is "super" even to the theologian himself by saying, "The worthy student of Systematic Theology, were he not qualified for the higher and more inclusive title of *theologian*, would be entitled to recognition as a *superscientist*, which he is."[52] Interestingly, this is the very opposite of the idea that is current in secular thinking, namely, that theology actually should no longer be called a "science" at all. Incidentally, "superscientist" is rather misleading, because it suggests something about the theologian ("superman") rather than his theology.

The idea of a "supernatural" or "sacred" theology, which implies an unbiblical overestimation of theology, has the same unacceptable background as natural theology. This background is the ancient nature-grace dualism, and the equation (more or less) of theology and Scripture. It is

---

[46] Bavinck (1883); Kuyper (EST).

[47] Kuyper (2008, 258, 260).

[48] This, incidentally, is exactly what Horton (1995, 55) wrote: "Only a theology that is *revealed* by God and anchored in Scripture...could plumb" the things of God.

[49] Kuyper (2008, 241); cf. Bavinck (*RD* 1:87), who even claimed that all Christian churches agree on this point.

[50] Kuyper (2008, 233–38).

[51] Kuyper (2008, 253–54), despite Kuyper's denial (266).

[52] Chafer (1983, 1:5.8).

302 THE WORLD IS CHRIST'S / **PART III**

therefore just as objectionable.[53] God is sacred (holy, Isa. 6:3), his Word is sacred (holy, Ps. 105:42), and his people are sacred (holy, 1 Pet. 2:9). But the sacredness of theology, which is a fallible, defective piece of human work, is equal to that of economics or chemistry. One could also put it in the reverse form: biology or psychology, done by serious Christians, starting from a Christian-philosophical view of cosmic reality, is just as sacred as theology. We could add that a linguistic or a social science that is rooted in biblical thought is more sacred than a theology rooted in apostate thought.

This notion of a sacred or supernatural theology is closely related to ideas concerning the (purported) study object of theology.[54] Even if it were correct to say that Holy Scripture is this study object, this would not make theology as such any more sacred than other sciences. But this idea of the Bible as theology's study object is itself a scholastic notion, supposing that the science of theology belongs to the higher domain of grace, to which Scripture is also thought to belong. The other sciences, including philosophy, are assigned to the lower domain of nature (NL2K: the common kingdom), to which also natural (autonomous) reason is supposed to belong. I repeat: all sciences, including theology, investigate *one and the same* revelation of God, because God's revelation in nature and his revelation in Scripture are not dualistically opposed, but they are basically one single revelation of God, of which Scripture is the centre (cf. §§3.3.3 and 4.2).[55]

11.5 OVERLAP WITH THE SPECIAL SCIENCES

11.5.1 Other Scientists' Interest in the Bible

To put this as clearly as possible: *anything* in cosmic reality can come under the scrutiny of the theologian, including things in nature, although they are always seen from the viewpoint of faith. Conversely, *anything* in Scripture can come under the scrutiny of *any* non-theological scientist, even though each scientist considers such a matter from his own specific viewpoint.[56] Here are some examples.

(a) *Mathematics*: In what Old Testament passages does the Hebrew word *ēleph* mean "thousand," and where does it mean "clan" or "squad"?

---

[53] Dooyeweerd (1960, 146); Strauss (1971, 65); Troost (1977, 180; 1982, 183; see extensively, 2004); Lategan (1989, 119-23).

[54] See extensively, Ouweneel (2013, chapter 7; 2014c, chapter 3).

[55] Troost (1978, 121).

[56] To know precisely how I intend this claim, see Ouweneel (2013, chapters 6–8; 2014a, chapter 3; 2014c, chapter 3).

What is the consequence of this for the supposedly exaggerated numbers of Israelites in Numbers 1? Although this is in the Bible, this is primarily a numerical problem, *not* a theological problem, although it may have theological consequences.

(b) *Geometry*: How can it be said that the "sea of cast metal" in the temple of Solomon measured ten cubits from rim to rim, and that its circumference was thirty cubits (instead of 31.42 cubits, according to the value of π) (1 Kings 7:23)? Did Jews at that time use a value 3 for π (which is hardly imaginable), or was the diameter measured from the outsides, and the circumference on the inside of the "sea"? Again, although this is in the Bible, this is primarily a geometrical problem, *not* a theological problem.

(c) *Physics*: The astronomer may be interested in the biblical model of the universe, as compared with models in other cultures and other time periods. Does this model presuppose a flat earth, or a globe-shaped earth?[57] What is the meaning of the "vault" over the earth, which we find many times, from Genesis 1 onward, a vault "in" which celestial bodies dwell along with the birds, and "beyond" which are waters?[58] This is primarily an astronomy problem.

(d) *Biology*: What is the possible biological, medical, hygienic, or sanitary significance of the distinction between the "clean" and "unclean" animals in the Bible (Lev. 11; Deut. 14)? What do the descriptions of the animal world in Job 38–41 tell us about biological knowledge at that time? To what extent was this knowledge accurate? These are strictly biology problems.

(e) *Perception and sensitive psychology*: The psychologist may pay attention to what the Bible has to say about heart, soul, and spirit, the many meanings of these terms, and their interrelationships.[59] These are strictly psychology problems.

(f) *Logic*: How do logical arguments function in the Bible, for instance, in letters like those to the Romans or the Hebrews? What syllogisms could we isolate in these arguments? Could we, with our present-day ideas about logic, identify possible logical flaws in the Bible?

(g) *Historiography*: The historian may be interested in what the Bible has to say about ancient history. For instance, can he identify the rather mysterious figure of Darius the Mede in Daniel 6? Or how does the "feast" of 180 days in Esther 1:4 relate to what we know of Persian history at that time? These are strictly history problems.

---

[57] See Ouweneel (2012b, §11.1.3).
[58] See Ouweneel (2012b, §11.1.2).
[59] See Ouweneel (2015).

(h) *Linguistics*: What is the precise linguistic meaning of what happened at the confusion of languages in Babel (Gen. 11:1–9), and the apparent removal of this confusion in Acts 2? What is the linguistic significance of glossolalia in general?[60] These are strictly linguistic problems.

(i) *Sociology*: When and how did the tribal community of Israel develop into a true nation, and into a real nation state? In what way, if any, were the typical tribal characteristics of Israel maintained, also after the Babylonian exile and in the New Testament? These are strictly sociological problems.

(j) *Economics*: The economist may be interested in the economic relationships in ancient Israel (e.g., Lev. 25)—which made both (extreme) capitalism (landlordism) and communism impossible—or in the early church (Acts 2–5, with possible economic consequences among later Messianic Jews in Palestine; cf. Rom. 15:26). These are strictly economic problems.

(k) *Aesthetics*: It is striking that the notion of "beauty" in the Old Testament is most strongly linked with feminine beauty. What sense of beauty does the Bible know apart from the beauty of human beings?

(l) *Legal sciences*: The legal scientist may pay attention to elementary juridical principles in the law of Moses, such as retribution, legal accountability, the relationship between crime and punishment, etc. These are strictly juridical problems.

(m) *Ethics*: Is there a progress in moral values from the earliest to the latest parts of the Old Testament, for instance, when it comes to marriage? What, if any, are the ethical differences between the Old and the New Testament?

11.5.2 Theology as a Helper

To be sure, most of the problems just mentioned will likely not be studied by other practitioners of the special sciences, but rather by theologians. That is because, in Scripture, all these matters are viewed from the religious[61] angle. But that does not change the fact that the problems mentioned are especially of a mathematical or geometrical or other such special scientific nature.

Every believing scientist—and of course this is what *every* scientist should be—will be able to make fruitful use of biblical insights and principles without thereby making his field of study "sacred," "supernatural," or "theological." And theology can study the totality of creational reality—always strictly from a religious viewpoint—without ever "profanizing" itself

---

[60] See Ouweneel (2007a, chapter 12).

[61] Dooyeweerdian philosophy prefers the immanent term "pistical" in order to prevent confusion with "religious" in the transcendent, existential sense; cf. Ouweneel (2014a; 2014c).

in this way. Scripture is *not* the exclusive domain of theology, just as nature and culture are not the exclusive domains of the natural and the cultural sciences, respectively. There is no single element in this world about which Scripture does not make some fundamental statement, and at the same time, there is no subject in reality about which theology speaks as the *only* speaker, as Reformed dogmatician Johan Heyns has nicely put it.[62]

Theology definitely plays a useful and important exegetical role in the *formation* of a truly Christian view of the world and of life by helping us properly understand the Scriptures on all the relevant points it covers. We could not very well imagine a "Christian worldview," no matter what kind, without any influence from Christian theology. We might even suspect such a—probably very biblicistic—worldview! But we keep remembering that such a (pre-theoretical) worldview as such is not theological in nature (and not philosophical either, for that matter). Therefore, I am very suspicious about the *theological* "big picture" to which VanDrunen refers.[63] It is the task of Christian *philosophy* to develop such a "big picture."

The place of theology should be modest; it should *influence* the formation of the Christian worldview, not *replace* it. Dutch philosopher and theologian Andree Troost, himself Reformed, mentioned the example that Herman Dooyeweerd several times expressed in his *confessional* prolegomena, which evidently had undergone the strong theological influence of the great Reformed theologians of his youth, Abraham Kuyper and Herman Bavinck.[64] If we desire a *Christian* worldview to underlie all scientific activity, it should be of an ecumenical character. That is, it should exhibit as few Catholic, Lutheran, Reformed, Evangelical, and Pentecostal idiosyncrasies as possible, but go back to the great central truths that all orthodox Christians throughout the centuries have shared, expressed especially in the Nicene-Constantinopolitan Creed.

11.5.3 "Christian Calculus"

By means of a specific example, let me try to explain the cheap shot of NL2K at its target of "Christian" sciences, as it all but ridicules such an idea. For example, VanDrunen writes: "Christ's resurrection, ascension, and establishment of the church have not changed the truths of calculus or the way that water flows. The fact that a plumber is converted to Christianity does not change his objective obligations as a plumber (even though he

---

[62] Cf. Heyns (1988, 60).
[63] VanDrunen (2010a, 175).
[64] Troost (1977, 147).

now has new motivation for being industrious and honest as he pursues his vocation)."[65]

Of course, the great facts of salvation did not change the natural laws of cosmic reality. I am unaware of any serious Christian scholar who has ever suggested that they did. Neither the Fall nor redemption ever changed God's creation ordinances as such; they changed only human *functioning* under these ordinances. However, VanDrunen's argument intends to suggest that not only calculus as such is not Christian (but rather common), but also the *science* of calculus, or more broadly, mathematics, cannot be a Christian science, either. Here lies a deep mistake, which we encounter throughout VanDrunen's book. In my words it is this error: 2 + 2 = 4, both for the Christian and the atheist, the Jew and the Muslim. So mathematics can never be a specifically Christian enterprise. If VanDrunen had only asked, What is the *ontic status* of the statement "2 + 2 = 4"?, he might have begun to think differently. But because he seems to refuse to consider the possible philosophical background of scientific questions, such a question as we have posed never crossed his mind. If he had also seen that philosophy, like any science, is always rooted in religious or ideological biases, he might have seen that, for this very reason, room exists for a *Christian* philosophy as well. And from there it would have been a small step toward a Christian approach to mathematics!

Let me work this out a little.[66] First, in the ancient paradigm of mathematics, the nature of the divine world order was basically viewed as mathematical (Pythagoras! d. 495 BC). People can know this mathematical world order through human reason, by means of the axiomatic-deductive method (that is, from a few self-evident axioms all the theorems of mathematics can be deduced).

Second, in the Reformational paradigm, this method of penetrating into the divine-mathematical world order was replaced by the empirical-inductive method (that is, our knowledge of the mathematical world order is derived from scientific observations); think of Johannes Kepler (d. 1630), Robert Boyle (d. 1691), and Isaac Newton (d. 1727).

Third, in the secularized paradigm (since the Enlightenment), the nature of cosmic reality is still basically viewed as mathematical, but no longer as a divine world order. Mathematics and physics have been secularized; they have nothing to do with the Creator anymore.

---

[65] VanDrunen (2010a, 170).
[66] See Ouweneel (1997, §6.3.3).

Fourth, in the critical paradigm, the idea of an objective mathematical world order was replaced by that of a subjective mathematical order, and even of mutually contradictory (Euclidian and non-Euclidian) orders. These newer orders turn out to be not only logically consistent, but also practically applicable within certain areas of reality. For the first time, a gap arises between a mathematical and a physical geometry, between pure rationality and empirical truth.

Fifth, now that the demand for and possibility of truth have been rejected, mathematics does not need to be true (i.e., corresponding with cosmic reality); it needs only to be workable. Thus, the reductionist paradigm places the ideal of logical consistency in the foreground. This ideal is pursued by trying to reduce mathematical relations to other modes of being, especially the logical mode (*logicism*: mathematics exists only in the *ratio*, not in external reality), the sensitive mode (*intuitionism*: we know of mathematical relations only through our intuition), and the lingual mode of being (*formalism*: mathematics is a "language" that does not refer to any external reality). Not only do mathematicians disagree about these various "isms," but since the philosopher of mathematics, Kurt Gödel (d. 1978), even *this* ideal no longer seems workable.

Sixth, Christian philosophers, working from a very different cosmology and epistemology, believe that mathematical relations do not exist only within human reason, or intuition, or language, but are rooted in the creation ordinances that God has instituted for cosmic reality.[67]

Yes, since the resurrection and glorification of Christ, 2 + 2 still equals 4. But that is not the point. Any philosopher of science will realize immediately what is the point: namely, what is the deeper *significance*, the *ontic status*, of this equation? What does it tell us about cosmic reality? The answers are very different, depending on whether they come from an ancient, early Protestant, humanist, or present-day Christian philosopher of mathematics. But precisely here lies the problem: NL2K advocates have no appreciation for the significance of (Christian) philosophy for our thinking.[68] They know only about theology in the realm of grace, and all the other sciences in the realm of nature. They believe that the equation and the reality, "2 + 2 = 4," belong to the common kingdom (common to both believers and unbelievers) without realizing the ideological background of this equation and reality, which makes it not common at all.

---

[67] See, e.g., Strauss (2009, 211–15).
[68] See especially VanDrunen (2010a, 174–77), where this lack of feeling for the (Christian-) philosophical roots of all science is painfully felt.

11.6 THREE GENERAL PARADIGMS

11.6.1   The Scholastic and Scientistic Paradigms

Let me add here a few thoughts about the notion of "paradigm," a notion developed by philosopher of science Thomas S. Kuhn (d. 1996).[69] This concept is also very significant for theology, as has been emphasized by many Christian thinkers.[70] NL2K advocates seem unaware of this, apparently because they have no room for philosophy in their thinking. Elsewhere I have described how we can distinguish three main paradigms.[71]

1. The *scholastic* paradigm of theology, based on the medieval dualistic amalgamation of ancient Greek and Christian thought. This is the systematic-theological paradigm of conservative Roman Catholic theology, as dominated by Thomism, but also, for instance, of NL2K thinking. The scholastic paradigm is based primarily not on Scripture, but on "the authorities," that is, in addition to Aristotle for the common realm, the church fathers, especially Augustine, for the sacred realm, and further particularly the conciliar dogmas and the papal doctrinal decrees, and for Reformed theologians, the Three Forms of Unity and/or the Westminster Standards.

This paradigm powerfully affected early Protestant theology, both among the Lutherans (e.g., Martin Chemnitz, Johann Gerhard, Johannes A. Quenstedt, David Hollaz) and among Reformed theologians (e.g., Theodore Beza, Amandus Polanus, William Perkins, Francis Gomarus, Gisbert Voetius). Synodical decrees, with the Canons of Dort being the best known example thereof, occupy *de facto* and *de iure* the same place as papal doctrinal decrees.

2. The *scientistic* paradigm of theology, based on the dualistic amalgamation of Christian and humanistic thought. This is the systematic-theological paradigm of liberal or modernist theology, marked especially by the results of so-called "higher biblical criticism" or the "historical-critical method." Scholasticism itself already had clearly rationalistic overtones, but in the eighteenth century, an entirely new, liberal approach arose, characterized by the rationalism of the Enlightenment of that time.

While many see a stark contrast between early Protestant orthodoxy and Enlightenment liberalism, several authors have clearly discerned

---

[69] Kuhn (1996).
[70] E.g., Küng in Küng and Tracy (1984); Avis (1986); Van Huyssteen (1987; 1997); Adriaanse et al. (1987, 29–34, 60); Mouton et al. (1988); Von Dietze (1998); Troost (2004); Koster (2005).
[71] Ouweneel (2013, chapter 13; 2014c, chapters 8–9).

the continuity between the two because of their underlying rationalism. Theologians who moved from early Protestant orthodoxy to Enlightenment liberalism had to make important changes in their thinking, but one thing did not change: the rationalistic methodology of theology. The products of a science that is considered to be neutral and objective, but in reality is rationalistic-positivistic, dominate the view of Scripture. Typical orthodox notions, such as creation, the Fall, redemption, the kingdom of God, the consummation of history, and so forth, are preserved but are transformed according to the demands of the ideals of humanism: those of autonomous humanity and of a manageable reality.

11.6.2   The Evangelical Paradigm

3. I care less about the name "Evangelical" than about knowing what it means: it refers to the systematic-theological paradigm of that "traditional" theology which builds on the Apostles' and the Nicene-Constantinopolitan Creeds, and that we therefore call "orthodox," without quibbling about the minute details. Negatively speaking, it is the paradigm that has not been affected too much by either the scholastic or the humanistic paradigms. Though being a negative statement, this is the crux, because so much of what is called "orthodox" theology is in fact heavily affected by traditional scholasticism, and sometimes also by the humanist paradigm. I identify those theologians as "Evangelical" who in the broad sense, as a matter or principle, wish to be guided by the content of Scripture, not by extra-biblical thought content, whether scholastic or humanist. These theologians do not study Scripture and Christian beliefs from perspectives that are alien to Scripture and Christian beliefs, but endeavour to understand Scripture and Christian beliefs from their own centre, without forcing them into conformity with a scientific system that is imposed upon them from the outside.

Is it realistic to assume that such a theology truly exists, and that it *can* exist, given the weaknesses of human nature? Scientistic theology's view of science is founded upon a long rationalistic tradition in Western civilization. As a consequence, scientistic theology consciously and repeatedly imposed upon Christian faith a secular view of reality and knowledge that is alien to it, and thus adulterated Christian faith. However, theologians who wish to remain faithful to Scripture often do the same, not because they deliberately apply foreign presuppositions but because they usually are insufficiently conscious of their premises. Consequently, they often unintentionally adopt either a scholastic worldview (like NL2K), or a biblicistic worldview (like fundamentalist schools), or one of the current secular worldviews (like more liberal schools), or an eclectic mixture of elements drawn from all of these worldviews. But, as the Lord makes clear, unintentional sins (Lev. 4) are also sins.

This leads me to the following description of an ideal Christian theology. This theology not only is faithful to Scripture's own self-understanding, but is capable of *critically accounting* for this fidelity on the basis of philosophical presuppositions that are themselves clearly congenial to Scripture.[72] Spiritual apostasy can be manifested not only in scientistic theology, but also in Evangelical theology, to the extent that the latter is usually an open fortress, with little *theoretically substantiated* resistance to all kinds of philosophical schools that seek to attack it.[73] Therefore, in my view, a truly Evangelical systematic theology can be designed and maintained only on the basis of a thorough, coherent theoretical-philosophical view of reality and knowledge, founded upon the same biblical faith principle as this theology itself. The latter phrase means that it must be based upon Scripture as accepted according to its own self-understanding as the divinely inspired and authoritative Word of God.

WORKING IT OUT: IS "CHRISTIAN PHILOSOPHY" INHERENTLY POSSIBLE?

Is not "Christian philosophy" inherently impossible?[74]

In my view, philosophy can be described as that foundational science—the "discipline of the disciplines"[75]—that endeavours to answer the most basic and vital questions about all our knowing and being, or about knowledge and reality. It is a *totality* science in the sense that it does not look at the various parts of reality separately, as do the special sciences, but tries to grasp the total picture.[76] Just like all science, such an endeavour can never be neutral, objective, unbiased. Those who think otherwise may perhaps think that a Christian philosophy is inherently impossible, because philosophy should be objective, i.e., bias free. In practice, such an objective philosophy does not exist. A philosophy is always rooted in a person's

---

[72] See extensively, Ouweneel (2013, chapters 6–14; 2014a).

[73] Troost (1977, 186).

[74] The answer to this question is a summary of Ouweneel (2014a, chapter 1). See there for a fuller answer.

[75] See Strauss (2009, title).

[76] The "big picture," as VanDrunen (2010a, 175) calls it—only he wrongly assigns this task to theology!

pre-theoretical worldview. That is, philosophy and all the special sciences (including theology) are of a theoretical nature, but are founded upon something that precedes all their theories: someone's *worldview*, a set of practical ideas about humanity, nature, culture, politics, history, society, justice, morality, religion, and so on.

Such a worldview itself is founded upon one's faith. A worldview is a set of *beliefs*, but your *faith* is much more than that. Your faith underlies your beliefs because your beliefs are (more or less) rational, whereas your faith is what I would call suprarational, that is, it transcends (surpasses) the rational. Note carefully: we are not saying that faith is non-rational, or even irrational; faith is not necessarily *against* reason, but faith is certainly *beyond* reason. Absurdities (like a square circle) are illogical, they are against reason; by contrast, mysteries surpass human logic, they are beyond reason. Faith can be formulated in rational thoughts and words; at that point faith becomes beliefs. In other words, faith can be logically accounted for. But this faith as such precedes and surpasses all such formulating and giving account.

Now, this faith always possesses a *religious* nature. I define religion here as the confidence a person has in Someone or something as an Ultimate Ground. This Ultimate Ground may be God, or some god, or many gods, or more vaguely, something divine, or even more vaguely, something that is absolutely awesome.[77] It is Someone or something that surpasses all visible things, or something *within* the visible world. This Someone or something functions as a kind of general, foundational principle from which the whole of reality can be explained. Such a principle could be matter, life, the spiritual, reason, development (evolution), society (or, for certain people, sex, football, fashion, alcohol, etc.). Everybody believes in Someone or something, some ultimate reality, or ultimate part or principle of reality. This Someone or something, this element or principle, explains the whole of reality, gives reality its meaning and purpose (or denies it any meaning or purpose), and is the thing in which a person places his ultimate confidence, or to which he is ultimately committed. To this Ultimate Ground his feeling, thinking, willing, and believing resorts, and beyond it, there is nothing else to which he can resort.

Atheism, agnosticism, nihilism, and solipsism are "-isms" that can be logically explained, verbally formulated, and rationally accounted for. Even irrationalism is a viewpoint that can be, and is, rationally accounted for. But in the end, these "-isms" cannot be rationally demonstrated beyond all doubt—just like faith in God, for that matter. This is the very reason why

---

[77] Cf. Rudolf Otto's (1970) idea of the "holy" in the sense of "numinous."

we call such convictions *faith*. Faith is beyond the rational (and beyond the emotional, the lingual, the social, etc.), and yet faith possesses certainty: a suprarational, transcendent, existential certainty of the heart. It is a person's ultimate commitment.

In summary: a person's scientific knowledge is ultimately grounded in his philosophical convictions, these convictions are ultimately grounded in his worldview, and his worldview is ultimately grounded in his suprarational, existential faith, which by definition is of a religious nature. In the so-called "common kingdom" of NL2K, it turns out that, in fact, nothing is common in the sense of neutral, secular, or non-religious: there are basically only Godward and apostate people, *and this ground attitude comes to light repeatedly* in the things people do and say.

When we see this, the answer to our question is no longer difficult: Can there be something like a Christian philosophy? Some philosophers in the Western world *are* Christians, but they often keep their philosophical work and their Christian beliefs quite separate. They may belong, or have belonged, to one of the most popular philosophical schools—determinism, utilitarianism, (neo)positivism, objectivism, existentialism, analytical philosophy, postmodernism, some liberation philosophy, some feminist philosophy, you name it—without their Christian convictions being fundamentally involved. To put it a bit bluntly: on Sundays and in their free time, they are Christians, but during working hours they work within some supposedly neutral, secular, non-religious philosophical framework. They are Christians-and-philosophers, but not Christian philosophers. That is, they do not adhere to, or they even reject outright, the notion of a "Christian philosophy," often because of some idea of a neutral, objective, unbiased, or non-religious philosophy.

Now if it is true that philosophy is always grounded in some faith, and that this faith is ultimately of some religious nature, then all philosophy is, at its deepest level, religious in nature. In my view, it is impossible to avoid that conclusion. If this is correct, then the choice is not between common, current (that is, secular) philosophy and some religiously biased philosophy, but *between philosophy based on false, and philosophy based on true, religion*. If the former choice were correct, I would not hesitate to choose the first option that I mentioned. But if all philosophy is indeed ultimately religious in nature, then I would certainly prefer a philosophy based on true religion.

Don't be ashamed to speak of a "Christian philosophy." I am a Christian, so for me, true philosophy cannot be anything else than a Christian philosophy. There is no such thing as a neutral philosophy, so I prefer a Christian philosophy. I truly believe that such a philosophy is not only possible, but also highly desirable, even indispensible. If you subscribe to the modern version of two kingdoms, namely, the kingdom of God alongside some common kingdom, then you believe that the word "Christian" may legitimately be applied only to matters in the former kingdom, whereas in the latter kingdom nothing is specifically Christian. Abandon that view. It is rather the reverse: with no idea of a Christian philosophy, you will not be able to properly understand theology as a theoretical enterprise! Now go and work *that* out for yourself![78]

---

[78] For help in doing this, you will want to read Ouweneel (2014a; 2014c).

12

A PHILOSOPHY OF THE STATE

PREPARATORY PONDERINGS

1. Do you think that in the present age, a truly Christian state could exist, in principle or in practice, if part of the population was non-Christian? Explain your answer.
2. If you think that such a Christian state could exist, what would be the characteristics of such a state?
3. In your opinion, how should people develop a Christian view of the state (or a view of the Christian state—is that the same or something else?)?
4. In what different ways would justice and morality function in a church, in a Christian family, and in a Christian state (assuming that such a thing could exist)?

12.1 "FROM WHERE DOES MY HELP COME?"

12.1.1   A "Theology of the State"?

In this last chapter, let us try to summarize everything we have been discussing up until this point, and to apply this to one specific problem: the *philosophy of the state* (German: *Staatsphilosophie*; Dutch: *staatsfilosofie*). As we have seen, there is no such thing as a "theology of the state," unless one means a theology *preached* by the (i.e., some totalitarian) state. This "theology" is like what the Chinese government tries to pursue in order to control Christians in its country, and like we find in certain Muslim countries where the authorities dictate the theological views of the population. But this is not what I mean. A "theology of the state" is a supposedly theological view of what the state is, or should be. If David VanDrunen can speak of a "theology of law,"[1] or a "theology of culture,"[2] then I presume he would not object to a "theology of the state," a "theology of politics," or a "theology of economics" (cf. §§9.4.3 and 10.4.1), or even a "theology of the environment," a "theology of social relationships," a "theology of history," a "theology of language," a "theology of aesthetics," etc.

After all we have considered, it is not difficult to see what error is being committed here. Theology must investigate all biblical passages that deal with authorities and citizens. These are either *descriptive* passages (ranging from ancient Israel to the Roman Empire), or *prescriptive* passages, which tell us how we citizens should behave toward the authorities (Rom. 13:1–7; Titus 3:1; 1 Pet. 2:13–17). But there is one thing that theology can never do: *tell us what a state is*—what is the state's nature, its origin, its development, its variety of forms, etc. The reason that theologians cannot do this is very simple: the Bible is not interested in such questions. So when a Christian thinker wants to form a view of the state, and compare this view with what, according to him, is a *Christian* view of the state, he must turn to Christian philosophy (assuming that such a thing exists, or at least has been attempted).

However, where this is so obvious, why do NL2K theologians keep speaking of a "theology of culture," or a "theology of the state," or things like that? Because they are speaking about two kingdoms in such a way that everything that can be properly called Christian by definition belongs to the first kingdom

---

[1] VanDrunen (2003, 30).
[2] VanDrunen (2010a, 12).

only. This is the kingdom that comprises both the church and theology. So if you want a Christian view of anything, ask the church and/or theology! If you want a Christian view of the state, NL2K advocates will answer that, either, such a view by definition cannot exist, or only the church and theology can provide you that view. What a disappointment—for neither the church *as church*, nor theology *as theology*, has any idea of what the state is, or should be. Church members, including theologians, may have an intuitive idea of what a state is, as all lay people do, but that is not what we are looking for. We want a scientific description of the state, its nature, its origin, its development, its variety of forms, etc., and all this from a Christian point of view. Neither the church nor theology can provide that.

Notice my desire to have a *Christian* view of the state. Am I not entitled to such a view? I am a Christian, and I intuitively sense that dictatorially governed states—oppressive states—cannot express God's ideal for a state. I also sense that a state where all the power is really in the hands of the country's great captains of industry cannot express God's ideal for a state, either. The same holds for a state where all the power is in the hands of one political party (either a communist or a fascist party). Nor can God's ideal be a state where the religious powers dominate the community (whether Hindu, Buddhist, Muslim, or even Christian powers, while oppressing people of other convictions), and the same is true for a state that itself dominates the religious communities in the country. However, these are only intuitions. I want a rational, coherent, systematic, theoretical view of the state from a Christian point of view.

NL2K will in fact never be able to give me an appropriate answer to my question about a Christian view of the state. The reason is that the sacred kingdom (church and theology) is not equipped to give me an answer, and in the secular kingdom there is neither Christian philosophy, nor Christian political science. So I am stuck. The sacred kingdom is not *able* to give me an answer, the common (secular, neutral) kingdom is not *allowed* to give me an answer. I am stuck—but, fortunately, only as long as I subscribe to NL2K. Not only does NL2K have no answer, it actually believes that *there is no Christian view of the state*, except the little wisdom that theologians might give me on the subject.

12.1.2 A Christian View of the State

Now, to be sure, I do *not* subscribe to NL2K; I may have made that clear. I do not believe in some natural law written on the hearts of all people, and functioning totally independent of Scripture (see chapter 4). Such a Scripture-independent natural law is nothing but a loincloth, a fig leaf, to hide the shame of refusing to acknowledge Christian philosophy, Christian political science, a Christian view of the state, etc. I do not believe in the kind of two kingdoms where only one kingdom allows me to use the word "Christian" at all. If there is no Christian philosophy, then I will never be able to develop a rational, coherent, systematic Christian view of humanity, either, nor a Christian view of nature, a Christian view of culture, a Christian view of history, a Christian view of emotional life, a Christian view of social relations, a Christian view of economics, a Christian view of aesthetics, and even a Christian view of the state, of politics, of taxpaying, of voting, etc. These are the very things that I, as a Christian philosopher, for decades have been terribly interested in, and I will not allow NL2K to take that away from me.

Do I really have to believe that there is no *Christian* evaluation of what is better: a democratic or an autocratic state? Is there no *Christian* answer to the question what is worse: a church-dominated state, or a state-dominated church? Is there no *Christian* analysis of whether it is better to have the capitalists in power, or the communists? Is it "sound popular sentiment" that has the answers to these questions (see §4.3.2)? But whatever your view of "natural law," an entity known as "the people" simply does not exist. Particular people have been formed by their history, their culture, their customs and traditions. Why are so many Europeans convinced of the *raison-d'être* of Christian-democratic parties, and why are so many Americans convinced of the necessity that political parties be religiously neutral (which they never are)? It is self-deception to believe that this has anything to do with "natural law" or "sound popular sentiment" (which are basically the same). It has everything to do with the enormous differences in European and American history, culture, customs, and traditions, respectively. As self-evident as Christian-democratic views are in Europe, so objectionable are they in the eyes of many American Christians.

Please realize that this is something that has to be thoroughly investigated by political science (as *has* been done)! And realize that any political science is always rooted in certain ideological presuppositions, and that these presuppositions are basically of a religious nature (see the previous chapter). Where this is so, what basic objection is there against a *Christian* view of the state, as rooted in a *Christian* philosophy of the state? The more humanist such a science is, the more it will emphasize the Enlightenment as the main source for the development of democratic principles. But to the degree that a political science is Christian, to that degree it will identify the important Christian influence on the development of democratic principles.[3] A Christian political science is biased, but so is any humanist

---

[3] See again Groen van Prinsterer (1975); "Groen" is not a first name but part of a surname.

political science. I prefer a biased Christian political science to a biased humanist (or scholastic, or biblicist) political science.

12.2 NL2K IDEAS OF THE STATE

12.2.1 The Sermon on the Mount

Let us now see how VanDrunen speaks of the state. His logic is as follows:

> Major premise: You cannot rule a state as you rule a church.
> Minor premise: The church is a Christian community.
> Conclusion: Therefore, the state cannot be a Christian community.

In my view, VanDrunen's logic is precisely analogous to this syllogism:

> Major premise: Soccer and tennis have different rules.
> Minor premise: Soccer is a sport.
> Conclusion: Therefore, tennis cannot be a sport.

If the reader thinks I am ridiculing VanDrunen's view, then study carefully this quotation:

> While Christians should desire civil government to promote justice, whatever justice it achieves is the justice of the common kingdom, not of the redemptive kingdom proclaimed by Christ.... The New Testament confirms the authority of civil magistrates to carry out this task.... The kingdom that Christ proclaimed is of a radically different character—a kingdom that is *not* to operate according to the principle of proportionate justice that should guide the state (see Matt. 5:38–42).... The two-kingdoms doctrine helps us to recognize that the Sermon on the Mount concerns the redemptive kingdom that finds expression in the church and says *nothing* about the obligation of the state to enforce the death penalty.[4]

Watch carefully what is going on here. Let us first look at what VanDrunen tells us about the Sermon on the Mount: it "concerns the redemptive kingdom that finds expression in the church." However, this Sermon is not speaking about the church at all. But even more importantly: the Sermon

---

4 VanDrunen (2010a, 195–96).

on the Mount is speaking only about the *personal* attitude of the believer. This Sermon does not involve rules for the state, *but neither for the church!* Several passages, especially 1 Corinthians 5, tell us how a local church must deal with evildoers. Does VanDrunen really think that the Sermon on the Mount is applicable for the order and practice of the church's life? If a person brings evil into the church, will Jesus then say to that church: "Do not resist the one who is evil. But if anyone slaps you on the right cheek, turn to him the other also" (Matt. 5:39)?[5] Of course not. Indeed, Matthew 5–7 does not give us guidelines for ordering the state—but neither does it give us guidelines for ordering the church.

The Sermon on the Mount is about the personal conduct of (individual) *disciples* (Matt. 5:1) in the kingdom of God. It does not tell us how families, or schools, or states must be ordered and governed, but neither does it tell us how churches must be ordered and governed. Actually, the matter goes much deeper than this. VanDrunen creates a difference between the Mosaic Law and the Sermon on the Mount with which I cannot agree at all.[6] I maintain that, as many commentators have pointed out, in Matthew 5–7 *not a single Mosaic commandment is trespassed, changed, or even cancelled.*[7] Reformed theology made the mistake of thinking that the Mosaic Law has been largely abolished, except perhaps for the Ten Commandments. *Nothing* of the Mosaic Law has ever been annulled. However, this Law is valid for Israel only (cf. Acts 15). Believers from the Gentiles are under the Law of Christ (1 Cor. 9:21; Gal. 6:2), whose moral kernel is identical with that of the Mosaic Law, though, but for the rest is very different. I must refer to other publications in which I have worked this out.[8]

To mention just one example to show that Jesus did not annul the Mosaic Law: he did not at all abolish the rule "an eye for an eye, a tooth for a tooth" (Matt. 5:38; cf. Exod. 21:24; Lev. 24:20; Deut. 19:21). What Jesus said is that this was *never* a rule governing the conduct of the individual Israelite, neither in the Old Testament nor in the New Testament. It was a rule to be implemented by the *authorities only*. In Old Testament times, the Israelite never had the right to personally take revenge for himself; this had to be left to the judges: "The *judges* shall inquire diligently, and if the witness is a false witness and has accused his brother falsely, then you shall do to him as he had meant to do to his brother. So you shall purge

---

[5] Cf. ibid., 110.

[6] Ibid., 109–110.

[7] One of the best Reformed introductions to this subject, in my view, is Ridderbos (1970, ad loc.).

[8] See especially Ouweneel (2016f).

the evil from your midst. And the rest shall hear and fear, and shall never again commit any such evil among you. Your eye shall not pity. It shall be life for life, eye for eye, tooth for tooth, hand for hand, foot for foot" (Deut. 19:18–21). This has not changed in the New Testament era: even the most Christian state has still to follow this *lex talionis*, that is, the legal standard of proportionate justice.

12.2.2 Various Types of Justice

The fact that justice works in different ways in the state and in the church does not prove that the church does, and the state does not, belong to the kingdom of God. (See the syllogisms at the beginning of §12.2.1.) In the view that I present in this book, the kingdom of God encompasses a large number of societal relationships: *Christian* church denominations (or local congregations), *Christian* families, *Christian* schools, *Christian* companies, *Christian* associations, *Christian* political parties, and sometimes even *Christian* states. In all these institutions, the one principle of divine justice is manifested in very different ways.

First, in the Christian church, justice means (among many other aspects): "Purge the evil person from among you" (1 Cor. 5:13), but also, for instance: "Brothers, if anyone is caught in any transgression, you who are spiritual should restore him in a spirit of gentleness. Keep watch on yourself, lest you too be tempted" (Gal. 6:1).

Second, in the Christian family, justice is governed by the love that exists between parents and children. There is a correspondence here with the church: in both relationships, justice is governed by the principle of love. One enormous difference is this: in principle, evil children are *never* purged from the Christian family.[9]

Third, if a state is very Christian—the great majority of its citizens are sincere Christians—even then the justice it is called to maintain *never* goes beyond *public* justice because this is proper to the state. Let us look here again at the first sentence in VanDrunen's quotation (§12.2.1): "Christians should desire civil government to promote justice...." *Why* should Christians do so? On what ground? Because of natural law? Or because of "sound popular sentiment"? No, rather, because it is the *divine calling* of the state—even though the authorities may not wish to acknowledge this—to promote justice. John the Baptist kept saying to King Herod: "It is not lawful for you to have your brother's wife" (Mark 6:18). Can a king not do anything he likes? Why did John keep telling him not to have his

---

9 This was different under the old covenant (Deut. 21:18–21).

sister-in-law? Was it against "natural law" or "sound popular sentiment" to take you brother's wife? No, it was against *God's* law. John was not ashamed to point this out to the king—perhaps because John did not believe in a separation between a sacred realm and a common realm.

In both realms—if we may at all split them in this way—it is the same divine law that rules. Churches must obey God's ordinances that are valid for churches (which must be explicated by Christian ecclesiology). Families must obey God's ordinances that are valid for families, and schools must obey God's ordinances that are valid for schools (which latter ordinances must be explicated by a Christian philosophy of education). States must obey God's ordinances that are valid for states (which must be explicated by a Christian philosophy of the state). Indeed, it is a Christian philosophy that has to explicate these various societal relationships, each with its own rules, its own type of justice.

12.2.3 Church Justice and State Justice

When VanDrunen points out that the sword belongs to the state, and not to the church,[10] he is perfectly correct. However, it does not at all follow logically that the state *therefore* belongs to some common kingdom, and not to the kingdom of God. What does follow logically is, again, the important fact that justice is explicated for the state in a way different from the justice that is explicated for the church. This has nothing to do with the Sermon on the Mount, as VanDrunen suggests, for this Sermon tells us only how the individual disciples should behave. The Sermon gives no rules for the state, but neither for the church, as we have seen. The Sermon on the Mount does not present us with any penal system or protocol, but the state does have these, *and so does the church*. These systems and protocols are rather different because the state and the church are rather different societal relationships. Similarly, families and schools have different penal systems and protocols, too, each according to the specific character of a given societal relationship.

In conclusion, when VanDrunen says, "Church discipline should look exceedingly different from civil justice in the state,"[11] he is perfectly correct again. He is simply drawing the wrong conclusion from this correct observation. The statement does indeed claim that churches and states are very different societal relationships. It does *not* prove, however, that the church belongs to the kingdom of God and the state does not. Moreover, I think

---

[10] VanDrunen (2010a, 122).
[11] Ibid., 141–42.

VanDrunen is exaggerating the differences between the state's penal system and the church's penal system.

First, in the state, the goal of any civilized penal system is definitely not only retribution, but *restoration* (rehabilitation, resocialization) as well. Those who have served their sentences in prison must be helped to re-enter society with dignity and value.

Second, in the civilized states that I know about, whether the evildoer shows remorse or not definitely plays a role. Sentences have been reduced because the criminal showed the judge (and in some countries, the jury) that he greatly regretted his evil act.

Third, if the evildoer in church has lived in gross sin for a long time, then is exposed and immediately confesses his sin, a church cannot act as if nothing has happened; for instance, he may be requested to abstain from the Lord's Supper for a while. There is definitely an element of retribution in this.

Of course, I cannot explicate all this here. I can only state that I view the differences between church justice and state justice as more gradual than essential. But that the two systems are very different is correct. This is not because church and state are in two different kingdoms, however, but because they are two very different types of societal relationships within the one kingdom of God.

12.3 ECONOMICS

12.3.1 Different Economic Systems

Another area in which VanDrunen wishes to prove the difference between what he calls the kingdom of God and the common kingdom is the area of economics.

> Worldly economics…explores the hard choices that people (and businesses and governments) have to make about how to use their inevitably limited resources. Individuals and institutions of the common kingdom may be full of good intentions, but they are constrained by an ethic of scarcity. In contrast, the New Testament reveals that an ethic of scarcity does not constrain the church. From a certain perspective it is true that churches set budgets based on expected giving and cannot cut checks to missionaries or the poor beyond the balance in their bank accounts. But as illuminating as worldly economics is for the

commerce of the common kingdom, it can make little sense of the church's giving and receiving as described in Scripture.[12]

Here we find a double error similar to the one identified in §12.2 (see the present and the next section). First, VanDrunen wants to illustrate for us the difference between the kingdom of God and the common kingdom by emphasizing the different economics of churches, on the one hand, and businesses and governments, on the other hand. To see the error here, let us compare the economics of a business and of a government. The very first economic principle of a business is to *make a profit*. If it would not follow this rule, it would soon go bankrupt. This principle must be constantly guided by economic wisdom, for instance, by not turning profits into salaries only, but by making wise investments, and by constantly operating within fiscal means available. Yet, profit making is its primary principle. In this sense, it differs essentially from a state, in which profit making is not at all a guiding principle. The state's task is to administer public justice, and its economic activity is totally subservient to this leading principle.

Now what does this prove? Does it prove that a company and a state belong to two different divinely instituted kingdoms? Of course not. Rather, it shows that in the one kingdom of God, each societal relationship *has its own type of economic activity*: churches, families, schools, companies, associations, political parties, states each engage in economic activity. There are basic economic principles that are valid for *all* these societal relationships, like making budgets to cover the expenses. But for the rest, their economic systems and activities differ significantly. A church does not have to make profit (it is not a business), and it does not have to administer public justice (it is not a state). Yet, this does not prove the existence of two different divinely instituted kingdoms, for within the supposed "common kingdom," the economics of a business and of a state differ just as much as the economics of a church and of a state.

12.3.2 Exaggeration

Second, VanDrunen exaggerates the differences again, apparently in order to make his case stronger—in this case, the differences between church economics, on the one hand, and business economics or state economics, on the other hand. To say, "the New Testament reveals that an ethic of scarcity does not constrain the church," is to spout nonsense. Churches,

---

[12] Ibid., 143.

too, face the limited availability of resources. They cannot keep spending more than they take in, just like any other societal relationship. They may appeal to their members to give, and to give generously; yet, they cannot spend more on their missionaries and their poor than they receive from such donors. VanDrunen admits this in the next sentence, apparently without realizing that he is thereby undermining his own argument. Church denominations and large local churches often use financial experts to monitor their budgets. Why? Because the basic economic rules are the same for all societal relationships. Churches can go bankrupt if they expect too much income from their members, or if they do not handle their finances according to proper economic principles.

Rather than concluding that church and state apparently belong to two different divinely instituted kingdoms, the conclusion is far more obvious that each societal relationship, including a church denomination or a local congregation, has its own type of economic principles. Yet, in all cases we are dealing with *economics* because there are economic principles common to every societal relationship. These economic principles are rooted in God's creational ordinances. I am very well aware of the fact that the worldwide church is a post-Fall (I would even say post-Pentecost) phenomenon. Yet, the social, economic, judicial, and ethical principles of the church are rooted in God's creation ordinances. We could not begin to distinguish such a thing as church *economics* if there were no economic principles operative in the church that are valid for all other societal relationships as well.

Let me add a minor point here. In the quotation given, VanDrunen speaks twice of an "ethic of scarcity." This is a remarkable confusion of two very different disciplines: ethics and economics. Scarcity is an economic starting point for economic thinking; this starting point has nothing at all to do with ethics. Ethics has to do with the principle, for example, "whatever you wish that others would do to you, do also to them" (Matt. 7:12). Economics has to do with the principle, for example, that "you can't keep spending more than you earn." These two principles may intersect in their applications; think of companies that spend money for charities, or states that spend money for welfare programs. But that does not make "scarcity" as such an *ethical* principle.

Incidentally, I also have a problem with the term "scarcity" as such. I will return to this point in the final "Working It Out" section at the end of this chapter.

12.4 MORE ON THE STATE

12.4.1 "Limited Government"

In previous chapters, I have referred repeatedly to the fact that the state is called to administer public justice, *and nothing more than that*. It does not meddle in the internal affairs of marriages, families, schools, companies, etc., unless crimes are committed within these societal relationships (rape, abuse, ill-treatment, theft, tax evasion, violence, and so on). VanDrunen says wise things about this matter,[13] but unfortunately without a coherent Christian view of the state (understandably so, for he does not believe in a Christian philosophy of the state).

One of the things VanDrunen says is this: "Christians should believe in limited government."[14] If he means that the task of the state does not extend beyond maintaining public justice, his statement is acceptable. However, I must admit that such statements often make me a little suspicious. The matter of "limited government" is a typically Republican issue. The argument goes like this: the smaller the government, the more individual freedom is guaranteed for citizens. One might even quote Bible verses to illustrate what a great good personal freedom is!

The point is, however, that Christians in the Democratic party might like to refer to other Bible verses, which are equally relevant: "Do not use your freedom as an opportunity for the flesh, but through love serve one another" (Gal. 5:13). "Take care that this right of yours [the freedom that you allow yourself] does not somehow become a stumbling block to the weak" (1 Cor. 8:9). "Live as people who are free, not using your freedom as a cover-up for evil, but living as servants of God" (1 Pet. 2:16). That is, never let your freedom turn into selfishness. On the contrary, use your Christian freedom to support the weak and the needy.

I can think of no *a priori* reason why dispensing charity should be limited to individual Christians, or to churches and special charity institutions. If the state is called to administer public justice, it must pursue this righteousness also toward the weak, the needy, and the disabled. The state cannot tell such people: "Go in peace, be warmed and filled" (James 2:16). Charity is not only an act of love; it is also an act of righteousness (justice). The state must take care of those who are little or incapable of looking after themselves. I

---

[13] Ibid., 197–98.
[14] Ibid., 198.

am not talking about the *lazy* ones: "If anyone is not willing to work, let him not eat" (2 Thess. 3:10)—I am speaking of the *weak* and *disabled*.

Of course, in practice it is not so easy to indicate how far this goes and what specific forms this must take. There will also be conflicts around this question: How far does the state's responsibility extend in general? Limited or extended government? A little or a lot of state control, or something in between? Where exactly in between? According to what criteria? These cannot just be ethical criteria; they must be criteria that are inherent to our Christian view of the state. Here again, we see how important it is for Christians to develop their own philosophy of the state.

12.4.2 Moral Issues

The central point that I am trying to make is that the state has to maintain public righteousness, and this also involves looking after the weak and disabled. It is absurd to think that being "social" is the same as "socialism." Caring for the needy is not socialism; it is a Christian duty, not only of individual Christians but also of Bible-rooted states, such as virtually all Western states once were. This principal element of any view of the state can never be given up. Socialism, as an "-ism," has absolutized the social aspect at the expense of individual freedom. This is going too far to one extreme. But the other extreme is not right either: emphasizing personal freedom to such an extent as to neglect the "widows and orphans:" "Religion that is pure and undefiled before God, the Father, is this: to visit orphans and widows in their affliction, and to keep oneself unstained from the world" (James 1:27; cf. Exod. 22:22; Deut. 10:18; 14:29; 16:11, 14; 24:19–21; 26:12–13; 27:19; Job 31:18; Isa. 1:17; Jer. 7:6; 22:3; Zech. 7:10).

VanDrunen does discuss the intersection between Scripture and politics:

A real difficulty arrives when believers consider public policy questions involving moral issues that *are* addressed in Scripture. In the contemporary American context questions about abortion, marriage, and war are among the most contested political issues. Scripture says many things relevant to these topics, so how much liberty do Christians really have when these topics become political controversies?[15]

VanDrunen answers his question by insisting that "the church [read: its theologians, teachers] must teach all that Scripture says about such topics *as moral issues* but should be silent about such topics *as concrete political or*

---

[15] Ibid., 199.

public policy issues,"[16] which he works out for the topic of abortion.[17] I am thankful that he makes a clear distinction between biblical principles and their practical implementation in political life. We cannot draw direct lines from biblical-moral issues to concrete political circumstances. This is very good. The only problem is that VanDrunen does not tell us *how* such moral principles must be "translated" in order to apply them to governmental legislation. He might answer: This is not the theologians' task—but then, whose task is it? Or, is that to be decided by the majority—but according to what criteria does the majority decide? If I understand him correctly, explicit biblical arguments are not allowed in the public square. So first, how can the believing politician publicly underpin his opinion on abortion? Only by an appeal to natural law? And second, what criteria help him to know how his moral principles must be practically applied?

My answer to these important questions is that the believing politician not only needs clear biblical principles on abortion, but also clear biblical principles on the state's responsibilities! *What he actually needs is a clear Christian philosophy of the state.* If VanDrunen does not believe in Christian philosophy, then he leaves the believing politicians out in the cold. The believing politician's main problem is not that so many people in his country advocate abortion rights. His main problem is that he *himself*, not having a Christian view of politics, does not know to answer such people. What *principle* can he adduce if other people say that he has no right to encroach upon the freedom of the woman who wants an abortion? What *principle* can he adduce if people argue that legal abortions are far better than back alley abortions? What principle can he adduce if people argue that early fetuses are not yet persons whose lives must be protected by the law?

Here is where the problem lies: apart from his biblical standpoint, the believing politician has little to offer except perhaps pragmatic, utilitarian solutions. What should he do? Does he acquiescently submit to the majority decision? Or does he have a Christian view of politics that helps him decide how to take a stand? Where does he obtain such a Christian view? *Not* from NL2K advocates; they deny the possibility of Christian views for any sphere of activity within what they call the "common kingdom." The believing politician can only hope to get answers from those who do believe in Christian philosophy, and specifically in a Christian philosophy of the state and of political science. I am not saying that such Christian philosophies are abundantly available, or that, when a person once has

---

[16] Ibid., 199–202.
[17] Cf. also VanDrunen (2009, 147–68).

them, there are no longer any practical political problems. But at least we should try to develop such a Christian philosophy of the state. Having an imperfect Christian philosophy of the state is always much better than having no Christian philosophy of the state, or than denying that such a Christian philosophy of the state can even exist.

12.4.3 Morality and the State

Earlier I argued that, as a matter of principle, ethics must not be viewed as part of theology, but as a special science, just like economics, aesthetics, legal science.[18] Just like any of these special sciences, including theology, ethics can be pursued on the basis of a radical-Christian worldview, but also on the basis of a scholastic, a humanist, or a biblicist worldview. "Biblical ethics" is a confusing term at best; what is actually meant is "biblical morality;" ethics is the *academic discipline* that studies morality. The Bible contains moral principles but ethics is a scholarly discipline developed by ethicists, on the basis of various worldviews.

I mention this because Darryl Hart has argued that since "biblical ethics" is based on faith, therefore the government should not promote morality.[19] Again, this is a tangle of confusion in one sentence.

First, there is no such thing as "biblical ethics;" at best, there is ethics based on Christian principles, just like any academic discipline can be based on Christian or any other principles.

Second, biblical morality is based on (the Christian) faith, but one can never say that the state has nothing to do with morality. Within any state, where Christians might not even be in the majority, there is always a variety of moral systems, biblical morality being only one of them. To be a "good" state, citizens may be called upon to live up to their "norms and values" as well as they can. This was one of the things that the Christian-Democrat Dr. Jan Peter Balkenende (b. 1956), who was prime minister of the Netherlands from 2002 to 2010, kept emphasizing throughout his time in office.

Third, indeed, the state as such does not promote morality, Christian or otherwise, because its task is only to administer public justice—but it may certainly underpin its measures and policies with moral arguments. It could hardly do otherwise: there can be no judicial system in any civilized country without some foundation in the governing moral values of the population.

---

[18] See Troost (2004; 2005); the theologian and philosopher Andree Troost specialized in ethics (1958; 2001).

[19] Hart (2006, 15–16, 90–97); for an extensive review of Hart, see Kloosterman (2008).

Fourth, if the state is a Christian state, it *ought* to underpin its policies with Christian moral arguments, and do so clearly and explicitly. John Frame said about this: "[Hart's] argument should really go the opposite way, since biblical morality is based on faith, government must promote precisely a morality based on faith. Biblical morality is required of everyone."[20] This moves somewhat to the other extreme, however. Biblical morality is indeed required of everyone, but this does not mean that it is the *state* as such that must promote it. Christian moral principles are primarily preached by Christian preachers, not by the state. Even if the state is a Christian state, it does not preach or promote Christian morality as such, although it may confess its Christian morality as a foundation for all its measures and policies. It should never lose sight of its actual task: public justice—not morality as such.

Nevertheless, Frame's approach is refreshing: if it is true that in principle every human ought to follow God's moral rules, then in principle every state ought to base its measures and policies on God's moral rules—and, I may add, not on some natural law, which anyone can interpret according to their own whim.

12.5 OTHER CONFUSIONS

12.5.1 God's Kingdom and the State

Michael Horton wrote: "So Christians are not called…to transform their workplace, neighborhood, or nation into the kingdom of Christ. Rather, they are called to belong to a holy commonwealth that is distinct from the regimes of this age (Phil. 3:20–21) and to contribute as citizens and neighbors in temporal affairs."[21] Again, we encounter much confusion here.

First, who ever said that Christians turn *anything* in this world into the kingdom of Christ? Christ himself will do that at his second coming.

Second, already now the kingdom of Christ exists in a hidden form, namely, practically and actually wherever people submit to the authority of the glorified Christ and where the Holy Spirit is working. That is, the kingdom is manifested not only in churches but in millions of Christian marriages, millions of Christian families, thousands of Christian schools and associations, hundreds of Christian companies, in dozens of Christian political parties, and even in some Christian states. I admit that the term

[20] Frame (2011, 261).
[21] Horton (2006).

"transform" is confusing here; it fails to recognize the vertical dimension. It is not the case that a person's workplace is transformed into the kingdom of Christ, as though it moves from one kingdom into another kingdom (horizontal), but in a person's workplace the kingdom of Christ may definitely be manifested more and more (vertical).

Third, we are *not* "called to belong to a holy commonwealth that is distinct from the regimes of this age (Phil. 3:20–21)" because by faith we already do belong to it ("our citizenship *is* in heaven, and from it we await a Savior, the Lord Jesus Christ").

Fourth, in my opinion, the reference to Philippians 3:20–21 supports my view rather than Horton's view. What does it mean that our citizenship (or commonwealth, or homeland) is "in heaven"? Compare this with this other statement by Paul: "seated in the heavenly places in Christ Jesus" (Eph. 2:6). Why there? God "raised him from the dead and seated him at his right hand in the heavenly places, far above all rule and authority and power and dominion, and above every name that is named, not only in this age but also in the one to come. And he put all things under his feet" (1:20–22). We see here that the notion of the "heavenly places" is closely related to that of the "kingdom of heaven:" believers are seated in him who is the King of the universe. *Of course*, this "regime" is "distinct from the regimes of this age"—but at the same time it is true that all the latter regimes are subordinate to the kingship of Christ. Thus, his kingdom is manifested in nation states, sometimes through, and often in spite of, the actions of earthly kings, presidents, and prime ministers.

John Frame wonders whether, when Horton refers to the "kingdom of Christ," he is even thinking of something that includes the church,[22] given the fact that NL2K sees the church as the present manifestation of the kingdom of God. Indeed, a family, a school, or a state is no church. However, in a Christian family, school, or state, the kingdom of Christ is manifested no less than in a church—and in a good Christian family, school, or state even better than in a deteriorating church. If Christians "seek the kingdom of God and his righteousness" (Matt. 6:33), they do so not only in church but in all societal relationships in which they submit themselves to the authority of the King and are led by the Holy Spirit.

The serious consequence of a view like Horton's is that it denies—not formally but effectively—this universal kingship of Christ and this universal working of the Holy Spirit, and limits them to the sacred realm. Horton & co. thereby play into the hands of all the atheists and agnostics who

[22] Frame (2011, 319–20).

propagate the neutral, secularized state and wish to restrict religion to the church and to the private religious lives of people. The growing number of non-Christians in North America should be thanking their new gods for the support they are receiving from NL2K advocates with their commitment to a secular state.

12.5.2 The Kingdom of God and the Kingdom of Christ

At this point I must discuss more extensively a matter that we mentioned earlier. It is the constant confusion between the kingdom of God in its universal sense (God's providential reign, from the beginning of time to the eternal state), and the kingdom of God in its specific form of the kingdom of Christ, the glorified Man at the right hand of God, who has been made King of the universe. We saw how this distinction is constantly ignored in the works of VanDrunen and Horton. In 1995 Horton wrote: "Christ rules in His kingdom through the miracle of grace, but He rules the world through the providence of natural laws."[23] Notice: in both cases it is *Christ*, which seems not very accurate. Therefore, in 2006 he wrote: "Is Jesus Christ Lord over secular powers and principalities? At least in Reformed theology, the answer is yes, though he is Lord in different ways over the world and the church. God presently rules the world through providence and common grace, while he rules the church through Word, sacrament, and covenantal nurture."[24]

Please note how, in the first part of the quotation, Horton refers to "Jesus Christ," but in the second part to "God," who providentially rules the world. Now I know that Jesus is God, but the point is that in the kingdom of Christ it is the glorified *Man* at God's right hand who is in charge, both in the church (as its head) and in the world.[25] Perhaps this is one of the gravest errors in NL2K. It sees the "two kingdoms" everywhere throughout the history of humanity, from Adam to the last day, but shows little awareness of the specific character of the kingdom in the present age. Elsewhere[26] I have pointed out how this view is related to supersessionism and the spiritualization of eschatology. But it is also a Christological problem: in fact, NL2K sees hardly any difference between the kingdom of God before the incarnation of the Logos and after the glorification of Christ. And *if* it sees it, it does not acknowledge the consequences of this difference.

Jesus Christ is the ruler of the kings of the earth, says the apostle John (Rev. 1:5)—already now. That is, Jesus Christ is the head of the United States of

---

[23] Horton (1995, 125).

[24] Horton (2006).

[25] Frame's position (2011, 321–22) would have been strengthened if he had pointed this out.

[26] See extensively, Ouweneel (2016e).

America and of the Netherlands, of Russia and of China, of North Korea and of South Africa. This is far more Christ-centred than the "providence" and "common grace" that Horton refers to. Let me put it as poignantly as possible: Jesus Christ is just as much the King of the United States as he is the King of, for instance, the Orthodox Presbyterian Church in America, just as he is King in Christian families and schools. Of course, he is this always in different ways—and NL2K loves to magnify these differences. This is fine with me, as long the Man Christ's universal kingship—and not only God's universal providential government—is acknowledged.

Jesus Christ is King formally over the entire world, and he is this actually wherever his authority is acknowledged, not only in individual lives but also in the societal relationships in which Christians exercise leadership. This does not mean that he is responsible for all the unholiness and out-right sins within these societal relationships, even in (so-called) Christian relationships. Jesus' kingship so far is a hidden kingship (cf. Col. 3:1–3); his *public* kingdom has not yet arrived in power and majesty, of which is said: "Every morning he shows forth his justice" (Zeph. 3:5), and: "Morning by morning I [i.e., the Messiah] will destroy all the wicked in the land, cutting off all the evildoers from the city of the LORD" (Ps. 101:8).

Today, we live under the indirect government of Christ, which means that all sins committed under his rule are punished only at the end, either judicially or militarily (cf. Matt. 13:41; 16:27; 19:28; 25:31–46; 2 Cor. 5:10; 2 Tim. 4:1; Rev. 14:14–16; 19:11–21). In contrast with this, in the future Messianic kingdom gross evil will be punished immediately:

> I will rejoice in Jerusalem and be glad in my people; no more shall be heard in it the sound of weeping and the cry of distress. No more shall there be in it an infant who lives but a few days, or an old man who does not fill out his days, for the young man shall die a hundred years old, and *the sinner a hundred years old shall be accursed* (Isa. 65:19–20).[27]

12.5.3 Is the State Satanic?

In Christian thought, I see four main positions concerning the state.

(a) The state is neutral or secular, that is, it belongs to the common kingdom (this is the position of NL2K).

(b) In the state, the kingdom of Christ may become manifested in a

---

[27] In spite of verse 17 ("I create new heavens and a new earth"), this passage cannot refer to the eternal state in the New Testament sense because in that state there can no longer be any sinners on earth. Old Testament revelation in fact never extends back beyond the beginning (Gen. 1:1) and ahead beyond the end of time (the end of the Messianic kingdom).

transformationalist sense; through their cultural activities, Christians transform the present world into the world as it will be fully realized in the new heaven and new earth (this is the neo-Calvinistic position, usually linked with a certain cultural optimism as well as with amillennialism).

(c) In the state, the kingdom of Christ may become manifested, but in a non-transformationalist sense (this is my position, which is most similar to the neo-Calvinistic position, but without any triumphalism and cultural optimism, and with a more premillennialist approach, although the latter is not essential for my view of the state).

(d) The state is Satanic.

Let us now briefly look at this fourth position, which so far has not yet been mentioned.

Coming from a premillennial-fundamentalist background, I fully understand the origin of the fourth view (although I cannot agree with it). We need only look at what states and empires have left behind throughout history: a trail of blood, violence, war, oppression. Yet, what is said here of the state reminds us of what we discussed before concerning the term "the world" (§§5.1.2, 6.3, and 8.1.2). Satan is the ruler of this world (John 12:31; 14:30; 16:11), "following the course of this world" is "following the prince of the power of the air, the spirit that is now at work in the sons of disobedience" (Eph. 2:2), and "the whole world lies in the power of the evil one" (1 John 5:19). However, "the world" is *not* the same as "the state" or "society."

Again, we are dealing here with a confusion of structure and direction (see §§3.2.2 and 4.5). There are only two kingdoms in this world: the kingdom of Satan and the kingdom of God (Matt. 12:25–28). This distinction is, as it were, perpendicular to the various societal relationships. That is, in every marriage, every family, every school, every association, every political party, *and every state*, it is either the kingdom of Satan that is manifested (in many varieties: communism, fascism, extreme Islam, extreme Hinduism, extreme Buddhism, or simply Western [post]modernism), or the kingdom of God.

Unfortunately, in some countries it is a mixture of the two. But at least the state is never neutral. In the words of John Frame:

> Insofar as the Kline–Horton view[28] obscures the religious nature of our cultural and political issues, it confuses Christians as to their responsibilities. In the general society as well as in the church, Christians should settle for nothing less than the comprehensive

---

[28] Today we would say: the Kline–Horton–Hart–Stellman–VanDrunen view.

lordship of Jesus Christ. He is King of Kings and Lord of Lords [Rev. 19:16]. To say this is not to advocate violent revolution in Jesus' name. He has forbidden us to take that course. But by his word and Spirit, by his love, and by wise use of means available to us, we seek to exalt him, not only in the church, but in the whole world.[29]

In this last phrase, the word "world" means society, not "world" as we identified it above: the realm of sin and Satan. We exalt our great King in *all* domains of cosmic reality, ranging from the church to the state.

WORKING IT OUT: BIBLICAL ANSWERS TO POLITICAL PROBLEMS
Are there uniquely and specifically Christian (i.e., Bible-based) answers and approaches to matters of social, economic, and environmental policy?

If you would ask NL2K advocates, the answer would probably be somewhat like this: there are matters on which the Bible makes explicit statements, and to which (if they have been properly expounded) we are bound. For the rest, we have to satisfy ourselves with natural law (which apparently for many people may mean very different things) to guide life in the common kingdom, a natural law that we share with many unbelievers. Sound popular sentiments and logical arguments must do the job in a neutral, secular domain of life. The Bible plays no role here, except perhaps in implicitly shaping believers' private opinions.

My own answer is very different: there are matters on which the Bible makes explicit statements, and to which (if they have been properly expounded) we are bound. However, our Christian framework of thought does not stop here, but only begins here. Biblical data are integrated and elaborated within a rational but pre-theoretical Christian worldview. Such data may be of a physical, biotic, anthropic, psychic, social, environmental, historical, economic, aesthetic, judicial nature, and so forth. Again, these must be properly interpreted. For instance, social, economic, and judicial principles from the Mosaic Law cannot be naïvely transferred in a cut-and-paste fashion to our own time and circumstances. First, Mosaic commandments were meant for Israel, and were never imposed upon Gentile Jesus-believers (cf. Acts 15). Second, even if they were, we must carefully develop proper criteria in order to apply them to our situation.

---

[29] Frame (2011, 324).

If in this way we have adopted a Christian (rational but pre-theoretical) worldview, we have a foundation for pursuing a Christian (rational *and* theoretical) cosmology and epistemology. These function as a foundation for a Christian philosophy of nature, a Christian philosophy of culture, a Christian philosophy of humanity (philosophical anthropology), of psychic and social phenomena (the special philosophy [*vakfilosofie, Fachphilosophie*] of psychology and sociology), of language (the special philosophy of linguistics [*taalfilosofie, Sprachphilosophie*]), of history (the special philosophy of the historical sciences [*geschiedfilosofie, Geschichtsphilosophie*]), of economics, of aesthetics, of ethics [*moraalfilosofie, Moralphilosophie*], of religious phenomena [*godsdienstfilosofie, Religionsphilosophie*].[30]

In many respects, it would be pure biblicism to draw lines too easily and quickly from biblical data to the various special sciences. There is always some amount of philosophical reflection between the Bible and its scientific application. This is simply because all special sciences have their own foundational philosophies. If you want to pursue psychology or economics in a Christian way, this usually comes to light not so much in your methodology and practical experiments, but rather *in the Christian-philosophical prolegomena of such sciences*. I have worked this out in several smaller volumes for beginners.[31] We do not pursue the sciences in a different way than other scientists do, but we pursue them from different philosophical starting points.

Let me limit myself here to some practical examples, in connection with the three disciplines hinted at in the question asked at the head of this section: sociology, economics, and environmental sciences. Sociology is the discipline of social behaviour, or human behaviour in groups. An obvious example is marriage. Imagine a discussion within a political party, or within parliament, or within the government, about what constitutes a real marriage. For instance, imagine the discussion about legalizing marriage for homosexuals. Imagine you are an adherent of NL2K, and you are against such marriages. You are in a difficult position, because you must keep your mouth shut about your Christian principles! You must appeal to "natural law" or "sound popular sentiment" without ever referring to the Bible. You discover that your opponents appeal to "natural law" or "sound popular sentiment," too: they argue that homosexuality occurs in the animal kingdom, and is therefore natural. Or they argue that marriage is

---

[30] These Dutch and German terms show the greater succinctness with which these things can be expressed in these languages.

[31] Ouweneel (2014a; 2014b; 2014c; 2015; 2016a).

a legal contract that establishes rights and duties between spouses, and that it would be discrimination to withhold this from homosexuals who wish to share such rights and duties. Or they argue that, no matter how much you may be against marriages between homosexuals, you have no right to impose your views on other people.

There you are. It is on the tip of your tongue to shout: "This is against God's Word!" But no, NL2K advocates forbid you to do that. You must limit yourself to natural law, whatever this is. Natural law can be interpreted in many ways, as one pleases. Scripture interpretation is not easy, certainly not in the matter of homosexuality. Moreover, we are fully aware of the fact that there are a lot of practical aspects to this matter that our biblical view as such does not cover. But as a starting point for the discussion, a biblical view is ten times better than a vague appeal to some natural law. You must "always [be] prepared to make a defense to anyone who asks you for a reason for the hope that is in you" (1 Pet. 3:15), even within the party, the congress or parliament, and the government. Christians should not *impose* their views on unbelievers; but they should certainly freely *witness* to their beliefs to unbelievers.

Or take economics. Almost every textbook of economics has somewhere on its first pages the term "scarce" or "scarcity" (cf. §12.3.1). People have many desires, but goods are limited. However, Reformed economist Andries Keizer has suggested that a *Christian* economics does not begin with the notion of scarcity (in answer to people's unbridled greed), but with the notion of greed.[32] There is enough for everyone if people would just limit their covetousness. In other words, economics, as being one of the humanities (the sciences of human behaviour), should begin with a Christian-anthropological analysis. In this context, Keizer showed how the economy of ancient Israel prevented communism by allowing every Israelite his own private property, but also prevented extreme capitalism (in his case: landlordism, the formation of huge estates) because in the year of jubilee all properties had to return to the original owners (Lev. 25). Thus, the greed of the state was checked (there was hardly any state property), and the greed of the large landowners was checked as well. Christian economics is not the science of scarcity, but of anti-greed.

Or take the environment. Imagine you are a Christian, which means that all your thinking about the environment is governed by your Christian view of God's good creation and of good human stewardship ("keeping" God's creation). But imagine you are also an adherent of NL2K, convinced

---

[32] Keizer (1986).

that, in the public square, you can *never* appeal to God's good creation and
our stewardship under God in your theory. You are bound to natural law,
so you come up with all kinds of pragmatic and utilitarian arguments why
we should be good to the environment. You have to appeal to the responsibility we have to our grandchildren when it comes to leaving behind a
deteriorated or improved environment, but you can never appeal to our
responsibility toward the Creator.

One of the candidates in the 2016 American presidential election suggested that, if he were to become president, he would annul the agreement
reached at the 2015 United Nations Climate Change Conference because
the measures suggested would be bad for American industry. Whether you
support such an action or not, consider the poles of the argument, earth
vs. industry. Can you imagine? The greed of today is more important than
the climate of tomorrow. It is easier to become president with the help of
the large industries than to feel responsible for the environment of the
coming decades.

Now, how would you respond to this in the public square? You come
up with your arguments from natural law. You bring up the best possible
pragmatic and utilitarian answers. But, if you are an NL2K adherent, you
are never allowed to say, *This is not what the Creator expects of us.* To put it
in stronger words, if you are an NL2K adherent, you must even believe that
God himself does not want you to speak up for him in the public square.
You may do that in church, or at home, but in society, especially in politics,
God himself *forbids* you to stand up for his honour. Why? Because God
himself supposedly instituted the common kingdom, a neutral, secular
sphere where believers and unbelievers work together. Well, even if there
were such a kingdom—which I firmly deny—then I still do not see why
Christians could not tell their unbelieving colleagues that *they* believe in a
Creator, in God's good creation, and in *their* responsibility toward this God
in preserving this creation as well as possible, as good stewards.

Such Christians do atheists and agnostics the greatest favour conceivable: in the public square they keep their mouths shut about their beliefs!
We do not want to cooperate in this unbiblical attitude. We keep telling the
adulterous leaders of this world: "It is not lawful for you [i.e., it is against
God's law] to have your neighbor's wife," like John the Baptist did (cf. Mark
6:18), even if it may cost us our head (as it did for John). We keep telling the
(political) world: Adultery, fornication, homosexuality, etc., are not what
the Creator had in mind when he created sexuality and instituted marriage.
Or, God does not want a society dominated by human greed. Or, God does
not want us to neglect the environment (God's good creation) only to satisfy

our short-term greed. To whose advantage is it if we are not allowed to proclaim in public: abortion is *sin*, homosexual behaviour is *sin*, greedy economics is *sin*, environmental neglect is *sin*? Is this to the honour of God, or does it rather play into the hands of the ruler of this world, Satan?

I hope and trust and pray that many Christians will not be prevented or intimidated by NL2K advocates from continuing to bear witness in the public square concerning God, his commandments, and his creation, and that they will continue to appeal to politicians concerning their deepest beliefs. Politicians, too, must one day "appear before the judgment seat of Christ, so that each one may receive what is due for what he has done in the body, whether good or evil" (cf. 2 Cor. 5:10). Let us not become weary of reminding the magistrates of this. As Paul wrote to Timothy:

> I charge you in the presence of God and of Christ Jesus, *who is to judge the living and the dead, and by his appearing and his kingdom: preach the word; be ready in season and out of season*; reprove, rebuke, and exhort, with complete patience and teaching. For the time is coming when people will not endure sound teaching, but having itching ears they will accumulate for themselves teachers to suit their own passions, and will turn away from listening to the truth and wander off into myths. As for you, always be sober-minded, endure suffering, do the work of an evangelist, fulfill your ministry (2 Tim. 4:1–5).

Old King Solomon said back in his day,

> Wisdom cries aloud in the *street*, in the *markets* she raises her voice [today we would add, not only in church]; at the head of the noisy *streets* she cries out; at the entrance of the *city gates* she speaks: "How long, O simple ones, will you love being simple? How long will scoffers delight in their scoffing and fools hate knowledge? Because they hated knowledge and did not choose the fear of the LORD...therefore they shall eat the fruit of their way...but whoever listens to me will dwell secure and will be at ease, without dread of disaster" (Prov. 1:20–22, 29, 31, 35).

To this he added:

> Wisdom has built her house.... She has sent out her young women to call *from the highest places in the town*, "Whoever is simple, let him turn in here...! Come, eat of my bread and drink of the wine I have mixed.

Leave your simple ways, and live, and walk in the way of insight....
Give instruction to a wise man, and he will be still wiser; teach a
righteous man, and he will increase in learning. The fear of the LORD
is the beginning of wisdom, and the knowledge of the Holy One is
insight. For by me your days will be multiplied, and years will be added
to your life" (9:1, 3–6, 9–11).

Divine wisdom is not just for the church; it is for all people. They need
divine wisdom in their churches, their marriages, their families, their
schools, their businesses, their associations, their political parties. In *all*
these societal relationships, *all* people need to learn that "the fear of the
LORD is the beginning of wisdom" (cf. Job 28:29; Ps. 111:10; Prov. 1:7; 15:33).
Therefore, let us freely and boldly proclaim God's wisdom to all people, for
all domains of life, so that they will receive a "heart of wisdom" (Ps. 90:12),
not just with regard to the way of salvation, but for their entire lives.

APPENDICES

APPENDIX 1
FOUNDATIONALISM VERSUS FIDEISM

The reader may have noticed that I have criticized not only the Klinean approach, but the Kuyperian approach as well. The latter also involves Reformed theologian and philosopher of Dutch origin, Cornelius Van Til (d. 1987), who has had an enormous influence on North American Reformed thinking. In my view, Van Til also failed to develop a proper view of the premises of both theology and the other special sciences. To show this, let me briefly describe here the well-known conflict between foundationalism and fideism.[1]

1. *Foundationalism*: truth—the truth of God, or truth in general—rests on a fixed, unassailable, axiomatic foundation. Although this is seldom mentioned, this foundation is of an emphatically *immanent* nature. Here we find in juxtaposition to each other:

(a) *Presuppositionalism*: faith is founded on clear and obvious presuppositions of a rational nature. This view goes back to Aristotle and Thomas Aquinas, and in more modern times to the French philosopher, René Descartes (d. 1650), who built his entire philosophy on what to him was

---

[1] Good introductions are White (1994; especially on C. Van Til, F. A. Schaeffer, C. F. H. Henry, D. A. Bloesch, and M. J. Erickson); the articles in *Modern Reformation* (March/April 1997); Cortois and Van Herck (1999); House and Jowers (2011).

an "evident" axiom: *Cogito, ergo sum*, "I think, therefore I am." Truth is considered to be a pyramid, in which one truth is deduced from the other, built on one or more axiomatic truths. These axioms are for all thinking people immediately obvious truths (think of Euclid's geometrical system). Recent representatives in theology were or are American theologians Cornelius Van Til,[2] Francis A. Schaeffer (d. 1984), Rousas J. Rushdoony (d. 2001), and Greg L. Bahnsen (d. 1995). The most important axiomatic presupposition is here Scripture as the Word of God; allegedly, one who starts from the authority of Scripture will come automatically to a knowledge of the truth.

(b) *Evidentialism*: faith is *not* founded on rational presuppositions but on empirical evidences; what is accepted as true is only what rests upon facts that are observable to everyone. This view does not automatically lead to empiricism or naturalism. On the contrary, this kind of empirical evidence—think of the resurrection of Christ (on the basis of the empty tomb and the testimonies of witnesses), prophecies fulfilled thus far, or striking radical conversions—is also used as evidence in apologetics. According to this view, truth is not found deductively, like in (a) above, but inductively: one moves from individual facts to general principles. In philosophy, this view goes back to British empiricism. Recent representatives in theology were and are American theologians John H. Gerstner (d. 1996), John W. Montgomery (b. 1931), Norman L. Geisler (b. 1932), Richard Swinburne (b. 1934), Josh McDowell (b. 1939), R. C. Sproul (b. 1939), and William L. Craig (b. 1949).[3]

2. *Non-Foundationalism*:[4] truth and apologetics are based not on (immanent) reason, nor on (immanent) observation, but on faith, that is, faith in either the irrational or the suprarational sense. Some people speak of the *post-foundationalist* task of theology now that it has become clear that, strictly speaking, Van Tilian presuppositionalism and Gerstnerian evidentialism can no longer be maintained.5 We distinguish between:

(a) *Fideism*: in line with (pre-)existentialism, especially Danish philosopher Søren Kierkegaard (d. 1855), faith is viewed here as an *irrational* condition for all knowledge of the truth—Kierkegaard's well-known "leap into the dark"5—which stands in opposition to reason. We are dealing here

[2] Van Til (1955; 1969).

[3] E.g., Montgomery (2003); Geisler and Turek (2004); Swinburne (2005); Craig (2008); Geisler (2009).

[4] See, e.g., Thiel (2000). Van Huyssteen (1997) and Shults (1999, *The Postfoundationalist Task of Theology: Wolfhart Pannenberg and the New Theological Rationality*); cf. Grenz and Franke (2001).

5 Kierkegaard (1980).

with a genuine *sacrificium intellectus* ("sacrifice of the intellect"), which goes all the way back to the way early Roman Christian thinker Tertullian (d. c. 225) and medieval British Christian thinker William of Ockham (d. 1347) linked faith with the absurd.

(b) The *Reformational epistemology* of American philosophers Alvin Plantinga (b. 1932), Nicholas Wolterstorff (b. 1932), and others:[6] truth begins with faith, but not an immanent faith that can be based primarily on reason or observation, nor an irrational faith. This view is closely related to the Christian-philosophical view that I have summarized elsewhere and that goes back to Dutch thinkers Herman Dooyeweerd (d. 1977) and Dirk H. Th. Vollenhoven (d. 1978), both of whom were Reformed.[7] Faith in the sense of *fides qua* ("the faith by which we believe") is neither rational, nor irrational, but suprarational. Therefore, faith does not stand *in opposition* to reason and observation, but only in opposition to the absolutization of it in presuppositionalism and evidentialism, respectively. Plantinga and Wolterstorff try to make this faith acceptable by appealing to the natural awareness of God that all humans supposedly possess.

The significance of such an approach for our present purpose is that this notion of human *suprarational* (transcendent, existential) faith helps us understand how both theology and all the other special sciences are rooted, not just in reason or empirical observation, but in the human heart, or Ego, this transcendent (suprarational and supra-empirical) center of human personality. And this heart is either born again and under the influence of the Holy Spirit, or it is in the grip of one or more apostatic impulses. As soon as this is recognized, we see that the nature of *any* science—not only theology—is either basically God-oriented or basically apostatic. In the works that I have now mentioned several times, I have attempted to explain that, if there cannot be a Christian biology or psychology or economics, there can be no Christian theology either. This insight may alone be sufficient to eliminate the scholastic splitting of reality into a sacred realm and a common realm.

---

[6] E.g., Wolterstorff (1988; 1995); Plantinga (2000); Plantinga and Wolterstorff (2009); and responses to this approach: Zagzebski (1993); also see Beilby (2006).

[7] Ouweneel (2013; 2014a).

MATTHEW TUININGA AND TWO KINGDOMS: IDIOSYNCRASY, INSTABILITY, AND INJURY

If at this point the reader still remains unpersuaded that NL2K is unhelpful for Christian living today, perhaps paying attention to the position(s) of one of its more public and articulate spokesmen may be useful.

Matthew Tuininga is the newly appointed[1] Assistant Professor of Moral Theology at Calvin Theological Seminary in Grand Rapids, Michigan. He has vigorously and publicly defended much of what I have been criticizing in this volume. For my analysis of Tuininga's position, two particular sources are very important, which consist of two public, somewhat popularized explanations of his views on "the two kingdoms."[2] What makes these sources unusually important is that Tuininga is seeking to explain his view of NL2K in a very plain and popular manner within a church context,

---

[1] September 2015.
[2] See Tuininga (2012; 2015).

aimed at being accessible to the ordinary church member. This format contrasts with the literary or academic explanations with which we have been interacting thus far.

I am characterizing Tuininga's view of NL2K as "idiosyncratic" because I have heard no other advocate explain or set it out in the way Tuininga does. Although various elements of Tuininga's explanation are presented by various representatives of NL2K, his exposition and application(s) remain *sui generis* (one of a kind).

I am also characterizing Tuininga's view as "unstable," principally because he uses an identical explanation of NL2K both to reject women's ordination to church office and to defend women's ordination.

This instability serves to illustrate clearly how dangerous and damaging NL2K can be to the church of Jesus Christ.

2.1 "THE TWO KINGDOMS" AS ESCHATOLOGICAL CONSTRUCT

Until now, I have been vigorously criticizing the notion that a common kingdom exists alongside the kingdom of God. For most NL2K advocates, the common kingdom is that place or realm within culture where secular, neutral activities occur under the rule of reason and natural law. The sacred kingdom is the church, which lives in the world under the rule of faith and the gospel.

For Tuininga, by contrast, the phrase and concept of "two kingdoms" refer not to two realms of life, nor to two domains of activity, nor to church and state, but these refer to "two ages:" the present age and the age to come. The present age is governed by the laws of creation, of providence, of reason, and of prudence. The age to come is governed by the law of Christ, by the gospel, by the principles of the new creation. For Tuininga, "the two kingdoms" is an *eschatological construct.*

The present age began after the Fall of humanity, and will continue until Christ returns. The new age began with the resurrection of Christ from the dead, and will continue into eternity future. Currently, then, there is an overlap of these two ages, insofar as the new age has already now become a reality with the finished work of Jesus Christ. This overlap means that Christians experience a tension throughout all of their life and activities in the world. This is the tension that many theologians describe with the phrase "already–not yet." This means that salvation is "already" present, but "not yet" completed. The kingdom of God has "already" begun, but is "not yet" completed. As a result, believers experience the tension between their continuing sin and fallenness, on the one hand, amid the in-breaking newness of divine grace, on the other hand.

However, in Tuininga's model, these two ages (the present age and the age to come) seem never to intersect each other in a way that would affect the world of everyday living. Because of their respective natures, governments, and durability, these two ages exist separately and remain separate. For the Christian, life in the present age belongs to the secular (the here-and-now) kingdom characterized by provisionality, temporariness, this-worldliness, and finiteness. For the Christian, life in the age to come is characterized by eternity, the reality of heaven, and the infinite permanence of all things made new in Christ.

To avoid all misunderstanding and mischaracterization of Tuininga's views, here are his own words, spoken in June 2012 in a United Reformed Church context:

> First, the two kingdoms doctrine is not about two realms, and it is not about two spheres. I have seen professors at Calvin College—one recently writing in the *Calvin Theological Journal*—get this wrong because they think it's about two realms, and then they think that must mean, "Oh, two spheres, just like Kuyper."
>
> This is not about two spheres. It is not about two airtight sections of life that you're keeping apart from each other as if Christ's only relevant to one and not the other. That's not what this is about.
>
> It is about two ages and two governments. It's about the present age, the age of creation before Christ's second coming, and the age to come, the kingdom of God. And then it's about the two governments that God has appointed to govern or order those ages: the political government of this age and the ministry of the Word and sacraments, which is the way Christ governs the kingdom of God that brings people into the age to come.

Notice, in this explanation, that the political government rules this age, and the ministry of the church rules the kingdom of God.

2.2 TUININGA'S "TWO KINGDOMS" AND WOMEN'S ORDINATION: 2012 VERSUS 2015

This eschatological construct of "the two kingdoms" does not mean that the new age has no relevance for Christian living in the present age. Quite the contrary. As new creatures in Christ, Christians live all of life before the face of God, in the power of the Holy Spirit, growing to be conformed more and more in the image of God in Christ.

Specifically and concretely, Tuininga has offered a number of examples of how his view would be applied to issues and problems in today's world.

One particular example will interest Reformed and Presbyterian believers in a special way, since this issue has been so divisive and contentious in their churches for the past thirty years. It is the issue of women's ordination to offices of leadership authority (teaching and ruling authority) in the church.

In connection with Tuininga's application of his own views, I am relying on the transcripts of two public events—one an address he gave at a church (June 8, 2012, Trinity United Reformed Church), the other a synodical interview for a teaching job at Calvin Theological Seminary (June 15, 2015, Christian Reformed Church synod). In each of these forums, Tuininga answered the same question: "May women exercise ruling authority in the church?"

But he gave two very different and contradictory answers, *each time with an appeal to his eschatological construct of "the two kingdoms."*

So, then, it would seem fair to claim that, if a theological construct can be used in defense of two contradictory applications, then that construct is implausible, unstable, and very unhelpful to the church.

Here is Tuininga's first answer: "No, women may not exercise ruling authority in the church." This answer was part of his 2012 speech given at Trinity United Reformed Church, in Caledonia, Michigan (38:00–39:15).

> Another example: gender roles in the church. The Bible teaches clearly that there is no male nor female in Christ Jesus. These things have no eternal significance in Christ, in that sense. So liberals are on good exegetical ground, then, aren't they, when they say that therefore we should allow women's ordination and we should throw out gender roles. If there's only one kingdom, if all of life is to conform right now without qualification with the kingdom of God, we should be ordaining women to all the offices of the church, and women should not be submitting to their husbands any more than the husbands submit to their wives.
>
> But what do you do about the fact that Scripture also says other things about those? That there are qualifications for office based on gender in the church? That wives are to submit to husbands? It seems as if there's rules for this age that aren't exactly the same thing as the kingdom to come. How do you make sense of that?
>
> Again, if you say there's only one kingdom, you've got to choose. And I would submit to you that if you do that, if you force yourself

to choose, you end up either being a legalist—you're a legalist if you go with the rules of this age and say that's your ultimate identity. If you say to a woman in the church, "Your ultimate identity is as a wife submissive to your husband," then you're a legalist. Then you're forcing her to conform to a set of rules and laws that she's going to fail.

Although his answer does not seem altogether clear and lucid, given his audience and context, we may conclude that in 2012, Tuininga was using his version of "the two kingdoms" to *disallow* women's ordination in the church.

When we come to 2015, however, one hears from his lips the opposite answer to the same question. In a synodical interview for a job at Calvin Theological Seminary, Tuininga was asked specifically about his view on women in ministry (54:22–57:50).

This time, in his answer, he first appeals to John Calvin's view of two kingdoms, suggesting that Calvin distinguished between moral and spiritual issues, on the one hand, and church polity issues, on the other hand. In Tuininga's opinion, regarding the first, Calvin insisted that there may be no compromise; regarding the second, Calvin noted that these issues can be influenced by circumstances and guided by prudence. Tuininga goes on, then, to claim: "And he [Calvin] unequivocally, explicitly puts women's roles in the church in the latter category." This means that gender roles in the church were, for John Calvin, matters of adiaphora (things that are morally indifferent), governed by prudence and reason.

Near 56:43 in the audio recording of his CRC interview, Tuininga claims that Calvin taught that whatever gender differences do exist here and now, for example, with respect to marriage, procreation, etc., they are temporal, and are going to be transcended in the kingdom of God. On the basis of these considerations, Tuininga has now come to accept women exercising authority in the church. This time (2015, CRC), Tuininga was using his version of "the two kingdoms" to *justify* women's ordination in the church.

2.3 CALVIN THE VENTRILOQUIST?

My question is simple: Are Tuininga's claims accurate, and is his most recent application of "the two kingdoms" doctrine, which was part of his job interview, faithful to John Calvin? In other words, did Calvin assign the matter of women exercising teaching authority in the church to the realm of church polity guided by circumstances and prudence?

Read, and decide for yourself. In his commentary on 2 Timothy 2:11–12, Calvin registers the following observations:

11 *Let a woman learn in quietness.* After having spoken of dress, he now adds with what modesty women ought to conduct themselves in the holy assembly. And first he bids them learn quietly; for quietness means silence, that they may not take upon them to speak in public. This he immediately explains more clearly, by forbidding them to teach.

12 *But I suffer not a woman to teach.* Not that he takes from them the charge of instructing their family, but only excludes them from the office of teaching, which God has committed to men only. On this subject we have explained our views in the exposition of the First Epistle to the Corinthians. If any one bring forward, by way of objection, Deborah (Judges 4:4) and others of the same class, of whom we read that they were at one time appointed by the command of God to govern the people, the answer is easy. Extraordinary acts done by God do not overturn the ordinary rules of government, by which he intended that we should be bound. Accordingly, if women at one time held the office of prophets and teachers, and that too when they were supernaturally called to it by the Spirit of God, He who is above all law might do this; but, being a peculiar case, this is not opposed to the constant and ordinary system of government.[3]

When Calvin refers to "the constant and ordinary system of government," it seems highly unlikely that he is relegating gender roles in the church to the realm of adiaphora. Clearly, Calvin affirms that God has entrusted the office of teaching to men only.

2.4   NL2K INJURES THE CHURCH

What we have seen, then, is the very same explanation of NL2K used to defend contradictory applications to living in the church.

Just as natural law is so flexible and unstable as to permit contradictory applications (such as: homosexual conduct is right and it is wrong), so too NL2K is far too flexible and unstable for Christians to lean on it for guidance and help in living their faith in today's world.

---

[3] John Calvin, *Commentary on Timothy, Titus, Philemon*, electronic version, http://www.ccel.org/ccel/calvin/calcom43.iii.iv.iv.html.

APPENDIX 3
THE REPUBLICATION HYPOTHESIS

3.1 AN ALLEGED COVENANT OF WORKS

One of the doctrines of NL2K, which I am calling "the republication hypothesis," lies a bit outside the many problems dealt with in the present book. Yet, I mention it here in an appendix because it is so characteristic of NL2K confessionalism. Of course, we cannot review the entire "Escondido theology" within the scope of this book, but the "republication hypothesis" seems to take up a special position. It has been called the "hermeneutical linchpin" to so much of the Escondido project that a few words about it may be appropriate. Actually, I have dealt with the matter extensively in my forthcoming volume on the Covenant, and also mention the matter in my forthcoming volume on the Torah in connection with the "law vs. gospel" ideas of Escondido.[1] I would suggest that these two volumes together with the present book form a rather full treatise on, and refutation of, the unbiblical Escondido theology.

---

[1] Ouweneel (2016g; 2016f).

Basically there are only *two* covenants that have been made specifically with Israel, though with a view to all of humanity. These are the "Old (Sinaitic) Covenant" and the "New Covenant" of Jeremiah 31:31–34, which is nothing but a renewal of the Old Covenant. *Both* are called an "everlasting" covenant because the Old Covenant was never annulled (cf. Matt. 5:17) but merges into the New Covenant.[2]

In general this corresponds with the traditional Reformed terminological inventions of the "covenant of works" (allegedly established initially with prelapsarian Adam, but "republished"—as the expression goes[3]—on Mount Sinai) and the "covenant of grace," both in all kinds of variations. I apologize for the word "inventions;" I am merely echoing the anonymous opponent of Reformed theologian Alexander Comrie (d. 1774), who claimed that the covenant of works was "newly invented" and in that time was "held to be the Shibboleth and slogan of Orthodoxy."[4] Comrie defended himself against these accusations, not so much with biblical arguments—that would be difficult anyway because Scripture does not know the term "covenant of works"—but by appealing to former theologians: Johannes Cocceius, Johannes Cloppenburg, and Johannes Piscator.[5]

In the broadest sense, the covenant of works is the name for any divine covenant in which God's demands of obedience are the alleged condition for receiving true life (adherents point to Lev. 18:5; Deut. 6:24–25; Neh. 9:29; Ezek. 18:9; 20:11–13; Amos 5:4, 6, 14; cf. Luke 10:28; Rom. 10:5; Gal. 3:12). The proponents of this idea believe that this covenant existed before the Fall, but some Reformed theologians, today especially NL2K advocates, believe that it received its form particularly in the Sinaitic covenant. They speak of the "republication" of the covenant of works on Mount Sinai. In the covenant of works, the gift of life is made to depend on human good works, whereas in the covenant of grace it is thought to depend purely on God's grace. Thus, the Old and the New Covenant are contrasted as the covenants in which everything depended on Man, or everything depended on God, respectively.

According to newer investigations, in which especially the Jewish explanation of the Sinaitic covenant has been studied and better understood, such

---

[2] See Ouweneel (2016f, chapter 4).

[3] Or "re-enacted"; cf. Hodge (1998, 433): "the law of Moses was a re-enactment of the covenant of works." Cf. Owen (1991, 70–78): the Mosaic covenant "is no other but the covenant of works revived.... Yea, in sundry things it re-enforced, established, and confirmed that covenant."

[4] See Ouweneel (2016g, §5.3.3).

[5] Graafland (1996, 363–64).

a view of the Sinaitic covenant as a covenant of works can now be considered as largely mistaken.[6] However, I have to say that among theologians, only a very few Reformed ones seem prepared to accept this evaluation. Apparently, the terms "covenant of works" and "covenant of grace" are too deeply embedded in the Reformed mindset; moreover, they have been solidified in perpetuity in the Westminster Standards. As a consequence, those who wish to call themselves true Presbyterians are bound to the "covenant of works" idea because of these Standards. (Incidentally, the three Forms of Unity do not mention a "covenant of works," although the Canons of Dort do speak of a "covenant of grace.")

Recently, the entire issue has become more urgent through the report on "republication" by the Orthodox Presbyterian Church in North America.[7] In this report, the notion of the "covenant of works" is taken for granted, so that not much good may be expected of the report. As Mark Karlberg recently wrote: "Though acknowledging that Scripture, not the *Westminster Standards*, has the last word in theological disputes, *in point of fact the [OPC] report reverses the priority, giving first place to the confessional teaching*."[8]

3.2 WAS THERE A COVENANT OF WORKS AT SINAI?

In my view, the idea of a *conditional* "covenant of works" versus an *unconditional* "covenant of grace" must be viewed as one-sided, if not simply wrong. In a certain sense, the Old Covenant is both a conditional and an unconditional covenant, and precisely the same holds for the New Covenant.[9] On the one hand, the Old Covenant, too, was rooted in God's redeeming grace. This becomes apparent already in the prologue (according to the Jewish enumeration: Word 1) to the Ten Words: "I am the LORD your God, who brought you out of the land of Egypt, out of the house of slavery" (Exod. 20:2; Deut. 5:6). All the subsequent nine Words must be seen in this light: they belong to a nation already delivered. The grace character becomes visible also in the mercy that God bestowed upon his people after they had broken the covenant, immediately after its establishment (Exod. 32–34). The Old Covenant was primarily a covenant of grace, with love that came basically from only one side.[10]

---

[6] See extensively, Ouweneel (2016f).
[7] https://www.opc.org/GA/republication.html.
[8] Karlberg (2016, 1); italics original.
[9] Cf. Wellum (2012, 608): "Viewing the biblical covenants as either unconditional or conditional is not quite right."
[10] H. D. Leuner in Kac (1986, 177); cf. Niell (2003, 133–36).

This grace was manifested most clearly in the sacrificial ministry: Israel stood before God on the basis not of its good works, but of the pleasing aroma of the daily burnt offerings (carefully read Exod. 29:38–46). If the Ten Words had been violated, the people could be restored in their communion with God through the sin offerings, which God himself had instituted as the way of restoration (Lev. 4–5; see especially 16:15–16, *Yom Kippur*, the "Day of Atonement"). This was the whole essence and function of the tabernacle (Exod. 25–27): it was God's dwelling place in the midst of Israel, as well as the place where the people could come near to him on the basis of the sacrifices, *not* on the basis of their "good works." It was a "tent of *meeting*" between God and his people, and its associated ministry was the only basis on which the people could stand before him: the ministry of sacrifice. Under the Old Covenant, Israel *never* stood before God on the basis of their own good works but only on the basis of God's grace. In other words, the *allegedly conditional* "covenant of works" is based on God's *unconditional* grace.

Conversely, the *New* Covenant is not *just* a covenant of grace; that is, it is *not* without responsible obedience. The very least is that entering into the New Covenant demands obedience to God's call for repentance (Deut. 30:1–10; cf. Ezek. 36:24–31); see more extensively my volume on the Covenant.

3.3 NO NATURAL LAW

The idea of an innate or natural law (see chapter 4 in the present book) is closely related to the republication hypothesis, according to which the essence of the Mosaic Law (the "moral law") was written in the hearts of the Israelites, as supposedly it had been written in the hearts of Adam and Eve. This notion did not make it into the Three Forms of Unity, but it did make it into the Westminster Standards, especially the Westminster Larger Catechism (answers 92, 93, and 98) and the Westminster Confession of Faith (4.2). In both cases—Eden and Sinai—the nature of the alleged "covenant of works" is thought to be the same: obedience to the "moral law" would bring righteousness (justification) by works.

Scripture nowhere says that Adam and Eve had "the law of God written in their hearts." The WCF refers here to Romans 2:14, which, first, does not speak of Adam and Eve, but of pagans, and, second, does not say that the pagans have the law of God written in their hearts, but the *work* of the law (see extensively §§4.1–4.2).

This entire notion of an innate law that allegedly came to Israel in the form of the Ten Commandments is basically foolish. At best, one can imagine that non-fallen people—and even some fallen people—may have a natural idea that it is wrong to kill or to steal, and even to commit adultery, because these are not in their own interest. If I were allowed to kill, to steal, or to commit adultery, then others are equally allowed to kill *me*, to steal from *me*, to touch *my wife*. It is also in people's own interest to honour their parents because (a) children are dependent on their parents—so you better show them respect—and (b) if we honour our parents, our children will honour *us*.

However, what innate law could ever teach a person that he has to observe the seventh day of the week? At best, intelligent people might come up with the idea that it would be wise to have a day of rest once in a while. But why every *seventh* day? And why such an absolute rest of household members, servants, and even cattle? Moreover, this was not for health reasons at all, but because "in six days the LORD made heaven and earth, the sea, and all that is in them, and rested on the seventh day" (Exod. 20:11), and because "you were a slave in the land of Egypt, and the LORD your God brought you out from there with a mighty hand and an outstretched arm" (Deut. 5:15). Certainly no innate law could ever have told us that. In my view, this is precisely why the Sabbath commandment is repeated so often (Exod. 16:23-29; 31:13–16; 35:2–3; Lev. 19:3, 30; 23:3; 26:2). Even the greatest sinners have a minimal sense of the wrong of stealing and killing—at least among themselves—but there is nothing obvious or self-evident about the Sabbath commandment. That is why it has been repeated time and again. Israel had to observe it, not because it was self-evident, or even because it was healthy, but because God told them to, for redemptive-historical reasons.

But then, does not the same hold for the first of the Ten Commandments? Theologians have often discussed the question of how far there is some innate sense of God in every human, also after the Fall. Even if there is such a sense of divinity (*sensus divinitatis*, as Calvin called it, or *semen religionis* ["seed of religion"]) in people, why would they necessarily acknowledge only one God ("You shall have no other gods before me")? By far most pagan nations worshiped many gods. Besides, what innate law would tell people, even non-fallen people, that they are not supposed to make a "carved image, or any likeness of anything" in heaven or on earth, whether of the one God or of the false gods? We know all these things because God revealed them to us. There is no such thing as an innate law that could have taught us these duties.

The Reformed (!) theologian Cornelis Van der Waal concludes:

The fact that seventeenth century Puritans have actually made Adam into just such a rational creature, who with the innate divine and legal knowledge could work out his own salvation, has played into the hands of [secular philosopher René] Descartes and of rationalism, as well as of work-holiness and of a perfectionism, but in fact it has strained the *gospel*.[11]

The point I wish to make again is this: *it is very difficult to convince people of wrong theological theories if these theories have made it all the way into their cherished creeds and catechisms.* Reformed Christians who adhere to the Three Forms of Unity are blessed. They may have their own reasons to defend notions such as the "covenant of works" and the "moral law," but at least they are not obligated to defend their creeds and catechisms on these matters. For Presbyterian Christians the situation is far more difficult because a refutation of the ideas in question affects the confessional ground on which they stand. For many Christians, who often are not unwilling to consider new ideas, this is almost unthinkable when it comes to ideas that fundamentally deviate from their creeds and catechisms.

3.4   A CASE STUDY

The "republication" controversy is of such a nature that, "it is claimed, the very integrity of the gospel is at stake."[12] The two sides of the present conflict have recently been described in two publications, one of which presents both sides.[13] The basic nature of the controversy is not so much the interpretation of Scripture but of the Westminster Standards: one party speaks of "The Faithful Plumb Line of the Westminster Confession of Faith,"[14] and the other party would probably agree. At stake are not the Westminster Standards themselves, but the interpretations of it and inferences from it.

Central to the controversy is the supposed "covenant of works." As I said, I do not accept the notion of a "covenant of works;" it is basically unscriptural, and I am thankful that there are also Reformed theologians who have come to the same conclusion. But for the genuine Westminsterians this is unacceptable, of course, because the "covenant of works" is taught in the Westminster

---

[11] Ouweneel (2008a, 54–55).
[12] W. Shishko in Elam et al. (2014, viii).
[13] Estelle et al. (2009); Elam et al. (2014).
[14] Elam et al. (2014, 38; cf. 39: "This plumb line has served as a faithful standard for faith and life for hundreds of years").

Standards, and these are "a faithful summary of the teaching of Scripture."[15] What happened at Westminster Theological Seminary (Philadelphia) was that several of its professors, such as John Murray, Norman Shepherd, and Meredith Kline,[16] deviated from the Westminster Standards in the eyes of their opponents. Their teachings "all need to be evaluated in light of, and measured against, the standard of this plumb line."[17]

Now I can imagine that those loyal to the Westminster Standards have great difficulty with the twofold notion, propagated by Meredith Kline and his disciples, of a "covenant of works" that was "republished" (or, reaffirmed) at Mount Sinai. Thus, the Sinaitic covenant comes to be viewed in some sense as a "covenant of works." In my view, the idea of a "covenant of works" is objectionable, but this "republication" theory is even worse. However, most critics of Kline's ideas fail to recognize that his erroneous teachings cannot be successfully opposed if their own criticisms also arise within a framework that holds to the doctrine of the "covenant of works."

What is even more shocking is the way the two parties accuse each other of jeopardizing the gospel. Kline's disciples claim that a rejection of the "republication" theory "will only leave us necessarily impoverished in our faith. We will see in only a thin manner the work of our Savior."[18] The opponents of the Klinean approach use similar strong language: "Ironically, the republication teaching, which was intended to preserve and protect the doctrine of justification, may (when consistently worked out) actually undercut this doctrine—the very doctrine by which the church stands or falls."[19] Allegedly at stake is not only the gospel, but, according to both parties, Reformed doctrine as well. Those advocating the "republication" doctrine insist that it "is part of the warp and woof of Scripture and sound doctrine," that is, Reformed doctrine.[20]

I myself see a few positive elements in Murray's teaching, the first of which is his allowance for a measure of grace in the covenant with prelapsarian Adam. His opponents cannot live with that; they prefer to limit the term "grace" to "specifically redemptive grace"—which, in my view, is a mistake.[21] Second, Murray wondered whether one can use the term "covenant" at all

---

[15] Ibid., 19.
[16] Some relevant publications: Murray (1954); Shepherd (2000); Kline (2006); see the brief summary by Karlberg (2016, 1–4).
[17] Elam et al. (2014, 19).
[18] Estelle et al. (2009, 19).
[19] Elam et al. (2014, 3–4).
[20] Estelle at al. (2009, 6).
[21] Elam et al. (2014, 18); see Ouweneel (2016g, §3.6).

for the prelapsarian situation. Yet, Murray maintained that prelapsarian Adam "was under obligation to perform perfect, personal obedience to the commandments as the legal basis of his attainment of the reward of life."[22] Norman Shepherd considered this to be an error: he saw "no place at all left for a covenant of works or meritorious human obedience."[23] Kline disagreed with both Murray and Shepherd, and even described their views as an "encroachment of this radical renunciation of the Reformation, this subtle surrender to Rome."[24] To complicate matters even further, some opponents of Murray and Shepherd also disagree with Kline.

A controversy like this makes one so very unhappy, since one can distinguish at least four parties, and one cannot agree with any them *because they all operate within the same paradigm embedded in the Westminster Standards.* We must take issue with the very *roots* of this paradigm; from wrong roots one can expect not only wrong fruits, but also heated controversies *between* these wrong fruits. The reason is that, if certain fruits are wrong, this is often discerned by other thinkers—but if these theologians are working within the same paradigm they necessarily combat these wrong fruits with other wrong weapons. The problem does not lie first of all with Murray, Shepherd, Kline, NL2K, or their opponents—in my view, the basic problems lie in the Westminster Standards themselves (more than in the Three Forms of Unity). As long as these Standards as such are not questioned—and in the Presbyterian world this is virtually impossible—new controversies, sometimes followed by new church divisions, will keep emerging.

3.5 AGAIN: THE SINAITIC COVENANT

In conclusion, *the Reformed distinction between the covenant of works and the covenant of grace is invalid.* We see this most clearly in all the meaningless discussions on the question whether the Sinaitic covenant was a covenant of works or a covenant of grace, or in a sense both at the same time, and whether the Sinaitic covenant involved a "republication" of the covenant of works, or not. Or even worse: "the covenant of redemption...was for Christ a covenant of works rather than a covenant of grace"[25]—as if there was a "covenant" between God and Jesus, and as if Jesus has obtained salvation (for himself or others) through his good works.

---

[22] Elam et al. (2014, 27).
[23] Ibid., 30.
[24] Ibid.
[25] Berkhof (1996, 268); cf. Brown and Keele (2012, 59).

Such questions—Were initially prelapsarian Adam, then Israel, then Christ, under some covenant of works?—are meaningless because they are rooted in wrong presuppositions. But as I said before, it is very difficult to attack the distinction between conditional and unconditional covenants, law and promise covenants, covenants of works and covenants of grace, *because it is contained in Presbyterian creeds and catechisms*. Fighting theological theories is one thing; it is quite another when theories that have become part of confessions have become sacrosanct, and are therefore far more difficult to combat. For many it feels as if one is combating Scripture itself.

Here we see the damaging consequences of all theologies that do not properly maintain the balance between God's sovereign grace and human responsibility; the mere mentioning of the latter is sometimes seen as a sign of Arminianism. From the outset, Reformed theology has badly suffered under this lack of balance, not only in its doctrine of predestination[26] but also in its covenant doctrine. And this lack became even worse in and through the debate with the Arminians (in the beginning of the seventeenth century).

Perhaps, the tension around the two notions, covenant of works and covenant of grace, is felt nowhere more painfully than in treatments of the Sinaitic covenant, which allegedly has aspects of both. Reformed (!) theologian Gerhard C. Aalders has rightly said about this: "How can one say that the one God of the one covenant forced his people [on Mount Sinai] into the harness of a works covenant, thus ordering them to strive for merit, while that same God revealed himself in his grace, and commanded them to live out of that grace only? How can one maintain, as a watered-down derivative of this, that the covenant of Sinai is given in a form that is strongly reminiscent of a covenant of works?"[27] What a relief that there are also Reformed opinions like this one!

According to this view, the Sinaitic covenant is, in Aalders' terms, "a covenant of grace wrapped up as a covenant of works," which he rejects. Equally Reformed Cornelis van der Waal adds to this: "Does one not sin against God, by ascribing to Him 'evil,' disloyalty to His one covenant administration?"[28] That is harsh language—but understandable over against those who impose a works-grace dualism upon the Sinaitic covenant. In my volume on the Covenant, I have argued, with special reference to Psalm 105 and Galatians 3, that actually the Sinaitic covenant was—not identical with

---

[26] See extensively, Ouweneel (2016i).
[27] Aalders (1939, 179).
[28] Van der Waal (1990, 59).

but at least—a direct continuation and elaboration of the Abrahamic covenant. It is the same God of grace and covenantal loyalty, who revealed himself to Adam before the Fall, to Adam after the Fall, to Noah, to Abraham, and to Israel at Mount Sinai.

Listen, for instance, to Deuteronomy 7:7–8, and wonder whether this is the austere language of a covenant of works, or whether this is the language of grace and love:

> The LORD your God has chosen you to be a people for his treasured possession, out of all the peoples who are on the face of the earth. It was not because you were more in number than any other people that the LORD set his love on you and chose you, for you were the fewest of all peoples, but it is because the LORD loves you and is keeping the oath that he swore to your fathers, that the LORD has brought you out with a mighty hand and redeemed you from the house of slavery, from the hand of Pharaoh king of Egypt. Know therefore that the LORD your God is God, the faithful God who keeps covenant and steadfast love [*chesed*] with those who love him and keep his commandments, to a thousand generations.

I know the next sentences (vv. 10–11) say: "…and repays to their face those who hate him, by destroying them. He will not be slack with one who hates him. He will repay him to his face. You shall therefore be careful to do the commandment and the statutes and the rules that I command you today." That is a necessary counterpart of God's love: covenantal vengeance upon those who consistently and rebelliously break the covenant. But that does not alter its basic character: ours is a God of love and *chesed* (covenantal loyalty), who enters into a relationship with a redeemed people, into a true "covenant of love," in which every blessing is based—not on work-holiness but—on God's being "merciful and gracious, slow to anger, and abounding in steadfast love and faithfulness, keeping steadfast love for thousands, forgiving iniquity and transgression and sin" (Exod. 34:6–7).

BIBLIOGRAPHY

Aalders, G. C. 1939. *Het verbond Gods: Een hoofdstuk uit de geschiedenis der openbaring.* Kampen: Kok.

Adams, J. E. 1986. *The Christian Counselor's Manual: The Practice of Nouthetic Counseling.* Grand Rapids, MI: Zondervan.

Adeyemo, T., ed. 2010. *Africa Bible Commentary: A One-Volume Commentary Written by 70 African Scholars.* Grand Rapids, MI: Zondervan.

Adriaanse, H. J., H. A. Krop, and L. Leertouwer. 1987. *Het verschijnsel theologie: Over de wetenschappelijke status van de theologie.* Meppel: Boom.

Althaus, P. 1967 (repr.). *Die Prinzipien der deutschen reformierten Dogmatik im Zeitalter der aristotelischen Scholastik.* Darmstadt: Wissenschaftliche Buchgesellschaft.

————. 1952. *Die christliche Wahrheit: Lehrbuch der Dogmatik.* 3rd ed. Gütersloh: Bertelsmann.

Aniol, S. 2013. *Two-Kingdom vs. Transformationalism: What's All This Fuss About?* http://religiousaffections.org/articles/articles-on-culture/two-kingdom-vs-transformationalism-whats-all-this-fuss-about/.

Aulén, G. 1960. *The Faith of the Christian Church.* Philadelphia, PA: Muhlenberg Press.

Avis, P. 1986. *The Methods of Modern Theology: The Dream of Reason.* Basingstoke: Marshall Pickering.

Bakker, F. 2009. *Van schepping naar herschepping*. Kampen: Kok.

Barker, K. L. 1985. *Zechariah*. EBC VII. Grand Rapids, MI: Zondervan.

Barth, K. 1936–1988: *Church Dogmatics*. Trans. by T. H. L. Parker et al. Vols. 1/1–4/4. Louisville, KY: Westminster John Knox.

_____. 1961. *Church Dogmatics: A Selection*. Edited and translated by G. W. Bromiley. New York: Harper.

Bartholomew, C. G. 2017. *Contours of the Kuyperian Tradition: A Systematic Introduction*. Downers Grove, IL: IVP Academic.

Bartholomew, C. G. and M. W. Goheen. 2013. *Christian Philosophy: A Systematic and Narrative Introduction*. Grand Rapids, MI: Baker Academic.

Bavinck, H. 1883. *De wetenschap der heilige godgeleerdheid*. Kampen: Kok.

_____. (1894) 1989. "Herman Bavinck's 'Common Grace.'" Translated by Raymond C. Van Leeuwen. *Calvin Theological Journal* 24.1:35–65.

_____. 1909. *The Philosophy of Revelation. The Stone Lectures for 1908–1909*. Princeton Theological Seminary. New York: Longman, Green, and Co. Available at http://www.neocalvinisme.nl/tekstframes.html.

_____. 2002–2008. *Reformed Dogmatics*. Edited by John Bolt. Translated by John Vriend. 4 vols. Grand Rapids, MI: Baker Academic.

Beasley-Murray, G. R. 1987. *The Book of Revelation*. New Century Bible. Grand Rapids, MI: Eerdmans.

Beilby, J. K., ed. 2006. *For Faith and Clarity: Philosophical Contributions to Christian Theology*. Grand Rapids, MI: Baker Academic.

Berger, K. 2004. *Jesus*. München: Pattloch.

Berkhof, H. 1986. *Christian Faith: An Introduction to the Study of the Faith*. Translated by S. Woudstra. Grand Rapids, MI: Eerdmans.

Berkhof, L. 1996. *Systematic Theology*. New edition. Grand Rapids, MI: Eerdmans.

Berkouwer, G. C. 1955. *General Revelation*. Studies in Dogmatics. Grand Rapids, MI: Eerdmans.

Berkouwer, G. C. 1962. *Man: The Image of God*. Studies in Dogmatics. Grand Rapids, MI: Eerdmans.

_____. 1972. *The Return of Christ*. Studies in Dogmatics. Grand Rapids, MI: Eerdmans.

Boettner, L. 1984. *The Millennium*. Phillipsburg, NJ: P&R Publishing.

Boice, J. M. 1986. *Christ's Call to Discipleship*. Chicago, IL: Moody Press.

Bolt, J. 1983. "Church and World: A Trinitarian Perspective." *Calvin Theological Journal* 18.1: 5–31.

Boot, J. 2016. "Open Forum on the Two Kingdoms Theology: 'Implications of Two Kingdoms Theology in the Call to Engage Culture.'" Unpublished address.

Bosch, G. 2000. *Reformatorisches Denken und frühneuzeitliches Philosophieren: Eine vergleichende Studie zu Martin Luther und Valentin Weigel*. Marburg: Tectum Verlag.

Bosmans, J. 2004. "The Primacy of Domestic Politics: Christian Democracy in the Netherlands." In *Christian Democracy in Europe since 1945*. Edited by M. Gehler and W. Kaiser. 47–58. Abingdon (UK): Routledge.

Bouma-Prediger, S. 2010. *For the Beauty of the Earth: A Christian Vision for Creation Care*. 2nd ed. Ada, MI: Baker Academic.

Bratt, J. D., ed. 1998. *Abraham Kuyper: A Centennial Reader*. Grand Rapids, MI: Eerdmans.

Brockhaus, U. 1972. *Charisma und Amt: Die paulinische Charismen-Lehre auf dem Hintergrund frühchristlicher Gemeindefunktionen*. Wuppertal: Rolf Brockhaus.

Brown, M. G. and Z. Keele. 2012. *Sacred Bond: Covenant Theology Explored*. Grandville, MI: Reformed Fellowship.

Brunner, E. 1946. *Revelation and Reason: The Christian Doctrine of Faith and Knowledge*. Translated by O. Wyon. Philadelphia, PA: The Westminster Press.

———. 1949. *The Christian Doctrine of God*. Translated by O. Wyon. Philadelphia, PA: The Westminster Press.

Brunner, E. and K. Barth. 1946. *Natural Theology*. London: Geoffrey Bless.

Bunyan, J. 2007. *The Pilgrim's Progress*. Chicago, IL: Moody Press.

Buri, F. 1956. *Dogmatik als Selbstverständnis des christlichen Glaubens*. Vol. 1: *Vernunft und Offenbarung*. Bern: Paul Haupt/Tübingen: Katzmann-Verlag.

Burtchaell, J. T. 1992. *From Synagogue to Church: Public Services and Offices in the Earliest Christian Communities*. Cambridge: Cambridge University Press.

Caird, G. B. 1966. *The Revelation of St. John the Divine*. Harper's New Testament Commentaries. New York: Harper & Row.

Calvin, J. 1960. *Institutes of the Christian Religion*. Edited by John T. McNeill. Translated by Ford Lewis Battles. 2 vols. Library of Christian Classics 20–21. Philadelphia, PA: Westminster Press.

Campbell, R. A. 1994. *The Elders: Seniority within Earliest Christianity*. Edinburgh: T&T Clark.

Caputo, J. D. 2006. *Philosophy and Theology*. Nashville, TN: Abingdon Press.

Carson, D. A. 1984. *Matthew*. EBC 8. Grand Rapids, MI: Zondervan.

Chafer, L. S. 1983. *Systematic Theology*. 15th ed. 8 vols. Dallas, TX: Dallas Seminary Press.

Churchill, W. 2008. *Churchill by Himself: The Definitive Collection of Quotations*. Edited by R. Langworth. New York: Public Affairs.

Clark, R. S. 2008. *Recovering the Reformed Confession: Our Theology, Piety, and Practice*. Phillipsburg, NJ: P&R Publishing.

Clouse, R. G. 1991. *War: Four Christian Views*. Downers Grove, IL: InterVarsity Press.

Cortois, P. and W. Van Herck, eds. 1999. *Rationaliteit en religieus vertrouwen*. Leuven: Peeters.

Craig, W. L. 2008. *Reasonable Faith: Christian Truth and Apologetics*. 3rd ed. Wheaton, IL: Crossway Books.

Danesi, M. and P. Perron. 1999. *Analyzing Cultures: An Introduction and Handbook*. Bloomington, IN: Indiana University Press.

De Graaf, S. G. 1939. *Christus en de wereld*. Kampen: Kok.

———. 2012. "'Christ and the Magistrate' and 'Church and State': Two Addresses by S. G. de Graaf." Translated with Foreword by Nelson D. Kloosterman. *Kingdoms Apart: Engaging the Two Kingdoms Perspective*, edited by Ryan C. McIlhenny. 85–124. Phillipsburg, NJ: P&R Publishing.

De Graaff, F. 1969. *Als goden sterven: De crisis van de westerse cultuur*. Rotterdam: Lemniscaat.

———. 1977. *Anno Domini 1000, Anno Domini 2000: De duizend jaren bij de gratie van de dode god*. Kampen: Kok.

Demarest, B. 1997. *The Cross and Salvation: The Doctrine of Salvation*. Wheaton, IL: Crossway Books.

Dennison, J. T., ed. 2008–2014. *Reformed Confessions of the 16th and 17th Centuries in English Translation*. 4 vols. Grand Rapids, MI: Reformation Heritage Books.

De Vleeschauwer, H. J. 1952. *Handleiding by die studie van die logika en die kennisleer*. Pretoria: J. J. Moerau & Kie.

Dooyeweerd, H. 1958. "De verhouding tussen wijsbegeerte en theologie en de strijd der faculteiten." *Philosophia Reformata* 23: 1–21, 49–84.

———. 1960. *In the Twilight of Western Thought: Studies in the Pretended Autonomy of Philosophical Thought*. Philadelphia, PA: P&R Publishing.

———. 1979. *Roots of Western Culture: Pagan, Secular, and Christian Options*. Edited by M. Vander Vennen and B. Zylstra. Translated by J. Kraay. Toronto: Wedge Publishing Foundation.

———. 1971. "Cornelius Van Til and the Transcendental Critique of Theoretical Thought." In *Jerusalem and Athens: Critical Discussions on the Philosophy and Apologetics of Cornelius Van Til*. Edited by E. R. Geehan. 74-89. Nutley, NJ: P&R Publishing.

———. 1984 (repr.), *A New Critique of Theoretical Thought*. Vol. 1: *The Necessary Presuppositions of Philosophy*. Vol. 2: *The General Theory of the*

Modal Spheres. Vol. 3: *The Structures of Individuality of Temporal Reality.* Jordan Station, ON: Paideia Press.

Douma, J. 1966. *Algemene genade: Uiteenzetting, vergelijking en beoordeling van de opvattingen van A. Kuyper, K. Schilder en Joh. Calvijn over "algemene genade."* 2nd ed. Goes: Oosterbaan & Le Cointre.

Douma, J., ed. 1987. *Oriëntatie in de theologie.* 2nd ed. Groningen: De Vuurbaak.

Ebeling, G. et al. 1986. "Theologie." In *Die Religion in Geschichte und Gegenwart.* Edited by K. Galling. 3rd ed. 6:754–82. Tübingen: Mohr (Siebeck).

_____. 1986. "Theologie und Philosophie." In *Die Religion in Geschichte und Gegenwart.* Edited by K. Galling. 3rd ed. 6:782–830. Tübingen: Mohr (Siebeck).

Eerdmans, B. D. 1909. *De theologie van Dr. A. Kuyper.* Leiden: Van Doesburgh.

Eggenberg, Th. 2010. *Kirche als Zeichen des Reiches Gottes: Eine Studie zur Bedeutung des Reiches Gottes für die Kirche in Auseinandersetzung mit Küng, Moltmann, Pannenberg und Hauerwas.* Diss. Heverlee: Evangelische Theologische Faculteit.

Elam, A. E., R. C. Van Kooten, and R. A. Bergquist. 2014. *Merit and Moses: A Critique of the Klinean Doctrine of Republication.* Eugene, OR: Wipf & Stock.

Ellul, J. 1967. *The Technological Society.* 2nd ed. New York: Knopf/Vintage.

_____. 1980. *The Technological System.* New York: Continuum.

Erickson, M. J. 1982. "Biblical Inerrancy: The Last Twenty-Five Years." *Journal of the Evangelical Theological Society* 25: 387–94.

_____. 2007. *Christian Theology.* 2nd ed. Grand Rapids, MI: Baker Book House.

Estelle, B. D., J. V. Fesko, and D. VanDrunen, eds. 2009. *The Law Is Not of Faith: Essays on Works and Grace in the Mosaic Covenant.* Phillipsburg, NJ: P&R Publishing.

Fee, G. D. 1987. *The First Epistle to the Corinthians.* NICNT. Grand Rapids, MI: Eerdmans.

Feyerabend, P. K. (1975) 2010. *Against Method: Outline of an Anarchistic Theory of Knowledge.* London: New Left Books.

Flusser, D. 2001. *Jesus.* 3rd ed. Jerusalem: Magness Press.

Frame, J. 2011. *The Escondido Theology: A Reformed Response to Two Kingdom Theology.* Lakeland, FL: Whitefield Media Productions.

France, R. T. 2007. *The Gospel of Matthew.* NICNT. Grand Rapids, MI: Eerdmans.

Gadamer, H.-G. 1998. *Truth and Method.* 2nd ed. New York: Continuum.

Gaebelein, F. E., ed. *The Expositor's Bible Commentary.* 12 vols. Grand Rapids, MI: Zondervan.

Galetto, N. 1990. *Christian Democracy: Principles and Policy Making.* Berlin: Konrad Adeneaur| Stiftun.

Geisler, N. L., ed. 1981. *Biblical Errancy: An Analysis of Its Philosophical Roots.* Grand Rapids, MI: Zondervan.

_____. 2009. *The Apologetics of Jesus: A Caring Approach to Dealing with Doubters.* Grand Rapids, MI: Baker Books.

_____ and F. Turek. 2004. *I Don't Have Enough Faith to Be an Atheist.* Wheaton, IL: Crossway Books.

Gentry, P. J. 2012. Chapters 4–15 in *Kingdom through Covenant: A Biblical-Theological Understanding of the Covenants.* Edited by P. J. Gentry and S. J. Wellum. Wheaton, IL: Crossway Books.

Graafland, C. 1996. *Van Calvijn tot Comrie: Oorsprong en ontwikkeling van de leer van het verbond in het Gereformeerd Protestantisme.* Vol. 3. Zoetermeer: Boekencentrum.

_____. 1999. *Gedachten over het ambt.* Zoetermeer: Boekencentrum.

Grant, F. W. 1901. *The Numerical Bible: Acts to 2 Corinthians.* New York: Loizeaux Brothers.

Godfrey, W. R. 2009. "Kingdom and Kingdoms." *Evangelium* 7.2: 16–19.

Goheen, M. W. and C. G. Bartholomew. 2008. *Living at the Crossroads: An Introduction to Christian Worldview.* Grand Rapids, MI: Baker Academic.

Graafland, C. 1973. *Waarom nog gereformeerd?* Kampen: Kok.

_____. 1989. *Kinderen van één moeder: Calvijns visie op de kerk volgens zijn Institutie.* Kampen: Kok.

Grenz, S. J. and J. R. Franke. 2001. *Beyond Foundationalism: Shaping Theology in a Postmodern Context.* Louisville, KY: Westminster John Knox Press.

Groen van Prinsterer, G. 1975. *Unbelief and Revolution: A Series of Lectures in History.* Edited and translated by H. Van Dyke. Amsterdam: The Groen van Prinsterer Fund (www.reformationalpublishingproject.com/pdf_books/ Scanned_Books_PDF/UnbeliefinReligionandPoliticsUnbeliefand RevolutionLectures_VIII_IX.pdf).

Hägglund, B. 1955. *Theologie und Philosophie bei Luther und in der occamistischen Tradition: Luthers Stellung zur Theorie von der doppelten Wahrheit.* Lund: G. W. K. Gleerup.

Haines, V. Y. 1982. *The Felix Culpa.* Washington, DC: University Press of America.

Halbrook, S. C. 2014. *God is Just: A Defense of the Old Testament Civil Laws.* Theonomy Resources Media.

Harinck, G. 2014. "Herman Bavinck and the Neo-Calvinist Concept of the French Revolution." In *Neo-Calvinism and the French Revolution.* Edited by J. Eglinton and G. Harink. 13–30. London: Bloomsbury T&T Clark 2014.

Hart, D. G. 2006. *A Secular Faith: Why Christianity Favors the Separation of Church and State*. Chicago, IL: Ivan R. Dee.

Hart, H. 1984. *Understanding Our World: An Integral Ontology*. Lanham, MD: University Press of America.

Hasenhüttl, G. 1979. *Kritische Dogmatik*. Graz: Styria.

Hauerwas, S. 2002. *With the Grain of the Universe: The Church's Witness and Natural Theology*. London: SCM Press.

Heering, G. J. 1944. *Geloof en openbaring*. 2nd ed. Arnhem: Van Loghum Slaterus.

Henderson, R. 2008. "Kuyper's Inch." *Pro Rege* 36.3: 12–14.

Hepp, V. 1936. *Dreigende deformatie*. Vol. I: *Diagnose*. Kampen: Kok.

Heyns, J. A. 1988. *Dogmatiek*. Pretoria: NG Kerkboekhandel.

Hill, C. E. 2001. *Regnum Caelorum: Patterns of Millennial Thought in Early Christianity*. 2nd ed. Grand Rapids, MI: Eerdmans.

Hodge, C. (1859) 1998. *A Commentary on I & II Corinthians*. Edinburgh: Banner of Truth.

Hoek, J. 2004. *Hoop op God: Eschatologische verwachting*. 2nd ed. Zoetermeer: Boekencentrum.

Hoekema, A. A. 1986. *Created in God's Image*. Grand Rapids, MI: Eerdmans.

———. 1994. *The Bible and the Future*. Grand Rapids, MI: Eerdmans.

Holmes, A. F. 1977. *All Truth Is God's Truth*. Grand Rapids, MI: Eerdmans.

Holzmüller, Th. and K.-N. Ihmig, eds. 1997. *Zugänge zur Wirklichkeit: Theologie und Philosophie im Dialog*. Bielefeld: Luther-Verlag.

Höpfl, H., ed. and trans. 1991. *Luther and Calvin on Secular Authority*. Cambridge: Cambridge University Press.

Horton, M. S. 2002a. *Where in the World Is the Church?: A Christian View of Culture and Your Role in It*. Chicago, IL: Moody Press 1995/Phillipsburg, NJ: P&R Publishing.

———. 2001b. *Covenant and Eschatology: The Divine Drama*. Louisville, KY: Westminster John Knox.

———. 2006. "How the Kingdom Comes." *Christianity Today* 50.1: 42. Available at http://www.christianitytoday.com/ct/2006/january/2.43.html?start=3.

———. 2011. *The Christian Faith: A Systematic Theology for Pilgrims On the Way*. Grand Rapids, MI: Zondervan.

House, H. W. and D. W. Jowers. 2011. *Reasons for Our Hope: An Introduction to Christian Apologetics*. Nashville, TN: B&H Academic.

Husbands, M. and D. J. Treier, eds. 2005. *The Community of the Word: Toward an Evangelical Ecclesiology*. Downers Grove, IL: InterVarsity Press/Leicester: Apollos.

Hylkema, C. B. 1911. *Oud- en nieuw-Calvinisme: Een vergelijkende geschiedkundige studie.* Haarlem: Tjeenk Willink.

Jaspers, K. (1953) 2010. *The Origin and Goal of History.* Translated by M. Bullock. New York: Routledge Press.

Johnson, A. F. 1981. *Revelation.* EBC 12. Grand Rapids, MI: Zondervan.

Johnson, G. L. W. and G. P. Waters, eds. 2007. *By Faith Alone: Answering the Challenges to the Doctrine of Justification.* Wheaton, IL: Crossway.

Kac, A.W., ed. 1986. *The Messiahship of Jesus: Are Jews Changing Their Attitude Toward Jesus?* 2nd ed. Grand Rapids, MI: Baker Book House.

Kaiser, C. B. 1991. *Creation and the History of Science.* Grand Rapids, MI: Eerdmans.

Kaiser, W. 2007. *Christian Democracy and the Origins of European Union.* Cambridge: Cambridge University Press.

Kalyvas, S. N. 1996. *The Rise of Christian Democracy in Europe.* Ithaca, NY: Cornell University Press.

Kant, I. (1798) 1991. "The Contest of Faculties." *Kant: Political Writings.* Edited by H. Reiss. Translated by H. B. Nisbet. 2nd ed. Cambridge: Cambridge University Press.

Karlberg, M. W. 2016. "Troubler of Israel: Report on Republication by the Orthodox Presbyterian Church Assessing the Teaching of Professor Meredith G. Kline." *The Trinity Review.* Special Issue. 1–17.

Keizer, A. 1986. *Wetenschap in bijbels licht: Handleiding voor de grondslagen van wijsbegeerte en vakwetenschap.* Amsterdam: Buijten & Schipperheijn.

Kelly, W., ed. 1894. *The Bible Treasury.* Vol. 20. Winschoten: H. L. Heijkoop.

Kersten, G. H. 1980. *Reformed Dogmatics: A Systematic Treatment of Reformed Doctrine Explained for the Congregations.* Translated by J. R. Beeke and J. C. Westrate. 2 vols. n.p: Netherlands Reformed Book and Publishing Committee (vol. 1), and Grand Rapids, MI: Eerdmans (vol. 2).

Kickel, W. 1967. *Vernunft und Offenbarung bei Theodor Beza.* Neukirchen-Vluyn: Neukirchener Verlag.

Kierkegaard, S. (1844) 1980. *The Concept of Anxiety* (ed. R. Thomte). Princeton: Princeton University Press.

Klapwijk, J. 1995. *Oriëntatie in de nieuwe filosofie.* 3rd ed. Assen: Van Gorcum.

Kline, M. (1993) 2006. *Kingdom Prologue: Genesis Foundations for a Covenantal Worldview.* Eugene, OR: Wipf & Stock.

Kloosterman, N. D. 2008. "The Bible, the Church, and the World: A Third Way." *Christian Renewal.* Vols. 26–27.

_____. 2012a. *Peering into a Lawyer's Brief: An Extended Examination of David VanDrunen's Natural Law and the Two Kingdoms.* Privately published.

_____. 2012b. "Natural Law and the Two Kingdoms in the Thought of

Herman Bavinck." *Kingdoms Apart: Engaging the Two Kingdoms Perspective,* edited by Ryan C. McIlhenny. 65–81. Phillipsburg, NJ: P&R Publishing.

Knowles, D. (1962) 1989. *The Evolution of Medieval Thought.* London: Longman.

König, A. 2006. *Die Groot Geloofswoordeboek.* Vereeniging: Christelike Uitgewersmaatskappy.

Koster, E. 2005. "Does Theology Need a Paradigm? Learning from Organization Science and Management Research." *European Journal of Science and Theology* 1.1: 27–37.

Kuhn, T. S. (1962) 1996. *The Structure of Scientific Revolutions.* Chicago, IL: University of Chicago Press.

_____. 2000. *The Road Since Structure: Philosophical Essays, 1970–1993.* Chicago, IL: University of Chicago Press.

Kuiper, H. 1928. *Calvin on Common Grace.* Grand Rapids, MI: Smitter Book Company.

Küng, H. 2001. *The Church.* Translated by R. and R. Ockenden. New York: Bloomsbury Academic.

Küng, H. and D. Tracy, eds. 1984. *Theologie–wohin? Auf dem Weg zu einem neuen Paradigma.* Zürich: Benziger/Gütersloh: Gerd Mohn.

Kuyper, A. 1880. *Sphere Sovereignty.* Translated by George Kamps. Available at http://www.reformationalpublishingproject.com/pdf_books/Scanned_Books_PDF/SphereSovereignty_English.pdf.

_____. [1911]. *Dictaten Dogmatiek.* Kampen: Kok.

_____. (1898) 2008. *Encyclopedia of Sacred Theology.* Edited by B. C. Richards. Translated by J. H. de Vries. New York: Charles Scribner's Sons. Available at http://reformedaudio.org/audio/kuyper/Kuyper%20-%20Encyclopedia%20of%20 20Sacred%20Theology.pdf.

_____. (1898) 2009. *Lectures on Calvinism: Six Lectures from the Stone Foundation: Lectures Delivered at Princeton University.* CreateSpace Independent Publishing Platform.

_____. (1902/1904) 2016a. *Common Grace.* Vol. 1: *God's Gifts for a Fallen World.* Edited by Jordan Ballor and Stephen Grabill. Translated by Nelson D. Kloosterman and Ed M. van der Maas. Abraham Kuyper Collected Works in Public Theology. Acton Institute for the Study of Religion and Liberty / Lexham Press.

_____. (1911–1912) 2016b. *Pro Rege: Living Under Christ's Kingship.* Vol. 1: *The Exalted Nature of Christ's Kingship.* Edited by John Kok and Nelson D. Kloosterman. Translated by Albert Gootjes. Abraham Kuyper Collected Works in Public Theology. Acton Institute for the Study of Religion and Liberty / Lexham Press.

Ladd, G. E. (1959) 1964. *The Gospel of the Kingdom: Popular Expositions on the Kingdom of God*. Grand Rapids, MI: Eerdmans.

Lakatos, I. 1980. *The Methodology of Scientific Research Programmes: Philosophical Papers*. Vol. 1. Cambridge: Cambridge University Press.

Lakatos, I. and A. Musgrave, eds. 1970. *Criticism and the Growth of Knowledge*. Cambridge: Cambridge University Press.

Lategan, L. O. K. 1989. *Die wese van die universiteit: 'n Histories-strukturele perspektief*. Bloemfontein: VCHO.

Lekkerkerker, A. F. N. 1971. *Oorsprong en funktie van het ambt*. 's-Gravenhage: Boekencentrum.

Lewis, C. S. 1973. *English Literature in the Sixteenth Century*. London: Oxford University Press.

Liebelt, M.2000. *Allgemeines Priestertum, Charisma und Struktur: Grundlagen für ein biblisch-theologisches Verständnis geistlicher Leitung*. Wuppertal: Brockhaus.

Liederbach, M. and S. Bible. 2012. *True North: Christ, the Gospel, and Creation Care*. Nashville, TN: B&H Academic.

Lischer, R. 2002. *The Company of Preachers: Wisdom on Preaching, Augustine to the Present*. Grand Rapids, MI: Eerdmans.

Littlejohn, B. 2012a. *The Two Kingdoms: A Guide for the Perplexed, Pt. 1: Introduction*. http://www.politicaltheology.com/blog/kingdoms-guide-perplexed-pt-1/.

———. 2012b. *The Two Kingdoms: A Guide for the Perplexed, Pt. 2: From Luther to Calvin*. http://www.politicaltheology.com/blog/kingdoms-guide-perplexed-pt-2-from-luther-calvin/.

———. 2012c. *The Two Kingdoms: A Guide for the Perplexed—Pt. 3: From Calvin to Hooker*. http://www.politicaltheology.com/blog/kingdoms-guide-perplexed-pt-3-calvin-hooker/.

———. 2012d. *The Two Kingdoms: A Guide for the Perplexed—Pt. 4: Richard Hooker*. http://www.politicaltheology.com/blog/kingdoms-guide-perplexed-pt-4-richard-hooker/.

———. 2012e. *The Two Kingdoms: A Guide for the Perplexed—Pt. 5: From Hooker to Locke*. http://www.politicaltheology.com/blog/kingdoms-guide-perplexed-pt-5-hooker-locke/.

Lohfink, G. 1998. *Braucht Gott die Kirche? Zur Theologie des Volkes Gottes*. 3rd ed. Freiburg: Herder.

Lucardie, P. 2004. "Paradise Lost, Paradise Regained? Christian Democracy in the Netherlands." In *Christian Democratic Parties in Europe Since the End of the Cold War*. Edited by S. Van Hecke and E. Gerard. 159–78. Leuven: Leuven University Press 2004.

MacArthur, J. F. 1988. *The Gospel According to Jesus*. Grand Rapids, MI: Zondervan.

McGrath, A. 2016. *Christian Theology: An Introduction*. 6th ed. Hoboken: Wiley.

McIlhenny, R., ed. 2012. *Kingdoms Apart: Engaging the Two Kingdoms Perspective*. Phillipsburg, NJ: P&R Publishing.

Mathison, K. A. 1999. *Postmillenialism: An Eschatology of Hope*. Phillipsburg, NJ: P&R Publishing.

Mattson, B. 2011. "Cultural Amnesia: What Makes Pietism Possible?" An Address to the Center For Cultural Leadership Annual Conference. http://static.squarespace.com/static/5005c8fe84ae929b3721501f/t/5057868fe-4b093884ee9a52f/1347913359774/

Mekkes, J. P. A. 1961. *Scheppingsopenbaring en wijsbegeerte*. Kampen: Kok.

Metzger, B. M. 1975. *A Textual Commentary on the Greek New Testament*. 2nd ed. London/New York: United Bible Societies.

Moffatt, J. 1979. *The First and Second Epistle to the Thessalonians*. The Expositor's Greek Testament. Vol. 4. Grand Rapids, MI: Eerdmans.

Moltmann, J. 1975. *The Church in the Power of the Spirit: A Contribution to Messianic Ecclesiology*. London: SCM.

Montgomery, J. W. 2003. *Tractatus Logico-Theologicus*. Bonn: Verlag für Kultur und Wissenschaft.

Moo, D. J. 1996. *The Epistle to the Romans*. NICNT. Grand Rapids, MI: Eerdmans.

Moore, R. D. 2004. *The Kingdom of Christ: The New Evangelical Perspective*. Wheaton, IL: Crossway.

———. 2015. *Onward: Engaging the Culture without Losing the Gospel*. Nashville, TN: Broadman & Holman.

Mouton, J., A. G. Van Aarde, and W. S. Vorster, eds. 1988. *Paradigms and Progress in Theology*. Pretoria: HSRC.

Murray, J. 1954. *Covenant of Grace: A Biblico-Theological Study*. London: Tyndale.

———. 1968. *The Epistle to the Romans*. NICNT. Grand Rapids, MI: Eerdmans.

Niebuhr, H. R. (1951) 2001. *Christ and Culture*. New York: Harper & Row.

Niebuhr, R. (1935) 1979. *An Interpretation of Christian Ethics*. New York: Seabury Press 1979.

Niell, J. D. 2003. "The Newness of the New Covenant." In *The Case for Covenantal Infant Baptism*. Edited by G. Strawbridge. 127–55. Phillipsburg, NJ: P&R Publishing.

Noordegraaf, A. 1980. *Gods bouwwerk: Aspecten van het gemeente-zijn in bijbels-theologisch licht*. 's-Gravenhage: Boekencentrum 1980.

_____. 1990. *Leven voor Gods aangezicht: Gedachten over het mens-zijn.* Kampen: Kok.

Noordmans, O. (1934) 2009. *Herschepping.* Barneveld: Nederlands Dagblad.

Ott, H. 1972. *Die Antwort des Glaubens: Systematische Theologie in 50 Artikeln.* Stuttgart: Kreuz Verlag.

Otto, R. 1970. *The Idea of the Holy.* New York: Oxford University Press.

Ouwendorp, C. 2012. *Jeruzalem & Athene: Een blijvende worsteling in de theologie.* Delft: Eburon.

Ouweneel, W. J. 1986. *De leer van de mens.* Amsterdam: Buijten & Schipperheijn.

_____. 1995. *Christian Doctrine: I. The External Prolegomena,* Amsterdam: Buijten & Schipperheijn.

_____. 1997. *Wijs met de wetenschap: Inleiding tot een christelijke wetenschapsleer.* Leiden: Barnabas.

_____. 2000. *De zesde kanteling: Christus en 5000 jaar denkgeschiedenis: Religie en metafysica in het jaar 2000.* Metahistorische trilogie. Vol. 3. Heerenveen: Barnabas.

_____. 2006. *Seks in de kerk.* Vaassen: Medema.

_____. 2007a. *De Geest van God: Ontwerp van een pneumatologie.* EDR 1. Vaassen: Medema.

_____. 2007b. *De Christus van God: Ontwerp van een christologie.* EDR 2. Vaassen: Medema.

_____. 2008a. *De schepping van God: Ontwerp van een scheppings-, mens- en zondeleer.* EDR 3. Vaassen: Medema.

_____. 2008b. *Het plan van God: Ontwerp van een voorbeschikkingsleer.* EDR 4. Vaassen: Medema.

_____. 2009a. *Het zoenoffer van God: Ontwerp van een verzoeningsleer.* EDR 5. Vaassen: Medema.

_____. 2010a. *Het heil van God: Ontwerp van een soteriologie.* EDR 6. Heerenveen: Medema.

_____. 2010b. *De Kerk van God (I): Ontwerp van een elementaire ecclesiologie.* EDR 7. Heerenveen: Medema.

_____. 2011. *De Kerk van God (II): Ontwerp van een historische en praktische ecclesiologie.* EDR 8. Heerenveen: Medema.

_____. 2012a. *De toekomst van God: Ontwerp van een eschatologie.* EDR 10. Heerenveen: Medema.

_____. 2012b. *Het Woord van God: Ontwerp van een openbarings- en schriftleer.* EDR 11. Heerenveen: Medema.

_____. 2013. *De glorie van God: Ontwerp van een godsleer en van een theologische vakfilosofie.* EDR 12. Heerenveen: Medema.

_____. 2014a. *Wisdom for Thinkers: An Introduction to Christian Philosophy.* St. Catharines, ON: Paideia Press.

_____. 2014b. *Power in Service: An Introduction to Christian Political Science.* St. Catharines, ON: Paideia Press.

_____. 2014c. *What Then Is Theology?: An Introduction to Christian Theology.* St. Catharines, ON: Paideia Press.

_____. 2015. *Searching the Soul.* St. Catharines, ON: Paideia Press.

_____. 2016a. *Probing the Past.* St. Catharines, ON: Paideia Press.

_____. 2016b. (in press). *Vindicating the Word.* St. Catharines, ON: Paideia Press.

_____. 2016c. (in press). *The Ninth King: The Last of the Celestial Empires: The Triumph of Christ over the Powers.* Jordan Station, ON: Paideia Press.

_____. 2016d. *The Heidelberg Diary: Daily Devotions on the Heidelberg Catechism.* Jordan Station, ON: Paideia Press.

_____. 2016e. (in press). *The Eternal Kingdom: An Evangelical Theology of Living under Christ.* St. Catharines, ON: Paideia Press [pre-publication].

_____. 2016f. (in press). *The Eternal Torah: An Evangelical Theology of Living under God.* St. Catharines, ON: Paideia Press.

_____. 2016g. (in press). *The Eternal Covenant: An Evangelical Theology of Living With God.* St. Catharines, ON: Paideia Press.

_____. 2016h. (in press). *Eternal Righteousness: An Evangelical Theology of Living before God.* St. Catharines, ON: Paideia Press.

_____. 2016i. (in press). *The Eternal Purpose: An Evangelical Theology of Living in Christ.* St. Catharines, ON: Paideia Press.

Owen, J. 1991. *Works.* Vol. 22: *An Exposition of the Epistle to the Hebrews.* Edinburgh: Banner of Truth.

Pannenberg, W. 2009. *Systematic Theology.* Vol. 3. Grand Rapids, MI: Eerdmans.

Planck, M. 1973. *Vorträge und Erinnerungen.* 5th ed. Darmstadt: Wissenschaftliche Buchgesellschaft.

Plantinga, A. 2000. *Warranted Christian Belief.* New York etc.: Oxford University Press.

Plantinga, A. and N. Wolterstorff, eds. 2009. *Faith and Rationality: Reason and Belief in God.* Notre Dame, IN: University of Notre Dame Press.

Plantinga Jr., C. 2002. *Engaging God's World: A Christian Vision of Faith, Learning, and Living.* Grand Rapids, MI: Eerdmans.

Polanyi, M. (1958), 1974. *Personal Knowledge: Towards a Postcritical Philosophy.* Chicago, IL: University of Chicago Press.

Polyander, J., A. Rivetus, A. Walaeus, and A. Thysius. (1625; 1881) 1964-1966. *Synopsis purioris theologiae.* Edited by H. Bavinck. 2 vols. Enschede: Boersma.

Popma, K. J. 1946. *De plaats der theologie*. Franeker: T. Wever.

Popper, K. R. 1979. *Objective Knowledge*. Rev. ed. Oxford: Clarendon Press 1979.

_____. 1992. *Realism and the Aim of Science*. Rev. ed. London: Routledge.

_____. 2002a. *The Logic of Scientific Discovery*. 2nd ed. London: Routledge.

_____. 2002b. *Conjectures and Refutations*. 2nd ed. London: Routledge.

Putnam, H. 1981. *Reason, Truth and History*. Cambridge: Cambridge University Press.

Putnam, H. 1985. *Realism and Reason*. Rev. ed. Cambridge: Cambridge University Press.

Putnam, H. 1992. *Realism with a Human Face*. Cambridge, MA: Harvard University Press.

Ratzinger, J. (Benedict XVI). 2008. *Jesus of Nazareth*. Vol. I: *From the Baptism in the Jordan to the Transfiguration*. San Francisco: Ignatius Press.

Ridderbos, H. N. 1962. *The Coming of the Kingdom*. Edited by R. O. Zorn. Translated by H. de Jongste. Nutley, NJ: P&R Publishing.

_____. (1965) 1970. *Het evangelie naar Mattheüs*. 2 vols. Korte Verklaring. Kampen: Kok.

_____. (1989) 1995. "The Kingdom of God and Our Life in the World." In *Confessing Christ in Doing Politics: Essays on Christian Political Thought and Action*. Edited by B. Van der Walt and R. Swanepoel. 10–24. Potchefstroom: Potchefstroom University for Christian Higher Education.

Ridderbos, J. 1935. *De kleine profeten*. Vol. 3: *Haggai, Zacharia, Maleachi*. Korte Verklaring. Kampen: Kok.

Ridderbos, S. J. 1949. *Rondom het gemene gratie-probleem*. Kampen: Kok.

Rietkerk, W. 2009. *De Titanic achterna?: Over de toekomst van de aarde*. Utrecht: Ankh-Hermes.

Rookmaaker, H. R. 1994. *Modern Art and the Death of a Culture*. Wheaton, IL: Crossway.

Rouvoet, A. 1992. *Reformatorische staatsvisie: De RPF en het ambt van de overheid*. Nunspeet: Marnix van St. Aldegonde Stichting.

_____. 2000. *Politiek met een hart: Beschouwingen over politiek en moraal*. Kampen, Kok.

_____. 2006. *Het hart van de zaak: Over de betekenis van geloven in de politiek*. Amsterdam: Bakker.

Rutherford, S. (1644) 1998. *Lex, Rex, or, The Law and the Prince: A Dispute for the Just Prerogative of King and People*. Berryville, VA: Hess Publications.

Saucy, M. R. 1997. *The Kingdom of God in the Teaching of Jesus in 20th Century Theology*. Dallas etc.: Word Publishing.

Sauter, G. 1998. *Zugänge zur Dogmatik: Elemente theologischer Urteilsbildung*. Stuttgart: UTB.

Schaeffer, F. 1968. *The God Who Is There*. Downers Grove, IL: InterVarsity Press.

Schaeffer-de Wal, E.W. 1993. "Het Koninkrijk van God als absolute eigentijdse werkelijkheid, I–III." *Radix* 19: 10–37, 60–108, 148–215.

Schilder, K. 1939. *Heidelbergsche Catechismus*. Vol. 1. Goes: Oosterbaan & Le Cointre.

_____. 2016. *Christ and Culture*. Translated by A. H. Oosterhof and W. Helder. Annotated by J. Douma. Hamilton, ON: Lucerna: CRTS Publications.

Schlink, E. 1983. *Oekumenische Dogmatik: Grundzüge*. Göttingen: Vandenhoeck & Ruprecht.

Schmidt, K. L. 1964. "Basileus." In *Theological Dictionary of the New Testament*. Edited by G. Kittel et al. Translated by G. W. Bromiley. Vol. 1. 564–93. Grand Rapids, MI: Eerdmans.

Schuurman, E. 1987. *Christians in Babel*. Jordan Station, ON: Paideia Press.

_____. 2003. *Faith and Hope in Technology*. Jacksonville, FL: Clements Publishing.

_____, C. Graafland, B. Goudzwaard, S. Griffioen, and A. Rouvoet. 1993. *Reformatorische cultuurvisie*. Nunspeet: Marnix van St. Aldegonde Stichting.

Schuyler English, E. 1986. *The Rapture*. 2nd ed. Neptune, NJ: Loizeaux Brothers.

Scofield, C. I. (1909) 1967. *The New Scofield Reference Bible*. New York: Oxford University Press.

Scott, W. 1920. *Exposition of the Revelation of Jesus Christ*. London: Pickering & Inglis.

Seerveld, C. 1995. *A Christian Critique of Art and Literature*. Toronto: Tuppence Press.

_____. 2000. *Bearing Fresh Olive Leaves: Alternative Steps in understanding Art*. Toronto: Tuppence Press.

_____. 2005. *Rainbows for a Fallen World*. Toronto: Tuppence Press.

_____. 2014a. *Biblical Studies and Wisdom for Living*. Sioux Center, IA: Dordt College Press.

_____. 2014b. *Cultural Education and History Writing*. Sioux Center, IA: Dordt College Press.

Shedd, W. G. T. 1889. *Dogmatic Theology*, dl. I–III. Edinburgh: T&T Clark.

Shepherd, N. 2000. *The Call of Grace: How the Covenant Illuminates Salvation and Evangelism*. Phillipsburg, NJ: P&R Publishing.

Shulam, J. (with H. Le Cornu). 1998. *A Commentary on the Jewish Roots of Romans*. Baltimore: Messianic Jewish Publishers.

Shults, F. L. 1999. *The Postfoundationalist Task of Theology: Wolfhart Pannenberg and the New Theological Rationality*. Grand Rapids, MI: Eerdmans.

Smith, J. B. 1961. *A Revelation of Jesus Christ*. Scottdale, PA: Herald Press.

Snyder, H. A. 2001. *Kingdom, Church, and World: Biblical Themes for Today*. 2nd ed. Eugene, OR: Wipf & Stock.

Spencer, H. 1864. *Principles of Biology*. Vol. 1. London: William & Norgate.

Spykman, G. J. 1988. "Christian Philosophy as Prolegomena to Reformed Dogmatics." In *'n Woord op sy tyd: 'n Teologiese feesbundel aangebied aan Professor Johan Heyns ter herdenking van sy sestigste verjaarsdag*. Edited by C. J. Wethman and C. J. A. Vos. 137–55. Pretoria: NG Kerkboekhandel.

_____. 1992. *Reformational Theology: A New Paradigm for Doing Dogmatics*. Grand Rapids, MI: Eerdmans.

Stackhouse Jr., J. G. 2002. "In the world, but…." *Christianity Today* 46.5: 80. http://www.christianitytoday.com/ct/2002/april22/8.80.html?start.

_____, ed. 2003. *Evangelical Ecclesiology: Reality or Illusion?* Grand Rapids, MI: Baker Academic.

Stegmüller, W. (1954) 1969. *Metaphysik, Skepsis, Wissenschaft*. Berlin: Springer.

Stellman, J. J. 2009. *Dual Citizens: Worship and Life between the Already and the Not Yet*. Sanford, FL: Reformation Trust Publishing.

Stott, J. R. W. 1959. "Yes." *Eternity* Sept.

Strauss, D. F. M. 1971. *Wetenskap en werklikheid: Oriëntering in die algemene wetenskapsleer*. Bloemfontein: Sacum Beperk.

_____. 1979. "Die teoretiese blootlegging van Skeppingsbeginsels." *Tydskrif vir Christelike Wetenskap* 15: 254–64.

_____. 1980. *Inleiding tot die kosmologie*. Bloemfontein: Sacum Beperk.

_____. 1991. *Man and His World*. Bloemfontein: Tekskor.

_____. 2009. *Philosophy: Discipline of the Disciplines*. Grand Rapids, MI: Paideia Press.

Strickland, W., ed. 1996. *Five Views on Law and Gospel*. Grand Rapids, MI: Zondervan.

Sullivan, F. A. 2001. *From Apostles to Bishops: The Development of the Episcopacy in the Early Church*. New York: Newman Press.

Swinburne, R. 2005. *Faith and Reason*. 2nd ed. Oxford: Clarendon Press.

Thiel, J. 2000. *Nonfoundationalism*. Minneapolis, MN: Fortress Press.

Thielicke, H. 1974–1982. *The Evangelical Faith*. Edited and translated by G. W. Bromiley. Vol. 1: *Prolegomena: The Relation of Theology to Modern Thought Forms*. Grand Rapids, MI: Eerdmans.

Tillich, P. 1964. *Theology of Culture*. Oxford: Oxford University Press.

_____. 1968. *Systematic Theology*. 2 vols. Digswell Place: Nisbett & Co.

Toly, N. J. and D. J. Block, eds. 2010. *Keeping God's Earth: The Global Environment in Biblical Perspective*. Downers Grove, IL: InterVarsity Press.

Towner, P. H. 2006. *The Letters to Timothy and Titus*. NICNT. Grand Rapids, MI: Eerdmans.

Trillhaas, W. 1972. *Dogmatik*. 3rd ed. Berlin: W. de Gruyter.

Troost, A. 1958. *Casuïstiek en situatie-ethiek*. Utrecht: Libertas.

_____. 1969. "De openbaring Gods en de maatschappelijke orde." *Philosophia Reformata* 34: 1–37.

_____. 1976. *Geen aardse macht begeren wij*. Amsterdam: Buijten & Schipperheijn.

_____. 1977. *Theologie of filosofie? Een antwoord op 'Kritische aantekeningen bij de wijsbegeerte der wetsidee' van Prof. Dr. J. Douma*. Kampen: Kok.

_____. 1978. "De relatie tussen scheppingsopenbaring en woordopenbaring." *Philosophia Reformata* 43: 101–129.

_____. 1982–1983. "Theologische misverstanden inzake een reformatorische wijsbegeerte." *Philosophia Reformata* 47: 1–19, 179–92; 48: 19–49.

_____. 2001. "Ethiek, vakfilosofie van de ethiek en wijsbegeerte." *Philosophia Reformata* 66.2: 189–207.

_____. 2004. *Vakfilosofie van de geloofswetenschap: Prolegomena van de theologie*. Budel: Damon.

_____. 2005. *Antropocentrische totaliteitswetenschap: Inleiding in de "reformatorische wijsbegeerte" van H. Dooyeweerd*. Budel: Damon.

Tuininga, M. J. 2012. "The Two Kingdoms Doctrine in Scripture." Trinity United Reformed Church. Public address. http://www.sermonaudio.com/ sermoninfo.asp?SID=71121445382

_____. 2015. "Interview at the 2015 Synod of the Christian Reformed Church in North America." https://www.youtube.com/ watch?v=ZWQCeFNFoao

_____. Forthcoming. *Christ's Two Kingdoms: Calvin's Political Theology and the Public Engagement of the Church*. Cambridge: Cambridge University Press.

Van Asselt, W. J. 2007. *Gisbertus Voetius*. Kampen: Kok.

_____ with T. T. J. Pleizier, P. L. Rouwendal and M. Wisse. 2011. *Introduction to Reformed Scholasticism*. Grand Rapids, MI: Reformation Heritage Books.

Van Bruggen, J. 1984. *Ambten in de apostolische kerk: Een exegetisch mozaïek*. 2nd ed. Kampen: Kok.

Van Campen, M. 2007. *Gans Israël: Voetiaanse en coccejaanse visies op joden gedurende de zeventiende en achttiende eeuw*. 2nd ed. Zoetermeer: Boekencentrum.

Van de Beek, A. 1996. *Schepping: De wereld als voorspel voor de eeuwigheid*. Baarn: Callenbach.

_____. 2005. *Toeval of schepping? Scheppingstheologie in de context van het moderne denken*. Kampen: Kok.

Vander Goot, H., ed. 1981. *Life is Religion: Essays in Honor of H. Evan Runner*. St. Catharines, ON: Paideia Press.

Van der Merwe, W.L. 1991. "Metafoor en teologie." *Tydskrif vir Christelike Wetenskap* 27.2: 65–108.

Vander Stelt, J. C. 1978. *Philosophy and Scripture: A Study in Old Princeton and Westminster Theology*. Marlton, NJ: Mack Publ. Co.

Van der Waal, C. 1990. *The Covenantal Gospel*. Neerlandia, AB: Inheritance Publications.

Van der Walt, B. J. 1974. *Die natuurlike teologie met besondere aandag aan die visie daarop by Thomas van Aquino, Johannes Calvyn en die 'Synopsis purioris theologiae': 'n Wysgerige ondersoek*. Potchefstroom: Potchefstroomse Universiteit vir CHO (unpublished dissertation).

VanDrunen, D. 2003. *Law & Custom: The Thought of Thomas Aquinas and the Future of the Common Law*. New York: Peter Lang.

_____, ed. 2004. *The Pattern of Sound Doctrine: Systematic Theology at the Westminster Seminaries: Essays in Honor of Robert B. Strimple*. Phillipsburg, NJ: P&R Publishing.

_____. 2006. *A Biblical Case for Natural Law*. Grand Rapids, MI: Eerdmans.

_____. 2009. *Bioethics and the Christian Life: A Guide to Making Difficult Decisions*. Wheaton, IL: Crossway.

_____. 2010a. *Living in God's Two Kingdoms: A Biblical Vision for Christianity and Culture*. Wheaton, IL: Crossway.

_____. 2010b. *Natural Law and the Two Kingdoms: A Study in the Development of Reformed Social Thought*. Grand Rapids, MI: Eerdmans.

_____. 2010c. "'The Kingship of Christ Is Twofold': Natural Law and the Kingdoms in the Thought of Herman Bavinck." *Calvin Theological Journal* 45: 147–164.

_____. 2014. *Divine Covenants and Moral Order: A Biblical Theology of Natural Law*. Grand Rapids, MI: Eerdmans.

Van Eikema Hommes, H. J. 1979. *Major Trends in the History of Legal Philosophy*. Amsterdam: North Holland.

Van Genderen, J. and W. H. Velema, eds. 2008. *Concise Reformed Dogmatics*. Translated by G. Bilkes and E. M. van der Maas. Phillipsburg, NJ: P&R Publishing.

Van Huyssteen, J. W. V. 1987. *Teologie as kritiese geloofsverantwoording: Teorievorming in die sistematiese teologie*. 2nd ed. Pretoria: RGN.

_____. 1997. *Essays in Postfoundationalist Theology*. Grand Rapids, MI: Eerdmans.

Van Ruler, J. A. 1995. *The Crisis of Causality: Voetius and Descartes on God, Nature and Change*. Leiden: Brill Publishers.

Van Til, C. 1955. *The Defense of the Faith*. Philadelphia, PA: P&R Publishing.

_____. 1962. *Christianity in Conflict*. n.p.

_____. 1969. *In Defense of the Faith*. Vol. 2: *A Survey of Christian Epistemology*. n.p.: Den Dulk Christian Foundation.

Veenhof, J. n.d. *Nature and Grace in Bavinck*. Toronto: Institute for Christian Studies.

Von Dietze, E. 1998. "Hans Küng's Paradigm Theology and Some Educational Implications." *Religious Education* 93.1: 65–80.

Vos, G. 1903. *The Teaching of Jesus Concerning the Kingdom of God and the Church*. New York: American Tract Society.

Walvoord, J. F. 1966. *The Revelation of Jesus Christ*. Chicago, IL: Moody Press.

Walsh, B. J. and J. R. Middleton. 1984. *The Transforming Vision: Shaping a Christian World View*. Downers Grove, IL: InterVarsity Press.

Weber, H. E. 1907. *Die philosophische Scholastik des deutschen Protestantismus im Zeitalter der Orthodoxie*. Leipzig: Quelle & Meyer.

Weber, H. E. 1908 (repr. 1969). *Der Einfluß der protestantischen Schulphilosophie auf die orthodox-lutherische Dogmatik*. Darmstadt: Wissenschaftliche Buchgesellschaft.

Weber, O. 1981. *Foundations of Dogmatics*. Translated by D. L. Guder. Vol. 1. Grand Rapids, MI: Eerdmans.

Wedgeworth, S. 2010. *Two Kingdoms Critique / Theology*. www.credenda. org/ index.php/Theology/ two-kingdoms-critique.html.

Wellum, S. J. 2012. Chapters 1–3 and 16–17. In *Kingdom through Covenant: A Biblical-Theological Understanding of the Covenants*. Edited by P. J. Gentry and S. J. Wellum. Wheaton, IL: Crossway Books.

Wentsel, B., *Het Woord, de Zoon en de dienst: Dogmatiek*, Vol. 1. Kampen: Kok 1981.

_____. 1982. *De openbaring, het verbond en de apriori's: Dogmatiek*, Vol. 2. Kampen: Kok.

_____. 1998. *De Heilige Geest, de kerk en de laatste dingen: De kerk als het saamhorige volk Gods: Dogmatiek*. Vol. 4b. Kampen: Kok.

White, J. E. 1994. *What Is Truth? A Comparative Study of the Positions of Cornelius Van Til, Francis Schaeffer, Carl F. H. Henry, Donald Bloesch, Millard Erickson*. Nashville, TN: B&H Publishers.

Wirzba, N. and F. Bahnsen. 2012. *Making Peace with the Land: God's Call to Reconcile with Creation*. Downers Grove, IL: InterVarsity Press.

Wolters, A. M. (1985) 2005. *Creation Regained: Biblical Basics for a Reformational Worldview*. 2nd ed. Grand Rapids, MI: Eerdmans.

_____. 1992. *Schepping zonder grenzen*. Amsterdam: Buijten & Schipperheijn.

Wolterstorff, N. 1988. *Reason within the Bounds of Religion*. 2nd ed. Grand Rapids, MI: Eerdmans.

_____. 1995. *Divine Discourse: Philosophical Reflections on the Claim that God Speaks*. Cambridge: Cambridge University Press.

Wood, A. S. 1978. *Ephesians*. EBC 11. Grand Rapids, MI: Zondervan.

Wright, N. T. 2002. *The Letter to the Romans*. New Interpreter's Bible X. Nashville, TN: Abingdon Press.

_____. 2010. *Simply Christian: Why Christianity Makes Sense*. New York: HarperOne.

_____. 2008. *Surprised by Hope: Rethinking Heaven, the Resurrection, and the Mission of the Church*. New York: HarperOne.

Zagzebski, L., ed. 1993. *Rational Faith: Catholic Responses to Reformed Epistemology*. Notre Dame, IN: University of Notre Dame Press.

Zorn, R. O. 1962. *Church and Kingdom*. Philadelphia, PA: P&R Publishing.

NAME INDEX

SUBJECT INDEX

abortion, 83, 95–96, 112, 277, 327–28

Abrahamic covenant, 30, 174, 193, 362

academy (theological), 12, 267–70

active obedience of Christ, 51

"age/world to come," 30, 137–38, 156–58, 223, 240–41, 348–49

amillennialism, 221, 227, 241–42

Anabaptist, 66, 118, 152, 208

anthropology, 55, 247,

apostasy/apostatic, 70, 105, 118, 310, 345

autonomy, 34, 133, 164

avenger of blood, 123

Babylon, 201–05, 214–17

Belgic Confession, 12, 16–18, 73, 161

"biblical" theology, 45–46, 264

biblicism, 5, 11–13, 29, 32, 45–50, 78, 256, 273, 291, 336

burnt offering, 191–94, 356

Byzantine Empire, 117

caesaropapism, 183

Canaan, 201–02, 211, 217, 221–22

Canons of Dort, 12, 17, 308, 355

Christology, xviii, 11, 220, 332

church (body of Christ), 152, 158, 161, 174, 179, 203, 220, 238, 252, 258

church (institutional), 117, 154, 156, 159, 184, 252, 255, 258–59, 261, 271, 275

churchism, 127, 153, 164, 243, 255, 261, 263–64, 271, 273

citizenship, 169, 211–12, 331

civitas Dei, 152

common grace, 35, 42, 60, 87, 96–97, 190–94, 332–33

SCRIPTURE INDEX

CPSIA information can be obtained
at www.ICGtesting.com
Printed in the USA
BVHW072000060521
606650BV00001B/40